CAMBRIDGE COMPANIONS TO LITERATURE

The Cambridge Companion to Greek Tragedy
edited by P. E. Easterling

The Cambridge Companion to Virgil
edited by Charles Martindale

The Cambridge Companion to Old English Literature
edited by Malcolm Godden and Michael Lapidge

The Cambridge Companion to Dante
edited by Rachel Jacoff

The Cambridge Chaucer Companion
edited by Piero Boitani and Jill Mann

The Cambridge Companion to Medieval English Theatre
edited by Richard Beadle

The Cambridge Companion to Shakespeare Studies
edited by Stanley Wells

The Cambridge Companion to English Renaissance Drama
edited by A. R. Braunmuller and Michael Hattaway

The Cambridge Companion to English Poetry, Donne to Marvell
edited by Thomas N. Corns

The Cambridge Companion to Milton
edited by Dennis Danielson

The Cambridge Companion to British Romanticism
edited by Stuart Curran

The Cambridge Companion to James Joyce
edited by Derek Attridge

The Cambridge Companion to Ibsen
edited by James McFarlane

The Cambridge Companion to Brecht
edited by Peter Thomason and Glendyr Sacks

The Cambridge Companion to Beckett
edited by John Pilling

The Cambridge Companion to T. S. Eliot
edited by A. David Moody

The Cambridge Companion to Renaissance Humanism
edited by Jill Kraye

The Cambridge Companion to Joseph Conrad
edited by J. H. Stape

The Cambridge Companion to William Faulkner
edited by Philip M. Weinstein

The Cambridge Companion to Henry David Thoreau
edited by Joel Myerson

The Cambridge Companion to Edith Wharton
edited by Millicent Bell

The Cambridge Companion to American Realism and Naturalism
edited by Donald Pizer

The Cambridge Companion to Mark Twain
edited by Forrest G. Robinson

The Cambridge Companion to Walt Whitman
edited by Ezra Greenspan

The Cambridge Companion to Ernest Hemingway
edited by Scott Donaldson

The Cambridge Companion to the Eighteenth-Century Novel
edited by John Richetti

The Cambridge Companion to Jane Austen
edited by Edward Copeland and Juliet McMaster

The Cambridge Companion to Samuel Johnson
edited by Gregory Clingham

The Cambridge Companion to Oscar Wilde
edited by Peter Raby

The Cambridge Companion to Tennessee Williams
edited by Matthew C. Roudané

The Cambridge Companion to Arthur Miller
edited by Christopher Bigsby

The Cambridge Companion to the French Novel: from 1800 to the Present
edited by Timothy Unwin

The Cambridge Companion to the Classic Russian Novel
edited by Malcolm V. Jones and Robin Feuer Miller

CAMBRIDGE COMPANIONS TO CULTURE

This volume addresses the work of women playwrights throughout the history of the American theatre, from the early pioneers to contemporary feminists. Women playwrights and their work are viewed through a number of lenses: cultural and historical, critical and theoretical, aesthetic and ideological.

The book is written for undergraduate students of drama, theatre, and women's studies. Each chapter introduces the reader to the work of one or more playwrights and to a way of thinking about plays. Together they cover significant writers such as Rachel Crothers, Susan Glaspell, Lillian Hellman, Sophie Treadwell, Lorraine Hansberry, Alice Childress, Megan Terry, Ntozake Shange, Adrienne Kennedy, Wendy Wasserstein, Marsha Norman, Beth Henley, and Maria Irene Fornes. Playwrights are discussed in the context of topics such as early comedy and melodrama, feminism and realism, the Harlem Renaissance, the feminist resurgence of the 1970s, and feminist dramatic theory.

A detailed chronology and illustrations enhance the volume, which also includes bibliographical essays on recent criticism and on African American women playwrights before 1930.

Brenda Murphy is Professor of English at the University of Connecticut. Her books include *American Realism and American Drama, 1880–1940* (1987), *Tennessee Williams and Elia Kazan: A Collaboration in the Theatre* (1992), and a study of Arthur Miller's *Death of a Salesman* for the Plays in Performance series (1995).

THE CAMBRIDGE
COMPANION TO
AMERICAN
WOMEN
PLAYWRIGHTS

EDITED BY

BRENDA MURPHY

CAMBRIDGE
UNIVERSITY PRESS

PUBLISHED BY THE PRESS SYNDICATE OF THE UNIVERSITY OF CAMBRIDGE
The Pitt Building, Trumpington Street, Cambridge CB2 1RP, United Kingdom

CAMBRIDGE UNIVERSITY PRESS
The Edinburgh Building, Cambridge CB2 2RU, United Kingdom
http://www.cup.cam.ac.uk
40 West 20th Street, New York, NY 10011–4211, USA
http://www.cup.org
10 Stamford Road, Oakleigh, Melbourne 3166, Australia

© Cambridge University Press

First published 1999

Printed in the United Kingdom at the University Press, Cambridge

Typeset in Sabon 10/13 pt. [CE]

A catalogue record for this book is available from the British Library

Library of Congress cataloging in publication data
The Cambridge companion to American women playwrights / edited by
Brenda Murphy.
p.   cm. – (Cambridge companions to literature)
Includes bibliographical references and index.
ISBN 0 521 57184 7 (hardback). – ISBN 0 521 57680 6 (paperback)
1. American drama – Women authors – History and criticism.   2. Women
and literature – United States.   I. Murphy, Brenda.   II. Series.
PS338.W6C36   1999
812.009'9287 – dc21   98–36593   CIP

ISBN 0 521 57184 7 hardback
ISBN 0 521 57680 6 paperback

CONTENTS

ILLUSTRATIONS

NOTES ON CONTRIBUTORS

THOMAS P. ADLER is Professor and Head of English at Purdue University, where he has taught since receiving his PhD from the University of Illinois in 1970. He is the author of many articles and a number of books on American drama, including *Mirror on the Stage: The Pulitzer Prize Plays as an Approach to American Drama, A Streetcar Named Desire: The Moth and the Lantern*, and his latest book, recently reprinted in paperback, *American Drama, 1940–1960: A Critical History* – which includes chapters on Hellman and Hansberry.

JAN BALAKIAN received her PhD from Cornell University in 1991, where her play, *The Ceiling Will Open*, won Cornell's playwriting award. She is currently Assistant Professor of English at Kean College of New Jersey. She has published critical essays on the plays of Arthur Miller, Tennessee Williams, and Wendy Wasserstein, as well as interviews with Wasserstein and Miller, and has just completed a book on Wendy Wasserstein's plays.

SARAH J. BLACKSTONE is Associate Professor and Chair of the Department of Theatre at Southern Illinois University at Carbondale, where she teaches theatre history. She is the author of *Buckskins, Bullets, and Business: A History of Buffalo Bill's Wild West*, as well as a number of articles on the nineteenth-century American theatre. She is currently engaged in a research project centered on Southern Illinois' extensive collection of American melodramas.

JANET BROWN holds a PhD in Speech and Dramatic Arts from the University of Missouri – Columbia. She is Education Director at the Center of Contemporary Arts in St. Louis, Missouri, and is the author of the groundbreaking *Feminist Drama: Definition and Critical Analysis* as well as *Taking Center Stage: Feminism in Contemporary US Drama.*

JERRY DICKEY is Associate Professor of Theatre Arts at the University of Arizona. He is the author of *Sophie Treadwell: A Research and Production Sourcebook*, as well as several essays on Treadwell which have appeared in *Speaking the Other Self: American Women Writers, Theatre History Studies,* and

Women & Theatre: Occasional Papers 4, and numerous essays and reviews on American theatre and drama in journals such as *Theatre Journal, Theatre Topics*, and *New England Theatre Journal*.

CHRISTY GAVIN is a Librarian and Professor at the California State University, Bakersfield, where she teaches research methodology and coordinates the University Library's instructional programs. Her publications include *African American Women Playwrights: A Research Guide* and *American Women Playwrights, 1964–1989: A Research Guide and Annotated Bibliography*.

CHRISTINE R. GRAY received her PhD in American Literature from the University of Maryland. Her publications include the introduction to the republication of *Plays and Pageants from the Life of the Negro*, "Mara, Angelina Grimké's Other Play," in the collection *As the Curtain Rises: Black Female Visions on the American Stage*, and a forthcoming book on African American playwright Willis Richardson. Gray teaches at Catonsville Community College and the University of Maryland. Her current research focuses on African American drama before 1930.

HELENE KEYSSAR is Professor of Communications at the University of California, San Diego, as well as an accomplished director and the author of *Feminist Theatre: An Introduction to the Plays of Contemporary British and American Women, The Curtain and the Veil: Strategies in Black Drama*, and *Robert Altman's America*, as well as many articles on drama and theatre, particularly on contemporary women playwrights. She has also edited *Feminist Theatre and Theory* and co-authored *Right in Her Soul: The Life of Anna Louise Strong* and *Remembering War: A US–Soviet Dialogue*.

AMELIA HOWE KRITZER is the editor of *Plays by Early American Women, 1775–1850* and author of *The Plays of Caryl Churchill: Theatre of Empowerment*. Her essays have appeared in a wide range of journals. As a specialist in women dramatists, she has directed plays by Caryl Churchill, Tina Howe, and Grace Livingston Furniss. She currently teaches in the joint theatre department of the University of St. Thomas and College of St. Catherine in St. Paul, Minnesota.

VERONICA MAKOWSKY is Professor of English at the University of Connecticut. She has published widely on American women writers, including *Susan Glaspell's Century of American Women: A Critical Interpretation of Her Work* and *Caroline Gordon: A Biography*, as well as a number of articles on southern writers and collections of the work of R. P. Blackmur. Her current project is a study of playwright Mary Coyle Chase.

BRENDA MURPHY is Professor of English at the University of Connecticut and the author of *American Realism and American Drama, 1880–1940, Tennessee Williams and Elia Kazan: A Collaboration in the Theatre, Miller: Death of a Salesman*, and a number of other books and articles on American playwrights. Her forthcoming book is *Congressional Theatre: Dramatizing McCarthyism on Stage, Film, and Television.*

LAURIN PORTER is Associate Professor of English at the University of Texas at Arlington, where she teaches drama, women's studies, and American literature. She is the author of *The Banished Prince: Time, Memory, and Ritual in the Late Plays of Eugene O'Neill.* Her articles on O'Neill, Horton Foote, Marsha Norman, Beth Henley, Paul Claudel, and Canadian playwright Ann-Marie MacDonald have appeared in *Modern Drama, Studies in American Drama, The Eugene O'Neill Review,* and *Claudel Studies,* as well as several anthologies. She is currently working on a book about Foote's nine-play cycle, *The Orphans' Home.*

STEPHANIE ROACH is an award-winning actor and playwright, whose play *The Platonics* was staged at Adrian College. She holds an MA from Case Western Reserve University and is currently a PhD candidate at the University of Connecticut.

PATRICIA R. SCHROEDER is Professor of English at Ursinus College in Pennsylvania, where she has won awards for excellence in teaching modern drama, American literature, and African American literature. She is the author of *The Feminist Possibilities of Dramatic Realism* and *The Presence of the Past in Modern American Drama,* as well as many articles on American playwrights, feminist drama, and dramatic theory. Her current project is a study of blues music as cultural performance.

JUDITH L. STEPHENS is Associate Professor of Speech Communication at Penn State University – the Schuylkill Campus. She is the author of *Borrowed Rites* and a number of articles on women playwrights in such journals as *African American Review, Theatre Journal, Theatre Annual, Text and Performance Quarterly,* and *The Journal of American Drama and Theatre.* She is co-editor of the forthcoming *Strange Fruit: Plays on Lynching by American Women* (1998), and is currently editing a second volume of lynching dramas.

MARGARET B. WILKERSON is Professor and Chair of African American Studies at the University of California, Berkeley. She has written many influential articles, particularly about African American drama and theatre, and is the editor of *9 Plays by Black Women* and *Kaiso!: Katherine Dunham, an Anthology of Writings.* She is currently writing a biography of Lorraine Hansberry.

PREFACE

Before the feminist resurgence of the 1970s, the prevailing wisdom among critics and historians was that the impact of women playwrights on the American theatre had been negligible. With the exception of a handful of respected plays – such as Susan Glaspell's *Trifles*, Lorraine Hansberry's *A Raisin in the Sun*, and Lillian Hellman's *The Children's Hour* and *The Little Foxes* – and a few spectacular Broadway successes like Anne Nichols' *Abie's Irish Rose* and Mary Chase's *Harvey*, women playwrights seemed invisible in the history of American drama and theatre. With the new wave of feminist criticism, however, came a rediscovery of the women playwrights who had written, sometimes anonymously or pseudonymously, a large body of work for the eighteenth- and nineteenth-century American stage, as well as a reevaluation of the work of women playwrights in the first half of the twentieth century. The new feminism also sparked a vibrant new feminist theatre, which in turn produced a whole generation of women writers and performers who worked with consciously feminist aesthetic principles.

This volume builds primarily on the critical, historical, and bibliographical scholarship of the last twenty years in addressing the work of women playwrights throughout the history of the American theatre, viewing women playwrights and their work through a number of lenses – cultural and historical, critical and theoretical, aesthetic and ideological. Each of the essays is meant to introduce the reader both to the work of one or more writers and to a way of thinking about plays. In the *Pioneers* section, Amelia Kritzer and Sarah Blackstone address the work of the most invisible American women playwrights, those who wrote for the eighteenth- and nineteenth-century theatre. Kritzer's chapter examines the emergence of women as comic playwrights at the end of the eighteenth century and their exploration of forms and possibilities in the early nineteenth, bringing to light the considerable contributions made by women playwrights to comic writing for the stage at a time when most of them labored in anonymity behind the scenes of theatrical production. Blackstone's chapter addresses the role of women playwrights in the development of the mode of drama that had the greatest impact on the American theatre in the nineteenth century – melodrama. From Mary Carr Clarke's *The Fair Americans* (1815) to the plays of the prolific Louisa Medina, whose adaptations of *Nick of the Woods* and *The Last Days of Pompeii* were major successes in the 1830s, to Julia Ward Howe's *Leonora* (1857), American women were constantly writing, shaping, and manipulating melodrama. Blackstone places this process in the context of recent critical and theoretical work which examines melodrama in relation to American culture, analyzing the consistent failure of academic critics to recognize the importance of melodrama. Marking the end of virtual anonymity and the beginning of a serious feminist agenda for playwrights, Patricia Schroeder's chapter analyzes the alliance of feminism, Progressive politics, and realist aesthetics in the first decade of the twentieth century. In the work of playwrights like Zona Gale, Rachel Crothers, and Marion Craig Wentworth, Schroeder demonstrates, realism was employed as an aesthetic strategy for promoting the feminist agenda within the general project of Progressivism.

It was only after this groundbreaking work of the teens that the playwrights who are designated here, after one of Susan Glaspell's plays, as *Inheritors*, were able to pursue their own individual interests and develop their own aesthetic and ideological agendas in the following decades. The chapters by Veronica Makowsky, Jerry Dickey, Brenda Murphy, and Thomas Adler demonstrate a broad spectrum of interests and of artistry in the work of Susan Glaspell, Sophie Treadwell, Rachel Crothers, and Lillian Hellman, each of whom achieved both commercial and critical success in the theatre of the twenties and thirties. As Judith Stephens and Christine Gray remind us, however, access to the commercial theatre was still severely restricted for women of color at mid-century, and accomplished playwrights like Zora Neale Hurston, Georgia Douglas Johnson, and Angelina Weld Grimké saw most of their work go unproduced, or produced only in alternative venues like high school auditoriums and church basements. It is only now that the work of women playwrights during the creative explosion by African American writers of the twenties that is known as the Harlem Renaissance or New Negro Movement is being rediscovered and read. The work of the next generation of African American playwrights is much better known, and has been highly influential. Margaret Wilkerson's chapter details in particular the work of three significant, and very different, playwrights who began their careers in Harlem in the 1950s: Lorraine Hansberry, Alice Childress, and Adrienne

Kennedy. Together these playwrights represent the broad spectrum of drama and theatre sparked by the Harlem theatre of the fifties as well as the diverse career paths these artists have followed.

The section on new feminists centers mainly on women playwrights who came of age in the late sixties and seventies, during the second-wave feminist movement. As the chapters by Helene Keyssar, Jan Balakian, and Laurin Porter show, all of these women were deeply affected by the new feminism, but in very different ways. The vitality and multiplicity of their responses to the feminist movement is evident in the work of such heterogeneous playwrights as Megan Terry, Maria Irene Fornes, Ntozake Shange, Wendy Wasserstein, Tina Howe, Marsha Norman, and Beth Henley. From a conscious attempt to create an avant-garde feminist aesthetics in the theatre to a conscious embracing of the most traditional theatrical forms in which to dramatize women's experience, these playwrights represent a broad spectrum of aesthetics and ideology. But, as these essays show, they share a deep interest in dramatizing the experience of women and the world as women see it.

Janet Brown's chapter on feminist theory and the chapters by Christy Gavin and Christine Gray on recent primary and secondary scholarship reflect the explosion of criticism by and about women since the seventies, as well as the tremendous diversity of aesthetic theories, ideologies, and interests that inform the critics who are writing about women playwrights. While these three brief chapters could not possibly be exhaustive or comprehensive, they serve to introduce the reader to the abundance of scholarly work that has been done on women playwrights, trace some of the threads of controversy, and indicate the wealth of material that is still to be explored.

As could only be the case with such an enormous subject, the goals of the volume are modest. Without any pretense to "covering" the subject of drama by American women, the hope is to suggest the richness of the field and to provide a foundation for further reading and study. For this reason, and for ease of use, the list of works cited has been collected at the back of the volume, and references are given in full there, while they are abbreviated in the text and notes. Stephanie Roach has prepared the Chronology with a view to quick identification of plays and playwrights for further study, as well as placing them within the history of the theatre and the larger culture.

The editor's chief regret is that, because space is finite, so many playwrights had to be left out of the volume or given less attention than they deserve. Christy Gavin suggests some of the contemporary writers who deserve attention in her list of "emerging playwrights": Lynn Alvarez, Jane

Chambers, Pearle Cleage, Velina Houston, Tina Howe, Wendy Kesselman, Karen Malpede, Cherrie Moraga, Suzan-Lori Parks, Sonia Sanchez, Milcha Sanchez-Scott, and Wakao Yamauchi. To this list can be added accomplished playwrights like Anna Deavere Smith, Emily Mann, Jane Wagner, Martha Boesing, Paula Vogel, and many others. And one immediately thinks of more playwrights from earlier decades who deserve study, such as Clare Boothe, Zoë Akins, Lula Vollmer, Clare Kummer, May Miller, Edna Ferber, Edna St. Vincent Millay, Djuna Barnes, and Carson McCullers. Thoughtful chapters on the playwrights who have been left out could easily fill another volume. Perhaps they will.

ACKNOWLEDGMENTS

This volume has accumulated many debts in the process of its creation. The first is to Sarah Stanton, whose editorial wisdom guided every step of its conception, development, and execution, and whose good sense and good humor helped to make it a pleasure to work on. Helen Azevedo Smith and Stephanie Roach provided invaluable assistance with the typescript at a time when their individual skill and expertise was crucial. And, as always, my husband George Monteiro provided help, constructive criticism, moral support, and sanity throughout. The University of Connecticut Research Foundation provided funds when they were needed most.

The staffs of several libraries contributed vitally to the project, particularly the reference librarians of the Billy Rose Theatre Collection, New York Public Library for the Performing Arts and the Schomberg Center for Research in Black Culture, New York Public Library; the University of Arizona Library Special Collections; Homer Babbidge Library, University of Connecticut; the University of Pennsylvania Libraries; and the Library of Congress. Wayne Furman, Vivian Gonzalez, and Annette Marotta were helpful and patient in the process of obtaining permissions.

Passages of "Realism and feminism in the Progressive Era" by Patricia R. Schroeder are adapted from her book, *The Feminist Possibilities of Dramatic Realism* (Madison, NJ: Associated University Presses, 1996). The author gratefully acknowledges Associated University Press's permission to reprint these passages.

The rights to Sophie Treadwell's works are owned by the Roman Catholic Church of the Diocese of Tucson: A Corporation Sole, from whom production rights must be obtained. The excerpts from Treadwell's works in Jerry Dickey's "The expressionist moment: Sophie Treadwell" are reprinted here by permission of the Diocese of Tucson. Proceeds from the printing or production of Sophie Treadwell's works are used for the aid and benefit of Native American children in Arizona.

Illustrations 1, 2, 3, 4, 5, 8, and 9 are prints from the Billy Rose Theatre

Collection (Vandamm and Friedman-Abeles Collections), the New York Public Library for the Performing Arts, Astor, Lenox and Tilden Foundations, and are reprinted with permission. Illustrations 6 and 7 are prints from the Photographs and Prints Division, Schomberg Center for Research in Black Culture, the New York Public Library, Astor, Lenox, and Tilden Foundations, and are reprinted with permission.

CHRONOLOGY

STEPHANIE ROACH

This chronology lists general events in American theatre history as well as biographical information on American women playwrights and the production and/or publication information of plays by American women playwrights. Under each date, general events are listed first. Events involving particular playwrights are listed in alphabetical order according to the playwrights' last names.

1665	Record of the first production in English in the Colonies, *Ye Bare and Ye Cubb* (non-extant) produced in Accomac County, Virginia
1687	Increase Mather begins Puritan attack on the theatre
1698	Harvard College's President indicates an interest in student dramatics
1705	Pennsylvania Assembly passes legislation against theatrical events
1709	Governor's Council in New York prohibits plays
1715	New York Governor Robert Hunter's *Androboros*, the first play written and published by an American
1724	First North American acting company established in Philadelphia
1728	Mercy Otis Warren born (d. 1814); Warren will become the first American-born woman to be known as a dramatic comedy writer

1730   Amateur New York production of *Romeo and Juliet* marks the debut of Shakespeare on the American stage

1750   General Court of Massachusetts passes legislation to prevent stage plays

1751   Judith Sargent Murray born (d. 1820); Murray will become the first American-born woman dramatist to have her plays produced professionally

1760   The *Maryland Gazette* prints the earliest known theatrical review

1762   Rhode Island passes legislation against stage plays
Susanna Haswell Rowson born (d. 1828); although born in England, Rowson grows up in Massachusetts; the Rowson family will be deported during the American Revolution, but Rowson and her husband William will eventually return to Massachusetts where they will have stage careers with the New American Company; Rowson will find playwriting success with her comedies and comic operas

1766   Major Robert Rogers' *Ponteach; or the Savages of America*, the first play about America published by an American

1767   New York's first permanent playhouse, the John Street Theatre, opens

1771–72   George Washington attends at least nineteen theatrical productions

1772   Mercy Otis Warren's first, though unproduced, play, *The Adulateur*

1774   The Continental Congress discourages stage shows, though no official resolutions are passed

1775   Mercy Otis Warren's *The Group*; published initially in installments in periodicals

1778   Several Congressional resolutions passed against plays and other diversions

1779	All theatrical entertainment in Pennsylvania is prohibited
1787+	With the end of the American Revolution, prohibitions and resolutions against theatrical activity begin to lift: Pennsylvania officially repeals its antitheatre legislation in 1789, Massachusetts and Rhode Island repeal their legislation in 1793; theatres throughout the nation begin to reopen and/or expand; women dramatists of this period include Judith Sargent Murray and Susanna Haswell Rowson
1793	A Charleston production of *The Tempest* sparks interest in the better use and design of stage effects Susanna Haswell Rowson begins her American stage career when she returns from her deportation to Britain
1794	Susanna Haswell Rowson's comic opera *Slaves in Algiers* performed at the Chestnut Street Theatre in Philadelphia
1795	Judith Sargent Murray's *Virtue Triumphant*; this and other Murray plays are produced by Boston's Federal Street Theatre, which Murray herself helped establish
1796	Judith Sargent Murray's *The Traveller Returned*
1797	Susanna Haswell Rowson's *Americans in England* staged at Boston's Federal Street Theatre; this same year Rowson quits the stage and opens a girls' school in Boston
179?	Mary Carr Clarke born (d. 183?); Clarke is one of the first American women to earn her living as a writer
1800	The first play to be called a "melodrama" is produced in France; the melodramatic form, especially as rendered by women dramatists of the nineteenth century, has a great impact on the American theatre
1813	Louisa Medina born (d. 1838); Medina will specialize in spectacular melodramas, especially adaptations of her own novels; Medina will also achieve a feat rare for her era by becoming a successful playwright, the most professionally produced female dramatist of her day who was not also an actress or manager

1815   The emergence of a professional theatre company in Frankfort, Kentucky marks the westward movement of American theatre Mary Carr Clarke's only comedy *The Return from Camp* (later published as *The Fair Americans*)

1816   Gas lighting installed in the Chestnut Street Theatre

1818   Sarah Pogson's *The Young Carolinians*

1819   Anna Cora Ogden Mowatt born (d. 1870); although her upper-middle-class family has religious objections to the theatre, Mowatt will be an avid drama reader and will become a successful actress with a profitable playwriting career

1823   Mary Carr Clarke's *The Benevolent Lawyers; or Villainy Detected*

1826   Gas lighting installed in New York theatres

1827   James Kirke Paulding makes a plea for a definitively "American" drama, *American Quarterly Review* (June)

1830s–40s American women dramatists turn from comedy to melodrama and tragedy; however, in 1845 Anna Cora Mowatt's comedy *Fashion* breaks on the theatre scene and is a stunning success; *Fashion* continues today to receive critical attention and is often still produced

1835   Louisa Medina's *Last Days of Pompeii* has a twenty-nine-performance run, setting the record for the longest running production at the Bowery Theatre, New York

1838   Louisa Medina's *Nick of the Woods* and *Ernest Maltravers* produced at the Bowery Theatre; Medina is the Bowery Theatre's house playwright

1840   First use of the term "vaudeville" in the United States

1843   First recorded matinee performance in New York

1845   Anna Cora Mowatt's *Fashion*; is reviewed twice by Edgar

Allan Poe for the *Broadway Journal*; also in this year Mowatt debuts as an actress

1847   Anna Cora Mowatt's *Armand, the Child of the People*

1848   First California theatre opens

1849   Frances Hodgson Burnett born (d. 1924); Burnett is born in England, but her family moves to Knoxville in 1865; Burnett will become a highly successful novelist and deft melodramatic dramatist

1850   As many as fifty theatre companies are operating nationwide

1853   Catherine Sinclair opens the Metropolitan Theatre in San Francisco

1854   Actor John Wilkes Booth's debut
Anna Cora Mowatt's final performance (June 3)

1855   Actress-manager Laura Keene opens the Laura Keen Varieties Theatre, New York

1856   First American copyright law
Mrs. Sidney Bateman's satire *Self*

1863   Charles W. Witham, the century's most prominent scenic artist/ designer, begins his career in Boston

1866   Extensive use of limelight

1870   Olive Logan's *Before the Footlights and Behind the Scenes*
Rachel Crothers born (birth date sometimes given as 1878, d. 1958); Crothers will become the most prolific and successful female playwright in the early part of the twentieth century; during her four-decade playwriting career, Crothers will bring twenty-four full-length productions to the New York stage

1874   The Lambs theatrical club established
Zona Gale born (d. 1938); Gale will become a successful writer of American domestic comedy and the first female winner of the Pulitzer Prize for Drama

Gertrude Stein born (d. 1946); although her fame will not come from her playwriting, Stein will write more than seventy-seven theatrical works; Stein's plays, often considered the dramatic equivalent of modernist painting, typically have no plot and bear little resemblance to traditional plays, making them extremely difficult to stage

1875   The emergence of complex sets, stagecraft machinery, and the modern concept of the director

1876   Nearly 100 theatre companies go on tour for the 1876–77 season
Susan Glaspell born (d. 1948); always on the cutting edge of American theatre, Glaspell will help found the Provincetown Players, a company that will produce her many and many-faceted plays

1878   Frances Hodgson Burnett's stage adaptation of her novel *That Lass o' Lowries*
Mrs. B. E. Woolf copyrights her melodrama *Hobbies; or The Angel of the Household*

1879   *Forget Me Not*, presented by Genevieve Ward

1880   Pauline Elizabeth Hopkins, African American playwright, writes, produces and stars in her melodrama *Slaves' Escape; or the Underground Railroad*
Georgia Douglas Johnson born (d. 1966); Johnson will become highly involved in the artistic community as a published poet, a skilled composer, and a socially aware dramatist honored for her work in several dramatic genres
Angelina Grimké born (d. 1958); Grimké will become the foremother of African American women dramatists with her groundbreaking *Rachel* (1916)

1881   The 14th Street Theatre, credited birthplace of the true vaudeville, tries to attract women to its performances by giving away sewing kits and dress patterns
Martha Johnson's *Carrots; or The Waif of the Woods*

1882   Aged and needy actors now assisted by the Actors Fund of America

1885	Annie Oakley joins "Buffalo Bill" Cody's Wild West exhibition Sophie Treadwell born (d. 1970); although she will also write realistically, Treadwell will become known as one of America's pioneers of expressionism
1889	Western theatres begin offering matinees for women and children Frances Hodgson Burnett's melodrama *Phyllis*; *Nixie* follows in 1890
1890	With the star system in place, actors begin hiring agents Minstrel shows are common
1891	Zora Neale Hurston born (d. 1960); prolific novelist, folklorist, playwright, Hurston becomes the most accomplished African American woman writer of the early twentieth century
1894	*Billboard* begins publication Eulalie Spence born (d. 1981); unlike many of her contemporaries, Spence will not focus on protest drama but will earn her fame through dramas depicting everyday Harlem life
1896	Kliegl Brothers lighting company founded
1897	Strauss Signs creates gas-lit marquees Frances Hodgson Burnett's *A Lady of Quality*
1899	May Miller born (d. 1995); Miller becomes the most widely published African American woman playwright to date
1900	Starting this year and continuing over the next eight years, more than eighty theatres will be built in the Broadway district (39th Street to 54th Street)
1901	Jane Addams and Laura Dainty Pelham found the Hull-House Players in Chicago for the purpose of community education and edification
1904	Frances Hodgson Burnett's stage adaptation *That Man and I*

1905   Harvard begins offering English 47, a playwriting course

1906   Lillian Hellman born (d. 1984); Hellman's plays of social consciousness win her the honor of election to the American Academy of Arts and Sciences (1960), the American Academy of Arts and Letters (1963), and the Theatre Hall of Fame (1974) Sophie Treadwell begins a short-lived vaudeville career as a character artist

1907   Playwright Martha Morton organizes the Society of Dramatic Authors because the American Dramatists Club will not accept female members

1909   Rachel Crothers' *A Man's World* (published 1915)

1910   There are twenty-six showboat theatres in operation
Florenz Ziegfeld discovers Fanny Brice

1911   An estimated 16 percent of New Yorkers attend a vaudeville show each week
Mary Austin's *The Arrow Maker*
Rachel Crothers' *He and She*

1912   Organization of Authors' League of America (now the Dramatists Guild) offers legal protection to (male) playwrights
Burlesque performers begin to strip for better revenues
Marion Craig Wentworth's *The Flower Shop*

1913   The Actors' Equity Association is founded
Rachel Crothers' *Ourselves*

1914   Rachel Crothers' *Young Wisdom*
Playwright and theatre critic Florence Kiper writes reviews "from the feminist viewpoint" in the journal *Forum*

1915   Susan Glaspell founds the Provincetown Players with George Cram Cook and others
Angelina Grimké's *Rachel* (published 1916) is produced at the Myrtill Minor School in Washington; *Rachel* challenges the

stereotypical and racist visions of African Americans promoted
by the film *Birth of a Nation* (1915)

1916   Susan Glaspell's *Trifles*
        Clare Kummer's *Good Gracious, Annabelle*

1917   Susan Glaspell's *The Outside* and *The People*

1918   Alice Dunbar-Nelson's *Mine Eyes Have Seen*
        Susan Glaspell's *Woman's Honor*

1919   Mary Burrill's *They That Sit in Darkness* appears in *The Birth
        Control Review*
        Mary Burrill's *Aftermath*
        Susan Glaspell's *Bernice*

1920s–30s Era of the Harlem Renaissance or the New Negro Movement,
        an explosion and celebration of African American letters and
        art; African American women playwrights such as Marita
        Bonner, Mary Burrill, Ottie Graham, Angelina Grimké,
        Dorothy C. Guinn, Frances Gunner, Maud Cuney Hare, Zora
        Neale Hurston, Georgia Douglas Johnson, May Miller, Myrtle
        Livingston Smith, and Eulalie Spence did not get all the
        recognition deserved or expected during this period, but they
        were a crucial part of the nationwide Little Theatre Movement
        occurring at the same time as the Harlem Renaissance; the
        Little Theatre Movement was intended to create amateur,
        community-based theatres that would be able to produce
        plays, especially one-acts, inexpensively

1920   A patent is granted for a counterweighted curtain opening
        mechanism
        Alice Childress born (d. 1994); Childress will become a
        celebrated playwright, director, actress, screenplay writer, and
        novelist; her art will be known for its poignant depiction of the
        common man and especially for its constant, dignified attack
        on racism
        Zona Gale's realistic drama *Miss Lulu Bett* wins the 1921
        Pulitzer Prize
        Edna St. Vincent Millay's *Aria da Capo*

one performances at the Plymouth Theatre in New York, reviving the popularity of expressionism on the commercial stage

1929   Marita Bonner's *Exit: An Illusion*
Rachel Crothers' *Let Us Be Gay*
Georgia Douglas Johnson's *Safe* pioneers innovative uses of various dramatic techniques in its depiction of the horrors of lynching
May Miller's *Graven Images*
May Miller publishes *Scratches* in University of North Carolina's *Carolina Magazine*
Eulalie Spence's *Undertow*
Spence's only full-length play, *The Whipping*, does not open as scheduled in Bridgeport, Connecticut; a subsequent movie deal with Paramount Studios also does not come to fruition

1930   After Broadway's commercial theatres experience their period of greatest success in the late twenties, the National Theatre Conference is established to assist and encourage non-commercial theatre
Just fourteen years after Grimké's *Rachel*, an estimated forty-nine African American women playwrights are at work
Avant-garde theatre artist Maria Irene Fornes born; Fornes' acclaimed work will earn her several Obies including one for Sustained Achievement
Susan Glaspell's final play, the Pulitzer Prize-winning *Alison's House*
Lorraine Hansberry born (d. 1965); Hansberry will achieve commercial and popular success and along with playwrights such as Alice Childress, earn critical, national acclaim for African American women playwrights
Georgia Douglas Johnson's *Blue-Eyed Black Boy*
May Miller's *Stragglers in the Dust* and *Plays and Pageants From the Life of the Negro*; *Plays and Pageants* earns Miller acclaim as one of the most promising contemporary playwrights

1931   Rachel Crothers' *As Husbands Go*
Zora Neale Hurston and Langston Hughes collaborate on *Mule Bone*, an authentic, yet unfinished, black folk comedy;

Mule Bone is eventually staged on Broadway in 1991
Adrienne Kennedy born; this future Obie-winning playwright
will share her theatre knowledge with young dramatists as a
lecturer in playwriting at Yale, Princeton, and Brown
Universities

1932   Rachel Crothers' *When Ladies Meet*
Shirley Graham's three-act opera *Tom Tom* produced at the
Cleveland Stadium marks the first professional production of a
black opera
Zora Neale Hurston creates and performs *The Great Day*, the
first of three musical programs of Negro folklore; *From Sun to
Sun* and *Singing Steel* follow in 1933 and 1934 respectively
Megan Terry (Marguerite Duffy) born; future writer in
residence for the Yale University School of Drama (1966–67),
founding member of the Women's Theatre Council (1972), and
Obie award winner, Terry will earn an international reputation
as the "mother" of American feminist drama

1933   May Miller's lynching drama *Nails and Thorns*
Sophie Treadwell's most experimental work, *For Saxophone*,
and her most realistic, psychological drama, *Lone Valley*

1934   Lillian Hellman's *The Children's Hour*; this play introduces
Hellman to the American theatre scene and enjoys the longest
run (691 performances) of any production in Hellman's thirty-
year playwriting career; Hellman will revive *The Children's
Hour* on Broadway under her own direction in 1952
Gertrude Stein's *Four Saints in Three Acts: An Opera to Be
Sung*, directed by John Houseman

1935   The Federal Theatre Project is organized and directed by Hallie
Flanagan
Zoë Akins wins the Pulitzer Prize for *The Old Maid*, adapted
from Edith Wharton's novel
Georgia Douglas Johnson's historical plays *Frederick Douglass*
and *William and Ellen Craft*
May Miller helps edit *Negro History in Thirteen Plays*, a
volume which contains Miller's own four history plays: *Harriet
Tubman*, *Sojourner Truth*, *Christophe's Daughters*, and
Samory

1936   Lillian Hellman's *Days to Come*

1937   Rachel Crothers' last play, *Susan and God*, runs for 288 performances
Tina Howe born; Howe will be known for her perceptive view of contemporary mores; her plays will often feature women artists as protagonists

1939   Lillian Hellman's *The Little Foxes*
Shirley Graham's *I Gotta Home*

1940   Shirley Graham's one-act *It's Morning*, and radio drama *Track Thirteen*

1941   Lillian Hellman's most overtly political play, *Watch on the Rhine*, wins the New York Drama Critics Circle Award for best American Play

1944   Lillian Hellman's last political drama, *The Searching Wind*

1945   Mary Chase's *Harvey* wins the Pulitzer Prize, running for 1,775 performances

1946   Lillian Hellman's *Another Part of the Forest*

1947   The first Tony Awards dinner is held
Marsha Norman born; Norman will win acclaim for her intense dramas which often subvert traditional narrative strategies

1948   Poet and playwright Ntozake Shange (Paulette Williams) born; Shange will become known for her artistic innovations, especially the "choreopoem"

1949   Alice Childress' *Florence*
Lillian Hellman's adaptation of Emmanuel Robles' *Montserrat*

1950s–60s Emergence of Off-Broadway, regional and university theatre

1950   Wendy Wasserstein born; Wasserstein will become a playwright known for creating strong women's roles and will be the first woman playwright to win a Tony Award

1951   Lillian Hellman's *The Autumn Garden*
Paula Vogel born; Vogel's plays will focus on the non-traditional family, and social issues such as AIDS, domestic violence, sexual abuse, and the feminization of poverty

1952   Alice Childress' *Gold Through the Trees*
Lillian Hellman directs a revival of *The Children's Hour*; in this same year she is called to testify before the House Un-American Activities Committee
Beth Henley born; Henley will be known for creating women characters who define themselves apart from men; her first New York production will earn her a Pulitzer Prize
Emily Mann born; Mann will become known for her documentary dramas, her focus on gender roles and sexual politics, and her several tours of duty as artistic director for theatres from Minneapolis to New Jersey and New York

1955   Alice Childress' *Trouble in Mind* wins an Obie
Lillian Hellman's adaptation of Jean Anouilh's *The Lark*

1956   Performance artist and writer Karen Finley born; Finley will earn an MFA in Performance Art at the San Francisco Art Institute; her work will focus on victimization, the dysfunctional family, and the eroticization of the body
Performance artist, director, actress Anna Deavere Smith born

1957   Lillian Hellman writes the book for *Candide*, a musical based on Voltaire

1958   Ketti Frings' *Look Homeward, Angel* wins the Pulitzer Prize

1959   Lorraine Hansberry's *A Raisin in the Sun* opens at the Ethel Barrymore Theatre and runs for 530 performances, winning a New York Drama Critics Circle Award; New York revivals in 1979 and 1983 will earn critical acclaim as will a musical version, *Raisin*, produced in 1973

1960   Association of Producing Artists founded
Lillian Hellman's last stage play, *Toys in the Attic*

1961	Jean Kerr's *Mary Mary* Megan Terry's *New York Comedy*

1962   Adrienne Kennedy's *Funnyhouse of a Negro*

1963   Adrienne Kennedy's *The Owl Answers*
        Suzan-Lori Parks born; carrying on the legacy of earlier
        African American women playwrights, Parks will earn praise
        in the *New York Times* as the most promising playwright to
        emerge in the 1989–90 season
        Megan Terry's *Eat at Joe's*

1964   Lorraine Hansberry's *The Sign in Sidney Brustein's Window*
        Adrienne Kennedy's *Funnyhouse of a Negro* wins an Obie

1965   National Endowment for the Arts established
        The annual gross for 1964–65 season on Broadway is
        $50,462,765; approximately 15 percent of the season is
        written by women dramatists
        Georgia Douglas Johnson receives an honorary degree from
        Atlanta University
        Megan Terry's *Calm Down Mother*

1966   Alice Childress' *Wedding Band*
        Megan Terry's *Viet Rock: A Folk War Movie*; *Viet Rock* is the
        first rock musical and the first Vietnam protest play; Terry
        receives international acclaim for writing and direction

1967   Barbara Garson's assassination satire *Macbird!*
        Rochelle Owens' *Futz* wins an Obie

1969   Alice Childress' *Wine in the Wilderness*
        Lorraine Hansberry's posthumous *To Be Young, Gifted and
        Black*
        Adrienne Kennedy's *A Rat's Mass*

1970s   Political/feminist theatre groups emerge: Anselma DelliOllio's
        New Feminist Repertory, the New Feminist Theatre, the
        Spiderwoman Theatre, At the Foot of the Mountain; such
        alternative groups begin forming in urban centers, employing
        radical techniques to challenge mainstream, middle-class,

commercial, linear, realistic theatre; these new groups are committed to collaborative theatre and multicultural awareness – the Spiderwoman Theatre, for example, is founded by Native American women
The emergence and proliferation of feminist theatre inspires the formation of lesbian ensembles: the Lavender Cellar in Minneapolis, the Red Dyke Theatre in Atlanta, the Lesbian-Feminist Theatre Collective in Pittsburgh

1970   Megan Terry's *Approaching Simone* wins an Obie

1971   Megan Terry begins her long career as the resident playwright and literary manager of the Omaha Magic Theatre, where she remains committed to community problem plays and social action dramas

1972   The Women's Theatre Council is formed
Adrienne Kennedy and Megan Terry earn grants from the National Endowment for the Arts; Terry will earn a National Endowment fellowship in 1989

1973   Tina Howe's *Birth and After Birth*
Jean Kerr's *Finishing Touches*
Megan Terry earns a Creative Arts Public Service grant

1974   The emergence of the dinner theatre fad

1975   Ntozake Shange's *For Colored Girls Who Have Considered Suicide/When the Rainbow Is Enuf*; *For Colored Girls* wins an Obie in 1977

1976   Julia Heward's performance piece *Shake! Daddy! Shake!*
Tina Howe's *Museum*
Adrienne Kennedy's *A Movie Star Has to Star in Black and White*

1977   Martha Boesing's *The Story of a Mother*
Obie to Maria Irene Fornes' direction of *Fefu and Her Friends*
Marsha Norman's first play, *Getting Out*, wins the John Gassner Playwriting Medallion, the Newsday Oppenheim Award, and a special citation from the New York Drama

Critics Circle; the play opens in Louisville and moves to New York the following year

Wendy Wasserstein's thesis play, *Uncommon Women and Others*, produced at the Yale School of Drama

1978   Approximately 40 feminist theatres can be counted; just three years later, some 112 exist

Susan Eisenberg founds Word of Mouth Productions, a theatre collective exclusively for women hoping to reach working-class female audiences; Women's Project and Productions also founded in New York

1979   Tina Howe's *The Art of Dining*; *The Art of Dining* wins an Obie in 1983

Ntozake Shange's *spell #7*

Paula Vogel's *Desdemona*

1980   Adrienne Kennedy's *Orestes and Electra*

Emily Mann's *Still Life*; Mann directs the 1980 Chicago production, the 1981 New York production, and the productions in Edinburgh and London in 1984

1981   Split Britches, a feminist/lesbian theatre company, is founded by Lois Weaver, Peggy Shaw, and Deborah Margolin; an off-shoot of the Spiderwoman Theatre performing in New York's East Village at the WOW Café, the company employs Brechtian techniques to critique rigid gender roles and compulsory heterosexuality

Beth Henley's first play *Crimes of the Heart* earns her a Pulitzer Prize and a New York Drama Critics Circle Award

Emily Mann wins an Obie for *Still Life*

Ntozake Shange's adaptation of Brecht's *Mother Courage* wins an Obie

Paula Vogel's *The Oldest Profession*

Wendy Wasserstein makes her debut as an actress in a play by Wallace Shawn

1982   Maria Irene Fornes earns an Obie for Sustained Achievement

Beth Henley's *The Wake of Jamey Foster*

1983 Maria Irene Fornes garners Obies for *Mud*, *The Danube*, and *Sarita*
Tina Howe's *Painting Churches* wins an Obie, an Outer Critics Circle Award, and a Rosamond Gilder Award
Marsha Norman's *'night, Mother*, a Pulitzer Prize and Susan Smith Blackburn Prize-winner
Anna Deavere Smith's *On the Road: A Search for American Character*
Wendy Wasserstein's Guggenheim Fellowship enables *Isn't it Romantic*

1984 Beth Henley's *The Miss Firecracker Contest*
Anna Deveare Smith's *Aye, Aye, Aye I'm Integrated* is produced Off-Broadway

1985 Maria Irene Fornes' *The Conduct of Life* wins an Obie
Marsha Norman's *Third and Oak* published; contains two one-acts that are mirror images of one another, *The Laundromat* (1980) and *The Pool Hall*

1986 Tina Howe's *Painting Churches* is televised on PBS's American Playhouse
Emily Mann's *Annulla*; Mann makes her Broadway directing debut with *Execution of Justice*
Paula Vogel's *And Baby Makes Seven*
Jane Wagner's *The Search for Signs of Intelligent Life in the Universe*

1987 Alice Childress wins the Harlem School of the Arts Humanitarian Award
Karen Finley's *The Constant State of Desire*
Tina Howe's *Coastal Disturbances*
Holly Hughes' *Dress Suits to Hire*

1988 Karen Finley's *The Theory of Total Blame*
Tina Howe's *Approaching Zanzibar*
Wendy Wasserstein's Pulitzer Prize-winning play and first play by a woman to win a Tony, *The Heidi Chronicles*

1989 First International Women Playwrights' Conference, Buffalo, NY

Karen Finley's *We Keep Our Victims Ready*
Suzan-Lori Parks' *Imperceptible Mutabilities in the Third Kingdom*; Parks wins an Obie and praise in the *New York Times*

1990   Adrienne Kennedy's *The Ohio State Murders*
Suzan-Lori Parks' *The Death of the Last Black Man in the Whole Entire World*

1991   The Broadway production of Marsha Norman's adaptation of Frances Hodgson Burnett's *The Secret Garden* is noted for its creative team of women: Norman, book; Lucy Simon, music; Susan H. Schulman, director; Jeanine Levenson, dance arrangements and associate conductor; Heidi Landesman, scenery and production team; Elizabeth Williams, producer
Suzan-Lori Parks' *Betting on the Dust Commander*
Anna Deavere Smith's *Fires in the Mirror*

1992   Tina Howe's *One Shoe Off*
Suzan-Lori Parks' *Everything*
Anna Deavere Smith's *Twilight Los Angeles*
Paula Vogel's *The Baltimore Waltz* and *Hot 'n' Throbbing*
Wendy Wasserstein's *The Sisters Rosensweig*

1993   Director Anne Bogart stages a Brechtian and feminist production of Clare Boothe Luce's *The Women*

1994   Martha Boesing's *Hard Times Come Again No More*
Lisa Loomer's *The Waiting Room*, a Best Play of 1994–95
Anne Meara's *After-Play*; Meara, of the comedy team Stiller and Meara, is noted for both performance and writing for the stage, screen, and radio
Suzan-Lori Parks' *The America Play*
Wendy Wasserstein speaks at a rally trying to save the endangered National Endowment for the Arts; a National Endowment for the Arts grant made Wasserstein's smash hit *The Heidi Chronicles* possible

1995   Emily Mann's *Having Our Say*

1996   Rita Dove's *The Darker Face of the Earth*; this is the first full-

length play by Dove, Poet Laureate of the United States
1993–95
Emily Mann's *Greensboro: A Requiem* chronicles the shooting
of anti-Klan protesters
Anna Deavere Smith begins working on her "Press and the
Presidency" project which will lead to a theatre piece and
several *Newsweek* articles in 1997
Wendy Wasserstein's *An American Daughter*, the first of
Wasserstein's plays to be produced directly on Broadway
without an Off-Broadway run

1997   ARTNOW, a grassroots celebration of and demonstration for
the arts and arts funding is held April 19
Beth Henley's *The Lucky Spot*
Tina Howe's *Pride's Crossing*

1998   Paula Vogel wins the Pulitzer Prize for *How I Learned To
Drive*

I

PIONEERS

I

AMELIA HOWE KRITZER

Comedies by early American women

Early American dramatists worked within a set of dramatic forms and theatrical traditions inherited from England. The most important comedic forms were sentimental comedy, social comedy, comic opera, and satire. Among theatrical traditions transmitted from England was the acceptance of women as playwrights: comedies by English women writers were among the most popular works in the theatres of early America. Early in the history of the new nation, American writers began using and reshaping drama to represent specifically American identities, experiences, and perspectives. While the American context offered new opportunities, however, it also presented unique obstacles. Strong antitheatrical attitudes, based on religious opposition to acting and cultural opposition to elite art forms, combined with thinly populated cities and scarcity of resources to make establishment of theatre difficult in the United States. To counter antitheatricalism, or perhaps merely to address unsophisticated audiences, writers of early American comedies assume a highly didactic tone and focus closely on issues of national identity. They present incidents in American history, demonstrate the dimensions of American citizenship, and exhort the audience to feelings of patriotism.

Women playwrights brought an additional item to this nationalistic agenda: they created characters that attempted to give tangible form to the idea of the American woman. Defining the United States in terms of the unparalleled freedom it offered women, despite the fact that it denied them the political rights it established for men, early American women praised and explored freedom in the comedies they wrote. They used the power of dramatic representation (perhaps, in some cases, as a conscious alternative to or intermediate step toward political representation) to demonstrate the energy, intelligence, and responsibility with which women of the new nation enjoyed their freedoms. The pursuit of happiness, a classic comedic theme but also one of the inalienable rights named in the preamble to the US Constitution, emerges as the central concern in comedies by early American women.

3

The first American woman to become known as a writer of dramatic comedy was Mercy Otis Warren. Born in 1728 in Massachusetts, Mercy Otis Warren gained wide exposure to books and ideas within her highly literate and politically active family. The cause of the American Patriots propelled Otis Warren into serious writing. As sister of the Patriot leader James Otis, wife of a high-ranking officer in Washington's army, and close friend of John and Abigail Adams, Warren lived at the center of Revolutionary activity in Massachusetts. When John Adams urged her to write satire, she joined her efforts to what Walter Meserve has called the "war of belles lettres" (*Emerging Entertainment*, 60) – the literary war between pamphleteers on both sides who anonymously but passionately attacked their opponents.

Mercy Otis Warren's best-known dramatic satire, and the only one for which she claimed authorship, is *The Group* (1775).[1] *The Group* first reached the public as installments in periodicals, then was published as a pamphlet. The play was not intended for performance, but may have been given dramatic readings in the camps of the Patriot army and in gatherings of those opposed to British rule. Only in a technical sense is this work a comedy; its tone alternates between outraged anger and lofty scorn. The sharp and literate satire focuses on the group of men appointed by England to govern Massachusetts in 1774, as part of what came to be known as the Intolerable Acts. Giving these men symbolic names like Hazelrod, Meagre, Hateall, Humbug, Spendall, and Dupe, Warren shows them preparing for war with the colonists who are "armed and all resolved to die" rather than allow this group to usurp the power of the elected assembly (31).[2] As they talk, the group's members reveal the base motives, cowardice, petty rivalries, callousness, and cruelty that Patriot polemic imputed to the Tories. While some express remorse for the ideals and people they have betrayed, others declare their readiness to use "brutal force" (34), invoking as models the Roman emperors Nero, Claudius, and Caligula.

While she does not include women in the primary action of the play, Warren makes it clear that the methods and mentality of her primary target, Hateall (based on Tory leader Timothy Ruggles) particularly threaten women's right to the pursuit of happiness. Renouncing compassion, Hateall declares that he would not abandon his position on the British governing council, even to save his wife, family, and friends. Hateall goes on to boast of beating his wife and recommends the same course to Simple Sapling if his wife objects to quartering soldiers in their home. Since Warren is known to have heightened her satire with genuine personal details (for example, by turning Tory leader Daniel Leonard, who dressed elegantly and was the only lawyer in Massachusetts to own a carriage, into the dandified and luxury-loving Beau Trumps), it is possible that these lines refer to real actions or character traits of Ruggles. In any case, the emphasis placed by Warren on Hateall's oppression of women points to a particular interest in the situation of women embedded in more general concerns about the issues that brought about the American Revolution.

Warren's woman-oriented perspective on the conflict becomes most apparent in the final lines of *The Group*. When the men, who have been meeting in the main room of a tavern, depart, a woman comes out of an adjoining alcove and speaks. It appears that she has heard the entire proceedings. In a soliloquy she speaks sadly of the bloodshed to come but confidently predicts victory by "freedom's sons" (53). Warren's description of this woman as "nearly connected with one of the principal actors in the group" (52) suggests that wives of Tories may separate their own pursuit of happiness from the interests of their husbands. Though the anonymous woman does not refer to spying, the situation that has permitted her to overhear everything hints at that possibility. Hateall's insistence that women be forced to quarter troops within their homes implies that wives of the Tory leaders would have access to important information and could hardly be blamed if they used it to undermine the efforts of the men who treated them so badly. Although a female character takes the stage only in this brief scene, her central position at the end of the play and her serious speech supporting the rebellion against England argue for consideration of the needs of American women at this time, even as they argue the Patriot cause.

Theatres, closed during the Revolutionary War, began reopening soon after it ended, and theatre in the United States expanded throughout the early national period, 1787–1815. Women dramatists of this period include Susanna Haswell Rowson (1762–1828), Judith Sargent Murray (1751–1820), Mary Carr Clarke (*fl.* 1815–38), and Sarah Pogson (*fl.* 1807–18).[3] Though no American women earned their living writing for the theatre at this time, or even persisted for long in a career with many difficulties and few rewards, a few did see their works produced and/or published. Their plays, like those of their male counterparts, emphasize issues of American identity. To the cast of distinctively American character types, of which the best known was the "Jonathan,"[4] women playwrights added the American woman – distinguished by her love of freedom and non-traditional strengths.

Susanna Haswell Rowson wrote comedies while a member of an acting company in Philadelphia. Though born in England, Rowson spent most of her childhood in Massachusetts, where she was a frequent visitor in the home of Mercy Otis Warren's brother. The outbreak of the Revolution, however, brought a rupture with these and other neighbors, since Susanna's father was a British naval officer; eventually the entire Haswell family was deported to Britain. There Susanna began writing novels, married William Rowson, and went on stage, touring in England and Scotland. Rowson and her husband came to the United States in 1793, as members of the New American Company. Rowson wrote several comedies for performance at her family's benefits,[5] but only *Slaves in Algiers* (1794) has survived. Rowson quit the stage in 1797 and opened a school for girls near Boston, which proved very successful. She continued writing, producing novels, poetry, and textbooks.

Slaves in Algiers, a comic opera with music composed by Alexander Reinagle, was first performed at Philadelphia's Chestnut Street Theatre, where Reinagle was manager, on December 22, 1794, after which it entered the company's repertory and was regularly performed. Dealing with the capture of American sea travelers by the Barbary pirates – a genuine international problem at the time – it contrasts two nations that, to Rowson, exemplified opposite extremes of freedom and oppression. The play presents two separate groups of characters: the captors, who inflict suffering on their victims but behave in a cowardly way when threatened, and the captives, who hold fast to their ideals while courageously struggling for freedom.

From the first scene, *Slaves in Algiers* emphasizes its theme that happiness and full human development depend on freedom of choice. Fetnah, the "chosen favorite" of the Dey (ruler) of Algiers, pronounces the house and clothing with which she has been provided "vastly pretty," but insists that she cannot be happy without liberty. Confiding that the Dey has commanded her to love him, she reports her reply: "I am sensible I am your slave ... you bought my person of my parents, who loved gold better than they did their child, but my affections you could not buy. I can't love you" (60). Continuing, Fetnah reveals that an American woman held by her father, the pirate Ben Hassan "nourished in my mind the love of liberty and taught me woman was never made to be the abject slave of man" (60). Fetnah envisions the home country of her American friend as "a charming place where there are no bolts and bars ... no guards ... a dear, delightful country, where women do just what they please!" (73). In the course of the play, Fetnah disguises herself, escapes from the palace, joins a band of ransomed captives plotting revolt, and offers to help them fight.

Fetnah's friend, Rebecca Constant, demonstrates the response of the exemplary American woman to being held in captivity. While waiting for friends to send the demanded ransom – not realizing that the sum has already arrived and been pocketed by the scoundrel Hassan – Rebecca prays for the safety of her teenaged son, considering her own situation inconsequential compared to the forced labor to which he is subjected. When her captor proposes that they "marry," thinking he can tempt her with the promise of three servants, she rebuffs him firmly. Meditating aloud, Rebecca reveals that she was separated from her husband and daughter during the Revolutionary War, and has long been traveling in the hope of finding them. When Rebecca later finds that Hassan has fled, leaving behind the money extorted from her, she determines to secure the freedom of other captives. Pushing aside the guard, she marches into the Dey's throne room and demands to be heard.

There Rebecca finds a group of American captives who have been playing out a second plot. Olivia, along with her father and fiancé, have been recaptured after an escape attempt. The Dey has offered to release the two men if Olivia becomes one of his wives; she has agreed, but is planning suicide as soon as the men are free. Rebecca offers to pay their ransom, but the Dey refuses, then gives Olivia a few minutes to say her goodbyes. When Rebecca insists there must be some way she can help, Olivia replies that her "fate, alas, is fixed" but asks the name of this sympathetic stranger. Olivia and her father then discover they are Rebecca's long-lost daughter and husband. This discovery prompts them to resolve that they "will die together" rather than allow Olivia to sacrifice herself (91).

The Dey orders their deaths, but is interrupted by the culmination of yet another subplot. The American sailor Frederic has initiated a rebellion of all the captives. This rebellion now reaches into the Dey's throne room, bringing in its wake Rebecca's son Augustus, Fetnah, and a chastened Ben Hassan. The villains instantly pledge reform, and Fetnah decides to defer her dream of going to America in order to supervise the promised changes. As the curtain falls, Olivia expresses the hope that "freedom spread her benign influence through every nation" (93).

Though the plot concludes at this point, Rowson was not yet finished with her audience; the epilogue she wrote for *Slaves in Algiers* makes a most provocative statement. Having exited after playing the role of Olivia, Rowson has herself summoned back by name, then reenters as playwright, and speaks directly to women:

> Well, ladies, tell me: how d'ye like my play?
> "The creature has some sense," methinks you say;
> "She says that we should have supreme dominion,
> "And in good truth, we're all of her opinion.
> "Women were born for universal sway;
> "Men to adore, be silent, and obey.   (94)

Rowson thus imagines out loud that women in the audience view the message of the play as female supremacy, but then assures them that women's real powers lie in soothing and caring for those around them, so that they "hold in silken chains the lordly tyrant man" (94). Whether Rowson used her tone of voice to advocate one of these opposing ideas of women's role, or made fun of both, cannot be known today. Nevertheless, this epilogue speaks on several levels about the potential power of women, the rights they might lay claim to, and the roles they might perform in the new nation.

Critics have, not surprisingly, seen in this play an expression of Rowson's interest in women's rights (see Brandt, *Susanna Haswell Rowson* Weil, *In Defense of Women*, and Parker, *Susanna Rowson*). Some have pointed to the parallel between marriage and slavery. It should be noted, however, that forced marriage and denial of female autonomy occur only within a society Rowson views as antithetical to American and Christian values. The more important agenda of the play is its attempt to represent the emergence of the American woman. Active, loyal, courageous, patriotic, thoughtful – the female characters of *Slaves in Algiers* demonstrate, and indeed seem to assume, equality with men. The American women of the play find themselves forced to confront a powerful system of tyranny; they defy this system, and in doing so define themselves, just as Americans gained their identity through defying British rule.

Judith Sargent Murray was the first American-born woman to have plays professionally produced. Born into a wealthy and politically active Massachusetts family, Murray gained an informal but impressive education and throughout her life advocated the education of women. After her marriage to John Murray, the founder of Universalism in the United States, she lived with him in Boston. Though best known for her essays, in which a prominent theme is the equality of women, Murray also wrote two sentimental comedies, *Virtue Triumphant* (1795) and *The Traveller Returned* (1796).[6] Both were performed at Boston's Federal Street Theatre, an institution Murray had helped to establish. *Virtue Triumphant* takes as its plot a familiar situation: Eliza, orphaned and penniless, and Charles, the heir to a fortune, fall in love. Their love is at first opposed by Charles' father, but the familiar scenario takes an unexpected twist when Eliza herself refuses to consider marrying Charles because of the status difference – and persists in her refusal even when Charles' father changes his mind. The play's subplot concerns the married couple with whom Eliza resides: Mrs. Bloomville's extravagance threatens to bankrupt her husband. *Virtue Triumphant* places the pursuit of happiness within the context of reason and responsibility. While emphasizing the importance of sensible and dutiful attitudes, Murray suggests that these attitudes can best be acquired through education and the exercise of choice.

The Traveller Returned focuses on a family broken apart nineteen years before the start of the action by the young wife's indiscretions. Because she engaged in a serious flirtation with another man, Mrs. Montague's husband left her, taking their young son, but leaving the infant daughter with her. He returns from his sojourn abroad on the eve of war between England and the American colonies, to observe her without revealing his identity. She, meanwhile, has long regretted her behavior. She has managed the household alone and reared not only her daughter, Harriot, but also a niece, Emily, and both are now of marriageable age. Camden, a young military officer, is courting Harriot; unknown to any of them, he is her brother, who has grown up with foster parents in another state. The subplot of the comedy, in which a dishonest innkeeper and his wife get the returned husband arrested as a spy so that they can steal his valuables, precipitates the play's happy ending. This play shows that freedom can permit a woman to make mistakes, but that she can correct her mistakes and succeed in the quest for happiness. Despite its didactic tone, the play offers amusing entertainment, with a droll "Jonathan," an eccentric old gentleman, and a couple of sly villains – a male with a comic Dutch accent and a female given to malapropisms.

Though one of the first American women to earn her living as a writer, Mary Carr (later Mary Clarke) remains almost unknown. Born in Philadelphia, Carr lived there and in New York. To support herself and her children after the death of her husband, Carr engaged in a wide variety of writing pursuits: starting and editing a weekly magazine, writing songs and poetry, writing and reviewing plays, doing journalistic reporting, writing biographies, and even ghost-writing the memoirs of a notorious female criminal.[7] A continuing association with the theatre is suggested by the success of a play written late in her life.[8] Carr Clarke's only comedy was probably performed at Philadelphia's Chestnut Street Theatre on January 6, 1815, under the title *The Return from Camp*, then published as *The Fair Americans* later that year.

The Fair Americans intertwines the outbreak of the war of 1812 with the affairs of two rural families who live near Lake Erie, adding theatrical interest with music, pageantry, and scenic spectacle. The peaceful life of this Pennsylvania community is disturbed when military recruiters come to the area with the news that war has been declared. Despite doubt over the validity of the conflict, most of the young men join the army. From this point, the play's action divides into two separate spheres. On the farm, the work of raising poultry and livestock, growing crops, spinning, weaving, sewing, knitting, dairying, baking, and brewing continues. In the military camp, preparations are made and battles launched. While the men are away, the women develop new strengths and consolidate their power within the sphere of the household; they also encounter danger when two young women, Sophia and Anna, are kidnapped by Indians. Life in the military reveals that some men, such as the doughty General Trueman, exemplify American virtues, while others, such as the vain and cowardly Ensign Freelove, do not. At the end, when the war is won, the two spheres reunite. That this reunion, as well as the welcoming of a British officer as a prospective son-in-law of the Fairfields, takes place on the farm, suggests that the farm household symbolizes the nation as a whole. Within this combined sphere, women work hard, but do so as equal partners in the familial and societal pursuit of happiness.

Sarah Pogson (also Sarah Pogson Smith), another virtual unknown,[9] arrived in Charleston, South Carolina, shortly after the Revolution and spent most of her life there. In addition to several plays, including one about Charlotte Corday,[10] Pogson's writings include a long poetic work and two novels. *The Young Carolinians*, published in 1818, takes a form similar to Rowson's comedy, but adds regional emphases. Ellinor, a young South Carolina woman, along with her brother and a female companion, are captured by the Barbary pirates while on a voyage to seek out Ellinor's fiancé, who has not been heard from in months. They find him and his servant Zeikel among the captives in Algiers. The men are forced to perform backbreaking labor, and Ellinor's companion Margaret is sent to be a servant in a private household. Ellinor finds herself desired by an Algerian prince. The plucky, backwoods-bred Zeikel and Margaret manage to free themselves and return to Charleston for help. Back in Charleston, Caroline, who has remained behind, breaks off her engagement with James because of his compulsive gambling. Miss Woodberry, who is aunt and guardian to several of the young people, immediately despatches money to ransom the captives. Before the ship with the ransom sails, however, the missing young people arrive home, having escaped by means of a complex plot involving feigned death, disguise, and hand-to-hand fighting. With this reunion, Caroline and James, who has given up gambling, also get back together.

With scenes alternating between South Carolina and Algiers, the play focuses on various forms of bondage – not only the slave status of the African house servant in South Carolina or the capture and forced labor of the "young Carolinians" in Algiers, but also the gambling habit, emotional excesses, sexual obsession, class prejudice, and ignorance of other characters. Pogson attempts to draw a distinction between the cruel and predatory

Algerian slave-drivers and the kindly South Carolinian woman who elicits expressions of affection from her elderly house slave, Cudjo. Unlike Rowson, Pogson does not dwell on the injustice of Americans being enslaved by the Barbary pirates; instead, she presents the view that such capture is merely one of the many ordeals humans must endure and through which they must try to improve themselves. In the view of Pogson's *raisonneuse*, Miss Woodberry, life itself imposes a kind of bondage, but "the mind well regulated and conscious of its powers, may by perseverance subdue all that would sink its dignity, or confine its faculties" (Pogson, *Essays*, 109–10).

These five comedies of the early national period all contest traditional power relations through the plays' structure. Rather than relegating female characters to secondary roles, they place them in the center, where they initiate action and speak their minds. This focus on the female takes place without apology or explanation. All the plays thus assume a basic level of power for women. In addition, the dramatists twist traditional comic form, which typically revolves around males' pursuit of one desirable woman. Depicting courtship as a search for the right partner rather than a conflict over the most desirable woman, the plays show the young women as much in pursuit as the men. Several of the female characters make journeys to find the men they love, and all speak openly and frankly when they proclaim love to the man of their choice. Male desire serves as an obstacle in the captivity plays and as an almost passive quality in others – for example, when Camden has trouble extricating himself from a presumed commitment to Harriot, even though neither loves the other. Some plays show comic role reversal, as when Ben Hassan, dressed as a woman to attempt escape, becomes the ridiculous object of pursuit by a drunken sailor.

The plays further revise comic form in their endings. Rather than emphasizing marriage or marriages, they conclude with the reunion of families or communities, with the couples linked in an egalitarian partnership and with some members of the group remaining unpaired but still very much a part of the whole. The presence of both mature and young characters, including long-married couples, emphasizes continuity rather than climax. The participants express their joy in the reunions by means of nationalistic rhetoric that projects the characters into the future. The endings thus offer a symbolic representation of America as a unified family or community in which both males and females pursue happiness as couples or as individuals.

All five plays make it clear in titles, prefaces, or character descriptions that their female characters are meant to be typical of American women.

The plays present communities of women, old and young, signaling a concern with collective, as well as individual, pursuit of happiness – and thus with the question of women's political power and status. Within these communities, the mature women serve as guarantors of stability and teachers of the national ideals to the young people under their care. The young women thus learn to make choices within the framework of the mother–child relationship – an idea consistent with the post-Revolutionary formulation of woman's political role as that of the "republican mother" (see Kerber, "Republican Mother"). These plays, however, seize upon the most independent, assertive, and socially active elements in the construct of the republican mother. When mature women face down a tyrant, as does Rebecca in *Slaves in Algiers*, engage in commercial dealings, as does Matronia Aimwell in *Virtue Triumphant*, or (even jokingly) propose a political role for themselves, as does Mrs. Fairfield in *The Fair Americans*, who says, "I wish I was Congress; I would always be at peace" (Kritzer, *Plays By Early American Women*, 198), they demonstrate that a public, even political, role for women in the new republic would require no stretch of logic.

Within these female-centered communities, the women develop non-traditional strengths as well as traditional virtues. All the female characters actively pursue goals: Olivia maneuvers to secure the freedom of her loved ones in *Slaves in Algiers*; Eliza emigrates to the United States alone in *Virtue Triumphant*; Margaret files open the bars that confine her in *The Young Carolinians*. Even those who must wait out a situation keep active. Harriot in *The Traveller Returned* engages in physical exercise, declaring after one walk that she has been "rambling ... half the town over" and is "delightfully fatigued" (119–20).[11] Sophia and Anna of *Fair Americans* similarly take long, vigorous walks. Rebecca in *Slaves in Algiers* reads while being held, Mrs. Montague in *The Traveller Returned* studies science while her husband is away, and Ellinor in *The Young Carolinians* insists on some work to keep her occupied during her captivity. Most exhibit an emotional strength that carries them through danger and adversity, en-abling them to place themselves in jeopardy to secure the safety or happiness of those they love. The virtue that most distinguishes the exemplary American women in these comedies is discretion. Since they develop discretion through the trial-and-error exercise of choice, this virtue depends on freedom.

The plays do acknowledge that independence carries risks. Freedom of choice implies the possibility of choosing wrongly. Murray's plays both present women whose behavior has led to unhappiness: Mrs. Bloomville, who wastes time and money, and Louisa Montague, who has caused the breakup of her family. These characters, however, demonstrate the ability to change and indicate that good character may develop over time. Several of the young women, including Anna and Sophia in *The Fair Americans*, who are seized by Indians while walking after dark, and Ellinor in *The Young Carolinians*, who is captured while traveling in search of her fiancé, experience violent abductions as a result of taking risks. The happy endings of the plays, however, provide reassurance that women do no permanent harm by their exercise of freedom, even if they encounter accidents.

Comedy, of course, implies movement toward pairing, and while these plays do show most of the young women pairing off with young men, they also claim for American women the choice of a single life as their path to happiness. When *Virtue Triumphant*'s Eliza tells Charles, "I never, but on equal terms, will plight my faith with yours," she envisions herself remaining single and insists she will be happy (Murray, *Gleaner*, 560–61). Although a surprise ending permits Eliza to marry the man she loves, the pleasant personality, important responsibilities, and numerous friends of the single, middle-aged Matronia Aimwell present a positive view of single life in the same play. Caroline, who breaks off her engagement in *Young Carolinians*, similarly expects to remain single and receives an equally encouraging view of life as an unmarried woman from her aunt.

Comedies by American women of the early national period thus express confidence that the unprecedented freedom accorded women in the new nation will naturally lead to their happiness. Though they do not explicitly argue for political rights, they demonstrate a consistent interest in the status of women. The female characters prove their ability to handle responsibility, and the playwrights signal optimism about their status in the future through the non-hierarchical groupings of men and women at the end, whose voices equally proclaim the greatness of the United States.

The optimism about new possibilities for women peaked during the early national period, then was lost in a wave of societal change that brought rapid urbanization, industrialization, and division of labor. Dramatic tastes changed as well, and the women who wrote for theatre in the 1830s and 1840s – Louisa Medina, Charlotte Barnes Conner, Elizabeth Ellet, Frances Wright – turned to melodrama and tragedy. Therefore, no comedies by American women have been recovered for the period 1815 to 1845. On March 24, 1845, the appearance of *Fashion* by Anna Cora Mowatt at New York's Park Theatre broke this long drought. *Fashion* became an instant hit, bringing Mowatt great recognition and success. This play alone among comedies written by women before 1850 has achieved a continuing place in American literature, being included in standard anthologies and receiving periodic production.

Anna Cora Ogden Mowatt (later Anna Cora Mowatt Ritchie) was born in 1819, and grew up in an upper-middle-class family in New York. As a child, she read all the plays of Shakespeare many times and staged impromptu performances in her home, but did not attend the theatre because of her family's religious opposition to it. While still in her teens, she married a well-to-do lawyer much older than she. In the early years of this marriage, she wrote and even published a play or two, but after her husband's financial failure she began to write in earnest. She also performed dramatic readings, then became a full-fledged actress, successfully touring the United States and England. Though she experienced social prejudice against her choice to go on the stage, she maintained her respectable reputation and helped to raise the estimation of the acting profession. After the death of her first husband, she married William Ritchie, a Southern journalist, but disagreement over the issue of slavery caused them to separate. She lived in Europe until her death in 1870. The scope of Mowatt's writing is quite broad: in addition to plays, she wrote novels, short stories, magazine articles, and her autobiography.

The action of *Fashion* takes place within the Tiffany household. Mrs. Tiffany, who has furnished her house in expensively garish style and covered herself with a veneer of spurious sophistication, attempts to ascend the social scale by marrying her daughter Seraphina to a French count. Mr. Tiffany, a merchant bankrupted by his wife's extravagance, has forged signatures to cover his debts; he hopes to marry the same daughter to his clerk-turned-blackmailer to secure silence. The household also contains an addled and gossipy old aunt, a French maid who feeds Mrs. Tiffany's obsession with everything European, a black valet dressed up in livery and renamed Adolph (from Zeke) to make him appear more fashionable, and Gertrude, a live-in music teacher for Seraphina.

As Mrs. Tiffany and her daughter are entertaining the collection of "drawing-room appendages" that comprise Seraphina's suitors, including the favored Count Jolimaitre, Trueman, an old friend of Mr. Tiffany, appears. Settling in for a stay in the household, he preaches "republican simplicity" and bluntly criticizes nearly everything he sees. The only person who gains his approval is the industrious and modest Gertrude. His confidence in Gertrude crumbles, however, when he comes upon her in a dark room with the Count. As it happens, Gertrude has set up a meeting with the Count in order to trick him into revealing that he is a fraud; the next day, a letter she has written makes the truth known to Trueman. He then reveals that he is Gertrude's grandfather, and possessed of a large fortune, to which she is heir.

Meanwhile, Seraphina is just prevented from eloping with Jolimaitre by

1. Scene from *Fashion* by Anna Cora Mowatt

the revelation of fraud. Trueman happily arranges for Gertrude to marry Colonel Howard, with whom a mutual attraction has developed, gets rid of the blackmailing clerk by informing him he could be charged as accessory to forgery, and offers to cover the Tiffanys' debts on condition that they will live in the country, giving up their social pretensions and extravagant habits.

Critics have generally praised *Fashion*, calling attention to its pivotal position in the development of American social comedy, or comedy of manners (see Havens, *Columbian Muse*). The play clearly and engagingly satirizes the social climbers and fortune hunters of a rapidly urbanizing nineteenth-century United States. Though a comedy – and a quite entertaining one – it serves as a serious warning to Americans that their constitutionally guaranteed right to the pursuit of happiness has been perverted into the pursuit of money and status. It also reminds its audience that they live in a world where appearance does not necessarily point to truth. The Tiffanys, who appear rich, are actually indigent; Gertrude, who appears poor, is heir to great wealth. The French count turns out to be an English cook and valet. Mrs. Tiffany, who egregiously mispronounces French, knows and actually cares little about actual European customs, and the bizarre behavior she presents as the latest fashion abroad represents only her own pretense and misunderstanding. Such rampant deceit makes pursuit of happiness not only complicated but almost futile.

The play, of course, offers a way out of the urban world of deceit and pursuit of dubious goals through its invocation of an idyllic rural world. Both Gertrude and Trueman represent that world. Even while living in the corrupt Tiffany household, Gertrude associates herself with this natural retreat by tending flowers in the conservatory. She has been reared by two selfless aunts, and her decision to work for the Tiffany family arose from her unselfish desire to become independent and not burden these elderly women further. Trueman acts as the touchstone of truth in the play; not even politeness can make him conceal his feelings of outrage at the travesty the Tiffany family has made of the pursuit of happiness.

Even as it presents a clear opposition between urban and rural life, however, *Fashion* operates on a deeper level. Its two sets of characters create a cultural and political contrast. The Tiffanys and their circle operate within the exciting and complex sphere of continual movement and change, where few constraints, no security, but great risk and great opportunity are the norms (see Halttunen, *Confidence Men*). Trueman represents those who cling stubbornly to tradition, enduring its limitations and lack of excitement for the sake of certainty and security. Rather than suggesting ways of modifying the contemporary urban world it depicts, to eliminate corruption, control competition, and reintroduce republican ideals while maintaining the momentum toward a broadening of opportunity, the play advocates a simple retreat into the rigid and placid realm of tradition. The play gives no consideration to the idea that this realm might present its own obstacles to the pursuit of happiness.

In its reverent view of tradition, *Fashion* represents a step backward in terms of its view of female identity and roles. While focusing on women, the play highlights weakness and folly rather than strength and capacity for reason. Seraphina, the young, desirable woman pursued by a large number of men, functions as a commodity to be used by her parents to achieve their goals – even when, at the end, she is to be bundled off to the country to save her parents from facing financial ruin and disgrace. Gertrude, the exemplary American woman, has left the kindly aunts who reared her, and is thus cut off from a supportive community that would allow her to find her own path to happiness. Perhaps for this reason, she never finds her own voice to proclaim the love she feels for Colonel Howard, instead playing a teasing verbal game. She gives her hand to Howard as a formal act of obedience to Trueman, when he reveals himself as her grandfather. In the end, Gertrude expects to return to the country, but her aunts have been supplanted by the patriarchal grandfather. Trueman is very eager to get Gertrude married; though he does want to make sure the marriage is a love match, he gives her no option of remaining single. Notably, the annoying maiden aunt in the Tiffany family presents an entirely negative view of the single woman. Though the solution to Mrs. Tiffany's errors provided at the end bears a faint echo of the view that women can improve their character and become exemplary Americans, it does not permit her to learn in an atmosphere of freedom; instead, the patriarch takes control of the Tiffany women's lives and dictates their choices. The definition of American at the end of the play, though it includes both men and women, is spoken by Trueman alone rather than by a chorus of citizens of both sexes. Ironically, this play that satirizes the desires of some Americans to ape European language abandons the idea that American women should be defined as different from – stronger and more independent than – their English counterparts. It counters the fast-moving pace of actual social change that offered potential as well as pitfalls to women, with a universalized model of weak women who need or prefer to subordinate their pursuit of happiness to the desires and control of men.

Comedies by American women of the late eighteenth and early nineteenth centuries demonstrate a strong and continuing interest in establishing a distinctive identity for the American woman. Their common pattern of linking freedom of choice with the pursuit of individual happiness points to a concern for the status of women. The alterations of comic convention and the daring character portrayals of the earlier plays, in which communities of women foster individual liberty, with both single and married older women serving as guardians and young women learning independence from them, indicate attempts to define the American woman in terms of new environments and experiences. When the plays show female characters acting responsibly, patriotically, and courageously, they imply that the American woman deserves to stand beside the American man in a national partnership of equals. By 1845, however, a more conservative vision of American womanhood is evident in *Fashion*'s confinement of women within domestic scenes and its idealization of feminine passivity. Comedies by early American women thus chart the change in attitudes from the relatively open-ended post-Revolutionary construct of the "republican mother" to a much more limiting definition of woman's sphere by the middle of the nineteenth century.

NOTES

1 Other satires attributed to Mercy Otis Warren include *The Adulateur* (1773), *The Defeat* (1773), and *The Blockheads; or The Affrighted Officers* (1776).

2 Page numbers refer to *The Group* in Amelia Howe Kritzer, ed., *Plays by Early American Women, 1775–1850*.

3 *The Chimera* by Mrs. Marriott, an actor with the Old American Company, was performed and published in Philadelphia in 1795; however, since Mrs. Marriott apparently spent only a brief period in the United States, her play is not included in this discussion.

4 The Jonathan character, introduced by Royall Tyler in *The Contrast* (1787) and later a stock type in many plays, was a backwoodsman whose good-natured simplicity was considered distinctively American.

5 Benefit performances, from which actors received the profits, supplemented their salaries. The actor whose benefit it was chose the play and roles to be performed; married couples or families usually shared a benefit.

6 The best of Murray's work, including her plays, is collected in *The Gleaner*, originally published in 1798 and recently republished by Union College Press.

7 *The Memoirs of the Celebrated and Beautiful Mrs. Ann Carson, Daughter of an Officer of the US Navy, and Wife of Another, Whose Life Terminated in the Philadelphia Prison* was originally published in 1822. The second edition, published in 1838, is available on microfilm.

8 *Sarah Maria Cornell; or the Fall River Murder*, performed at the Richmond Hill Theatre, New York, in 1834.

9 Recognition of Sarah Pogson as a playwright has been complicated by the fact that *Essays Religious, Moral, Dramatic, and Poetical* (1818), which contains three of her plays, was erroneously attributed to Maria Pinckney (see William S. Kable, "South Carolina District copyrights: 1794–1820").

10 *The Female Enthusiast*, 1807, included in Kritzer, ed., *Plays by Early American Women*.

11 Page numbers refer to *The Traveller Returned* in Kritzer, ed., *Plays by Early American Women*.

2

SARAH J. BLACKSTONE

Women writing melodrama

From Mary Carr Clarke's early play *The Benevolent Lawyers; or Villainy Detected* (1823), to the many successful novel adaptations by the prolific Louisa Medina, to Pauline Hopkins' *Slaves' Escape; or the Underground Railroad* (1880), to the widely varied work of Francis Hodgson Burnett, whose stage adaptations of her own novels span several decades, American women have been writing melodrama. These women, and others like them, played an important role in the development and success of the mode of drama that had the greatest impact on the American theatre in the nineteenth century.

The study of nineteenth-century melodrama has traditionally been on the fringes of scholarly work. This is due in large part to the concerted efforts of early twentieth-century theatre practitioners to create new forms completely divorced from melodrama, which by that time had held the stage for nearly a century. The writers and producers of the new styles of realism, naturalism, and symbolism had to slay the giant of melodrama in order to gain control of the theatre of the twentieth century. Writers such as George Bernard Shaw, Eugene O'Neill, Anton Chekhov, and Susan Glaspell began writing plays that demanded new acting and production styles. These writers, as well as designers, theorists, and producers, were passionate in their defense of a new aesthetic for the theatre and their arguments against melodrama gained in strength and validity as the old mode of communication failed to respond to the new age. Eventually scholars and practitioners began to speak with scorn of anything thought to be melodramatic, as they simultaneously spoke glowingly of all efforts to create a sense of realism. The final step in this process occurred when scholars began to look for the beginnings of realism in the works of authors who wrote melodrama. Those who showed signs of attempting realistic characters and situations were seen as good playwrights and earned a place in history books and the literary canon while those who wrote true melodrama were seen as lesser artists and were marginalized and forgotten.

The few studies of melodrama completed after realism became the dominant form concentrated on production techniques and theatre architecture, and on the famous actors and managers who worked with the few melodramas that would be remembered. Thousands of plays and playwrights were forgotten, and the scripts destroyed, lost, or collected in archives and forgotten. Few anthologies of even the most famous examples of this genre exist, making the plays very difficult to study.

The marginalization of melodrama as a flawed and failed form has been institutionalized in theatre training, scholarship, and general usage. Introductory theatre textbooks and histories of the theatre tend to vilify the form or dismiss it out of hand, melodramas are rarely produced even in academic settings, melodramatic style is not included in acting classes, and the form has become synonymous with overblown acting and poor writing. The term "melodrama" is defined by *The Random House Dictionary*, a supposedly neutral source, as "a drama in which exaggeration of effect and emotion is produced and plot or action is emphasized at the expense of characterization." The dominant dramatic form and production technique of the nineteenth century has been generally dismissed and essentially forgotten.

Over the past fifteen years, however, melodrama has been revisited by scholars because the plays are full of hints about the social practices and political attitudes of a former century. A number of interesting articles and several book-length studies have been published since 1980 which reconsider the plays and playwrights who worked in this genre. Much of the work completed so far has used the techniques of cultural history to investigate social attitudes and practices as they changed and developed during the nineteenth century.

In order to investigate what the plays have to say about the culture that produced and embraced them it is necessary to understand the genre as it was written and defined in the nineteenth century. These plays were generally scenarios, or outlines, for dramatic action rather than carefully crafted pieces of literature, and are sometimes very difficult to read and understand as written works. However, they should be studied, and their worth determined, by the requirements of the melodramatic genre and not by the standards of modern realism or other twentieth-century forms.

The history of the melodrama as a genre is fairly clear. The first play to be called a melodrama was produced in France in 1800 by René Pixérécourt, and the form was brought to England by Thomas Holcroft when he produced a translation of a Pixérécourt melodrama called *A Tale of Mystery* in 1802. The form swiftly spread, and as Vera Mowry Roberts explains in *The Nature of Theatre*:

Everywhere – in England, France, Germany, and America – melodrama was
the genre most performed during almost the whole of the nineteenth century.
It drew the largest audiences, filled the most theatres, and engaged the largest
number of actors, not excepting even Edwin Booth and Henry Irving. It
reached its peak of popularity about 1880 and since has been in a long, slow
decline ... on the stage of Western theatres. (218)

So exactly what is a melodrama? Determining the answer to this question
is not an easy task. The basic definitions of the genre are confusing and
contradictory, and most are tainted by negative language and are based on
too few examples of the form. The plays that are currently being recovered
from archives and other storage places are dizzying in their variety,
complexity, and subject matter. What was considered known must be
reexamined in the light of new discoveries, and old prejudices and
resistances must be overcome. A new comprehensive definition of melodrama must be developed as scholars reach a better understanding of the
genre.

However, a few general traits or characteristics can be listed with some
confidence at this time. Melodramas were "plays with music" as the term
implies. Scholars disagree as to whether each play was accompanied by a
complete score as movies are today, but all seem to believe that the
moments of highest emotion were accompanied by appropriate music. This
music was provided by a piano in smaller venues, but in the best theatres
entire orchestras were used. Many melodramas also contain incidental
songs and dances, some specifically written for a particular play and others
drawn from popular music of the day. *Camptown Races* is an example of a
popular song that was simply appropriated by a melodrama author. David
Belasco used this song in both *The Girl I Left Behind Me* and *The Girl of
the Golden West*. Most melodrama manuscripts that survive do not include
their musical scores, but many include the placement, and sometimes the
names, of songs and dances as stage directions, others simply call for
"specialties" at certain points in the action.

The diction of some melodramas, particularly those written early in the
nineteenth century, is extremely elevated to aid the emotional appeal of the
scripts. This was expected by audiences in the nineteenth century, but
sounds archaic to modern ears. This convention was replaced by efforts to
recreate authentic dialects in later melodramas. The dialogue in melodramas often seems stodgy or difficult to understand, regardless of when
the plays were written, and this aspect of the style must be overcome to
study them.

Melodramas develop the theme of good vs. evil in the way that heroic
tragedy developed the theme of love vs. honor. Often defined as plays on

serious subjects with happy endings, melodramas are thought to employ the device of poetic justice, where the good are rewarded and the evil punished on a scale commensurate with their actions. While poetic justice is often in evidence, this part of the definition must be stretched a good deal to cover the contents and endings of many melodramas now being studied. Heroines fall from grace and still obtain their happy ending, as is seen in *My Partner* by Bartley Campbell, where Mary actually gives birth to an illegitimate child during the play and still marries the hero. In other cases, heroines remain true to the values of their culture and are denied a happy ending. In Louisa Medina's *Nick of the Woods*, the star character Tellie Doe dies at the end of the play, receiving only a soulful epitaph from the hero as the reward for her virtuous behavior.

Much has been written about the stereotypical nature of the characters in melodrama who are held to be all good or all bad, and are immediately recognizable by their costumes and demeanor. This part of our current definition of melodrama also needs revision. Every script has an identifiable hero, heroine, and villain, but heroes sometimes fall prey to drink or gambling, virtuous women fall from grace, and villains reveal perfectly good motivations for their evil actions. Supporting characters seem less varied and do tend to fall into stereotypical categories. Most characters are affected by actions outside themselves and make decisions based on the social and moral codes of their day rather than reach any profound individual realizations about themselves, even when they show a mixture of good and bad in their characters. While at odds with the tenets of psychological realism, this does not mean that the plays are lesser works. Several great theatrical forms, most notably the *commedia dell'arte*, have been based on similar casts of recognizable characters who follow a loose scenario based on well understood social codes to tell their stories.

Because character development is generally not a focus of the melodramatic form, the plays are driven by plot and rely heavily on spectacle to elaborate the theme of good vs. evil. Characters face all kinds of obstacles, placed in their way by the playwright, to show their dedication to the requirements of good behavior as defined by nineteenth-century culture. Each act ends with some spectacular effect that leaves the audience anxious to know how the hero or heroine will escape. People are tied to railroad tracks or threatened by buzz saws; buildings or other structures burn to the ground; the mine entrance collapses; or the train runs off the track. Such twists and turns of plotting brought about the colloquial phrase "cliff hanger," and the technique is still used to good effect in television drama. Playwrights often had to manipulate the logic of the plot to bring about the happy ending that was a feature of the form. These contrived endings are seen by critics as another example of poor construction, although the Greeks often brought on a god at the end of the play to tie up all the loose ends left dangling by the playwright, yet these plays are not subjected to the same criticism.

The effect of melodrama is principally on the emotions rather than the intellect. For this reason, as well as the complicated plots which seem to make little logical sense, and characters that are perceived as stereotypical, the form has long been held to be mere entertainment and not really an art form. Recently scholars have begun to question this judgmental approach and urge a more measured study of the plays and the historical forces that produced them. Bruce McConachie, in his book *Melodramatic Formations: American Theatre and Society, 1820–1870* makes clear the project facing theatre historians:

> The relevant issue for theatre historians is not whether these diverse melo-
> dramas were any good ... Nor is it particularly helpful to rail against
> melodrama for encouraging its spectators to escape from reality ... Rather,
> the question is what types of melodramatic experiences did nineteenth-
> century theatre goers participate in and what meanings did they construct
> from them. In a sense, we need to understand not what audiences were
> escaping from, but what they were escaping to, and what impact this willing
> suspension of disbelief may have had on their lives ... Consequently, theatre
> historians need to explore what the experience of melodrama did with, for,
> and to their willing participants. (x)

If the study of melodrama itself is on the fringes of scholarship, the study of women who wrote such plays is even further from the center of theatrical investigation, and study of works by women of color almost completely absent. The work of early feminist scholars was concentrated on recovering the work and lives of women playwrights who were exceptional enough in their careers to gain notice in their own times and to leave a record of their accomplishments, and to include women of note in histories and antholo-gies. This project grew to include the investigation of known works by women for discussions of women's issues and/or advocacy for women's causes. Many important plays have been rediscovered and analyzed, and important biographical work has been completed as these issues are studied. Scholars are now beginning to study the works of those women who worked in all genres and at all levels of accomplishment throughout American history, and who may have had little recognition or success in their careers.

Over the years the examination of various theatrical documents has produced the names of many women playwrights and the titles of many plays written by women in the nineteenth century. But manuscripts of many of these plays have been lost, making evaluation of the careers of these playwrights impossible. However, the growing interest in melodrama has led to the rediscovery or reexamination of archival collections that contain many previously unknown works, some by women. For instance, a newly cataloged collection of 2,000 melodramas at Southern Illinois University contains 120 plays written by 91 different women. The earliest was copyrighted in 1878, the latest in 1931. Such discoveries are exciting and will undoubtedly lead to new knowledge about women writers of the nineteenth century.

Research is complicated by the lack of copyright laws during most of the nineteenth century, and the common practice of play piracy that resulted. Many play pirates simply obtained a printed copy of a script, changed the title and/or the character names, and copyrighted the resulting "new play" under their own names. Some of these pirates even sent stenographers to local theatres to copy down popular plays as they were being performed. These practices make it very difficult to determine who wrote what version of what play.

Other factors also complicate the process of attributing work to women authors. Anyone could adapt a novel for the stage, and many versions of certain stories existed, making it difficult to determine who wrote what, and where certain versions were performed. Rosemarie K. Bank has noted that Louisa Medina adapted at least two novels that had alternative stage versions on the boards at the same time her work was being produced ("Theatre and Narrative Fiction," 66–67). Women often used pen names, though rarely the names of men, to hide the fact that they were active in the public sphere, and actors often bought scripts outright from their authors and copyrighted the works in their own names, leaving the actual playwright out of the process altogether. Finally, many of the surviving manuscripts have no authors listed at all, leaving the researcher with the task of consulting copyright listings, which are often unreliable as shown above, and newspaper reviews and stories, when they can be located, for further information.

Biographical information about women of the nineteenth century is also difficult to obtain. Only the most independent and successful women were recognized in their own right and not as the wives or daughters of men. Women found it difficult or impossible to own property or transact business. The theatre was seen as a questionable place of employment, and some women were reluctant to admit their connection with plays or producing companies. Even when the details of a woman's theatrical connections can be discovered, it is often difficult to find even the most basic information about the rest of her life. New research techniques are being developed to help gain the information needed. New sources of information, particularly public documents, are being examined and old sources are being revisited with women particularly in mind.

As the surviving collections of melodrama manuscripts are mined for information about the nineteenth century, the works of women, including good plays and bad, melodramas and farces, comedies and tragedies, are being found and studied. The difficult work of recovering information about productions and public reception of these plays has begun, and biographical information about the women who wrote them is being extracted from a wide array of sources. We still know disappointingly little and there is much work yet to be done, but interesting facts have begun to emerge.

The lives of several American women playwrights who wrote melo-dramas have been carefully researched, and copies of their plays have become widely available. June Schlueter, ed., *Modern American Drama: The Female Canon*, Amelia Howe Kritzer, ed., *Plays By Early American Women, 1775–1850*, and Vivien Gardner and Susan Rutherford, eds., *The New Woman and Her Sisters: Feminism and Theatre 1850–1914* are excellent sources. A number of essays and individual articles have been published in theatrical journals over the past few years and many of these also contain excellent, if generally scanty, information about women writing melodrama. Some of the data below is drawn from these sources, but I have also included information on women who have not previously been discussed. Their work came to my attention in a large collection of melodramas that has just been cataloged, and in my efforts to understand their work I have discovered a little about their lives which is included here.

Many women who wrote for the stage also wrote novels, biographies, and/or poetry, and many were actors and managers as well. In some cases these women wrote memoirs, autobiographies, or prefaces that give us a glimpse into their lives. Mary Carr Clarke (179?–183?) was such a woman. Much of what we know about her appears in the preface to a book for which she was the ghost-writer. According to Amelia Howe Kritzer, she wrote four plays, three of which were published and two of which are extant (*Plays By Early American Women*, 16). That Mary Carr Clarke wrote *The Benevolent Lawyers; or Villainy Detected* (1823) is undisputed, but whether or not the play received a production is unknown. None-theless, it is the earliest known melodrama written by an American woman and the text does survive. Her other melodrama, *Sara Maria Cornell; or The Fall River Murder* had a long run at New York's Richmond Hill Theatre in 1833, but does not survive. This play used the common device of basing a play on a current and sensational murder case. This technique is still used by television writers, the direct artistic descendants of nineteenth-century melodrama writers. Mary Carr Clarke also wrote popular songs and biographies (Kritzer, *Plays by Early American Women*, 17).

Following close on the heels of Mary Carr Clarke's *Sara Maria Cornell* and perhaps inspired by its success, came Louisa Medina's *Nick of the Woods*, which was produced at the Bowery Theatre in New York in 1838. Medina was the house playwright at the Bowery, and Clarke wrote a biography of its manager, Thomas Hamblin, as told by Elizabeth, his first wife. It is quite likely that these women were familiar with each other's work, if not actually acquainted with one another. According to Rosemarie Bank, Medina may have written as many as thirty-four plays, although only eleven have been definitely identified as her work ("Theatre and Narrative Fiction," 55). Three of her plays were actually published, and two of these are classic melodramas. Both *Nick of the Woods* (1838) and *Ernest Maltravers* (1838) contain information from the author about specific scenic and costume requirements, and about musical accompaniment at particular moments in the plays. *Ernest Maltravers* contains several long songs, and *Nick of the Woods* contains several spectacle scenes. One of these shows a character going over a waterfall in a blazing canoe, and another features characters clinging to a bridge dangling over a precipice.

In 1878 Mrs. B. E. Woolf copyrighted a play entitled *Hobbies; or the Angel of the Household*. This seems to have been her only published work, and little is known about its production history. The play takes place in the household of Major Garroway Bangs and is a series of comic situations instigated by preparations for an amateur theatrical. The play is of very poor quality, relying on bad puns and silly disguises for its humor. The villainous Major Bangs is easily fooled and punished by the young lovers, and never poses much of a threat. The only scene of any interest features a series of impersonations of famous melodrama actors by the hero. Mrs. Woolf, whose maiden name was Josephine Orton, was an actress with the Boston Museum Stock Company at the time she wrote the play, and it may be a piece performed at one of her benefit performances.[1] This theory is supported by the many incidental songs and dances sprinkled through the play, all assigned to the leading lady, Minnie Clover. Mrs. Woolf's husband, Benjamin Edward Woolf, was the conductor of the orchestra at the Boston Museum, and later at the Chestnut Street Theatre in Philadelphia, and is credited with writing at least sixty light operas and plays during his lifetime.

Another actress/singer of this period, Genevieve Ward, is listed in many sources as the author of the sensational melodrama *Forget Me Not*, which she first presented in 1879. She performed the play more than two thousand times during her career, making the heroine Stephanie her signature role. References to her performances in the play appear throughout George C. D. Odell's *Annals of the New York Stage*, almost always heaping praise on Ward as "impressive," "an admirable actress," "excellent as always in the role," and almost as frequently declaring her supporting cast as inadequate to the task. Buried in these references is the information that Ward did not, in fact, write this popular play. Odell states that Ward had to go to court for the rights to the play, which she had purchased outright from the author, Palgrave Simpson. After winning this court battle, Ward copyrighted the play in her own name, and her performance of the role of Stephanie in England, America, and Australia from 1879 until 1887, led to the mistaken belief that she was the playwright as well as the actress who created the role.

One of the African American women authors known to have written a melodrama in the nineteenth century is Pauline Elizabeth Hopkins. Only recently recognized as a prolific writer of novels, short fiction, and essays during a literary career that spanned thirty-six years, Hopkins wrote, produced, and starred in her melodrama *Slaves' Escape; or the Underground Railroad* in 1880. The only recorded performance of this play took place in Boston at the Oakland Garden on July 5, 1880. The company called themselves Hopkins' Colored Troubadours and featured not only Pauline Hopkins, but her mother and stepfather as well. The play received a few favorable reviews, but was not performed a second night. It is known that Hopkins later revised the play, changing the title to *Peculiar Sam; or The Underground Railroad*, and changing the number of acts, but no other information survives. Hopkins toured with the family group for at least two years after her play was produced and, according to Jane Campbell's article on Hopkins in the *Dictionary of Literary Biography*, she was referred to as "Boston's Favorite Soprano" (183). One other play was written by Hopkins but never published. Called "One Scene from the Drama of the Early Days" it was a version of the story of Daniel in the lions' den. Pauline Hopkins' literary career is being reexamined and her novel *Contending Forces: A Romance Illustrative of Negro Life North and South*, which was originally dismissed because of its melodramatic qualities and its concentration on domestic issues, is being studied again due to the new interest in nineteenth-century publications.

Two years later, in 1881, Martha Johnson copyrighted her play *Carrots; or The Waif of the Woods*. This frontier melodrama tells the story of a young, red-headed tomboy, known to all as Carrots. The villain is determined to take Carrots out of the woods and make a lady of her. In Act III he says, "The prettiest and freshest thing I have seen in a woman in years. Only let me get her to town and completely in my power and the rest will be comparatively easy. The wild bird of the forest may fret against the gilded bars of her cage for a while, but in the end she will take it kindly, they all do, these women." In the course of the play, her ability to shoot a gun, fight hand-to-hand, and use her wits to avoid the villain stand Edith (Carrots) in good stead. Eventually the hero wins out over the villain and the two lovers settle down in the woods to live happily ever after. Nothing is known about the author of this well-written melodrama and Odell makes no mention of New York productions. Careful research is needed to discover more about Martha Johnson.

Actress Rosina Neuville, who was known for her appearances with such greats as Edwin Forrest, the elder Booth, and the father of E. H. Sothern, spent much of 1886 touring in a melodrama called *The Boy Tramp; or The Maniac Mother* with her son Augustus. All references refer to this as "her play" and the play was copyrighted in her name. It is possible that this is another case of a play purchased by an actress from the playwright and then referred to as her own work, but no evidence to that effect has been discovered. Odell lists a number of performances in New York during 1886 and he has nothing good to say about the play, calling it "their ancient thriller," "the abiding horror," and stating that New York has "for some time been eager to escape" the play. Whoever the author may be, it would seem that this was not a popular melodrama. The play is not very well crafted, either. The story is extremely convoluted, a failing that is compounded by the way the author has thrown in the many specialty songs and dances at any point where the plot runs into a dead end. Slapstick humor is included at inappropriate times and the ending is almost impossible to understand. Nonetheless, Rosina Neuville made her living in the lead role of this play on the stages of New York for well over a year.

Recently the work of Frances Hodgson Burnett has been rediscovered. New versions of *The Little Princess* and *The Secret Garden* have brought this prolific writer of the nineteenth century to the attention of late twentieth-century readers. Remembered now for her stories for children, and the stage and film versions of those stories, Burnett also wrote adult fiction during the late nineteenth and early twentieth centuries, some of which she adapted for the stage. Born in 1849 in Manchester, England, Burnett's family moved to Knoxville, Tennessee in 1865, and she spent most of her life in the United States. She was married twice and had two children. Her experience with stage versions of her novels began with the adaptation of her very popular novel *That Lass o' Lowries* in 1878. Other adaptations followed. *A Lady of Quality* (1897) featured a heroine who was reared as a boy and killed her husband with a riding whip. A more gentle heroine is found in her play *That Man and I* (1904), which is an adaptation of her novel *In Connection with the De Willoughby Claim*. Both *Phyllis* (1889) and *Nixie* (1890) are plays in the melodramatic form. Her famous children's tales use the devices of melodrama, particularly the theme of good vs. evil, and spectacular effects, to create exciting and engaging theatre. Early in her career, Burnett was considered a serious artist and was compared to George Eliot. Her success with more popular forms, however, led to a reappraisal of her talent by critics. She began to be seen as a formulaic writer who cared more for money than for art. As scholars revisit her works in the light of the new interest in melodrama, perhaps a more balanced critique of her work will emerge.

Another successful woman melodramatist was Madeleine Lucette Ryley, who wrote, according to her *Variety* obituary, a score of successful plays in the last two decades of the nineteenth century. Ryley began her career as a comic opera comedienne, and was married to English comedian John H. Ryley, but she seems to have left the stage to concentrate on writing sometime around 1888 or 1889. Her two best-known plays are *Christopher, Jr.*, which starred Nat C. Goodwin, and *An American Citizen*, which was a vehicle written specifically for John Drew and Maude Adams. Neither of these plays follows the strict melodramatic form as they are really comedies, not serious plays with happy endings, but many features of both plays are based in the melodramatic tradition. Characters fit the stereotypical categories of melodrama, and plot is the central focus of both plays. A kind of poetic justice operates in the plays as the comic resolution brings the world of the play back into balance. As might be expected from the work of a comic opera star, there are musical interludes throughout both plays.[2]

Mrs. Romualdo Pacheco married her Mexican-born husband in 1863. Her maiden name was Mary McIntire and she was known as a playwright at the time of their marriage. Romualdo Pacheco was the governor of California for a year (1875) and eventually became a Congressman and an American minister plenipotentiary (diplomatic agent) to the Central American republics. Little has been discovered about Mrs. Pacheco, but her plays *Loyal to Death*, *Nothing But Money*, and *Incog* were popular melodramas that received good reviews. Further research should reveal more about this playwright as she and her husband led a very public existence, and documents regarding their lives are sure to exist in the records of California and the US Congress.

Melodrama did not disappear with the advent of the new century. Many of the writers of the Progressive Era wrote in this genre as well. Most of these plays have been ignored or scoured for evidence of realism, but few have been studied for the information they reveal about the changing values of the time or for their adherence to what was by that time an outdated set of dramatic conventions. Success in the commercial theatre was seen more and more as a failure of artistry and popular writers were not admired by critics. Melodramas of this period, by such well-known figures as Mary Roberts Rinehart, Marguerite Merington, and Angelina Grimké, have yet to be studied as examples of the genre. Such a study might lead to a clearer understanding of the changes in society during this turbulent period.

It is clear from this brief discussion of only a few of the women who wrote melodrama that there is much work yet to be accomplished. The difficulties in locating the names of women playwrights and their plays, finding manuscripts and biographical information, and overcoming prejudices against the melodrama have kept scholars from making much progress in the study of nineteenth-century women playwrights. Recent discoveries in manuscript collections and the methodologies of feminism and the new historicism have led to an exciting new area of research. Future work in this area should lead to new and interesting information that will help to rewrite the history of the nineteenth-century American stage.

NOTES

1 Benefit performances were common in the nineteenth century. The performer, or a group of performers, received all the profits from an evening's performance. The material for the performance was chosen to showcase the particular talents of the performer being benefited.

2 The most recent and thorough study of the work of this playwright is the unpublished dissertation "New Women Dramatists in America, 1890–1920: Martha Morton and Madeleine Lucette Ryley" by Sherry Engle, which was completed in December 1996 at the University of Texas, Austin.

3

PATRICIA R. SCHROEDER

Realism and feminism in the Progressive Era

It has become a commonplace in recent feminist theory to dismiss stage realism as fundamentally incompatible with feminist interests. The reasons for this dismissal have changed through time. In the 1970s some feminists rejected realism simply because they saw its linear form as designed to reflect male experience exclusively.[1] More recently, others have denounced realism because it apparently normalizes the traditionally unequal power relations between genders and classes.[2] Still others have charged that realism reinscribes this inequality in a particularly dangerous way by pretending to be an objective recording of the world while representing woman as sexual "Other" and excluding female subjectivity.[3]

While it is certainly true that stage realism has often been guilty of these offenses, I fear that the dismissal of realism by feminists might have several undesirable effects. First, abandoning stage realism means abandoning much important theatre history, especially in America, and especially the works of early twentieth-century feminist playwrights who used realism to illustrate the entrapment of women characters in traditional roles. Second, the outright rejection of realism ignores the built-in subversive possibilities of this endlessly adaptable form. Finally, since realism is still the most prominent mainstream dramatic form in American theatre, rejecting it as a vehicle for feminist issues would deprive feminist playwrights of a widespread audience.

American women realists of one period did, in fact, employ realism as a means to express feminist views. This chapter focuses on three playwrights of the Progressive Era – the first few decades of the twentieth century – because it was a time of widespread changes in the position of women as they fought for the rights to vote, to become educated, to support themselves, and to live independent lives. The plays of Zona Gale, Rachel Crothers, and Marion Craig Wentworth will demonstrate how realism could once – and possibly still can – be used to promote positive social change for women.

The development of realism

Realism has dominated the American theatre since the late 1800s. In its original form, realism was designed to replicate the offstage world – the social milieu of the writer's time and place – as accurately as possible. While all theatre reflects some notion of "reality," the "reality" of realism was, at its inception, specific to the exterior world we all share; that is, the plays dramatized external or social situations rather than inner psychology or subjective visions.

Developing out of the pioneering work of Henrik Ibsen, realism was soon codified into a set of stage conventions that are still in use today. Most often the action takes place in a domestic setting, such as a drawing room or kitchen, which has an imaginary fourth wall – the invisible barrier between stage and audience. Characters in a realistic play are recognizable, commonplace people (neither kings nor clowns), with clearly delineated motivation for their actions, and who speak in the vernacular, the everyday language appropriate to their situation and their era. The action of realistic drama is linear (occurring in chronological order) and causal (based on actions and events that produce predictable consequences), and often revolves around the revelation of a secret from the past and the reactions of the characters to a new, perhaps more truthful version of their lives. Finally, the plot of a realistic play often ends in closure, that is, with issues resolved – at least temporarily.

While this description of realism seems fairly tame to late twentieth-century audiences (after all, most dramatic television shows follow this realistic format), realism was quite controversial at the beginning of the century. One primary reason for this controversy was that realism was created in reaction to the popular dramatic forms of the nineteenth century, farce and melodrama, which provided entertainment through humor or sentimentality. Realism, in contrast, was designed to deal with serious social issues (such as the emancipation of women or the double standard of morality) and their repercussions on private lives. Furthermore, in depicting middle-class reality, realism often implicitly criticized the accepted pieties of bourgeois life, thereby outraging those who had the most to gain by keeping accepted social conventions intact. It was within this highly charged political and theatrical environment of the early twentieth century that feminist playwrights entered the fray.

Feminism in the Progressive Era

Writing in the journal *Forum* in 1914, theatre critic and playwright Florence Kiper surveyed the previous New York theatre season, in her words, "from the feminist viewpoint." In this review essay, Kiper first defines as "feminist" issues a wide and varied array of social, political, and economic controversies affecting women's lives. Her list includes everything from divorce to working conditions for young girls to the suffrage movement. Kiper then predicts that "the woman movement" would be the most important political trend of the twentieth century. After thus broadly defining feminist concerns, Kiper goes on to lament the dearth of socially aware realist playwrights to engage these topics in the American theatre: "We have at present no Ibsens, Shaws, Bjørnsons, Strindbergs, Brieuxs ... Almost none of our clever writers for the stage are bringing to these vital themes [i.e., those women's issues noted above] a conscious philosophy or an informed understanding" ("Some American Plays," 921). By directly connecting these prominent realist playwrights with the stage representation of women's issues, Kiper suggests that in her era, realism was not only suitable for feminist exploration of social issues, but virtually equivalent to it.

While Florence Kiper was correct that the 1913 Broadway season offered few realistic plays that explored the social issues surrounding the woman question, a number of women playwrights of the era were beginning to do just that.[4] Among the many women's issues these playwrights tackled, their plays prominently depict the entrapment of women in confining domestic roles (largely a consequence of women's financial dependence on men) and document changing social mores as women moved into the workforce and began to cast their votes.

Domestic entrapments

One play that offers a serious critique of women's familial entrapment is Zona Gale's *Miss Lulu Bett* (first performed in 1920). *Miss Lulu Bett* depicts an unmarried woman's domestic enslavement to her unappreciative and demanding family. However, it also scrutinizes the plight of the other women in the household – those with ostensibly more "enviable" positions – and ends with the suggestion that autonomy and self-support may offer the only escape from enforced domestic roles.

Gale's three-act play focuses on the title character, who performs all the household work for her sister Ina's family, her labor the price paid so that she and her mother can exist as dependents of Ina's husband Dwight. The family mythology has defined Lulu as not "strong enough to work" (*Miss Lulu Bett*, 91), thereby emphasizing both Lulu's dependency and the belief that performing all the household duties for four adults and two children does not constitute "work." This devaluing of Lulu's contribution to the family permits Dwight and Ina to see Lulu as a faceless drone, not as a person with desires and aspirations of her own. They criticize everything she does, from the color of the bread she toasts for them to her purchase of flowers to brighten their table (at which she rarely gets to sit). Although Lulu owns nothing but what they provide for her, including a wardrobe of Ina's cast-off clothes, they complain about Lulu's appearance, finding her presence in front of company to be an embarrassment (90). Dwight's kindhearted brother Ninian sums up Lulu's plight when he tells her, "They make a slavey of you. Regular slavey. Damned shame I call it" (103).

In *Miss Lulu Bett*, Gale made powerful use of the realistic set to emphasize the protagonist's restrictions. Act I, in which Lulu functions solely as a household servant, takes place in the family dining room, an enclosed space which Lulu enters and exits from the kitchen while the rest of the family sit and eat. At the end of Act I, however, Lulu marries Ninian, and the scene thereafter shifts to a side porch of Dwight's house. This space, attached to the house but with fewer confining walls, parallels Lulu's partial break from Dwight's family. After traveling briefly with Ninian, Lulu has seen something of the world and has been recognized as an individual instead of a mere functionary filling a role. Unfortunately, when Ninian confesses that he had lost touch with his first wife fifteen years previously and does not know for certain if she is dead (and, therefore, if his marriage to Lulu is legal), Lulu feels she must return to Dwight and Ina's home. At this point, however, she is, like the porch, attached to the household but not entirely confined by it, and she begins to assert herself against Dwight and Ina by keeping their daughter's secrets from them, appropriating a dress of Ina's without permission, and reading Dwight's letter from Ninian despite Dwight's express order not to. This movement to an exterior space thus symbolizes Lulu's emerging consciousness of her own identity and desires, desires that cannot be contained within the walls of Dwight's house.

In Gale's original script, Lulu's desires also exceeded the boundaries of realistic closure, an important innovation in an otherwise realistic play.[5] In that original ending, Ninian's first wife is found to be alive, thus invalidating Lulu's marriage. Rather than marrying Cornish (another suitor) or maintaining her position in Dwight's household, however, Lulu chooses a life of uncertain independence. Refusing to let Cornish explain her decision to Dwight and Ina, Lulu insists on speaking for herself. Furthermore, she leaves town alone to seek employment, needing, as she says, "to see out of my own eyes. For the first time in my life" (161). The play thus originally concluded with Lulu's escaping her lifelong imprisonment, but without any resolution of her economic or social problems. Like the shift in set, then, the original ending of Gale's play indicates the rebellion of Lulu's desires against the forces of oppression, forces represented, in part, by the realistic set and resisted by Lulu's refusal of containment.

Unfortunately, this open ending caused so much controversy in the original 1920 production that the author felt compelled to change it to ensure the play's successful run. In the revised ending, Ninian's first wife turns out to be dead, and he returns to rescue Lulu from her life of drudgery in Dwight and Ina's house. While Cynthia Sutherland sees this change as Gale's capitulation to public opinion – in her view, an example of women increasingly choosing to act as mediators rather than revolutionaries after women's suffrage was won – Carole L. Cole notes astutely that both versions retain Lulu's basic evolution as she strives to define herself rather than merely accept Dwight and Ina's definition of her; the way the play concludes is not its whole meaning.[6] The merit of Cole's interpretation is further suggested by other elements in Gale's realistic text, elements hinting that domestic entrapment was common among women of the era and suggesting some of the social and economic forces that sustained it.[7]

The primary reason women accepted roles like Lulu's within Dwight's family was economic necessity, a condition Lulu recognizes and laments on several occasions. First she discusses the problem with Ninian, revealing her awareness of her plight as just one example of a widespread social condition. She says: "I can't do any other work – that's the trouble – women like me can't do any other work" (*Miss Lulu Bett*, 103). Later, she makes a similar remark to Cornish, explaining her desire for independence and the economic difficulties that prevent her achieving it. She tells him that although she is a locally renowned cook, "I can't earn anything. I'd like to earn something" (131). Lulu's perceptions of her limited earning power accurately reflect the conditions of the time. Despite the political gains women apparently achieved with the passage of the Nineteenth Amendment in 1920 (the year of *Miss Lulu*'s premiere), political rights did not bring economic equality. As historian William Chafe has noted, almost all the women who joined the labor force in the 1920s were motivated by economic need, yet they were treated on the job as marginal employees whose primary responsibilities – and chief sources of support – were in the home (*Paradox*, 78). While clerical opportunities for refined, middle-class, white women were expanding, uneducated women like Lulu rarely had the chance to "earn something" and so support themselves.

Given these economic limitations, marriage might seem to be the most desirable option a middle-class woman had to ensure her financial support. Yet Gale's play emphatically suggests otherwise, even given the revised ending in which Lulu is reunited with Ninian. Close scrutiny of the other female characters reveals the strictures placed on all women within the traditional patriarchal family, even if those women were not primarily responsible for domestic work. Lulu's mother, for example, states outright that marriage offers no better alternative to Lulu's position. When Ninian asks Mrs. Bett if Lulu wouldn't be better off with a husband, Mrs. Bett replies: "Wouldn't make much difference. Why look at me. A husband, six children, four of 'em under the sod with him. And sometimes I feel as though nothin' more had happened to me than has happened to Lulie ... Only she ain't had the pain" (107).

In Ina, the female head of the household, we see the clearest example of how limiting marriage could be, especially to women married to petty tyrants like Dwight. Despite his contradictions and repeated sexist remarks, Ina follows her husband's lead in all actions, accepting his every notion, no matter how illogical or insulting. In everything from the proper preparation of potatoes to the value of family life, Ina echoes Dwight's remarks with her own "That's what I always think." When Dwight attempts to coerce Lulu's obedience with a family vote, Ina mindlessly follows his lead, consolidating his power and making a mockery of the democratic process. In short, Ina is a cipher, a useless woman literally unable to boil water without Lulu's instructions or to conceive a thought without Dwight's direction; she is yet another victim of Dwight's manipulation, even as she practices the same arts on the other, less powerful members of her household. As Cole has explained it, the play "is a study of the power relationships within the nuclear family. Indeed, the play constitutes a devastating portrait of the male autocrat who holds absolute power in ways both petty and profound and the hierarchy that forms among the female family members based on each one's relationship and usefulness to him" ("The Search for Power," 116). Given a social reality in which most women lived as economic dependents of possibly despotic men, some form of entrapment for women was virtually inevitable. And while Gale's play does focus on a domestic world where women are "others" with little possibility for self-fulfillment or even self-definition, *Miss Lulu Bett* uses the conventions of realism to criticize those limitations and to suggest some of the widespread cultural conditions that create and sustain them. In this way, the play makes a strong political statement regarding the rights of women. Some feminist critics have argued that realism is without value for feminist dramatists because it is incapable of exploring individual dilemmas in terms of a broad social context.[8] *Miss Lulu Bett*'s attention to historical context, social convention, and women's economic realities challenges the universal applicability of this dismissal.

Women in the workforce

While Gale and others were using realism to document how social conventions and economic restrictions often forced women into narrow domestic roles that offered no choice or potential for growth, other playwrights were portraying women who had already moved outside the domestic sphere. This depiction of single women pursuing careers and creating alternatives to patriarchal living arrangements reflects a social trend of the early 1900s. As historian William Chafe has observed, at the end of the nineteenth century, "half the graduates of the best women's colleges remained single, and they constituted the core of female professional workers" (*Paradox*, 111). These career women – often ridiculed as humorless, sexless "New Women" in the popular press – faced a number of social problems that sound distressingly familiar to 1990s feminists: hostility to women working outside the home (especially from men competing for their jobs), lack of role models in other than traditionally female fields such as teaching and nursing, disparagement of female aspirations, malicious rumors about independent women's sexual orientation, and the apparent need to choose between marriage and a career (Chafe, *Paradox*, 107–11). So while female playwrights of the era were eager to depict autonomous working women with interests beyond the domestic, as working women themselves they recognized the potentially paralyzing problems the New Woman faced. As playwright Martha Morton observed in a 1909 interview, "Woman is going out into the world and helping to do the world's work, and adapting herself to the new condition hurts" (Patterson, "Chat," 128).

A number of playwrights writing between 1900 and 1920 explored these sometimes hurtful adaptations in their realistic plays, documenting the personal and professional problems faced by career women and protesting social conditions that interfered with women's pursuit of economic independence. By their very existence these plays counter the criticism that realism was limited to portraying and therefore validating the domestic world of the patriarchal nuclear family. The feminist plays I have chosen to explore here show the conflicts between and within individual working women, conflicts created by social mores and internalized by the women characters of these realistic plays. In this way, these plays illustrate the current feminist belief that female identity is, at least in part, a product of cultural mythology. Furthermore, they delineate the problems that arise when the forces of convention or individual desires conflict with a woman's wish for autonomy. These plays reveal that realism could be used in the theatre to depict what women might accomplish, as well as what price they would have to pay, as they moved outside traditional domestic spheres.

Two plays that use realism to explore the plight of the career woman are Rachel Crothers' *A Man's World* (1909, published 1915) and Marion Craig Wentworth's *The Flower Shop* (1912). Both plays focus on independent women with satisfying work to do, and both emphasize the central character's connections with a community of women who exhibit various stages of feminist awareness. Both plays explore the economic and social forces that propel women into marriage, and both depict women in conflict with the men they love when it comes to balancing a home and a career. However, the similarities between the plays end at their conclusions, as the two central characters find different ways to reconcile their romantic attachments with their feminist ideals.

A Man's World takes place primarily in the apartment of Frank Ware, a female novelist and social reform worker who lives with her small adopted son, Kiddie. While Frank's drawing room is conventionally appointed and focused on the domestic, it certainly offers a counterpoint to the male-dominated living spaces inhabited by Gale's *Miss Lulu Bett*. For Frank's parlor is located in a rooming house occupied by an assortment of struggling artists, musicians, and writers, male and female, who each occupy a private space but who nonetheless move rather freely from one room to another. The extent to which Frank's bohemian drawing room differs from that of a traditional patriarchal family is illustrated vividly in the first act, when Frank arrives home from work to find a group of male friends entertaining Kiddie – that is, engaging in child-care activities traditionally associated with women. As Frank flops onto a chair, the men gather to wait on her, offering her food, stoking her fire, and helping her off with her gloves. Lois Gottlieb has noted that this scene *reverses* the patriarchal norm in which the male breadwinner enters a domestic space expecting service from the subservient women who work within the domestic space and whom he supports (*Rachel Crothers*, 40–41). Yet despite the fact that she is the only one of the group who is financially successful, Frank asserts no authority; she is simply depicted, as the stage directions clarify, as an equal, exuding "the frank abandon of being one of them – strong, free, unafraid" (*Man's World*, 10).

Unlike most of the other inhabitants of her building, Frank takes her work outside her home: she not only publishes critically acclaimed novels about the exploitation of impoverished women, she is also deeply involved in setting up a "girls' club" for former prostitutes. While Frank may write in her apartment (her exact writing habits are never made clear), her work in both publishing and social reform extends her influence beyond the domestic scope. As Sharon Friedman has argued: "Through her social welfare activity and her writing, Frank makes these private grievances [i.e., unequal sexual relations and man's exploitation of women] a matter of public concern, and in the process gives herself a platform. As social housekeeper, mother to destitute girls, Frank makes maternity her career outside the home" ("Feminism," 78). Frank's life work is therefore the inverse of Miss Lulu Bett's. Rather than showing us the impact of social concerns on the home, Crothers has created a feminist-activist protagonist who takes the values of home and care and attempts to infuse them into society at large.

Margaret Kendall of Wentworth's *The Flower Shop* is a similar character: an independent career woman (formerly an opera star, currently a shop owner) with an interest in social reform and in building community with other women. The setting of Wentworth's play, moreover, moves out of domestic spaces entirely and into the flower shop of the title, an enterprise owned and managed by Margaret. While the set is realistic in its functioning doors and its attention to detail, it depicts a public space controlled by Margaret and populated with her staff, her customers, and occasionally her women's group, which holds its meetings in the shop. Margaret's social work differs from Frank's, however, in that she is attempting to enlighten women of her own upper-middle class to the dangers of being financially dependent on men. For Margaret, economic freedom is the greatest freedom of all, the one on which all other liberties depend. As she tells a friend, "I shall always be my own mistress because I have my own work, my own pocket-book" (*Flower Shop*, 23). For her, many of the members of her women's club – her "followers" – "seem like a lot of frightened slaves . . . and the husbands masters and owners by right of the household purse" (20). Perhaps Margaret's work to "abolish" this form of domestic slavery is not so different from Frank's work with "fallen" East Side women after all, since Margaret views marriage based on financial dependence as just another form of prostitution (91).

Building communities of women for their mutual support is thus important to both Frank and Margaret. Frank defends her rooming-house arrangement against a detractor as "rather good for me . . . The house is filled with independent women who are making their own living" (*Man's World*, 24); she also experiences great satisfaction in her reform work with poor girls. Margaret likewise is dedicated to her "followers," claiming that the interests of a family (were she to have one) would not make her forget "the *other women*, their helplessness and their needs" (*Flower Shop*, 62). Yet both plays do an excellent job of depicting the differences among the varied women each independent protagonist encounters. What Doris Abramson has noted about *A Man's World* is true of both plays: not all the women characters are at the same level of emancipation, so the plays illustrate a moment of historical transition ("Rachel Crothers," 61). Each female character has to make decisions between new freedoms and old customs and prejudices.

In *A Man's World*, this transitional moment for women is perhaps best reflected in the character of Clara, an aspiring miniaturist from a wealthy family who (as one of the other artists describes her) would "like to tiptoe through bohemia, but she's afraid of her petticoats" (17). While Clara admires everything about Frank, from her self-sufficiency to her generosity and kindness, she herself is without marketable skills and feels "absolutely superfluous" (52). Complaining about the double standard that relegates unmarried women to "old maid" status, Clara asserts: "If I were a man – the most insignificant little runt of a man – I could persuade some woman to marry me – and could have a home and children and hustle for a living – and life would mean something" (53). But Clara is not the only counterpoint to Frank. Lione, a singer, while more independent and also more talented than Clara, also rails about the unfair position of women who must depend on men for financial support and social position. Her response to the problem, however, is a self-centered acceptance of the *status quo*. She tells Frank: "Men are pigs of course. They take all they can get and don't give any more than they have to. It's a man's world – that's the size of it. What's the use of knocking your head against things you can't change? I never believed before that you really meant all this helping women business. What's the use?" (57). Despite these women's differences from each other and from her, Frank responds to both of them with sympathy and support. While Frank herself values autonomy and fosters sisterhood, she realizes that not all women would or could make the choices she has made. In response to Clara, who accuses her of believing "in women taking care of themselves," Frank asserts: "I believe in women doing what they're most fitted for. You should have married, Clara, when you were a young girl – and been taken care of all your life" (52). Given this backdrop of social reform work and varying states of feminist consciousness, Crothers' play avoids projecting one proper course of action for all women, focusing instead on the complex network of environmental forces complicating all women's choices.

The Flower Shop also depicts the various conflicts faced by women, both the independent New Woman of the period and her more traditional sisters, during this transitional historical period. In Wentworth's play, these differences emerge most clearly in the discussions about marriage in which Margaret's flower shop staff frequently engage. For Polly, young and pretty and enamored of her beau, traditional marriage beckons appealingly. Noting that "It is a man's place to provide for the woman he loves" (27),

Polly proclaims that she wants "a real *old-fashioned* marriage," in which she will quit her job, devote her time to caring for the household, and never object to asking her husband for money (94–95). Lena, another shop worker, sees marriage not as a romantic adventure but as an opportunity to rest from toil. Like Crothers' Clara, Lena is aging, unmarried, and alone. She sees marriage to a decent carpenter whom she does not love as "a good chance" to achieve financial security, to avoid lifelong loneliness, and to have a child, which she desperately wants. These experiences with other women, while they do not change Margaret's ultimate choices for herself, do allow her to see (as Frank does) that not all women have the fortitude or the training to face daily economic demands and a solitary life. Both of these plays, then, document the difficult choices and limited options women faced in the early twentieth century, thus providing a tapestried background against which to evaluate the actions and decisions of the central characters.

Against this backdrop, Frank and Margaret look all the more courageous in overcoming the many obstacles to their freedom. For Frank, most of these obstacles are placed in her way by social convention and public opinion. The strength of these forces against an independent woman are made clear in the very first scene, when Frank's male friends are discussing her book in her absence. First they read aloud from a glowing review, which finds Frank's novel especially impressive in its "strength and scope" now that she has been revealed to be a woman. This brings them to wonder where she finds her material – that is, what man is ghost-writing for her. Their gossip then moves to her love life, and they wonder about the exact nature of her relationship with Malcolm Gaskell: whether he and Frank are, in fact, lovers, and whether he is the man supplying her material (*Man's World*, 7–8). That Frank's alleged friends have such doubts about her veracity and ability suggests the wave of hostile criticism and innuendo faced by women active in public life.

Frank's problems in maintaining her autonomy are compounded by her love for Gaskell, a successful newspaper man and a staunch supporter of the gender-divided *status quo*. He disparages her book as "clever as the deuce" but not "big" (23); he asserts that "Women are meant only to be loved – and men have got to take care of them" (25); he protests that her settlement work is "disagreeable" (26); and he summarizes proper relations between men and women this way: "Man sets the standard for woman. He knows she's better than he is and he demands that she be – and if she isn't she's got to suffer for it" (23). In addition to his belittling of Frank's work and beliefs, he insists that she reveal her entire history (especially how she came to adopt Kiddie), while insisting that she has no need to know his. It may seem unlikely that the independent Frank could actually fall in love with such a man. That she does suggests two things: that independent women have as much a need for love as traditional women do; and that, as products of the social system they are trying to reform, women like Frank have nonetheless internalized much of their patriarchal culture. As Florence Kiper noted in the 1914 review that I cited earlier:

> [Frank] is a type of the modern feminist. And the conflict of the drama is waged not so much without as within her own nature, a conflict between individual emotion and social conviction. What many of our writers for the stage have missed in their objective drama that uses the new woman for protagonist is a glimpse of that tumultuous battlefield, her own soul, where meet the warring forces of impulse and theory, of the old and the new conceptions of egotism and altruism. ("Some American Plays," 928)

The conclusion of the play indicates exactly how painful this conflict between "impulse and theory" is for Frank and how much she is willing to pay for her feminist ideals. Just after Frank reveals to Gaskell that she reciprocates his love, they discover the secret of Kiddie's parentage: Gaskell is actually Kiddie's father and, therefore, a man Frank has long hated for abandoning the boy's biological mother. When Gaskell refuses to admit any responsibility for the affair, Frank refuses his marriage proposal. In a reversal of Nora's slamming the door to Ibsen's *Doll's House*, Gaskell leaves Frank's apartment, closing the door behind him.

While the door may be shut on Gaskell's relationship with Frank, the debate between the New Woman and the traditional man, and thus the issues of the double standard and equality for women, are left open at the end of the play. The play thus beautifully illustrates Kiper's point about the New Woman's inner conflicts. Because the play ends, as Kiper describes it, with "no sentimentalism, no attempt to gloss over the situation with the pet American dramatic platitude that love makes right all things" ("Some American Plays," 928), we are left inspired that Frank has stood up for her principles but saddened that her stand has cost her emotional fulfillment. In short, Crothers' realistic treatment of an increasingly common predicament of the era, combined with the varied background characters and with her innovative refusal to provide an easy solution, forces an audience to feel something of the losses women face when their feminist ideals collide with their very human hunger for love.

In *The Flower Shop*, Wentworth does an even more thorough job of depicting the "warring forces" within career women of the day. Her task is made easier because Margaret has already rejected her version of Malcolm Gaskell, the extremely chauvinistic William Ramsey, who years before had wanted Margaret to renounce her career as an opera singer in order to marry him. Her current problems are twofold: the first involves helping her old friend Louise, also a former opera star and now married to Ramsey, to return to her career over her husband's objections; the second concerns reconciling her insistence on financial independence with her deep love for Stephen Hartwell, who is currently running for a judgeship under much public scrutiny.

When the wealthy Hartwell first proposes, he simply assumes that Margaret will give up her flower shop. Once she convinces him of the absolute necessity, for her, of maintaining a separate income and therefore her own business, he capitulates, realizing that "It is easy to be romantic ... – set woman on a pedestal as a saint for devotion and all that, – it is harder to help her live her own life, but perhaps after all that is the most genuine devotion – real chivalry in the end" (113). Given his public position, however, it soon becomes clear to Margaret that her independence may cost him both the support of his traditional family and the judgeship he seeks. Her conflict, then, is internal – her desire for autonomy versus her love for Hartwell – but also includes public repercussions for the man she loves.

In Act III, as she waits in the darkened flower shop to hear if Hartwell has found some way to reconcile their love and his public interests, and as Polly and Lena come in separately to tell her of their wedding plans, Margaret vacillates in agony. This scene of Margaret's turmoil, while perhaps suffering from unrealistic coincidences, brilliantly encapsulates the "tumultuous battlefield" within themselves that independent women of the era suffered. First Margaret thinks of her "followers," lamenting that she cannot give up her business without disappointing them. Then, haunted by the dance music filtering in from across the street and tormented by the sensuous fragrance of the flowers surrounding her, she surrenders to her emotions and desires, feeling that she cannot lose Hartwell's love. Margaret cries out: "Is this what it is to be merely a woman – no will – no head – all heart – nothing but heart, with a cry in it that will not be stilled. *I want him* ... Ah, my sisters, I have understood your needs – now I see your temptation" (98). Just as Margaret decides to send for Hartwell and renounce her flower shop, however, Louise returns with the news that she has abandoned her career plans for fear of losing her husband's love. Louise's lack of persistence reinvigorates Margaret's own, and she vows to "renounce the sweetness" in order to promote the new order she envisions between women and men.

Unlike *A Man's World*, however, *The Flower Shop* ends with a conventional reconciliation. It seems Hartwell's publicity director has found a way to avoid "the woman question" during his campaign, so Hartwell and Margaret are free to marry under their original agreement: Margaret keeps her shop and her economic independence. This forced closure does falsely simplify the complex issues raised by the play. However, Hartwell's resolve to stand by Margaret no matter what the cost suggests a more positive vision for social reform than the one Crothers envisioned in *A Man's World*. Margaret's happy ending suggests that men as well as women can suffer from sexist public criticism, that some men are willing to support women's autonomy, and that heterosexual love is not necessarily a cage designed to restrain women and regulate their activities. It also vividly paints the conflicts and agonies that career women faced in trying to lead full emotional lives.

In these plays of women in the workforce, both Crothers and Wentworth dramatize the conflict between career ambition and the desire for love that working women of the early twentieth century faced (to say nothing of their late twentieth-century sisters). Using a realistic set, everyday characters, increasingly commonplace situations, and the linear logic of realism, the plays accurately depict and protest the barriers to achievement faced by women of the 1910s. Realism has historically been used in this way more than once. As Michelene Wandor has observed, "artistic movements which seek to represent the experiences of oppressed groups reach initially for a realistic and immediately recognisable clarity ... Such realism has a radical impact when the content is new, when the selection of ordinary everyday elements in life are shaped into a work of art" (*Strike*, 11). By using realism in this way, these playwrights made the new and sometimes radically revised ideas about gender roles and gender relations more accessible to theatregoers of their era, inviting audiences to see these changes as a part of everyday reality.

Rethinking realism

In this chapter, I have used my analysis of three plays to illustrate some crucial points in the ongoing debate about realism's usefulness to feminist drama. Most obviously, I have tried to show that historical context is crucial in determining meaning. In the Progressive Era, realism was considered the highest and most modern form of dramatic writing, the only form appropriate for critical exploration of social problems. Many feminist playwrights of the period thus wrote realistic plays as the best way to have their voices heard and their ideas taken seriously. We would do them grievous disservice to dismiss their work as inadequate because realism is sometimes seen, in late twentieth-century criticism, as an outmoded or debased form.

But it is not only in distant historical contexts that I want to rethink the relationship between feminism and realism, for realism as dramatic form has persisted now for over a hundred years, and perhaps contemporary feminists can learn some lessons by looking at its history. While realism is based on the specific theatrical conventions described at the beginning of this essay, it can also be adapted and modified by innovative playwrights; indeed, many feminist playwrights from the Progressive Era to the present have mingled realistic conventions with antirealistic ones to create hybrid forms, suitable for many purposes.[9] Furthermore, even the most traditional realism can still reach wide audiences and protest the social conditions it presents. Let the continuing lesson of Gale, Crothers, and Wentworth be this: depicting what is can be a step toward creating what should be.

NOTES

1 See, for example, Anne Commire, in Kathleen Betsko and Rachel Koenig, eds., *Interviews with Contemporary Women Playwrights*, 90; Rosemary Curb, "Re/cognition, Re/presentation, Re/creation in Woman-Conscious Drama: the Seer, the Seen, the Scene, the Obscene," 302–03; and Nancy Reinhardt, "New Directions for Feminist Criticism in Theatre and the Related Arts," 35–37.

2 See, for example, Sue-Ellen Case, *Feminism and Theatre*, 124; and Jill Dolan, "'Lesbian' Subjectivity in Realism: Dragging at the Margins of Structure and Ideology," 44.

3 See, for example, Catherine Belsey, "Constructing the Subject: Deconstructing the Text," 51–57; Jill Dolan, *The Feminist Spectator as Critic*, 84; Elin Diamond, "Mimesis, Mimicry, and the 'True-Real,'" 61; Jeanie Forte, "Realism, Narrative, and the Feminist Playwright – a Problem of Reception," 115–17; and Janelle Reinelt, "Beyond Brecht: Britain's New Feminist Drama," 154.

4 For an examination of more feminist-realist playwrights of the period, see chapter 2 of Patricia R. Schroeder, *The Feminist Possibilities of Dramatic Realism*.

5 See Judith E. Barlow's "Introduction" to *Plays by American Women: 1900–1930*, xxiv.

6 Cynthia Sutherland, "American Women Playwrights as Mediators of the 'Woman Problem,'" 324–25 and Carole L. Cole, "The Search for Power: Drama by American Women, 1909–1929," 119–20.

7 In her 1985 essay on "The Compatibility of Traditional Dramatic Form and Feminist Expression," Judith L. Stephens, like Cole, argues that *Miss Lulu Bett* is a feminist play because of the choices Lulu makes in defining herself. What I hope to add to this discussion is an analysis of the economic and social forces Gale critiques as impingements on Lulu's developing agency.

8 Jill Dolan, for example, in discussing Marsha Norman's *'night, Mother*, has observed that the play is "like most traditional American dramas" in its "focus on individual suffering" and its "unwillingness to discuss [a central character's] dilemma in terms of a wider social context" (*The Feminist Spectator as Critic*,

36–37). While Dolan's comments may have some validity in describing Norman's play, her contentions have too often been generalized by feminist drama theorists and used as reasons to dismiss all realist texts.

9 For more discussion and examples of such hybrid realism, see Patricia R. Schroeder, *The Feminist Possibilities of Dramatic Realism*, especially chapters 2 and 4.

2

INHERITORS

4

VERONICA MAKOWSKY

Susan Glaspell and modernism

As for so many early twentieth-century women writers, modernism for Susan Glaspell (1876–1948) was at once a blessing and a curse. It stimulated her best work, and then scorned her aesthetic. It incorporated her theatrical innovations, and proceeded to ignore their creator. It made her reputation, but only to repudiate it. In order to understand these seeming paradoxes, that slippery term, "modernism," or, more accurately, "modernisms," must be defined in its gendered American historical context before we turn to Susan Glaspell herself.

Much of the exuberance of American nineteenth-century literary culture arose from the belief that art and life are indivisible. As Ralph Waldo Emerson, who greatly influenced Glaspell, concludes in "The Poet" (1842), "The poets are thus liberating gods ... They are free, and they make free" (236). Although Emerson addressed his exhortations to "men," women, too, believed that their writings would and should affect the lives of their compatriots. One of the major goals of the so-called domestic and sentimental novelists of mid-century was to evoke feeling or "sentiment" in their readers, but feeling was the means to an end, not the end itself. In her "Concluding Remarks" to her best-selling *Uncle Tom's Cabin* (1852), Harriet Beecher Stowe admonished her readers, "There is one thing that every individual can do, – they can see to it that *they feel right*" (624), and then act upon that feeling to end slavery. When Abraham Lincoln addressed Stowe in 1863 as "the little lady who made this big war," his condescending comment did acknowledge that Stowe's art moved her readers to profound change in American life. Over sixty years later, Susan Glaspell, in her second novel *The Visioning* (1911), similarly hoped to move her compatriots to support socialist reforms as propounded by the Emersonian male protagonist and the newly converted heroine. The literary tide changed, however, and *The Visioning* did not express the current hopes of the people, but separated Glaspell from them, in the artistic avant-garde.[1]

In the early years of the Provincetown Players, from the group's founding

49

in 1915 through the United States' entry into the First World War in 1917, Glaspell and her fellow artists operated under the premise that art and life were inextricably linked. In *The Road to the Temple* (1927), her memoir of her husband George Cram Cook, a founder and the moving spirit of the Provincetown Players, Glaspell quotes a letter from him to her: "One thing we're in need of is the freedom to deal with life in literature as frankly as Aristophanes. We need a public like his, which has the habit of thinking and talking frankly of life. We need the sympathy of such a public, the fundamental oneness with the public, which Aristophanes had" (250). Cook wanted the Provincetown Players to provide the venue for a specifically American drama in a synergistic relation with the American people. The structure, dialogue, and staging could exhibit various degrees of "making it new," but the art of Provincetown would remain connected with life. The prewar works of the Provincetown Players represent an early form of modernism, what Andreas Huyssen calls "the historical avant-garde's insistence on the cultural transformation of everyday life" (*After the Great Divide*, 7) through thematic and technical breaks from the past. For women writers, however, this break from the past also meant dividing themselves from the rich literary tradition of their foremothers, the popular women novelists of the nineteenth century (See Clark, *Sentimental Modernism*). In plays such as *Trifles* (1916), *The People* (1917), *The Outside* (1917), and *Woman's Honor* (1918), Glaspell's women protagonists resist this new cultural imperative in their attempt to bring the best parts of the past forward while attempting to create new forms in the present that will, in turn, benefit the future.

In the aftermath of the First World War, modernism became associated with largely conservative male artists and essayists, the New Critics, who, paradoxically, wanted to define a modernist tradition based on once startling, but now codified techniques, not further innovation. The canon valorized Ezra Pound, not H.D.; Ernest Hemingway, not Gertrude Stein; and, of course, Eugene O'Neill, not Susan Glaspell, one of American literature's greatest but least-known writers. *Bernice* (1919), *Inheritors* (1921), and *The Verge* (1921), Glaspell's last plays of the Provincetown years, were written in the immediate aftermath of World War I and demonstrate her resistance to late modernism's calcification into a new set of constricting conventions and its disparagement of the life of the people and mass culture. Glaspell's disillusionment and despair were cautiously manifested a decade later in her last produced play, the Pulitzer-Prize-winning *Alison's House* (1930), in which a woman poet's legacy, safely sanitized and defused by the passage of decades, is inherited by a young male poet.

2. Scene from *Trifles* by Susan Glaspell

Glaspell's Provincetown plays, however, are modernism at its best: fresh, innovative, inclusive, and challenging.[2] Her first and best-known play *Trifles* (1916) epitomizes early modernism's attitude toward the past and its art. As is characteristic of all of Glaspell's work, *Trifles* advocates rejecting what is bad from the past, that which is outmodedly constricting, while preserving what is good, that which transmits hints for originality and progress. As is also typical of Glaspell, *Trifles* expresses women's fears as well as hopes for modern times and modernist art.

The nineteenth-century domestic novel advocated what has become known as the cult of domesticity: the idea that woman's sphere was limited to the home, but that within this sphere she was empowered to create a haven of morality, order, comfort, and sympathy. When joined with the pioneer myth, this tale envisions a frontier woman heroically creating such a domestic refuge in the wilderness. In the bleak, cold, and disordered kitchen of *Trifles*, Glaspell tries to ascertain why this myth was such a failure that it drove a farm wife, Minnie Wright, to behavior that was its antithesis, the murder of her husband when he was supposedly safe in his bed. Indeed, Glaspell is questioning the value of the sentimental domestic novel as Minnie Wright transforms it first into a modernist revenge tragedy for herself and her husband, and then into a potentially feminist detective story for the two local women, Mrs. Hale and Mrs. Peters, who are confronted with the crime scene.

When the County Attorney arrives at the Wright farm to investigate, he reads Minnie's kitchen as would the scornful male reader of the sentimental novel: he is willing to give it a hasty perusal, and then dismiss it as a failed exemplar of a trivial genre. He remarks that Mrs. Wright was "not much of a housekeeper" (38) and that "I shouldn't say she had the homemaking instinct" (39): Minnie Wright not only lacks the technique to create a scene of domestic bliss, but also what the County Attorney would regard as the essential womanliness or "instinct." Despite its failure as the sentimental *mise-en-scène*, the County Attorney is unwilling to change it. His immediate concern on entering the room is maintaining the past: "has anything been moved? Are things just as you left them yesterday?" (36).

Speaking for Glaspell, who played the part in the original production, Mrs. Hale comments on the unfairness of "trying to get [Minnie's] own house to turn against her" (40). This injustice stems from the fact that, to Glaspell, Minnie Wright is not responsible for the failure of her life to conform to that of the sentimental novel, for she has had authorship wrested away from her by her husband. Minnie's maiden name is "Foster," indicative of the nurturing domesticity which she was capable of producing. Minnie, however, married John Wright, who now "writes" the script for her life according to what he considers "right." John transforms the domestic sphere into a woman's prison, solitary confinement at that. He will not allow Minnie money to dress decently enough to attend church and its women's association. Not yet satisfied that his control over Minnie's life's plot is total, he destroys the domestic sphere as he damages the bird cage. Further, he apparently believes that he breaks Minnie's spirit as he breaks her pet canary's neck since, as many critics have noted, the unmarried Minnie has sung beautifully in the context of the communal art of the choir.

Through the image of caged bird as imprisoned woman artist, Glaspell is also challenging the sexism of many male modernists, particularly one of their great influences and avatars, Friedrich Nietzsche, avidly read by Glaspell and her husband. In *Beyond Good and Evil*, Nietzsche writes: "Men have so far treated women like birds who had strayed to them from some height: as something more refined and vulnerable, wilder, stranger, sweeter, and more soulful – but as something one has to lock up lest it fly away" (166). Nietzsche is happy to become the modern artist as superman while imprisoning women in their traditional role of moral and spiritual exemplars who are too delicate, and too valuable as property, for flight into modernity. John Wright similarly preempts the future for Minnie. When an aspect of modernity arrives that could relieve Minnie's mental, if not physical, isolation, the telephone, John refuses to have it installed. Like the County Attorney, he resists change. Minnie can neither have the benefits of the old "plot" for women, nor reap the advantages of modernity because she has been denied "author"ity.

Because John will not allow her the authority over the domestic sphere which society has falsely promised in return for relinquishing her public agency, Minnie is compelled to write a plot with which she has no essential affinity, a modernist revenge tragedy. Because she is cut off from the communal art of domesticity, and indeed any community, her new art is an isolated one, much as the woman modernist is separated from the tradition and support of her nineteenth-century predecessors. The scene she creates before the murder is quintessentially modernist. In the kitchen, where we expect cosiness, we are shocked not only by dirty towels, exploded jars of jam, and a crumb-covered table, but within a beautiful box is the corpse of the broken bird, modernist juxtaposition at its delicate but jarring best.

Minnie can no longer participate in the women's communal art of singing in the choir, so she has tried another usually communal art, quilting, which she is forced to do alone. As with the singing bird in its cage, Minnie at first tried to invoke a traditional plot by making a log cabin quilt, but in her increasing agitation before the murder, she can no longer conform to the measured stitches necessary for that form. As Mrs. Hale later notes of the sewing, "All the rest of it has been so nice and even. And look at this! It's all over the place! Why, it looks as if she didn't know what she was about!" (*Trifles*, 41), a typical reaction when comparing modernist art to the traditional art of the past. A few lines later, Mrs. Hale also terms the sewing "queer," which is Glaspell's word throughout her works for avant-garde art, that which points the way to the future, but appears grotesque in its isolation when viewed from the vantage point of the crowded past.

In her kitchen, Minnie leaves us the modernist scene of her break from the past, but she is unable to cope with a future beyond that disruption. Mr. Hale recalls that when he visited the Wright farm and Minnie told him of John's death, "She had her apron in her hand and was kind of – pleating it" (37). Her apron represents the domestic arts of the past; she can no longer employ it in its prescribed way, so she tries to make the utilitarian garment into fancy pleats. But pleats are simply repeating folds: for every fold forward, there is a fold back, indicative of Minnie's inability to move boldly forward into the future. Mr. Hale also notes that she is sitting in her rocking chair and "rockin' back and forth" (37). She oscillates between past and future, and makes no progress; this movement also futilely cancels itself. Although she has been compelled by her circumstances to regain authorship of her life by murdering her husband, she cannot see herself permanently in the role of playwright or heroine. As she talks with Mr. Hale, she moves from the rocking chair at center stage to another chair in the corner. Like many women artists thrust into modernity, in the words of Mr. Hale, Minnie acted "as if she didn't know what she was going to do next" (37).

When Mrs. Hale and Mrs. Peters arrive at the scene of Minnie's modernist break with the past, they also feel compelled to make some decisions about the future, but, in order to do so, they must first evaluate the past. While Minnie may have been thrust into a male version of domesticity, that of a woman's prison, Mrs. Hale and Mrs. Peters learn that they have acquiesced by refusing to read the past as it was and choosing to read it sometimes as the frontier saga and sometimes as the domestic novel. Mrs. Peters knows that frontier life does not conform to the soothing image of a pioneer family comfortably ensconced in a sturdy log cabin against the background of a noble and inspiring forest for, as she tells Mrs. Hale, "I know what stillness is. When we homesteaded in Dakota, and my first baby died – after he was two years old, and me with no other then –" (44). She also knows that the sentimental novel's picture of the domestic sphere as a harmonious meeting place for both genders is false; she remembers, "When I was a girl – my kitten – there was a boy took a hatchet, and before my eyes ... If they hadn't held me back I would have –" (43), presumably done what Minnie Wright did after the death of her canary. As Glaspell's characteristic and modernistic use of dashes indicates, Mrs. Peters is groping toward knowledge for which the traditional books of the past have given her no words, no script, while the men of the present ridicule women's hesitant attempts at articulation.

Mrs. Hale also realizes that she has allowed herself to be cozened into the domestic plot. She has thrown herself wholeheartedly into life with her relatively decent husband and her beloved children so that she blinds herself to less comfortable resolutions of the domestic narrative, like that of Minnie Wright. During the course of the play, Mrs. Hale repeatedly begins to understand what Minnie has done and why, and then pulls back from her understanding, much as Minnie has pleated her apron and rocked back and forth. When Mrs. Hale picks up the jaggedly cut loaf of bread, she then *abruptly drops it. In a manner of returning to familiar things* (39). Her preconceptions about domestic life continue to be challenged until Mrs. Hale realizes that if Minnie Wright may have been forced out of domesticity into her "crime," she herself has chosen to collude in the circumstances that produced it. She cries, "Oh, I *wish* I'd come over here once in a while! That was a crime! Who's going to punish that?" (44).

The ending of *Trifles* epitomizes the modernist woman artist's dilemma. Mrs. Hale and Mrs. Peters refuse to end what has become a detective story with the traditional male punishment according to traditional male standards of justice. They do not reveal to the County Attorney and their husbands the motive that they need to pin the crime on Minnie Wright, but, like Minnie, they are unable to foresee a radically different future. They are distressed that Minnie's jars of preserves have burst from the cold and are delighted to find one unharmed. They cling to this remnant of preserved traditional domesticity, and so decide to tell Minnie that all her preserves are fine. They want to behave as if her radical act has changed nothing; the past is preserved.[3] Tellingly, Mrs. Hale rips out Minnie's "queer" modernist stitching and replaces it with the neatly repetitive stitches of the past. Yet Mrs. Hale and Mrs. Peters now know that their dream of domesticity is a dangerous illusion, and that they will have to force themselves and Minnie to believe that it is true.

Although Mrs. Wright, Mrs. Hale, and Mrs. Peters appear stalled between the deceptive past and an unknown future, their *shared* consciousness of their state constitutes Glaspell's hope that they will eventually move into the future out of an untenable past, as Glaspell herself has subtly and quietly moved her audience from clinging to a fictitious past to raising questions about potential futures. For Glaspell, in *Trifles*, after a necessary stage of solitary realization and breaking from the past, modernist art must return to communal decisions about the future.

In *The People* (1917), Glaspell continues to explore the themes of the relationship between art and life, the catalytic role of women in questioning and subverting men's penal or artistic laws, and the challenge of bringing what remains alive from the past into the future without its incarceration in dead forms. In contrast to the muted questioning of *Trifles*, Glaspell explicitly examines the relationship of the avant-garde artist to the broader community.

Like *Trifles*, *The People* opens on a scene of disorder, in this case that of a messy and disorganized radical publication called *The People*, loosely and satirically modeled on *The Masses*, the leftist publication of Glaspell's Greenwich Village and Provincetown years. Like the domestic novel, radical art is not prospering. The magazine is about to fold, ostensibly for lack of funds, but in reality because of the fatigue and disillusionment of its editor, the ironically named Edward Wills, who has lost his will to persevere, and dispiritedly comments, "we don't change anything" (47). The publication's impotence, and its imminent demise, arise from a number of problems. Despite the communal aspirations of its title, as Ed Wills bitterly notes, "Everybody is plugging for his own thing. Nobody caring enough about the thing as a whole" (40), or, indeed, for "the people." Despite the fact that no work appears to be in progress, representatives of the people are repeatedly refused a hearing and summarily ushered out of the office.

In the case of editor Ed Wills, however, lies the crux of the people's and *The People*'s dilemma: the avant-garde artist should inspire the people, and in that sense, lead them into a better future, but the avant-garde artist may consider himself "avant," too far ahead of the people to understand them or affect them. Worse yet, he may translate "avant" not as signifying a forerunner, but as indicating natural superiority. Only four of the twelve characters in the play have conventional names; the other eight have appellations such as The Woman from Idaho, The Earnest Approach, and The Man from the Cape. Glaspell is borrowing from modernist theatre, that of expressionism, to suggest representative types rather than individuals.[4] The danger, though, for modernist artists including Ed Wills, is that these types will appear somewhat dehumanized and easily manipulable rather than symbolically significant. Ed Wills wants to be the modernist god-like creator but despondently states: "The People ... Oh, I got so tired looking at them – on farms, in towns, in cities. They're like toys that you wind up and they'll run awhile. They don't want to be expressed" (48).

Two women, reminiscent of the farm wives in *Trifles*, belie Ed's despair and his condescending attitude toward the people. Oscar Tripp, the associate editor, points to a woman like Minnie Wright, an absence who becomes a presence, in this case for the staff of *The People* and for the audience: "Just last night I heard of a woman in Bronxville who keeps *The People* under her bed so her husband won't know she's reading it" (42). She is also like Mrs. Hale and Mrs. Peters in that she is as yet unwilling to confront her husband and the patriarchal order, but, potentially like Minnie Wright, her weapon is poised where he is supposedly safest, in the domestic haven of his bed. While he remains asleep, she is awakened, but not yet ready to arise.

Another awakening representative of the people, The Woman from Idaho, played by Glaspell in the original production, makes her actual presence felt in the office. In her native state, she earned a living as a seamstress, but she was actually more interested in earning her death since she was saving for the respectable and conventional goal of buying her own tombstone. The words that would be carved in stone, however, failed in comparison with the words she found in a copy of *The People* that she serendipitously encountered. The local storekeeper asked her to take it out of the store because of the cover: "if some folks in this town see it, they'll think I'm not all I should be" (54). The storekeeper responds to modern art by removing it in the interest of his reputation for conformity.

In contrast, The Woman from Idaho is so moved by the magazine's contents that she uses her tombstone money, that of death and stasis, for a trip to move to New York, life and mobility. She reminds Ed that modern art should not be focused solely on the future where it would become isolated and deracinated like Ed and his magazine. Instead, she shows him how his words of the present in *The People* led her to connect to the living past of Lincoln's words that Ed quoted, not to the dead past of tombstones, and then to forge a bond with the future in her trip to New York and her reinspiration of Ed. She exhorts, "Let life become what it may become! – so beautiful that everything that is back of us is worth everything it cost" (58). Living words and inspirational forms create an endless chain, which Ed recognizes when he affirms, "This paper can't stop!" (58).

Although Glaspell has apparently provided us with a happy ending, with Ed restored to his true art and The Woman from Idaho resurrected into a new life, the fact remains that the male character is the artist while the woman is the muse. This paradigm is characteristic of much of Glaspell's work, particularly her late novels, but we cannot be sure that the woman is getting the lesser role. If we regard The Woman from Idaho and her later spiritual sisters, not as muses, but as Jamesian artists-in-life, Glaspell's intent becomes clearer. For Glaspell, art should never be separate from life; in fact, life is an art, so that the women who work in this medium, rather than paint or pen, may be those who most fully express themselves and inspire others.

Mrs. Patrick and Allie Mayo of *The Outside* may be regarded as two aspiring, but temporarily stymied, female modernist artists-in-life. Once again, Glaspell's play opens on a scene of abandonment and discomfort, in this case a defunct life-saving station near the end of Cape Cod where Mrs. Patrick, formerly a summer resident, now lives permanently with her servant Allie Mayo. The male characters are life-savers, but they are engaged in the hopeless project of resuscitating the corpse of a drowned man. Although their project should be moving and uplifting, for them, it is just another job: "Work – tryin' to put life in the dead" (48), to which they are inured by "Force of habit, I guess" (48), and led by precisely followed, mechanical routine: "Lucky I was not sooner or later as I walk by from my watch" (48). The ironically named life-savers can be seen as male artists trying to revive a dead form of male art, despite the futility of their uninspiring "work" and "habit."

Allie Mayo lost her husband to the sea twenty years ago and Mrs. Patrick recently lost hers to another woman, so that their current abode does not suggest conventional domesticity, any more than did the kitchen in *Trifles*. Tony, a local Portuguese-American, remarks, "A woman – she makes things pretty. This not like a place where a woman live. On the floor there is nothing – on the wall there is nothing. Things ... – do not hang on other things" (*The Outside*, 49). Despite the triteness of his view of woman's traditional art, making "things pretty," his description accurately describes the isolated state of the women as expressed in their medium, the room in which they live. The past is gone, but there is "nothing" to replace it. There is no continuity between past, present, and future: "Things do not hang on other things." Indeed, Mrs. Patrick does not spend much time in her house, preferring to watch the sand as it attempts to bury the contorted vines that struggle to grow beyond the forest. Just as she wants to bury the potential of the future, Mrs. Patrick explicitly rejects the past in its entirety when she says to the men, "This isn't the life-saving station any more. Just because it used to be – I don't see why you should think – This is my house! And – I want my house to myself!" (49).

While one could read Mrs. Patrick's denunciation of the life-savers as a bold feminist statement, reclaiming her physical and spiritual space, and as a rejection of the conventional art of the past, the way "it used to be," Glaspell, through the voice of Allie Mayo, the part she played in the original production, suggests that the woman artist should neither be isolated from other human beings nor disconnected from the past, though this alienation may be a necessary stage of recovery on the way to the future, much like Minnie Wright's rocking in *Trifles*. Halfway through the play, Allie's first word is "Wait"; she says it to Mrs. Patrick as if suggesting that she must pause and reassess before plunging into the future.

Through Allie, Glaspell uses the metaphor of the vines that reach out beyond the town and the forest to "the outside" of sand and water to suggest the role that she foresees for Mrs. Patrick and for women artists. These "strange little things that reach out farthest," a metaphor for modernist avant-garde art, do not merely point to the future, "avant," but guard, or "garde" the best part of the past: "And hold the sand for things behind them. They save a wood that guards a town ... where their children live" (53). As The Woman from Idaho renounced her tombstone, so Allie Mayo wants Mrs. Patrick to reject her burial of her potential: "Don't bury the only thing that will grow. Let it grow" (52).

With the help of her new community with Allie Mayo, the last lines of the play show Mrs. Patrick rising to the challenge of the woman artist-in-life, "(*feeling her way into the wonder of life*) Meeting the Outside! (It grows in her as CURTAIN lowers slowly)" (55). Glaspell's stage directions, "*feeling*," "grows," and "slowly," suggest that modernity must evolve gradually from a communal past, like the growth of a cluster of plants. While one might regard the women's devotion to the strange twisted vines as about as unappealing as the corpse-care of the "life-savers," the vines only look odd until we remember their connection to the past and their role of conserving its life in order to bring it into the future, in much the way

Glaspell hopes that her audience will evaluate her seemingly strange female modernist art with its hesitantly articulate and unconventional women.

In her next three major plays, *Woman's Honor*, *Bernice*, and *Inheritors*, Glaspell presents the idea of life as we live it as a fiction developed by males, and challenges it through a variety of dramatic heroines, artists-in-life. In *Woman's Honor* (1918), Glaspell makes two modernistic breaks with the past. First, she reveals the title concept as a euphemism for the sacrifices by women that men need to maintain their self-affirming fictions of themselves and the society that they have created. Secondly, as in *The People*, Glaspell eschews the device of individual names for the use of expressionistic representative types: The Shielded One, The Motherly One, The Scornful One, The Silly One, The Mercenary One, and The Cheated One. As the names indicate, these women are not autonomous beings, but exist only in relation to others, men who diminish them while paying lip service to the concept of a woman's honor. By the end of the play, however, the women have turned their lack of individual names into communal strength as they band together and reject the traditional male plot for/against them, along with the men. Instead of saving accused murderer Gordon Wallace, for whom they were initially willing to sacrifice their "honor" by providing an alibi, the women become interested in saving their sisters "through Gordon Wallace" (155): they are now the subjects and he is the tool. The last line of the play indicates that the women have become such powerful communal artists-in-life that the now "feminized" Gordon Wallace succumbs to their script. As he "staggers back to LAWYER'S arms," he moans, "*Oh, hell. I'll plead guilty*" (156). The women of *Woman's Honor* examine the past, reject parts of it, but retain enough female solidarity from the nineteenth-century separation of spheres to build together a bridge into the future: this is Glaspell's goal for the female avant-garde artist, her vision of modernism.

After these powerful one-act dramas, Glaspell's first three-act play, *Bernice* (1919), seems somewhat anticlimactic in theme and in technique. The title character never appears on stage, but her family and friends gather as she lies dead in a room offstage. Bernice has died of natural causes, but she has made her devoted maid Abbie, played by Glaspell in the original production, promise to tell Bernice's husband Craig that she killed herself, presumably over his infidelities, in order to give Craig a sense of self-worth. Bernice's dear friend Margaret, a labor organizer, is at first devastated by the supposed suicide, and then by her later knowledge of Bernice's deception. In the last lines of the play, however, Margaret realizes that Craig has changed for the better and that Bernice was exemplary: "Oh, in all the world – since first life *moved* – has there been any beauty like the beauty of perceiving love? ... No. Not for words" (230). Bernice, as artist-in-life, moves others by moving beyond the medium of words from life into death back into a metamorphosed life.

The problem is, obviously, that in order to achieve this reformed scenario, Bernice must die, another apparently self-sacrificial woman derived from the nineteenth-century domestic plot. Glaspell, however, is suggesting that Bernice, like the women in *Trifles*, is perpetually stymied in achieving cosy domesticity through the poor material provided by a patriarchal society: her baby dies, her father withdraws from life and authority, her husband philanders and writes trash. It is no wonder that Bernice's doctor diagnoses her ultimately fatal illness as "ulcers in the stomach" (180). Through the "fiction" of her suicide, Bernice is actually telling the truth: her life has killed her, gradually and inexorably, but on her deathbed she decides to use her death to rewrite the script and make some meaningful changes, to anticipate some satisfaction in the little time she has left after a lifetime of frustration, much as does Milly Theale in Henry James' *The Wings of the Dove*.

Through Bernice's friend Margaret, Glaspell reiterates her belief in the artist's mission. Margaret points out that the people "continue to look to *writers*" (*Bernice*, 202) to get "a little farther than others can get ... at least the edge of the shadow" (202), a shadow that Bernice approaches on her deathbed. Once again the writer is the avant-gardiste, the one on the outside, who provides inspiration for the people, as Bernice moves her friends and family. Margaret excoriates the cowardice of American writers' refusal to enter the shadow as she confronts Craig.

> What is it the matter with you – with all you American writers – 'most all of you. A well-put-up light – but it doesn't penetrate anything. It never makes the fog part. Just shows itself off – a well-put-up light [*Growing angry.*] It would be better if we didn't have you at all! Can't you see that it would? Lights which – only light themselves keep us from having light – from knowing what the darkness is. (199)

The darkness of Minnie Wright in *Trifles*, The Woman from Idaho in her tombstone phase in *The People*, Mrs. Patrick in *The Outside*, and the women in *Woman's Honor* must be confronted, not avoided, in order to "penetrate the fog" and reach the light on the other side of a better future.[5] In *Bernice*, Glaspell engages the miasmic darkness of women's fatal frustrations in the hope that her audience, still alive, can reach the light on the other side.

Glaspell's plays until 1918 are largely representative of the avant-garde version of modernism, what Huyssen calls the "insistence on the cultural transformation of everyday life" (*After the Great Divide*, 7). From 1918, though, her plays manifest another aspect of modernism, what Matei Calinescu terms "its outright rejection of bourgeois modernity" (*Five Faces of Modernity*, 42) and "its ideals of rationality, utility, progress" (10). In that most repressed play, *Bernice*, the muted hostility toward bourgeois modernity is demonstrated mainly through the satirical portrait of Bernice's ultra-conventional, hyper-organizing sister-in-law Laura, but it becomes a major theme of Glaspell's last two Provincetown plays, *Inheritors* (1921) and *The Verge* (1921). The change lies in Glaspell's perception that the cataclysm of World War I did not erase the stultifying aspects of the past and nurture its best parts into the future, but instead reinforced the repressive, xenophobic, and biased elements of society, as epitomized in the Espionage Act of 1917 and the Sedition Act of 1918.

On the Fourth of July 1879, *Inheritors*' Silas Morton decides to commemorate the best aspects of the past, such as independence and a pioneering spirit, and to make reparations for the worst, the crimes against Native Americans, by contributing a valuable hill on his property for the founding of a college, a place where young men and women could find "All the things men have found out, the wisest and finest things men have thought since first they began to think" (111). By time-present, when Silas' granddaughter Madeline is a student at Morton College, the college appears to be a place which promotes the worst men have thought and done: it supplies strike-breakers to local industries and is, indeed, a steady supporter of the military-industrial complex, modernity at its worst. The college is also helping to deport some students from India who would be punished for their views in their native land and, ironically, in this self-proclaimed bastion of democracy as well.

Despite *Inheritors*' bitter denunciation of repressively bourgeois modernity, Glaspell does hold out hope for the future through Madeline's conversion to the avant-garde. Like *The People*'s Ed Wills and The Woman from Idaho, the Indian students quote some revolutionary words of Lincoln in their defense. Madeline, until this point a fairly typical tennis-playing coed, is indirectly affected by Lincoln's words as she impulsively defends the Indian students from police brutality by striking the officers with her tennis racket, and later confronts the police a second time, despite repeated warnings from her quite influential and highly bourgeois relatives. Madeline's spontaneous acts lead to her more reasoned radicalization as she begins to interpret clues around her and discovers that "We seem here, now, in America, to have forgotten we're moving. Think it's just *us* – just now. Of course, that would make us afraid, and – ridiculous" (151). Madeline refuses to believe in stasis and asserts a chain of inspiration from her pioneering ancestors through her toward the future: "The wind has come through – wind rich from lives now gone ... Then – be the most you can be, so life will be more because you were" (156).

As this ending suggests, *Inheritors* can be read as Glaspell's scornful modernist counter-propaganda to prevailing bourgeois ideologies, combined with her optimistic avant-garde stance. In *The Verge*, however, she explores what would become high modernism, characterized by its rigid separation from mass culture (Huyssen, *After the Great Divide*, viii). Through Claire Archer, the protagonist, Glaspell explores the causes and the tragic consequences of the high modernist's alienation from the life around her.

Claire Archer's early life was much like that of Bernice or the women in *Trifles* in that she was frustrated in her expectation of fulfillment through conventional women's roles. Her first husband was a "stick-in-the-mud artist" (*The Verge*, 69), and the current three men in her life, soulmate, lover, and husband, are ultimately as conventional as their names suggest: Tom, Dick, and Harry. Like Bernice, Claire lost her son in infancy. Her daughter Elizabeth is a mindlessly conformist debutante. Amid the disappointments of the quotidian, Claire looked to modernity for reinvigorating transformation. She married her current husband Harry because he was an aviator; Claire hoped that this modern technology would change man's perspective, "to look from above," but discovered that "man flew, and returned to earth the man who left it" (69). She also regarded World War I's destruction of the stifling past as a chance for positive metamorphoses, "But fast as we could – scuttled right back to the trim little thing we'd been shocked out of" (70). Her husband Harry is more correct in his diagnosis than he knows when he wants Claire to see a nerve specialist who "fixed up a lot of people shot to pieces in the war" (65), but for Claire the war itself was not responsible for her incipient madness, but its failed aftermath was.

Claire retreats from the bourgeois world by becoming a high modernist artist in her chosen medium of horticulture.[6] With the help of her servant Anthony, she jealously guards her greenhouse from intruders. In Act I, in the midst of a snowstorm, Claire diverts all the heat from the house to her greenhouse for her delicate plants and then tries to prevent her family and friends from entering because the temperature drops whenever the door is opened. This is a scene of exclusivity as high comedy, but the mood darkens as the audience begins to perceive how thoroughly Claire cuts herself off from those around her. In one of Glaspell's ugliest and most confrontational scenes, Claire strikes her daughter Elizabeth and rejects her, saying, "To think that object ever moved my belly and sucked my breast!" (78). Claire refuses to see that her decision to have Elizabeth raised by her conventional sister Abigail, leaving Claire free for her high modernist pursuits, might be the cause of what she regards as Elizabeth's repugnant conformity. As she feigns madness in Act II, she rejects mass culture as represented by the phonograph records the others play. In the last act, she strangles Tom Edgeworthy when she discovers that he is not the fellow explorer that she believed him to be, but simply wants to keep her "safe" (99). The conclusion of the play exhibits her final and total alienation as she retreats into madness and sings "Nearer My God to Thee" since she is certainly far from everyone else. Claire has done what is expected of the high modernist artist: she has rejected human society along with mass culture and devoted herself to her art to the point of madness. In her rigid devotion to this role, she is as much a conformist as those around her, and her chosen role is as constrictingly sacrificial as her socially assigned gender role.

What, then, of the results of all this exclusive artistic devotion? Claire produces two works of art, the Edge Vine and Breath of Life. The Edge Vine certainly resembles the bourgeois notion of modern art: "*The leaves of this vine are not the form that leaves have been. They are at once repellent and significant*" (58). Claire regards the vine as a failure because "It doesn't want to be – what hasn't been" (61). Consequently, Claire turns to her remaining experiment, Breath of Life, which "is outside what flowers have been" (63), and, in contrast to the Edge Vine, does not turn back. Breath of Life, however, is not yet complete: it lacks a fragrance which Claire calls "Reminiscence" because "What has gone out should bring fragrance from what it has left" (63, 62). This legacy from the past as represented in human community is what Claire herself lacks. She, like her plants, is a high modernist experiment, and she is also a failure because she has isolated herself from the past and from community. She is as mentally dead as Bernice is physically dead, but, unlike Bernice, she has left nothing for others.

Glaspell herself, though, did leave us this cautionary tale about modernity's dangerous tendencies before her decade-long hiatus from playwriting, in which she continued her experiments in radically innovative novels such as *Fugitive's Return* (1929). *The Verge* is a fitting conclusion to Glaspell's Provincetown years since it is technically the most modernist of her work: the language is highly fragmented, with a plethora of Glaspell's characteristic dashes, and the greenhouse and "thwarted tower" are expressionistic representations of Claire's mental state.[7] In contrast, the Pulitzer Prize that Glaspell won for *Alison's House* (1930) signifies bourgeois approval of traditional technique and thematic correctness, a conventional epilogue to a radical career.[8] Like Bernice, Alison Stanhope is dead before the play begins. She is a nineteenth-century poet, based on Emily Dickinson, who renounced a married lover for the good name and feelings of her family and devoted the rest of her life to her art. She seems to have learned these lessons from a poet of her past, Ralph Waldo Emerson, two of whose poems are quoted in the play as signposts to Alison's decision: "Forbearance," requiring her sacrifice, and "The House," concerning the enduring quality of art. Since he is generally known as a radical thinker whose watchwords are non-conformity and self-reliance and who advocated living in the present, Emerson, like Alison and *Alison's House*, seems camouflaged for the demands of social conformity.

Unlike the avant-garde art earlier espoused by Glaspell, Alison's poetry seems to leave few positive influences, in art or life. The young male poet who comes to see her house on the last night of the nineteenth century, John Knowles, writes trite un-Dickinsonian verse: "Perhaps I could even write a poem about it – how the river flowed by the sea, as her century flowed – to eternity" (96). Although the characters, male and female, say that "Alison wrote those poems for me," her family is enmeshed in unhappy marital and extramarital relationships, such as her niece Elsa's living with a married man and provoking her father's rejection. Even the nephew whom Alison regarded in infancy as heaven's angelic messenger is trying to exploit spurious memories of his famous aunt as a bribe to his English instructor for passing his college course. The only positive effect of Alison's art is that, with the discovery of her love poems, Elsa is reconciled with her father. If Alison's poetry has changed anything, that change is subtle almost to invisibility.

In a sense, *Alison's House* can be regarded as the dutiful exemplar of modernism between the wars when art was supposed to exist, timelessly, for and in itself, with little relationship to the life around it, the type of art praised by the rapidly ascending New Critics. This is the kind of art Alison Stanhope/Emily Dickinson ostensibly wrote, which is why Dickinson was usually the only woman in the old canon of nineteenth-century American literature. By 1930, Glaspell may have felt that any ostensibly timeless or universal quality that her works possessed would be their only claim to notice. She was right, temporarily, as the Pulitzer Prize demonstrated, but wrong in the longer run since most women modernists were erased from the literary canon anyway. We now read Dickinson as a woman both beyond and of her time as we see the American Renaissance in its historical and cultural perspectives. As we similarly revise our view of modernism into modernisms and refuse to valorize its latest and most marmoreal phase, we can now see Glaspell as her own kind of avant-garde modernist, who valued the best of the past, present, and future, and never lost sight of the relationship between art and humanity, so that of her works "there will be those in the future to say, She wrote them for me" (*Alison's House*, 153).

NOTES

1 For an analysis of Glaspell's fiction, see my *Susan Glaspell's Century of American Women*.

2 Due to difficulties of distinguishing contributions, I am not discussing Glaspell's two collaborations with George Cram Cook, *Suppressed Desires* (1915) and *Tickless Time* (1918), nor *The Comic Artist* (1928), her later collaboration with her lover or common-law husband Norman Matson. I am also excluding Glaspell's unpublished *Chains of Dew* (1922) and her one-act play *Close the Book* (1917), a slight and farcical precursor to *Inheritors*.

3 Judith L. Stephens argues that *Trifles* is typical of Progressive Era plays because it "both challenged and reinforced the dominant gender ideology of the period" ("Gender Ideology," 53). I agree, but think that the challenge is what Mrs. Hale, Mrs. Peters, and Glaspell's audience subliminally and ultimately retain; after viewing the potential for change, the past can no longer be accepted complacently and unquestioningly.

4 For accounts of American expressionism, including Glaspell's *The Verge*, and its antecedents, see Ronald H. Wainscott's chapter 6 in *The Emergence of the Modern American Theater*: "The Vogue of Expressionism in Postwar America" and Mardi Valgamae's chapter 1 in *Accelerated Grimace*: "The Spell of Expressionism," and chapter 2: "The Provincetown Players."

5 When we consider Glaspell's close association with Eugene O'Neill in the Provincetown Players, her use of fog imagery here could be read as an implicit critique of the despair of his plays as symbolized by their now-famous, seemingly never-lifting fogs.

6 Barbara Ozieblo ("Rebellion and Rejection," 71) and Kathleen L. Carroll ("Centering Women Onstage," 197) see Claire as a female Nietzsche, and I would agree since Nietzsche is a precursor of this type of high modernist artist.

7 For a discussion of Glaspell's structural and linguistic innovations in *The Verge* and other plays, see Linda Ben-Zvi, "Susan Glaspell's Contributions." For an account of expressionism in *The Verge*, see Wainscott, *The Emergence of the Modern American Theater*, 114–15 and Ozieblo, "Susan Glaspell," 13–14.

8 Carroll sees this as a muting of Glaspell's feminism in particular ("Centering Women Onstage," 191), while I see the repressed feminism as part of Glaspell's strategic repression of her avant-garde beliefs in social transformation because of the high modernist cultural climate.

5

JERRY DICKEY

The expressionist moment: Sophie Treadwell

Until recently, most standard accounts of twentieth-century American theatre have virtually ignored Sophie Treadwell. At most, Treadwell's best-known play, the explosive 1928 drama *Machinal*, receives mention as a last gasp example of 1920s expressionism on the commercial Broadway stage. With a renewed attention to *Machinal*, however, first with its reappearance in print in an anthology in 1981 and then in prominent revivals by the New York Shakespeare Festival in 1990 and the Royal National Theatre in London in 1993, Treadwell has begun to attract more scholarly and artistic interest. With her theatre career spanning six decades, including the writing of forty plays in a variety of styles and subjects, as well as acting in, directing, and producing her own works for the Broadway stage, Treadwell may be viewed as one of America's pioneering, early twentieth-century women dramatists. Her writings consistently examine the conditions of modern society which inhibit women's personal struggles for independence and equality. Especially in her most experimental works, *Machinal* and *For Saxophone*, Treadwell may also be seen as one of the first American women playwrights to utilize non-realistic innovations in style and narrative to create a decidedly feminist aesthetic in the theatre.

Sophie Treadwell was born in Stockton, California in 1885. Her mother, Nettie Fairchild Treadwell, was part of a ranching family which helped settle the Stockton area. Her father, Alfred B. Treadwell, was of Mexican and European descent. His desertion of the family in favor of a career as a lawyer and elected judge in San Francisco severely disrupted Sophie's formative years. Despite the fact that she would often spend summers in San Francisco with her father, Sophie frequently experienced embarrassment and humiliation over her mother's persistent attempts to follow and reunite with Alfred. Many of these early family experiences reappear in Treadwell's dramatic writing: devotion to a life built on working the land; patriarchal responsibility and absence; individuals struggling with a lineage of mixed races; the struggles of a woman yearning for independence yet tied emotionally to the love of a man; and the plight of a young working girl trying to make her way alone in the big city.

When Treadwell entered the University of California at Berkeley in 1902, she soon found numerous outlets for her considerable creativity. She regularly performed in dramatic productions, edited the college humor magazine, participated in ladies' crew, and gained employment teaching foreign students at a night school. Treadwell also entered the field of journalism, working as a campus correspondent for the *San Francisco Examiner* and in the circulation department of the *San Francisco Call*. Money she earned from these jobs went to support her education (Alfred was unreliable in providing financial assistance) and to help her financially destitute mother. By her senior year, Sophie was suffering from near nervous exhaustion, and though she began missing periods of school, she nevertheless graduated *in absentia* with her classmates in the spring of 1906 after the San Francisco earthquake disrupted normal activities.

After brief stints as a teacher and tutor in remote areas of northern California, Treadwell decided to pursue her first love: acting. With her mother in tow, Treadwell moved to Los Angeles where she went on the vaudeville stage as a character artist, performing three songs with changes of costume. Her disappointment with theatre life grew rapidly, however, when she discovered first-hand the squalidness of the performance conditions in vaudeville theatres. She quit acting and, with the aid of Constance Skinner, a drama critic she had befriended, worked as a typist for Helena Modjeska while the great Polish star wrote her memoirs. Treadwell was awestruck by Modjeska, and "Madame" took a special interest in the young would-be actress. Modjeska provided tutelage and sponsorship, and soon wrote personally to New York theatre managers in support of a play written by her new protégée. Modjeska helped instill in Treadwell a firm resolve to retain artistic control over her own writings for the theatre, and Treadwell's subsequent insistence on this, along with her tireless efforts as an advocate for the rights of dramatists, undoubtedly earned her a reputation with managers and producers as a difficult artist with whom to work. Treadwell left Modjeska's employ after a few months to be with her ailing mother, and then turned quickly to pursue dual careers in playwriting and journalism, first in San Francisco and then following her new husband, the renowned sportswriter William O. McGeehan, to New York.

Treadwell's earliest plays reveal an willingness to explore a range of stylistic and structural approaches. These works vary from short comic or character sketches to three-act, domestic "problem" plays. Her earliest departures from realism were *To Him Who Waits* (1915–18) and *The Eye of the Beholder* (1919), two one-act efforts employing symbolist and expressionist devices. The latter, especially, echoes Alice Gerstenberg's *Overtones* (1913), in which varying personas of a female character are depicted onstage. These two works were largely aberrations, however, and Treadwell's early writing reveals a propensity for the realistic situations generally presented within the structures of the "well-made play."

Treadwell's thoughts on play structure and her writing process may best be seen in surviving notes from three lectures she gave to the American Laboratory Theatre in New York in 1925. These notes reveal Treadwell's familiarity with the "well-made play" format and the importance of working from a detailed scenario which grows organically, either during preplanning or during the actual writing process, out of a carefully designed "situation ... one moment when opposed forces come together in a particularly thrilling or amusing moment" ("Writing," 5). On the other hand, these lecture notes clearly indicate that as a playwright Treadwell remained much more interested in the initial phase of creative invention than in structuring dramatic action. Treadwell used her writing as an extension of her actor training; writing afforded her the opportunity to explore creatively a variety of roles springing from her dramatic imagination. She explained to students at the Lab the reason for her turn from acting to playwriting: "In writing plays I wasn't limited to just the parts, the stereotyped parts that might be handed out to me [through typecasting]. In writing I played, and I played from the very beginning of their creation, any and all parts that entered my fancy" ("The Playwright," 1).

Treadwell's plays, then, tend not to be tightly constructed well-made plays on the model of Scribean dramaturgy. Her interest in creative exploration over formal structure may partially explain why the many revisions she made to her plays rarely yielded substantial focusing of dramatic action in the traditional Aristotelian sense. This fact may also explain why Treadwell frequently met with difficulties in marketing her plays with commercial theatre producers; often her works favored characterization at the expense of a clearly defined line of action. Treadwell concluded as much at the end of her first lecture to students at the American Lab: "I have been interested in the HOW of writing rather than the WHAT of a play. If any of you thought to learn from me anything really about a play, what is a play, what makes a play and what doesn't, it is inevitable that you have been disappointed. You see I know quite less about that than I do about this" ("Writing," 8).

These lectures also prove noteworthy because they demonstrate Treadwell's underlying dissatisfaction with the American commercial system of play production. Treadwell received her first Broadway production in 1922 (*Gringo*, produced and directed by Guthrie McClintic), and at the time of these Lab lectures she was experiencing difficulties getting her comedy *O Nightingale* produced after George C. Tyler unceremoniously dropped the play despite successful tryouts featuring Helen Hayes in the central role. Like Lab founder and director Richard Boleslavsky, with whom Treadwell had spent the summer of 1923 studying as part of a collective of theatre artists, Treadwell states in her notes that American commercial theatre discouraged artistic experimentation, limited actors to a small range of roles based solely on their physical type, and blunted the creative imaginations of dramatists by insisting on the use of "play doctors" (professional rewrite specialists who reworked scripts to realize their commercial potential), a set four-week rehearsal period, and an unwillingness by directors to discuss a play's content with actors. "I do not in the least exaggerate," Treadwell said, "when I say that many plays go into their dress rehearsal without the actors knowing ... what the play is about, what the parts are about and what the words really mean" ("Producing," 11). Marketing and selling scripts for such a system of play production consisted of a repeated series of artistic compromises for Treadwell, ultimately constituting for her "a whole tragedy in itself" ("Producing," 1).

Treadwell responded to her frustrations with commercial theatre practices by vehemently defending the creative rights of the dramatist and by lobbying for the playwright as the controlling visionary artist in the theatre. Unlike her mentor Boleslavsky, who believed the director should be the artist who shaped theatrical production, Treadwell believed the playwright to be not only "the biggest creative force in the theatre" but "perhaps the only really creative force." By necessity, then, Treadwell's ideal dramatist "should be very definitely a craftsman of the theatre ... knowing definitely and to the last detail how to make [his] dream materialize to its fullest within the world of the theatre, a world that can sometimes turn out to be so dull, so mean, so cruel" ("Producing," 4). By the winter of 1925, Treadwell had concluded that if her own brand of playwriting was to gain a voice on the Broadway stage, she must take matters into her own hands. In April of that year, *O Nightingale* opened at the 49th Street Theatre in New York, with Treadwell acting in a supporting role and directing and co-producing. While not a smash hit by Broadway standards, *O Nightingale* nevertheless garnered enough critical praise and box-office sales to give Treadwell further encouragement to pursue directing and producing her own works and to feel more at liberty to explore non-realistic dramatic structures.

New York theatre in the 1920s afforded Treadwell numerous examples of a new form of non-realistic playwriting and staging. The twenties featured a wave of European and American plays written and/or staged in the style of expressionism. Significant earlier efforts in expressionism had occurred in the New York theatre by 1920 or before, most notably Alice Gerstenberg's *Overtones* (1913) and Eugene O'Neill's *The Emperor Jones* (1920), a vigorous and sustained exploration of the style manifested itself after the US release of the influential German film, *The Cabinet of Dr. Caligari*, in the spring of 1921. In the ensuing years, New York theatre audiences witnessed a string of revivals of European expressionist plays: Georg Kaiser's *From Morn to Midnight* (1922); Ernst Toller's *Man and the Masses* (1924); August Strindberg's *The Spook Sonata* (1924) and *A Dream Play* (1926); Frank Wedekind's *The Earth Spirit* (produced under the title, *The Loves of Lulu*, 1925); and Franz Werfel's *The Goat Song* (1926). Audiences of the twenties could also choose from a host of plays with expressionist features written by American dramatists: Susan Glaspell's *The Verge* (1921); O'Neill's *The Hairy Ape* (1922), *The Great God Brown* (1924), and *All God's Chillun Got Wings* (1924); Elmer Rice's *The Adding Machine* (1923) and *The Subway* (1929); George S. Kaufman and Marc Connelly's *Beggar on Horseback* (1924); and *Roger Bloomer* (1923) and *Processional* (1925) by John Howard Lawson.

Despite differences in tone, setting, theme, and degree of stylization, these works typically featured some common characteristics. Above all, they attempted to reject representation of surface reality in favor of a depiction of inner, subjective states of emotion and experience. Visual and emotional qualities often featured an element of distortion, exaggeration, or suggestive symbolism, frequently achieving a dream-like or nightmarish quality to the action. The effects of mechanization and urbanization resounded in the compressed syntax and telescopic dialogue of the characters, who with the exception of the central character often appeared as abstracted types or caricatures. Music and sound effects helped communicate the varying emotional states of the play's focal characters, sometimes being used as substitutes for words and action. These plays also tended to reject a linear, sustained exposition of story in favor of a rapidly changing sequence of short scenes which sometimes dissolved one into the other in cinematic fashion.

Although very little documentation exists in Treadwell's papers to reveal the extent of her interest in this emerging dramatic style of expressionism, she clearly became very familiar with its features. In January of 1926, Treadwell wrote a guest review for the *New York Tribune* of productions of Werfel's *The Goat Song* and O'Neill's *The Great God Brown*. While she thought the former an archetypically "German play, a Big Bertha, heavy booming, devastating," she was still moved by the "magnificent" epic production. And while Treadwell expressed concerns that O'Neill's youthful fame and success had encouraged him to expose "all the wares that the back shelves of his mind possess, no matter how commonplace, how uninteresting, how cheap these wares may be," she nevertheless admired the "depth and truth" of the play, as well as its expressionist staging by Robert Edmond Jones (Treadwell, "*Goat Song*"). This review demonstrates that while Treadwell did not always approve of expressionist plays' heavy didacticism on the one hand or idiosyncratically personal statements on the other, she clearly recognized the potentially powerful impact that such a style offered in the theatre.

At this point in her career, Treadwell appeared eager to tackle such extreme forms of non-realistic dramaturgy herself, and her interest the following year in a sensational murder trial provided her with a point of departure in subject matter. In the spring of 1927, a Long Island housewife named Ruth Snyder and her corset-salesman lover, Judd Gray, were put on trial for the sordid murder of Snyder's husband. Despite the substantial evidence which suggested that in her marriage Ruth Snyder and her nine-year-old daughter were victims of several beatings and violent threats, both Gray and the media painted Snyder as the monstrous initiator of the crime, a sinister, scheming temptress who led Gray down the road to debauchery. Daily columns reported the details of her clandestine affair with Gray, thus whetting the vicarious appetites of respectable readers who could see no aspect of themselves in the inhuman Snyder.[1] The trial so captivated the public's interest that 180 reporters were assigned to the case. The Manhattan press gave so much attention to the trial that even the sensational *New York Graphic* proposed that each of the New York papers limit their daily courtroom summaries to 500 words each (Hadden and Luce, *Time Capsule*, 221). The media frenzy continued unabated, however, until the couple was executed by electric chair at Sing Sing on January 12, 1928. Although Snyder and Gray both had been on trial and executed, Snyder received the vast majority of the media's microscopic attention. Not even her death would remain a private affair. A reporter for the *New York Daily News* smuggled a camera into the execution chamber strapped to his leg under his pants and his gruesome photo of Snyder at death appeared in print the following morning. Edmund Wilson reported that prominent New York dailies devoted more column inches to Snyder's execution than to the death the day before of Thomas Hardy, and he wondered why this act of violent retribution against this one woman would so intrigue and please the public (Wilson, *The American Earthquake*, 161–63).

Treadwell must have wondered the same thing. Having maintained a professional career as a journalist since 1908, Treadwell had covered other sensational murder trials involving women defendants. In San Francisco in

1914, Treadwell wrote a series of daily columns describing the trial of Leah Alexander for the murder of J. D. Van Baalen, an advertising man and her lover of several years. Two years later, for the *New York American*, Treadwell reported on the Providence, Rhode Island trial of Elizabeth Blair Mohr for hiring her chauffeur and accomplices to murder her physician husband and disfigure his housekeeper lover. In each of these instances, Treadwell's reportage suggests that the truth in the cases remained far more elusive and complicated than the official court testimony and traditional media coverage would indicate. Treadwell blended her reporting of the factual evidence of the cases with subjective observations on the women being tried. She would record the manner in which a defendant held her mouth in moments of repose, a snatchet of women's conversation heard outside the courtroom commenting on the murdered man's good looks, or the silent gasping for breath by one of the distressed women during the prosecution's closing arguments. Through an emphasis on such details, what one of Treadwell's contemporary journalist-turned-playwrights Susan Glaspell would refer to in a popular one-act play as "trifles" typically dismissed as unimportant by men but recognized as significant and telling actions by women, Treadwell insinuated that the women's relationships to their lovers or spouses, and the reasons for their subsequent violent actions against them, emerged as perhaps more complex than the all-male juries, and society in general, would recognize. As Treadwell concluded in her first report on Alexander's trial: "Next Tuesday morning, before Judge Dunne, a woman – young, handsome and radiant with health – goes on trial for her life. This thing is coming towards her, silent, powerful, inexorable" ("Girl Slayer"). This "thing" to which Treadwell refers implies more than a single, particular act of retribution for a crime committed, but suggests the crushing weight of an entire society whose masculine laws and orientations stifle the voices and emotional needs of women.

Treadwell echoed this belief in response to the trial of Ruth Snyder. Although she did not cover the trial officially for any of the New York papers, Treadwell regularly attended the proceedings. Her response this time consisted not of a series of articles but of a play, *Machinal*, titled after the French word used to describe actions of an automatic, mechanical, or involuntary nature. Treadwell most likely drafted the play in the summer and fall after the Snyder trial, but her work on it accelerated after Snyder's execution. *Machinal* was copyrighted on April 21, 1928 and began its ninety-one-performance run at the Plymouth Theatre in New York beginning September 7 of that year.

One of the earliest drafts of *Machinal* confirms that Treadwell based her play on Ruth Snyder. But Treadwell's interest in the specifics of Snyder's

3. Scene from *Machinal* by Sophie Treadwell

case consisted mainly in her attempt to use them as a springboard for her own critique of gender inequity in modern society. Later versions omit the Snyder reference and note that the plot pertains to "an ordinary young woman, any woman" (*Machinal*, 173). By focusing more on actions leading up to the murder and subsequent trial, and by employing archetypal character names such as the Young Woman instead of Snyder, Treadwell effectively moves the play's subject from the specific to the general. Ruth Snyder may have been one particular woman, but Treadwell's *Machinal* suggests that the forces which drove her to violence could do the same for "any woman" similarly disempowered by modern society.[2]

Machinal is written in nine scenes, each of which depicts "the different phases of life that the woman comes in contact with, and in none of which she finds any place, any peace" (*Machinal*, 173). These "different phases" often take the form of a specific social institution or a situation which defines expected feminine behavior. Scene One, "To Business," shows the Young Woman as economically dependent on her office job, with the prospect of marriage to her older, physically repugnant boss as the only visible alternative to her social station. The second scene, "At Home," depicts the Young Woman's devotion to her lonely, dependent mother, who cares more for her own future security than her daughter's happiness in finding love in marriage. Scenes Three and Four, "Honeymoon" and "Maternal," portray first the Young Woman's anxieties on her wedding night and then her rejection after giving birth to a baby girl of the traditional notion that all women possess maternal instincts. In the latter scene, Treadwell's Young Woman recoils at the prospect of motherhood and laments the loss of control over her own body to which she has been forced to succumb. The subsequent two scenes dramatize the Young Woman's foray into what traditional society of the twenties would define as an illicit love affair. In "Prohibited," she encounters in a speakeasy (a bar that sells liquor illegally during Prohibition) an expatriated American adventurer, A Man (Richard Roe), who has recently returned from Mexico where he killed two "bandidos" to escape captivity. In "Intimate," the Young Woman blossoms into happiness after making love with her gentle, romantic partner. Scene Seven, "Domestic," contrasts the tenderness of the preceding scene with the crudity of the Young Woman's married life, as husband and wife sit on opposite ends of a divan, he reading headlines of economic profit and material possession, she of episodes of domestic violence and desperate escapes to freedom. In "The Law," the audience witnesses the Young Woman on trial for the murder of her husband. After a betrayal by her former lover, Roe, the Young Woman confesses. A concluding scene, "A Machine," portrays the Young Woman in her final moments in prison awaiting execution. The play ends with the Young Woman incoherently pleading with her mother to communicate the details of her life, and the social forces dictating behavior for all women, to her daughter.

As this plot summary reveals, Treadwell presents the action of *Machinal* in an episodic, fragmented manner. The action unfolds in fits and starts and appears noteworthy especially for what it does not present onstage. *Machinal* avoids the type of confrontational scenes normally found in both realistic and expressionist dramas: there is no scene in which the jealous husband accuses his wife of infidelity, no emotionally contrived scene in which the Young Woman's daughter appears for sentimental effect, no tearful farewell episode between the Young Woman and Roe when he returns to Mexico, and most obviously no scene depicting the actual murder or subsequent arrest. Instead, Treadwell augments her short, suggestive scenes with a wide variety of expressionist devices to encourage audiences to project into the skeletal action the motivations and factors affecting the behavior of the characters. *Machinal* employs an extensive network of sound effects imitative of radio dramas, a medium which Treadwell felt theatregoers had grown accustomed to imbuing with their active imaginations. Additionally, offstage voices and figures expand the implications of the action to the world beyond that of the Young Woman. The language ranges from the staccato rhythms of the office workplace and the crude punning of the Husband to the simple lyricism of the Young Woman with her lover.

The most extreme form of emotional distortion and subjectivity in language, however, comes in the form of lengthy interior monologues by the central character. In a stage direction from an unpublished typescript of *Machinal*, Treadwell states her purpose in employing these introspective monologues: "Does their place in the plan of the play – connecting links, or better, – connecting channels of action – demand that the thought move through them in an approximately straight line, or can one be permitted a nearer approach to the scatteredness, unexpectedness of the relaxed meditating mind?" Treadwell hoped that her use of these monologues and other expressionistic techniques would create an overpowering stage effect "by accentuation, by distortion ... and by the quickening of still secret places, in the consciousness of the audience, especially of women" (*Machinal* ts.).

The stage directions quoted above contain a couple of noteworthy features. First, Treadwell clearly intended for *Machinal* to stimulate the subconscious mind of the theatregoer. She abandons linear exposition of thought or story in favor of an appeal to the "still secret places" in the emotional lives of her audience. In this regard, Treadwell shares a strong affinity with her main collaborator on *Machinal*'s premiere production, Arthur Hopkins. By the mid-1920s, Hopkins as a director earned wide recognition for helping usher in a subtle form of psychological realism to the American theatre. Yet he had also directed influential productions employing an expressionist style, most notably Eleanor Gates' *Poor Little Rich Girl* (1913) and Shakespeare's *Macbeth* (1921). Regardless of the style, Hopkins sought through his direction the realization of what he termed his theory of "Unconscious Projection." Most clearly articulated in his 1918 publication, *How's Your Second Act?*, this theory involves an attempt to stage a play's action suggestively so that the drama will, somewhat like hypnotism, attain complete illusion by appealing to the audience's unconscious. The key for attaining such illusion involved extreme simplification in the staging of the action. Hopkins stated, "It is the elimination of all the non-essentials because they arouse the conscious mind and break the spell I am trying to weave over the unconscious mind" (16). Hopkins' "non-essentials" refer to any acting tricks or self-conscious stage business. In *Machinal*, Treadwell offers a dramaturgical extension of this theory of Unconscious Projection, using sounds, monologues, lighting, and fragmentary dialogue to suggest rather than to define the action for the audience.

The other noteworthy passage in Treadwell's unpublished stage directions pertains to her belief that this approach might have its greatest effect upon the female spectator. In her influential study, *Feminism and Theatre*, Sue-Ellen Case discusses the possibility as to whether or not a dramatic form exists which particularly expresses female sensibility or experience. Influenced by French feminist theorists of *l'écriture feminine*, most notably Hélène Cixous and Luce Irigaray, Case outlines a concept of dramatic "contiguity," a structural methodology which she describes as "elliptical rather than illustrative, fragmentary rather than whole, ambiguous rather than clear, and interrupted rather than complete" (129). Although the French theorists argue that such a contiguous narrative structure may be found in much of women's writing, it should be noted that such a theory eludes universal acceptance by feminist theorists and critics. Some theorists, for example, believe that the theory reinforces notions that gender is biologized or fear that its potential acceptance as a more valid form of women's writing would actually serve to inhibit women from writing in a variety of forms for fear of critical censure. Whether or not such a contiguous structure gains widespread critical acceptance as an accurate reflection of female experience, it should be recognized that Treadwell suspected that such an alternative, non-linear dramatic form might best be understood by female spectators. Perhaps along with Susan Glaspell then, Treadwell emerges as one of the first women playwrights in America to try to adapt a prevailing aesthetic style, expressionism, to appeal to a female sensibility.

A few critics concluded that *Machinal* possessed such a particularly feminine quality. Reviewing the play for the *New York Graphic*, Walter Winchell believed that Treadwell's careful examination of the female sex would make the play particularly appealing to women. And Arthur Ruhl, writing for the *New York Herald Tribune*, believed the play bore the stamp of a feminine writing style, one that contained "a kind of desperate intensity, at once wistful, defiant, and fiercely in earnest." In support of his conclusion, Ruhl cited the scene in the speakeasy, in which at one table a young woman argues with a man about whether or not she should have an abortion. In the moment when the woman suddenly rebuffs the man with a simple, "I know! I know!" Ruhl interpreted the understatement to contain "an uncanny touch of feminine authenticity" which revealed the woman's frustration about "the man, herself, about life in general and the particular tragedy into which it has drawn her" ("Off-Stage"). In an earlier review of the play, Ruhl had similarly cited the drawing-room scene in "Domestic," in which the presence and laugh of the Husband "makes the spectator's flesh, no less than that of the Young Woman herself, 'curl,'" even though "Almost nothing is said" ("Second Nights"). Such a comment confirms that audiences were actively filling in the gaps of the play to create meaning out of allusion.

Critics afforded Hopkins' production of *Machinal* an overwhelmingly enthusiastic response. Many reviewers compared the play to earlier examples in the expressionist mode, with Rice's *The Adding Machine* drawing the most comparisons for its similar treatment of a beleaguered office worker who resorts to violence in response to his frustrations and who finds love only outside of marriage. Critics also compared *Machinal* to the plays of O'Neill, and many saw in the character of the Husband an echo of Sinclair Lewis' Babbitt.

More importantly, however, a number of critics praised *Machinal* for its unique fusion of European expressionism and domestic American realism. Pierre de Rohan's review in the *New York American* typically summarizes Treadwell's unique achievement: "She has created a complete picture of life's bitterness and essential meanness, painted with the small, oft-repeated strokes of the realist, yet achieving in perspective the sweep and swing of expressionism" ("*Machinal* Ugly"). Scenes such as "At Home" and "Intimate," for example, contain a simplicity and directness in graphic detail like that found in numerous realistic American family dramas. Such scenes, Arthur Pollack felt, dropped the expressionist style "when it would seem pointless or too pointed" ("Plays and Things"). Robert Littell, in *Theatre Arts*, praised Treadwell for resorting more to "a reporting of the bare facts" in the play's final episodes, thus abandoning the expressionist style which gives the play its "depth and strangeness" ("Chiefly About," 774). Littell especially applauded Treadwell's ability to use suggestiveness and allusions in both expressionist and realist scenes for emotional effect: "All sorts of things that do not strictly belong to the play, things that would be excluded by other playwrights, stray into *Machinal* and sink out of sight again, giving us overtones and glimpses and other dimensions which the ordinary self-contained play is too 'well-made' ever to tolerate" (777–80). Oliver M. Sayler perhaps paid Treadwell the greatest compliment when he concluded that *Machinal* was "one of the first [plays] by an American dramatist successfully to merge expressionist form and expressionist content," and in doing so "frequently touches more startling heights of lucid vision than Eugene O'Neill's *The Emperor Jones* or *Strange Interlude*" (*Footlights*). Such reviews reveal a fascination with *Machinal*'s tempering of the bombastic quality of much expressionist drama.

One remarkable aspect of the critical response to *Machinal* in 1928 consists of the nearly total absence of discussion of the play's damning social indictments. Instead, critics remained preoccupied either with what they believed to be a new theatrical style of production and writing or with the play's supposed basis in the Snyder murder trial, the latter point being debated almost equally among those who saw in the Young Woman a personification of Snyder and those who did not. Surprisingly, critics did not elaborate on the play's treatment, albeit suggestive, of homosexuality or abortion. The scene of illicit love between the Young Woman and Roe did not receive substantial condemnation, but rather was often singled out for its lyrical beauty and subtlety. When the play was produced in London in 1931, under the title *The Life Machine*, these features, as well as the play's indictment of religion, marriage, motherhood, materialism, and urban mechanization, initially led to its banning by the Lord Chamberlain and subsequent dismissal by critics as lurid and sensational.

In 1928, *Machinal* had largely served to revitalize the fading popularity of expressionism on the commercial American stage. In an essay entitled "Applying the Pulmotor to Modernist Drama," Richard Watts, Jr. congratulated Treadwell on giving the expressionist form "credibility" by having the style match her theme perfectly. Treadwell, Watts argued, had rescued expressionism from its current state of "degradation," especially as propagated by the dramas of the New Playwrights Theater, who perhaps turned to the style out of an inability to master "the conventional form." But if Treadwell is to be credited with such a rescue, her accomplishment proved shortlived. As America entered the Depression of the thirties, expressionist drama largely fell into the province of agit-prop drama and all but disappeared from the commercial stage.

Treadwell herself even seemed to abandon this new-found style, at least for a time, after the success of *Machinal*. Her next play was a New York comedy of manners, *Ladies Leave*. Critics who had been impressed with Treadwell's creative invention in *Machinal* could not reconcile their expectations with their experiences as they watched this polite comedy. It was dismissed, perhaps a bit too perfunctorily, as lightweight and undeserving of Treadwell's efforts.

Treadwell's interest in adapting the expressionist mode returned, however, after a visit to Russia in 1933. This trip occurred at a most opportune time in Treadwell's career, coming as it did after one of her biggest disappointments in the commercial American theatre. In March of 1933, Treadwell opened her realistic, psychological drama, *Lone Valley*, at the Plymouth Theatre, the same site as her triumphant *Machinal*. Treadwell had been offering *Lone Valley* in tryout performances as far back as 1927, initially under the direction of Howard Lindsay and the production of

Crosby Gaige. For the Broadway version in 1933, however, Treadwell once again assumed the roles of director and producer. The play received exceptionally poor notices and closed after only three performances.

Undoubtedly, then, Treadwell eagerly accepted an invitation two months later to go to Moscow to participate in Alexander Tairov's revival of *Machinal* at the Kamerny Theatre. Treadwell had long had an affinity for Russian theatre, studying under Boleslavsky and developing a lifelong friendship with former American Lab instructor and Russian drama critic Alexander Koiransky. It was through the efforts of Koiransky that *Machinal* received a translation into Russian by Sergei Bertenson, a member of the literary staff at the Moscow Art Theatre, and in turn it was Bertenson who helped place the play with Tairov after the MAT board rejected it for its lack of a suitable proletarian hero. With the dismal failure of the last two of Treadwell's traditionally structured plays on Broadway, the trip afforded her the opportunity to reacquaint herself with the stylistic approach which had proven so successful in *Machinal*.

Tairov's production lived up to all of Treadwell's expectations. She repeatedly praised Tairov's expressionist interpretation, a conceptual approach which highlighted the backdrop of the modern cityscape in which American materialistic values crushed and regularized even the most basic human desires for individuality. She told the Soviet press: "I had to come here, to such a distant country as yours ... to see for the first time my authorial ideas not only carried out, but also significantly deepened and broadened" (Treduell, "Avtor," 604). What she witnessed "for the first time" was Tairov's emphasis on the overall social tragedy inherent in the play rather than the earlier American and British tendencies to underscore the script's naturalistic elements.

Upon her return to America in the summer of 1933, Treadwell soon turned her energies to the most introspective and experimental play of her career, *For Saxophone*. In many respects, *For Saxophone* appears as a dramatic extension of *Machinal*. Like that earlier play, *For Saxophone* takes as its subject a hypersensitive young woman who seeks sexual and emotional fulfillment outside of her stifling marriage. While in both *Machinal* and *For Saxophone* Treadwell sympathetically portrays female sexual desire, both plays end with the young women's inability to reconcile their desires with social expectation and constraint. As importantly, the style and narrative structure of *For Saxophone* takes up where *Machinal* left off: it employs many of the same expressionist devices, such as fragmented, episodic scenes, a barrage of sound effects, archetypal and symbolic characters, and a variety of language constructs. But with *For Saxophone*, Treadwell added a couple of features which were present in

Tairov's production of *Machinal* – the use of spotlighting for emotional intensification or cinematic transitions between scenes and the employment of near-continual musical underscoring. By incorporating these new techniques, the resulting effect in *For Saxophone* is a work of dazzling if uneven originality, a drama which extends the work begun with *Machinal* in establishing a new theatrical aesthetic.

In her opening stage directions for the play, Treadwell states that *For Saxophone* is "really words for music." The extensive use of musical underscoring along with other expressionist devices was once again conceived in order to activate the imaginations of the audience. Treadwell expounds on this intent in her preliminary remarks to the play:

> This script is written to be played with an almost unbroken musical accompaniment . . .
>
> . . . much use is made of voices (of people not seen) – bits of conversation here and there – incomplete – suggestive . . .
>
> The play is done in sixteen scenes, seven of which are voices with only one moment seen – the focal moment (something like a close-up in pictures). All the scenes of each act go one into the other through lights, voices, and music, so that the effect is of something seen, moving-by, and something overheard, – from all of which, a bit here and a bit there inconsequential and seemingly unrelated, the audience discovers, – writes the play.   (*For Saxophone* ts.)

Throughout the play, Treadwell achieves dramatic power through hinting, interruption, and circumvention, rather than overt delineation, of a scene's fundamental action. By calling upon the audience to "write" the play, Treadwell again avoids the overt didacticism of many expressionist dramas. Only in piecemeal fashion do audiences finally come to see a complete picture of the subtle mechanisms by which society inscribes gendered behavior in women. Lily, the young woman of *For Saxophone*, learns indirectly, like the audience, and then ultimately resists society's traditional imperatives concerning feminine desire: endure marriage, no matter how stultifying; avoid open expression or pursuit of sexual fulfillment; defer self-interest and egoism to the concerns of male partners. The tragic dimension of *Machinal* and *For Saxophone* arises from the young women's inability even to conceive of themselves as the subjects of their own lives. The fault, Treadwell argues, resides not so much in the women but in an unconcerned society which subtly undermines their pursuit of personal and sexual fulfillment.

Although Treadwell revised *For Saxophone* over a period of eight years and marketed it over a period of fourteen, the play remains unproduced. Early versions garnished virtually unbridled enthusiasm from the likes of Arthur Hopkins, Donald Oenslager, and Robert Edmond Jones, the latter once stating to Treadwell in a letter that with this play she had created the beginnings of a new theatrical idiom (Wynn, "Sophie Treadwell," 175–76). Jones tried unsuccessfully for three years to raise the money to produce the play. Other commercial producers and agents, however, were less interested in the work, at times dismissing its structure in terms such as "bizarre" and "eccentric," and at other times decrying the lack of star turns in the central role.

For Saxophone would prove Treadwell's final venture into adaptations of the expressionist aesthetic. Perhaps as a result of her inability to market this play successfully, her writings in the 1940s and fifties turn solidly toward psychological realism, and her themes, while never totally abandoning her inquiries into gender inequities, lack the depth and insight of her earlier dramas. Treadwell's last Broadway production was *Hope for a Harvest*, a simple play about America's lost work ethic, which was produced by the Theatre Guild in 1941.

Sophie Treadwell's dramatic writings encompass a wide range of subjects and styles. Her lifelong desire for gender equality and her willingness to experiment with form led to two strikingly innovative dramas, *Machinal* and *For Saxophone*. Unlike many other expressionist plays of the period, these works avoid literal, uncontested readings, favoring instead suggestiveness achieved through a network of non-realistic devices. These plays perhaps mark Treadwell as America's first playwright to devise a decidedly feminist aesthetic in the theatre, one which places women in the position of subject in drama while attempting to appeal to a female sensibility in her audience.

NOTES

1   For detailed discussions of the Snyder–Gray case, see John Kobler, *The Trial of Ruth Snyder and Judd Gray* and Ann Jones, *Women Who Kill.*
2   In her essay, "In Defense of the Woman: Sophie Treadwell's *Machinal*," Jennifer Jones articulates both the similarities and differences between Ruth Snyder and the Young Woman, Helen Jones.

6

BRENDA MURPHY

Feminism and the marketplace: the career of Rachel Crothers

By all objective standards, Rachel Crothers is the most significant woman playwright the United States produced in the early twentieth century, and one of the four or five major American playwrights who did their best work before World War II. An actress, director, and the author of more than thirty plays, most of which were commercially successful, Crothers was a consistent and acknowledged presence in the American theatre between 1906, when her first hit appeared, and 1937, when her last play achieved a run of 288 performances and won the Theatre Club's award for the outstanding play of the 1937–38 season. Crothers has consistently been undervalued by drama historians and literary critics, however. Like that of most women writers in the early twentieth century who wrote about the relations between the sexes, the institutions of marriage and the family, and the struggle of women to define their values in the face of the conflicting demands of nurturing a family and pursuing a career, Crothers' work was marginalized by her contemporary critics and reviewers. The influential academic critics of American drama continued this marginalization during the thirties by setting Crothers' work outside the "mainstream" of male playwrights and dismissing it as a "feminine" footnote. Arthur Hobson Quinn's chapter, "Rachel Crothers and the Feminine Criticism of Life," in the standard prewar history of American drama, is typical of this treatment.[1]

The feminist theatre movement of the seventies and several second-wave feminist critics recovered some of Crothers' early feminist work, particularly *A Man's World* (1909), her play about the double standard, which was reprinted in Judith E. Barlow's *Plays by American Women* (1981), and *He and She* (1911), her play about the conflicts between motherhood and career.[2] Although no one objects to Crothers' rejection of the double standard, feminist critics have been uneasy with her presentation of a protagonist who chooses full-time domestic duties over a very promising career as a sculptor in *He and She*, particularly since part of the reason for her choice is that her husband, also a sculptor, has a hard time dealing with her success. Even more troubling has been *Young Wisdom* (1914), a play that has been portrayed as a satire of the feminist movement (Gottlieb, *Rachel Crothers*, 71). It is, however, *Young Wisdom*, and *Ourselves* (1913), the least studied of Crothers' plays, that, along with *He and She*, provide the key into what has been seen as a major ideological shift from the earnest Progressive Era feminism of Crothers' early discussion plays to the witty, satiric treatment of women and women's issues in Crothers' plays of the twenties and thirties.

Just prior to her original version of *He and She* (1911), Crothers had achieved a good deal of notoriety with *A Man's World*, which not only ran for two seasons on Broadway between 1909 and 1911 before it began a successful tour, but was a critical success as well.[3] The play's treatment of a young woman's refusal to accept her fiancé's rationale for deserting his former lover and their child based on different sexual mores for men and women sparked a heated discussion of the double standard in the popular press. It also inspired the most prominent male dramatist of the period, Augustus Thomas, to write an answer to it in his play *As a Man Thinks* (1911), where the protagonist argues that it is not, as "that woman dramatist with her play" said, a "man's world" but a woman's world, moved by "the mainspring of man's faith in woman – man's *faith*" (87). In the context of the play, this "faith" amounts to the necessity for a woman to be monogamous so the man can be assured of the paternity of his children. Thomas fully supports the notion that it is a woman's responsibility to be "better" than a man. While he generally supports sexual exclusivity for both husband and wife, he suggests that a man can be forgiven for straying occasionally, but a woman cannot.

Crothers made full use of the general interest generated by the two plays to write a third play about the double standard, *Ourselves*, but in between she wrote one of her best-known and best-written plays, *He and She*. The play is a serious investigation of the decisions about her life that the "New Woman" faced in 1911. Each of its three female characters faces the dilemma of trying to join marriage and career. Ruth, a magazine editor who is forced by her fiancé to choose between her work and marrying him, decides on her career because she cannot imagine a fulfilling life without it. Daisy, who has been taking care of herself because she had to and not because she wanted to, jumps at the chance to get Ruth's fiancé on the rebound, quit her job, and settle into taking care of him and their apartment.

These two minor characters serve to emphasize the choices open to the protagonist Ann, a sculptor who has just won a competition for a major

4. Rachel Crothers directs a rehearsal of *A Man's World*

commission. She must decide between taking the major step of accepting the job, and thus launching a full-fledged professional career, or fulfilling her ideal notion of her duty as a wife and mother. She resists the pressure to give up the commission in order to preserve the pride of her husband, whom she has beaten in the competition, but when her sixteen-year-old daughter announces that she has fallen in love with the chauffeur at her boarding school, Ann decides that she must put aside her work and let her husband execute her design so that she can exert a closer influence over her daughter. As might be expected, Crothers presents a number of discussions about marriage, career women, motherhood, and the relations between the sexes in the course of the play.

The popular responses to these plays constitute a chronicle of the pressures that a playwright like Crothers, who chose to write serious plays about feminist issues, confronted when she placed a discussion play before the American theatre audience in the teens. *A Man's World* fared best with the press, as it did in ticket sales, partly because of a carefully orchestrated publicity effort to advertise its support for the single standard for sexual morality, and thus make it appealing to conservative middle-class women as well as reform-minded Progressives. Most reviewers quoted the lines from the play that appeared on the program: "This is a man's world. Man sets the standard for woman. He knows she's better than he is and he demands that she be – and if she isn't she's got to suffer for it. That's the whole business in a nutshell."[4] This set the issue clearly before the audience, with the serious and highly moral tone Crothers wanted to take. In order to enhance the seriousness, and the play's respectability with audiences, free tickets were offered to clergymen in the conservative city of Philadelphia, with the statement that, "while it is ... in no sense a sermon, [the play] is yet so directly in line with the movement being carried on from the pulpit for a single moral standard, that it has pleased ministers in many cities" (Crothers, Clippings, April 10, 1910). The reviews show that the effort worked for the most part. A review from the New York *Sun* is representative of the attitude the newspapers took:

> It is a pretty strong case that Miss Crothers makes out. She argues through her play that if women would not accept men knowing that they were bad they would be good. That is to say that women themselves, by condoning men's offences [*sic*] against the moral law, are responsible for the existence of the double standard of which they complain so much ... Whatever may be one's view on this subject, it is a subject proper for dramatic discussion; and Miss Crothers has made an interesting though not a great play about it.
>
> (Clippings, n.d.)

The majority of reviews show the resistant attitudes Crothers was up against in her audience. The *Los Angeles Examiner* expressed a fatalism about social change that was not about to be affected by any discussion play:

> The sermon is that the same rule of "purity" should apply to the man as is made to apply to the woman.
>
> This is absurd because men will not have it that way; this settles it; there is no appeal, never has been and never will be.
>
> But it is a good thing – very occasionally for men to realize that being men, and therefore being brutal and cruel, is not a part of their philosophy of which to be proud. (Clippings, n.d.)

There were also plenty of antifeminist voices to be heard, of which this writer in the *Blue Book* for May 1910, after the play had been running for eight months in New York, is typical:

> "A Man's World" has been pronounced "a great American play" ... I would amend these estimates and suggest that "an uncommonly good *woman's* play" amply covers Miss Crothers' work. It is typically and aggressively a woman's argument throughout ... She fails to reflect that Nature, not Man, is the inexorable arbiter in the matter of sex responsibility and that, however unjust Nature's dictum may be on purely ethical grounds, she is powerless to change it.
>
> Yet, woman fashion, she will have her say. (Clippings)

Crothers had her knowledge of this audience behind her when she launched a trial run of *He and She* in 1911, and again, as *The Herfords*, in 1912. Introducing the central issue of the play as marriage vs. career, the Boston *Traveler* ran a contest the week before it opened in 1912, with free tickets awarded for the best answers to the question: "Should an artist's wife be an artist also?" In an interview that appeared in the *Boston Herald* the day after the play opened, the star Viola Allen said, "the play is about the question whether the profession of a married woman is not the greatest in the world. I love the role ... After all, when it comes right down to choosing what is best in the world, the best thing a woman can be is a mother" (Henderson, "Interview"). This from a woman who raked in a tidy $2,000 a night in profits on tour with her own company while her millionaire husband stayed at home breeding horses in Kentucky.

The Herfords opened in Boston, and toured in the South and West, but never made it to New York in 1912. Two reviews, from the *Boston Transcript* and from the *Atlanta Journal*, should give an idea of the spectrum of resistance it was up against. The Boston critic called Crothers "the only prominent woman playwright of America who has any definite notions about the world in general," but continued with a veiled invidious comparison to George Bernard Shaw, "we are only just learning to expect such unalloyed seriousness of thought upon the stage; and those who have written in this vein have found it necessary to write brilliantly, to make every 'discussion,' every line, sparkle. Miss Crothers cannot do this. She argues thoroughly, earnestly and well; but she cannot fascinate" (Keightley, Scrapbook, January 28, 1912). The Atlanta writer was more blunt about the local audience's lack of interest: "It is pretty safe to say that Atlanta as a community is not particularly interested in the thing written of in the magazines as 'women's rights.' Women here have always had everything they asked for, without having to fight or argue for it" (Keightley, Scrapbook, n.d.).

As an extension of her argument in *A Man's World*, and partly as an answer to Thomas, Crothers wrote *Ourselves* in 1913.[5] A straightforward melodrama ending in a fifteen-minute discussion scene that provides both rhetorical and formal closure, the play is less complex than the two earlier ones dealing with the relations between the sexes. Its plot is simple. Beatrice Barrington, a society lady who wants to do volunteer work, comes to a Manhattan halfway house for "girls" between the ages of fourteen and thirty who have been convicted of prostitution. She ends up taking one of the inmates, Molly, into her home in order to try to reform her by making her into a social secretary. She succeeds fairly well until Molly falls in love with Beatrice's brother Bob, an artist, who has an affair with her. When Bob's wife Irene finds out about it, he cuts off the affair, and, with Beatrice's consent, sends Molly away from Beatrice's house, presumably back into the streets. This is the end of Act III. Crothers added a fourth act to this conventional melodramatic plot, however, which consists primarily of the discussion that occurs when Irene and Beatrice arrive at Bob's studio while Molly is there getting her belongings.

The issue Crothers addresses in the play is primarily the double standard, but she shifts the focus from the struggle between men and women to the responsibility of women for the behavior of men. The first thing she does is explode the nineteenth-century myth that "good women" have no sexual desire, and that any woman who does is by nature "bad." Miss Carew, the matron of the halfway house, explains the behavior of her charges by insisting that sexual attraction is powerful, and that most girls are trapped into a life of prostitution after having been deceived into a "first fall" by a boyfriend. Going beyond this fairly standard Progressive explanation for prostitution at the turn of the century, Crothers suggests that not only lower-class girls, but society ladies, are sexual beings. In the discussion scene, Bob advances the usual male "explanation" for his behavior, suggesting that Irene, the "good woman," is a different order of being from

Molly, the "bad girl." When Irene questions this, he responds that she condemns him because she is a cold-blooded saint who doesn't understand the power of male sexuality.

The crux of the discussion comes when Irene refuses to accept this tired nineteenth-century formulation of the physiology of the "good woman." When she says it is not true that women are cold-blooded saints, Bob replies that women have no idea what animal passions men have to resist, because their pulses beat evenly and slowly. Irene sets him straight about her sexuality with a clarity that was quite unusual on the American stage in the teens, telling him not to count so much on the slow, even pulses of a woman, and that she would be just like him if she had given in to her sexual impulses rather than controlling them.

The play's statement about male sexuality is essentially the same as that in *A Man's World*, as is the play's insistence on the man's responsibility for his behavior. What is new here is the notion that women are in part responsible for the moral laxity of men because they have allowed them to get away with it. Rather than blaming the prostitute, personified in the play by Molly, for the "social evil," Crothers presents her as a victim of her environment, her own sexuality, and the men who have exploited her. But she also blames the "good women," like Irene, who have tolerated their husbands' behavior.

Crothers uses the discussion to provide the play's closure, disrupting the conventional melodramatic resolution that ended Act III. Instead of sending Molly away, she has Beatrice realize that driving Molly out of her house is the one thing for which she is to blame. This gives Molly the self-confidence to make a new start, based on independence and self-reliance, and a determination to cut loose from her pimp. Although Irene leaves the scene, saying that she cannot forgive Bob, Crothers leaves the door open to a reconciliation, as Bob is persuaded to come home to her. The overall effect is to suggest a new hope for American society if it is willing to face the truth about male and female sexuality and the moral issues attending it.

While *Ourselves* was admired by the critics, it was not nearly the popular success that *A Man's World* was. Part of the cause of this lack of popular response can be read in the reviews, which betray a certain jadedness about Progressive studies of urban vice as well as an impatience with the discussion-play genre. The *New York Times* noted that, "If 'Ourselves' ... had been the first instead of one of the last of the modern vice plays, it would have been a tremendous box-office success. It is a drama full of interest up to the moment the final curtain drops on the fourth act, but whether or not theatregoers have tired of this particular style of play is a question" ("Rachel Crothers," 11).

Always keenly perceptive about the audience response to her plays, and always ready to adapt to the changing cultural climate, Crothers made a major aesthetic and ideological shift in her next play, *Young Wisdom*.[6] The play is an unabashed comedy, which has been dismissed by the few critics who have written about it as a send-up of feminism. The play is actually more a satiric treatment of the cultural modernism of the teens than of feminism or the women's movement *per se*. The comic structure is based on the romantic relationships of two sisters, Victoria and Gail Claffenden, played in the theatre by sisters Edith and Mabel Taliaferro. Victoria is a recent college graduate of twenty-one, who has been introducing her nineteen-year-old sister Gail to "advanced ideas" about the relations between the sexes and the institution of marriage. As the play opens, Gail is balking at the traditional wedding her parents are planning for her and her fiancé, Peter van Horn. Victoria has convinced her that the advanced idea is to live with her fiancé, abstaining from sex, before she marries him, because it is the only thing that will make the union of men and women pure and noble. Once this "trial marriage" becomes established, Victoria says, men will hold women through love and respect rather than the law and fear.

Victoria subscribes to the "moral uplift" school of first-wave American feminism, which holds that women have the responsibility for taking the moral lead in civilizing men. She has made up her own version of moral uplift, however, based on her misunderstanding of Progressive ideas about social Darwinism. She explains to Gail that women are more highly "evolved" than men, and thus have the responsibility to lead them forward through "advanced ideas," such as trial marriage. Taking her sister's ideas to heart, Gail tries to persuade Peter to skip the wedding and go off on their honeymoon together – a "motoring trip" across the country – in order to find out whether they really are suited to each other in the "highest" sense. Peter, a very conventional young man, resists this idea until Victoria's fiancé Christopher Bruce talks him into going along with the idea in order to scare Gail into marrying him. For good measure, Chris talks Victoria into putting her advanced talk into words and going away with him as well, and the men plan to meet at a house in the country where they will reveal their plan and show the women their ideas are mistaken.

Act II takes place in the country, where a comedic green-world confusion reigns. Peter and Gail arrive at the house, and are taken in by the occupants, an artist named Max Norton and his French servant Jean. Max immediately falls in love with Gail, and, after mistakenly attacking Peter as a "dirty little blackguard" when he learns the couple is traveling together without being married, is introduced to Gail's version of the "advanced ideas," and is determined to enlighten her. Victoria and Chris arrive at the house and are at first shocked when they think Peter and Gail are sleeping together. Victoria backs down from her position on trial marriage, insisting that nobody understands what she really meant. Victoria demands that they take Gail home so she doesn't "disgrace herself"; Chris counters that they should all go to the next town and be married; Gail refuses to do either. Finally Max, in a sweeping gesture of male decisiveness and power, takes Gail in his arms and carries her out as the curtain falls.

In Act III it becomes clear that Max has saved them all from "advanced ideas." The curtain opens on the Claffenden living room, where it is becoming evident that Gail has gone off with Peter, and the girls' father, The Judge, articulates the traditional patriarchal social views she has tried to escape. When the young people return, The Judge promptly locks Gail in her room and announces that she will marry Peter that night, despite the fact that Victoria tells him Gail does not love Peter, and forcing her to marry him would be benighted and medieval. Between the two poles of the "advanced" and the medieval, Crothers introduces two other positions on marriage in Act III. One is Mrs. Claffenden's enunciation of the sentimenta-lized nineteenth-century code of selflessness responsible for the "angel of the hearth" typology of much mid-nineteenth-century domestic fiction and drama. When Victoria hears her mother describe the peace, dignity, and happiness of her self-sacrificing life as wife and mother, she backs down immediately from her "modern" ideas, saying that she feels silly and her mother is as wise as the sphinx.

The most important position on marriage in the play, however, is that articulated by Max Norton, who asks the other men whether there is anything on earth so rotten as two people marrying unless they're so in love that they can't live without each other. When he convinces Victoria that he cares more for Gail than he's ever cared about anything in his life (on the basis of one evening's acquaintance), Victoria replies that love is the most wonderful thing in the world. Victoria confesses feeling a funny little suffocating sinking of the heart for her fiancé Chris, which can't be explained by anything but love. Chris' response is to kiss her. Presumably, the audience's is to affirm the position that the most important factor to be considered in marriage is physical attraction, perhaps elevated a step to romantic love. The play's romanticizing of physical attraction, combined with its positive presentation of domestic selflessness as a vocation for women and its denigration of trial marriage, hardly amounts to a radical feminist position on marriage.

Crothers eschews the most patriarchal view of the institution, however, by undermining The Judge's position and rendering him powerless. After trying to take full control of his daughter's life and give her away to the unwilling Peter despite both their wishes and the fact that she loves another man, The Judge is effectively excluded from the family when Gail and Max go off with Victoria and Chris to be married, significantly bringing Mrs. Claffenden with them, but not The Judge. What the comic form affirms is a new order where marriage is no longer in the patriarchal control of the older generation, and where the values controlling it are no longer the maintenance of social traditions and appearances. In the new order, the operative values are romantic love or sexual attraction, depending on who describes it; the man's assertion of power over the woman, based on this attraction; and the woman's selfless devotion to hearth and home. Crothers' comic resolution gets the woman out from under her father's control, but certainly not her husband's, and presents her as subject to biological and emotional forces within herself as well.

Crothers' use of comedy and her most conservative treatment of the relations between the sexes up to this point was welcomed by the critics. *Life* was delighted that "In 'Young Wisdom' Rachel Crothers seems to have come back into sanity and wholesomeness after her recent excursion into the unpleasant recesses of the underworld," suggesting that, even in this comedy, "she does perhaps a little too much preaching, but even the preaching is refreshing, as it is mostly directed against the prevailing tendency of untrained minds to find immediate solutions for questions that have baffled the world's wisdom since the world began" ("Drama," 150). Another reviewer commented that, "In 'Young Wisdom' Miss Crothers has taken up advanced ideas, out of which a problem play might have been made, but which is, through and through, a comedy." The reviewer admitted that he had thought "the announcement that the play was to concern trial marriage was unpromising, but she has treated the subject as perhaps only a woman could do whose art ennobled her to touch it lightly and whose refinement guided her every step. The play is imbued with feminine delicacy ... It is a strong sweet, pure, thoroughly entertaining play" (Clippings, n.d.).

This was a long way from the Rachel Crothers of *A Man's World*. As American audiences lost their taste for the impassioned debate of the discussion play, Crothers quickly adapted to their demands, subjugating feminist ideology to the formal demands of comedy and reducing the issues surrounding marriage to the question of sexual attraction. Defending herself from the charge of hypocrisy in a newspaper interview, she said, "I hope I have proved myself a natural woman's champion, the most ardent of feminists, for I certainly believe in women and their capacity to earn their daily bread in the same field and on the same footing with men. Therefore, while my new comedy is a satire on the theories involved in the advanced women I am not laughing at them but with them" (Gottlieb, *Rachel Crothers*, 74–75). As Crothers very well knew, however, there is more to comedy than laughter, and her comedy clearly placed the men in power and the women in the bedroom and the kitchen.

Capitalizing on what they had learned from the audience response to the earlier plays, Crothers and her producers, the Shubert brothers, tried to make *He and She* seem almost innocuous when they produced it in 1920 with Crothers herself in the lead role of Ann. They claimed in their press release: "This new play strikes a new note in the ever-growing battle of the sexes. From a different angle [Crothers'] searching pen has drawn a picture of American life which reveals all the tenderness and love and strength of family life and shows inevitably how the call of home must everlastingly come first."[7] The public was not fooled into thinking *He and She* was either new or uncontentious. Coming down hard on the play's subject, the reviewer for the Brooklyn *Eagle* wrote that "the play contributes not a single new thought to the old discussion. It is dramatic occasionally, but the writing is conventional and the point of view provincial. On the whole, a pretentious play that does not make good its pretensions" (Keightley, Scrapbook, February 13, 1920).

With help from the Shuberts' press release, *He and She* was generally misunderstood by both the public and the reviewers. The New York *Sun* wrote that "in this play of married life poor old Feminism never had a chance" (Keightley, Scrapbook, February 13, 1920) and the *Evening Telegram* took the producers' bait, declaring that "Miss Crothers takes a conservative view of the woman question. Herself a woman who has made a career, and manifestly believing in careers for women, she wisely puts the task of wife and mother in the first place" (Keightley, Scrapbook, February 13, 1920). More perceptive critics like Kenneth MacGowan and Alexander Woollcott saw Crothers for what she was, a feminist in the nineteenth-century school of Charlotte Perkins Gilman and Susan B. Anthony, who held that a woman had the right to choose between a career and the demands of marriage and a family, but did not believe it was possible to do both well, as her younger contemporaries were suggesting.[8]

It is clear from the newspaper reports that the points of view articulated in the reviews were well represented in the general audience, though their reports of the proportions vary according to the reporter's own bias. One reporter noted that "the majority of the masculine contingent applauded long and defiantly the philosophy of a young and assertive male reflecting the familiar doctrines of the anti-suffragists. They laughed proudly at his sallies. On the other hand, most of the feminine portion gave enthusiastic approval to the idea of a woman carving out a career for herself at the same time that she lives a normal domestic life. The voting was about even at the particular performance this writer attended" (Keightley, Scrapbook, n.d.). The conservative Burns Mantle, on the other hand, deprecated the women's support for this point of view at the same time that he showed his own contempt for working women: "The audience last night was enthusiastic. True, near us sat a group who did not approve of the heroine's decision, but they were evidently professional women satisfied with their careers. They looked it" ("'He and She'"). Louis Gardy of the *Call* was so taken aback by the reaction of the women in the audience that he ascribed what he called Crothers' choice of a "stock finale" for her play to her need to "make concessions to the limitations of her audience":

> It is unfortunate, of course, that most of the women in the audience applaud sentiments which praise men, but most likely the dear little darlings in evening dress are just trying to flatter their male escorts. Maybe, and this is an unkind thought, the dear little darlings don't understand Miss Crothers' viewpoint at all, and respond to all the antique rules which they got from their great-great-grandmother because that's the only stuff they can sense. Or is it that they are all of the domestic type and are jealous of the independent business woman? (Keightley, Scrapbook, February 15, 1920).

Two interesting characteristics of the American audience surface from the response to *He and She* in 1920. The first is the general belief that the question whether a woman could have a career and still be a good wife and mother had become an outdated issue between the first production in 1912 and the revival, and the discussion was no longer considered relevant to the current concerns of women. The second is the deep lack of consensus about women, careers, and motherhood that led audiences to see the play either as a hymn to the overwhelming importance of motherhood or as an assertion of a woman's right to combine a career with a fulfilling domestic life. For the most part, those who saw Crothers' play seem to have constructed its meaning from their own perspective within this dichotomy.

The historical reality was that the older feminist position Crothers was reasserting – that a woman had to renounce marriage in order to dedicate herself seriously to a career – was no longer acceptable to a new generation who thought, as Dorothy Dunbar Bromley wrote, "that a full life calls for marriage and children as well as a career" ("Feminist," 552). The new generation of women in the twenties did not want to hear that they couldn't "have it all." What's more, as Bromley commented in 1927, "if a blundering male assumes that a young woman is a feminist simply because she happens to have a job or a profession of her own, she will be highly – and quite justifiably – insulted: for the word evokes the antithesis of what she flatters herself to be" ("Feminist," 552). What the word evoked for these young women was "the old school of fighting feminists who wore flat heels and had very little feminine charm, or the current species who antagonize men with their constant clamor about maiden names, equal rights, woman's place in the world and many another cause" ("Feminist," 552). The New Woman was emphatically not a culture heroine of the majority of women who came of age in the twenties. On the other hand, the majority of the audience for the New York theatre in the twenties, the middle-class women who stayed at home, and the middle-class men who supported them while they did it, were ready to see any criticism of women working outside the home as an affirmation of their own values. Crothers' calculated attempt to negotiate between these two positions in presenting her play was ultimately a failure. She was ultimately unable to package the feminist ideology of the 1890s in a form that appealed to the 1920s.

It was *Young Wisdom*, which affirms a conservative stance on marriage while it contains enough discussion of the institution to engage its audience in serious consideration of some important issues, that provided the essential plan for Crothers' social comedies in the twenties and early thirties, the plays that were most successful with audiences and that earned her the title of America's "foremost woman playwright," plays like *Nice People* (1921), *Mary the Third* (1923), *Expressing Willie* (1924), *Let Us Be Gay* (1929), *As Husbands Go* (1931), *When Ladies Meet* (1932), and *Susan and God* (1937). In these lightly satirical treatments of the values, mores, and ideas of the American middle and upper classes, Crothers achieved, with an unerring sense of style, a mordant, witty dialogue which became the hallmark of the brittle American society comedies of the twenties and thirties. Combining a natural ingenuity with long years and practice as playwright, director, actor, and producer, she achieved a mastery of comic construction, pace, and tempo. She also managed to address the perennial social issues that interested her and her middle-class audience, primarily those related to marriage, divorce, the family, and the various social and intellectual fads that characterized the period, such as Freudianism, the cult of self-expression, and the religious fad of "Moral Re-Armament," or Buchmanism, that emanated from the Oxford Group.

Crothers' main target during these years was the generation that came of age in the twenties and its various extremes and follies. In *Young Wisdom*, it is not the women's movement that is satirized, but a debased version of it, which rejected the social-reform agenda of the Progressive movement, and made the serious concerns of the New Woman – economic independence, the freedom to choose one's career and develop one's talent, and the freedom to marry a husband of one's choice, or not to marry – into excuses for hedonism and irresponsibility. Crothers' attitude toward the Jazz Age generation is most evident in *Nice People*, a treatment of the flapper that followed F. Scott Fitzgerald's *This Side of Paradise* by only a year. *Nice People* featured the young Tallulah Bankhead, Katharine Cornell, and Francine Larrimore as three spoiled young flappers, who, in 1920, have allowances of $20,000 a year, and spend $80.00 on a single spree. Crothers spends the first act displaying the vacuous materialism of these young women, and then has the protagonist, Teddy Gloucester, rescued from her empty life by a young man who shows her the joys of a rural life raising chickens. Like other Crothers heroines, Teddy discovers the satisfaction of economic independence, even from an extremely wealthy family. When her father offers to buy her young man for her in the end, she replies: "I'd like to see you try. Why do you want to dispose of me? Let me do it myself. First of all, I want to be left alone – to think. Men aren't everything on earth ... Regardless of you – or any other man in the world, I'm going to take care of myself" (*Nice People*, 184).

The most skeptical of Crothers' plays, *Mary the Third*, returns to the notion of "trial marriage," placing Mary's attempt in 1923 to decide whether to marry her boyfriend against the background of the unhappy marriages of mother and grandmother and their handling of them according to the cultural values of their generations. At the same time that the play undermines the traditional marriage by exposing the pragmatic motives for entering and continuing it, the ending suggests, through Mary's engagement, that marriage based on sexual attraction is inevitable in contemporary American culture, as is disillusionment of the cultural expectation that love and marriage will last forever. The only difference between Mary and her mother and grandmother is that divorce will be more socially acceptable for her, and along with her determination to be economically independent, will provide an escape when her marriage becomes intolerable.[9]

With *Expressing Willie*, Crothers beat Fitzgerald by a year, anticipating Jay Gatsby in her Willie Smith, a young man who has made millions in toothpaste and is now surrounded by a crowd of social sycophants in his Long Island mansion. The target of the satire is the cult of self-expression arising from the popularization of Freudian psychology. After exposing the hypocrisy and silliness of its disciples, Crothers leaves the audience siding with Willie's wholesome mother, who says, "if we were all running around without any *suppressions*, we might as well have tails again" (*Expressing Willie*, 72). The later social comedies attack the middle-aged rather than the youthful products of the new values of the Jazz Age. *Let Us Be Gay* takes on the values related to marriage and divorce among the fashionable upper class and *As Husbands Go* examines the effect of Parisian freedom on two middle-aged women from Dubuque. Crothers' two most successful social comedies, *When Ladies Meet* (1932) and *Susan and God* (1937), made use of her well-practiced formula of combining a topical social issue with recognizable society types as characters, witty dialogue, and a humorous comic plot. In this context, Crothers could get away with debating social issues that were as serious as those in her discussion plays of the teens without alienating an audience that was primarily interested in escapist entertainment. *When Ladies Meet* treats seriously that stock situation of the farce, the love triangle, from the neglected perspective of the "other woman." Crothers' last produced play, and her most successful, was *Susan and God*, which, with Gertrude Lawrence in the role of Susan Trexel, ran for 288 performances on Broadway. It satirizes the attempt to import meaning into the empty lives of the idle rich by latching onto "spiritual" fads and enthusiasms – in this case, Buchmanism imported from England. In the course of the play, Susan finds that her newly found religious conviction is a sham, but that she can fill her empty life with a real family relationship with her husband and daughter.

Throughout her career, Crothers was primarily and fundamentally a theatre professional. Her plays provided a timely, intelligent, and often witty commentary on middle- and upper-class America from the under-represented perspective of a woman negotiating the shifting economic and social conditions and cultural values surrounding the issues of marriage, divorce, sexuality, economic independence, family responsibility, class, generational conflict, materialism, and spirituality. Her perspective on these issues was that of a feminist who came of age in the 1890s, but her plays reflect a feminism that is by no means static or monolithic. Her playwright's ear was always attuned to the interests of her audience, the audience of the New York commercial theatre. Crothers was consistently successful in the volatile Broadway marketplace because, like George Bernard Shaw, she learned how to package her ideas in forms that her audience accepted as entertainment, and she had the extraordinary talent to carry it off.

NOTES

1   *A History of the American Drama*. See also, Thomas H. Dickinson, *Playwrights of the New American Theatre* 182–88.
2   The most substantial piece of criticism is Lois Gottlieb, *Rachel Crothers*. For articles, see: Carolyn Forrey, "The New Woman Revisited"; Yvonne B. Shafer, "The Liberated Woman in American Plays of the Past"; Deborah S. Kolb, "The Rise and Fall of the New Woman in American Drama"; Sharon Friedman, "Feminism as Theme in Twentieth-Century American Women's Drama"; and Doris Abramson, "Rachel Crothers: Broadway Feminist." For placements of Crothers' career in a historical context, see Patricia R. Schroeder, *The Feminist*

Possibilities of Dramatic Realism, 61–97; Sally Burke, *American Feminist Playwrights*, 37–51; and Brenda Murphy, *American Realism and American Drama*, 96–109 and 159–68.

3 For a full discussion of *A Man's World*, see Patricia R. Schroeder, "Realism and Feminism in the Progressive Era," in this volume.

4 Program, *A Man's World*, Billy Rose Theatre Collection, New York Public Library for the Performing Arts.

5 The discussion of *Ourselves* is based on the unpublished typescript in Special Collections, University of Pennsylvania Libraries.

6 The discussion of *Young Wisdom* is based on the unpublished script of the play in the Billy Rose Theatre Collection, New York Public Library for the Performing Arts.

7 Press release, appearing in several clippings, Cyril Keightley Scrapbook, Chamberlain and Lyman Brothers Theatrical Agency Collection, New York Public Library for the Performing Arts.

8 See Alexander Woollcott, "'He and She'" and Kenneth MacGowan, "'He and She.'"

9 For a fuller discussion of *Mary the Third*, see Schroeder, *Feminist Possibilities*, 81–97.

7

JUDITH L. STEPHENS

The Harlem Renaissance and the
New Negro Movement

The 1920s and 1930s form an important period in our cultural history that is famous for its legacy of creative work focusing on the lives and concerns of African Americans. This flowering of art and literature is variously referred to as the Harlem Renaissance, New Negro Movement, or New Negro Renaissance. Among the many outstanding black writers associated with the period are Langston Hughes, Countee Cullen, Georgia Douglas Johnson, Claude McKay, and Zora Neale Hurston. The enduring value of the work produced by black artists from this era has prompted literary scholars to recognize the Harlem Renaissance as "the one period in black letters that stands out above all others" (Harris and Davis, *Afro-American Writers*, xi) and theatre scholars to acknowledge the contemporary development of a serious theatre that could "speak to and for African Americans" (Hatch and Hamalian, *Lost Plays* 18).

Although the Harlem Renaissance is so named because of the great number of black artists who flocked into Harlem, making it the black cultural capital of the world, significant artistic activity was also occurring in cities such as Washington DC, Chicago, and Boston. Just as the movement cannot be limited to one location, neither is it easily reducible to exact dates, but it is generally conceded that an unprecedented surge in activity among African American artists, reflecting a renewed race consciousness and pride, began around World War I and extended into the decade of the the 1930s.[1]

Since important literary and artistic movements are constantly reexamined and reevaluated, understanding the Harlem Renaissance is a continuing project. One of the more recent contributions to this ongoing project is a reexamination of the movement by feminist critics and scholars who focus on women writers and artists. In *Color, Sex, and Poetry: Three Women Writers of the Harlem Renaissance*, Gloria T. Hull examined the work of Angelina Grimké, Alice Dunbar-Nelson, and Georgia Douglas Johnson and concluded that in the New Negro era, women were penalized, in subtle and blatant ways, for their gender. In *Women of the Harlem Renaissance*, Cheryl Wall found that writing by African American women communicated a very different sense of the Renaissance than did the work of their male counterparts. Comparing two contemporary (1925) essays that are representative of these differences, Wall found Alain Locke's "The New Negro" conveys an energetic sense of renewed race consciousness and pride, while Marita Bonner's "On Being Young – A Woman – and Colored" evokes images of silence, paralysis, and entrapment. While Locke was recognized as a leading intellectual and his "New Negro" essay is widely accepted as the manifesto of the period, Marita Bonner regularly published her work in the leading black journals of the day, but remained almost unknown among generations of scholars until 1974 when her provocative play, *The Purple Flower* (first appearing in the magazine *The Crisis*, 1928) was published in Hatch and Shine's landmark anthology, *Black Theatre USA*. If, as Hull and Wall suggest, our perception of the Harlem Renaissance has been generated by a focus on male writers and the "New Negro" is gendered male, a fuller understanding of the period may be reached through a reexamination of the Renaissance in terms of writing that reflects women's struggles and accomplishments. This chapter will focus on the work of African American women playwrights of the era who were pioneers in expanding women's opportunities in theatre and developing black drama.

Nellie McKay has recognized the Harlem Renaissance as a special time in the evolution of black women playwrights in America because they produced a drama that is both woman centered and racially conscious while struggling to find a place for themselves in a developing theatre tradition ("What Were They Saying?" 129–46). The first anthology to focus on African American women playwrights of the Harlem Renaissance era is Kathy Perkins' *Black Female Playwrights: An Anthology of Plays before 1950*.[2] While presenting the work of seven outstanding playwrights from the period, Perkins' groundbreaking study culminates in a listing of over 150 works by forty-six women, providing a springboard for further research into this neglected area of American theatre. While acknowledging that black women playwrights of the 1950s, such as Lorraine Hansberry and Alice Childress, were the first to receive coveted playwriting awards and national recognition, Perkins notes that it was the black women during the first half of the twentieth century who set the stage for these later, more commercially successful writers. Elizabeth Brown-Guillory's *Their Place on the Stage: Black Women Playwrights in America* and *Wines in the Wilderness: Plays by African American Women from the Harlem Renaissance to the Present* reveal the presence of an artistic tradition that links black women playwrights of the Harlem Renaissance to their contemporary counterparts. By noting common themes, forms, and techniques, both Brown-Guillory and Perkins provide foundations for a wider study of black women's drama.

In light of the insights provided by these recent studies, this chapter will examine the lives and work of Harlem Renaissance women playwrights as a reflection of the black female tradition of self-help and mutual support that has been passed down through generations of African American women since slavery. This approach provides a framework for discussion based on the historical experience of African American women and a woman-centered perspective that both encompasses and transcends the period known as the Harlem Renaissance.

The self-help/mutual support tradition

According to National Council of Negro Women president Dorothy Height, the black tradition of self-help and mutual support can be traced back to the days of the transatlantic slave trade when,

> It was up to us to either forge ties of mutual support or perish as a people. Those unbreakable bonds sent people searching for one another after the forced separations of slavery. They are still evident in our custom of calling one another brother and sister – and mother, aunt, and uncle – even when there is no blood relationship. There's an entire history behind these interactions that is precious to our sense of self-worth and identity as a people.
> ("Self-Help," 136)

Black feminist scholars such as Jacqueline Jones, Patricia Hill Collins, and Elsa Barkley Brown have documented the presence of a self-help and mutual support tradition specifically among black women. Whether in the form of a slave woman clandestinely providing food for runaways, middle-class black women of the early twentieth century organizing benevolent societies for poor families, or black housewives of the Depression bartering for services ("I'll do your hair; you let me borrow your pots and pans"), black women's resistance to racism and sexism has created a unique cultural legacy of self-sufficiency and collective cooperation (Jones, *Labor of Love*, 229). Black women's networks, in all historical periods, provide a site for examining a "womanist consciousness" in which the concepts of self and community are not seen as separate entities. As Patricia Hill Collins notes in *Black Feminist Thought*, "self is not defined as the increased autonomy gained by separating oneself from others. Instead, self is found in the context of family and community ... Rather than defining self in opposition to others, the connectedness among individuals provides

Black women deeper, more meaningful self-definitions" (105–06). A black feminist or "womanist" consciousness is one in which black females are encouraged to discover their own strengths and share them with the whole community. This unifying philosophy was expressed in the work of nineteenth-century black women leaders, such as Anna Julia Cooper and Ida B. Wells, and appears in the writing of contemporary black feminists who stress that resistance to race, sex, and class oppression is one struggle (Brown, "Womanist Consciousness," 176–77).

The black female legacy of self-help and mutual support is reflected in the lives and work of African American women playwrights of the Harlem Renaissance. Their specific contributions to the tradition can be seen in the self-defined images of black women these playwrights created and in the ways they both responded to and helped shape the artistic community in which they worked.

The creative environment

Black women playwrights of the 1920s and 1930s were not professional playwrights in that they did not make their living from writing but supported themselves with other full-time jobs. Most were teachers, a few were government workers, others worked at a variety of jobs, but all were aware that opportunities for black women playwrights in the white-dominated professional American theatre were non-existent. These women wrote for the love and challenge of writing and for their communities. Their dramas were primarily published in black-owned journals such as *The Crisis* and *Opportunity*, and produced in black-owned and operated community theatres, churches, schools, social club halls, and homes. Some of this pioneering group of female dramatists saw their plays produced at newly formed black amateur theatres such as the Harlem Experimental Theatre, the Krigwa Players (Harlem, Baltimore, Washington DC, and Denver), the Howard Players, (Howard University, Washington DC), and the various Negro Units of the Federal Theatre Project. As they gain belated recognition as important playwrights in American theatre history, it must be acknowledged that many of these women were multitalented artists who wrote poetry, fiction, essays, or musical compositions as well as plays. They were theatre pioneers because they wrote during a period when black artists were eager to create their own images on stage but still developing as playwrights, directors, and designers. As women, they performed a unique role by providing the burgeoning black drama with feminine perspectives.

The Harlem Renaissance occurred during the "Little Theatre Movement," a nationwide movement to create community-centered, amateur (not for profit) theatres where plays (mostly one-acts) could be inexpensively produced. At the same time, American playwrights were attempting to forge a "native drama" by drawing on the folk life, customs, and speech patterns common to a particular people, culture, or region. While white playwrights had previously written about black life, most of their portrayals of black people were degrading or, at best, unconvincing because they reproduced the old familiar and degrading stereotypes such as: (for males) the lazy buffoon or razor-toting criminal, or (for females) the mammy or oversexualized floozy. Addell Austin sums up the situation succinctly: "Blacks believed that their own writers could portray themselves more realistically. What was needed were vehicles to promote these writers and their works" ("Opportunity," 235).

Since the white-dominated American theatre did not welcome either black artists or audiences, leaders in the African American community took it upon themselves to create the necessary opportunities for black artists. One of the most dynamic and versatile leaders was sociologist W. E. B. Du Bois who, as editor of the NAACP's (National Association for the Advancement of Colored People) *The Crisis* magazine, launched a literary contest for black playwrights that offered cash prizes and publication for the best one-act plays that dealt with black history or experience. Du Bois also organized the Krigwa Players Little Negro Theatre to produce "a real Negro theatre" that would address itself to the black community. In the words of Du Bois, the theatre would be, "About us, By us, For us, and Near us" (Hatch and Hamalian, *Lost Plays*, 447). While mandating that the emphasis would be on promoting plays written by black playwrights and intended for black audiences, Du Bois emphasized that artists of all races would be welcome, as would "all beautiful ideas." Charles S. Johnson, editor of the Urban League's *Opportunity* magazine, also offered cash prizes and publication for the best black-authored one-act plays dealing with black experience. According to Kathy Perkins, women outnumbered men in submitting plays to these contests and most of the winners were women.

Among the other cultural leaders who created opportunities for black theatre artists were Alain Locke and Montgomery Gregory. As professors at Howard University in Washington DC they established the Howard Players and the Department of Dramatic Arts as a professional training ground for black Americans in the theatre. In addition to overseeing the Howard productions, Locke and Gregory edited *Plays of Negro Life* (1927), the earliest anthology of plays focusing on black life. While all of these leading figures were dedicated to promoting black artists and the development of black drama, important differences existed. Discussions of black theatre in the Harlem Renaissance are often based on the different philosophies of black drama held by Locke and Du Bois. Du Bois favored "propaganda plays" that revealed the racial prejudice and violence encountered by black Americans, while Locke promoted "folk drama" that focused on authentic black themes and characters but without emphasizing racial oppression. Most of the women playwrights of the era wrote both types of drama and some, such as Georgia Douglas Johnson, often combined strands of each type in a single work. Plays with historical themes and subjects, such as African heritage, slavery, or heroic ancestors, formed a third category of drama that served to inform audiences about the traditions of black culture and to reinforce racial pride.

The black women playwrights of the Harlem Renaissance era were, to a certain extent, considered privileged women in their day because they were college educated and possessed a cultural awareness that was rare among the masses of black people. Fully conscious that they were writing at a time when the majority of black women, rural or urban, earned meager wages by working in some type of domestic service, these playwrights wrote plays about all classes of black people in an attempt to create authentic portraits of black life. Into this highly creative atmosphere of a developing black drama, black women playwrights brought their own unique approaches to creating self-defined images, resisting stereotypes, and responding to new opportunities to share their artistic talent with a wider public.

The playwrights

The four most prolific black women playwrights of the 1920s and 1930s were Georgia Douglas Johnson, May Miller, Eulalie Spence, and Zora Neale Hurston. Spanning both decades, their plays demonstrate black women's contributions to the dramatic themes and forms that were prominent in the developing black theatre. Examining their plays in conjunction with their individual lives and community involvement reveals the ways in which early black women playwrights both relied upon and contributed to a legacy of self-help and mutual support.

The life and work of Georgia Douglas Johnson (1880–1966) provide a focal point for understanding how artistic, political, and social skills become unified within a tradition of self-help and mutual support. Poet, playwright, and composer, Johnson brought to her artistic endeavors the talent, community involvement, and perseverance that were necessary for black women artists to survive in this era. Born in Atlanta, Georgia, she was educated in the public schools of the city and at Atlanta University. She

5. Georgia Douglas Johnson

went on to attend Howard University in Washington DC and Oberlin Conservatory of Music in Ohio. By the time she tried her hand at play-writing, Johnson had already established her reputation as a poet with two published volumes, *Heart of a Woman and Other Poems* (1918) and *Bronze: A Book of Verse* (1922). According to scholar Winona Fletcher, Johnson was a leader and energetic participant in most of the groups and organizations in the Washington area committed to concerns of women and minorities. After her husband's death in 1925 Johnson supported herself and her two sons by assuming various jobs with the government and taught periodically, in Washington DC, as a substitute teacher. Johnson is known to have written close to thirty plays, but only a few scripts have survived. She wrote various types of drama: propaganda plays, lynching dramas, and historical dramas. As an active participant in the artistic community of her day, she entered her work in the newly organized play competitions. Her 1926 play *Blue Blood* won honorable mention in the *Opportunity* contest, and was produced by the Krigwa Players. The play subtly broaches the subject of white men's sexual exploitation of black women and skillfully builds to a shocking revelation as two black mothers discover that their children, who are engaged to be married, have the same white father. *Plumes* (1927), which treats the struggle of a rural Southern black mother to deal with poverty and her daughter's death, won *Opportunity*'s first prize and was produced by the Harlem Experimental Theatre.

Johnson used her playwriting skills to speak out against many forms of racial injustice. Several of her plays take a strong stand against lynching, a brutal form of racial violence carried out against African Americans (primarily black men) by white mobs. Johnson wrote during a time when white mobs, predominantly in the South, killed black men by shooting, knifing, hanging, or burning and received no repercussion from the law for these murders. Johnson was the most prolific of all playwrights who wrote dramas protesting the crime of lynching and she was an active participant in the anti-lynching movement during the 1920s. Her six known dramas representing the anti-lynching tradition in theatre are: *Safe*, *Blue-Eyed Black Boy*, two versions of *A Sunday Morning in the South*, and two lost plays: *A Bill to Be Passed* and *And Still They Paused*. The first three reflect the human struggle for survival within the context of black southern families resisting the brutality and injustice of lynching. With *A Sunday Morning in the South* (1925), she became one of the first playwrights to deal truthfully with the issue of alleged interracial rape of white women and to dramatize white women's complicity in the lynching ritual. She was also a pioneer in writing plays in the anti-lynching tradition in which a lynching incident occurs during the dramatic action. Understanding the nature of theatre and its power to make offstage events as powerful as those occurring on stage, she paved the way, with *Safe* (c. 1929) and *Blue-Eyed Black Boy* (c. 1930), for the use of sound and lighting effects, vivid oral description, and audience imagination to convey the horrors of lynching and its impact on families. Unlike her plays on non-lynching themes, none of her lynching dramas were published or produced in her lifetime. According to Winona Fletcher, Johnson submitted at least five plays, three on the theme of lynching, to the Federal Theatre Project between 1935 and 1939 but none was accepted.

Both of Johnson's historical dramas were published and produced in her lifetime. *Frederick Douglass* (1935) is set in a humble two-room hut in "slavery days" and focuses on the early life of the great orator and abolitionist. Frederick escapes from slavery in the nick of time but only with the help of Ann, his fiancée, and Jake, an old slave. Johnson's *William and Ellen Craft* (1935) takes place before the Civil War and depicts a young couple plotting their escape from slavery. Through the help of Aunt Mandy, an old slave woman, William and Ellen escape to the North disguised as a white gentleman and his black servant.

Georgia Douglas Johnson not only contributed to the New Negro

Renaissance as a playwright and poet but she also offered her home on S Street in Washington DC as a meeting place for numerous black artists of the period. Early Harlem Renaissance figures such as Langston Hughes, Alain Locke, Willis Richardson, and Jessie Fauset were in attendance at Johnson's "S Street Salon." Other sister playwrights included in these Saturday night gatherings were May Miller, Marita Bonner, Mary Burrill, Alice Dunbar-Nelson, Zora Neale Hurston, and Angelina Weld Grimké. Johnson helped to nurture and sustain creative activity by providing a casual setting for black artists to meet, socialize, discuss their work, and exchange ideas. Hull has suggested that Johnson's role as a cultural sponsor was all the more important because she played it outside of Harlem, thus providing an impetus for the intercity connections that helped to make the movement a truly national one.

Johnson ultimately found more success as a poet than a playwright. She received an honorary doctorate from Atlanta University in 1965 and continued to publish poems until her death in 1969. When Johnson died, at the age of eighty, May Miller, one of her sister playwrights of the 1920s and 1930s and a former participant in the Saturday night salon gatherings, sat by her bedside stroking her hand and repeating the words, "Poet Georgia Douglas Johnson" (Harris and Davis, *Afro-American Writers* 163).

As a playwright who unflinchingly fused dramatic art with the brutal theme of lynching, sustained a focus on women characters while helping to develop various forms of black drama, and fostered a vital network for the artistic community, Johnson left her own legacy to both the theatre of Harlem Renaissance and black women's self-help/mutual support tradition.

May Miller (1899–1995) was the most widely published black female playwright of the period. She grew up on the campus of Howard University where her father, Kelly Miller, was a prominent professor of sociology. Miller graduated from the famous Paul Laurence Dunbar High School in 1916 where two of her teachers were early Renaissance playwrights, Mary Burrill and Angelina Grimké. While Miller was still a high school student, Burrill encouraged her to write her first play, which was published in the school magazine. As a student at Howard University, Miller received further encouragement in her playwriting skills from professors Locke and Gregory. According to Elizabeth Brown-Guillory Miller wrote, directed, and performed in plays while at Howard. Following graduation Miller taught speech, drama, and dance at Frederick Douglass High School in Baltimore for twenty years. In addition to writing nearly twenty one-act plays, she joined the Baltimore Krigwa Players and contributed her talents as a director and performer. On weekend trips to Washington DC, she frequented Georgia Douglas Johnson's "S Street Salon." She enrolled in playwriting courses at Columbia University where she studied under Frederick Koch, founder of the Carolina Playmakers at the University of North Carolina, Chapel Hill. Her play *Scratches*, revealing how a sense of community and fair play survives among urban blacks living under harsh conditions, was published in the 1929 issue of the university's *Carolina Magazine*. Like her sister playwright Georgia Douglas Johnson, Miller wrote various forms of drama: folk, protest (or propaganda), and historical. She also participated in the newly created opportunities for black playwrights. Her play *The Bog Guide* treats the destructive effects of racism in both white and black communities and won third place in the 1925 *Opportunity* play contest. *The Cuss'd Thing* (1926), in which a husband and wife face serious conflict over the man's dream to become a professional musician, won honorable mention in the same contest.

While most black women wrote their plays with an all-black cast, Miller frequently incorporated white characters. Her lynching drama *Nails and Thorns* (1933) is set in the white home of a southern sheriff and his wife where their attitudes regarding an impending lynching are contrasted with those of Annabel, a black domestic servant. In *Stragglers in the Dust* (1930) Nan, a black charwoman who cleans the area around the tomb of the Unknown Soldier, believes her son, who was killed in World War I, is buried in the tomb. The character of Nan is contrasted with a white politician whose sick and confused son, wounded in the war, dies while trying to enter the tomb. Miller skillfully shows how Nan and the politician, who both lost sons in the war, are united by experience but divided by class and race. *Graven Images* (1929) deals with racism in biblical times and is based on the Old Testament verse, "And Miriam and Aaron spoke against Moses because of the Ethiopian woman he had married" (Numbers 12:1). After Miriam taunts Moses' young son, Eliezer, for being black, she is punished by God for her words. Miller was moved to write this play because her father had often referred to the biblical verse as the first mention of prejudice on account of color, causing Miller to wonder how the young child might have felt when he was taunted by Miriam.[3]

Like her sister playwrights, Miller gave most of her plays female protagonists. *Riding the Goat* (1925) is a comedy in which two women teach a young black doctor to respect the rituals and beliefs of the black community in which he works. When the play was published in *Plays and Pageants From the Life of the Negro* (1930), editor and black theatre pioneer Willis Richardson referred to Miller as one of the "most promising" playwrights. Miller would later refer to this play as her "most popular" and remembered the many $5 royalty checks that came in from Little Theatre groups all over the country.[4]

Miller's historical plays were an especially significant contribution to the developing black drama. As a teacher, Miller saw the need to instill racial pride and cultural awareness in her students and she understood the need for young people to see black heroes and heroines portrayed on stage. Miller acknowledged professors G. Carter Woodson and Randolph Edmonds as major influences who instilled in her a strong commitment to dramatize Negro history. As a result of her commitment, Miller wrote the greatest number of historical plays of the era that focus on women's lives and experiences. Two of Miller's plays set in mid nineteenth-century America are *Harriet Tubman*, which depicts an escape from slavery directed by the famous leader of the underground railroad, and *Sojourner Truth* in which the legendary, pipe-smoking, itinerant preacher successfully employs her wit and wisdom to convert a group of young white trouble-makers. Miller's *Christophe's Daughters*, set in 1820 Haiti, portrays the loyalty and courage that two royal daughters show for their father, King Henry Christophe, who is surrounded by traitors during the final days of his reign. In *Samory* Miller focuses on the African hero who, in 1881, led a successful native army in the Sudan against French troops. Miller was urged by Woodson to create a play honoring Samory's military skills and tactical knowledge but, even in this all-male play, Miller creates a subtle but strong female presence by demonstrating the respect Samory holds for the memory of his mother. Since his mother sold kola nuts to make her living, Samory knows that messages arriving at his camp, hidden in kola nuts, can be trusted and are from his most loyal officer who is also his closest friend. All four of Miller's history plays were published in *Negro History in Thirteen Plays* (1935), an anthology Miller edited with Richardson.

Since she was the most widely published African American woman playwright of the 1920s and 1930s, Miller's plays offer the widest variety of self-defined black female images. Like Georgia Douglas Johnson, Miller both drew support from and contributed to the self-help/mutual support tradition. As a prolific playwright, she undoubtedly struggled to find the times of solitude a writer needs to create, but she also possessed a deep sense of community. As a mentor, she encouraged Zora Neale Hurston to attend Howard University to study theatre and literature and, later, to attend the Saturday night gatherings at the home of Georgia Douglas Johnson. As an editor, she included the historical dramas of Johnson in the anthology *Negro History in Thirteen Plays* and, as a friend, she was at Johnson's bedside to offer words of comfort in the face of death. Her teaching career demonstrates her ability to unify the roles of teacher and artist and reflects her self-help/mutual support interaction with the community. As a teacher/playwright, Miller acknowledged her school's art, music, and physical education departments as "a built in support system" (Miller, "Georgia Douglas Johnson," 352 n.6). Her school provided her with an important platform on which to mount her dramatic works and, through her plays, she provided a compelling way for students to learn about black heroes and heroines by seeing them come to life on stage.

The life and work of Eulalie Spence (1894–1981) reveals how a legacy of self-help and mutual support enabled black women playwrights of the period to strongly assert their artistic independence and individuality while continuing to be important contributors to the community. Unlike many of her sister playwrights, Spence chose not to write dramas of protest or propaganda but to focus her plays on everyday life in Harlem. According to Perkins, her rationale for avoiding protest drama issues was that she knew nothing about lynchings, rapes, nor the blatant racial injustices in this country. As a West Indian, she claimed these issues were not a part of her background. She believed that "We go to the theatre for entertainment, not to have old fires and hates rekindled" (Hatch and Hamalian, *Lost Plays*, 466). Spence is known to have written fourteen one-act plays, and at least seven were produced. Her only full-length play, *The Whipping* (1929), was to open in Bridgeport, Connecticut but was not produced, and subsequently optioned by Paramount Studios, but never made into a movie.

Spence was born in 1894 on the island of Nevis, British West Indies. When her father's livelihood as a sugar planter was destroyed by a hurricane, the family emigrated to New York, settling first in Harlem and later moving to Brooklyn. She received her BA from New York University in 1937 and an MA from Columbia University's Teachers College in 1939. Perkins reveals that Spence was the backbone of a family of seven sisters and was inspired to write by her mother, who often read stories to her daughters. One of the few women dramatists to receive formal training in playwriting, she studied under professors such as Hatcher Hughes and Estelle Davis at Columbia. She taught elocution, English, and dramatics at Eastern District High School in Brooklyn from 1927 until her retirement in 1958. She contributed her directing talents to Eastern District's drama club and the Krigwa Players. Even though Du Bois tried to persuade Spence to use her writing skills for protest drama, she continued to create folk dramas for fun and entertainment. Despite her differences with Du Bois, Spence remained an active member of his Krigwa Players from 1926 until its demise in 1928 and the group produced three of her plays, *Fool's Errand* (1927), *Foreign Mail* (1926), and *Her* (1927). *Fool's Errand*, a satire on gossipy church women, won a $200 prize as one of the Krigwa Players entries in the Fifth Annual Little Theatre Tournament.

Spence established a relationship with Du Bois' philosophical rival, Alain Locke. She frequently corresponded with Locke and her play *The Starter* appeared in his pioneering anthology, *Plays of Negro Life*. Awarded third place in the 1927 *Opportunity* contest, *The Starter* is set in Harlem and concerns the romantic relationship between a young man who is an elevator "starter" for a department store and a young woman who is a "finisher" in a dress shop. Spence's command of dramatic dialogue is evident in her skillful creation of the verbal banter between the young couple. *Hot Stuff* (1927) focuses on the life of Fanny King, a Harlem numbers runner, dealer in stolen merchandise, and prostitute. Fanny, described by Spence as "The Red Hot Mama" is both villain and victim: she scoffs at all the suckers in Harlem who trust their money to her and she is brutally beaten by her husband; she is Spence's unflinching portrait of a woman surviving in a "dog eat dog" world. In contrast to *Hot Stuff*, *Episode* (1928) is a comedy set in an expensive Harlem apartment house. In this satirical look at marriage, a wife first argues with her husband about never staying home with her and then threatens to leave him when he constantly stays at home to practice a horn that he plays often, loudly, and badly. *Her* is a suspense drama in which supernatural events bring about long-delayed justice under the watchful eye of a black woman carrying out routine washing and ironing. *Undertow* (1929) concerns an unhappily married couple's conflicts which end in death when the husband's long-lost love returns to claim him.

Like her sister playwrights, Spence chose to create plays with strong female characters and like May Miller, she contributed her playwriting, directing, and teaching skills to the developing black drama in her community. Her work reveals her unique approach to balancing a commitment to both self-reliance and community involvement. While she was aware of differing philosophies of black drama, Spence remained loyal to her own artistic sensibilities, creating the plays she felt inspired to create, while maintaining connections with both Du Bois and Locke. Her strong female characters reflect her own inner strength and self-reliance that, instead of fostering alienation, served to shape her own form of participation in the artistic community.

Zora Neale Hurston (1891–1960) is known primarily as a novelist and folklorist but she was also a significant contributor to the theatre of the Harlem Renaissance. From the 1930s through the 1960s Hurston was the most prolific and accomplished black woman writer in America. In addition to four novels, two books of folklore, an autobiography, and fifty short stories and essays, she wrote close to twenty plays and musical reviews. Her novel *Their Eyes Were Watching God* (1937) is considered her masterpiece. The fact that by 1950 she was working as a maid and in 1960 died in a county welfare home without enough money to pay for her own funeral, is a telling commentary on the struggles that even the most talented black women writers faced.

Hurston was born in 1891 in Notasulga, Alabama but spent the greater part of her childhood in Eatonville, Florida, an all-black town five miles from Orlando. Eatonville was to become an important source of black cultural traditions that form the core of Hurston's writing. She attended Morgan Academy in Baltimore where she was persuaded by May Miller to enroll at Howard University to study drama under Locke and Gregory. During her years at Howard (1919 to 1924) she developed her writing skills and in 1925 her play, *Color-Struck*, placed second in the *Opportunity* awards. *Color-Struck* focuses on the character of Emmaline, a black woman who has internalized white racism's hatred of her dark skin. Her envy of light skin drives her boyfriend away and eventually contributes to her own daughter's death. Within this tragic story Hurston deftly incorporated a slice of black cultural life (a dance hall scene) that includes orchestral music (banjo, guitar, accordion, church organ, and drum) and the jubilant dancing of the "cake walk."[5] The play was published in *Fire!* (1926) a one-issue, avant-garde journal edited by Hurston and other young black artists of the Harlem Renaissance. Emmaline's preoccupation with skin color and feelings of inferiority were not shared by Hurston. In a 1928 essay entitled "How It Feels to Be Colored Me," she asserted that she did not belong to "the sobbing school of Negrohood who hold that nature somehow gave them a lowdown dirty deal and whose feelings are all hurt about it ... No, I do not weep at the world – I am too busy sharpening my oyster knife" (Walker, *I Love Myself*, 153). The sentiments Hurston expressed in this essay are reflected in her 1927 play *The First One*, published in the anthology *Ebony and Topaz*. *The First One* is based on the biblical story of Noah and his son Ham but, in the hands of Hurston, the inclusion of a strong female character determines the outcome. Taking place in the Valley of Ararat, three years after the Flood, the play depicts how Noah came to place a curse on his youngest son, Ham, for showing disrespect to him. Under the influence of too much wine, Noah rages, "He shall be accursed. His skin shall be black! Black as the nights, when the waters brooded over the Earth! ... Black! He and his seed forever ..." Noah remains steadfast in his rage and will not "unsay the curse," despite the tearful pleadings of his wife and other children. When Noah finally orders the stricken Ham to "go out from among us that we may see thy face no more," it is Eve, Ham's wife, who offers her wisdom and ability to face the future with courage:

6. Zora Neale Hurston

EVE: Ham, my husband, Noah is right. Let us go before you learn to despise your father and your God. Come away Ham, beloved, come with me where thou canst never see these faces again ... where never thy happy voice can learn to weep. Come with me to where the sun shines forever, to the end of the Earth, beloved the sunlight of all my years. (*She kisses his mouth and forehead. She crosses to door of tent and picks up water bottle. Ham looks dazedly about him. His eyes light on the harp and he smilingly picks it up and takes his place beside Eve.*)

HAM *(lightly cynical to all)*:   Oh, remain with your flocks and fields and
vineyards, to covet, to sweat, to die and know no peace. I go to the sun. *(He
exits right across the plain with his wife and child trudging beside him ...)*
(Perkins, *Black Female Playwrights*, 88)

Reflecting the sentiments of Hurston's 1928 essay, the play's ending
portrays a small community (Ham, Eve, and their child) pulling together in
the struggle for survival instead of focusing on blacks as victimized people.
Hurston records woman's valued place as a leader and counselor in the
community through the character of Eve.[6]

With the help of Annie Nathan Meyer, an influential white woman who
recognized Hurston's talents and shared her interest in writing, Hurston
obtained a scholarship to Barnard, where she received her degree in
anthropology. With the encouragement of famous anthropologist Franz
Boas and the patronage of wealthy matron Charlotte Osgood Mason,
Hurston traveled throughout the South collecting stories, songs, dances,
and games from small black rural communities. She believed that a
measure of a people's self-respect was the love they had for their own
customs and that the rituals of daily life in African American communities
could form the foundation of a "real Negro Theatre." In 1931 she
collaborated with Langston Hughes, one of the most highly esteemed
writers of the period, to create *Mule Bone*, an authentic black folk comedy
based on her memories of Eatonville. Unfortunately the collaboration
brought an end to their friendship and the (unfinished) play was not staged
until 1991 when Michael Schultz directed a production on Broadway.

Hurston is one of the few black playwrights of the period who
attempted to pursue a life in the professional theatre. In the 1930s she
created and performed in musical programs of Negro folklore: *The Great
Day* (1932), *From Sun to Sun* (1933), and *Singing Steel* (1934), all based
on the folk material she had gathered in her southern travels. She
performed in these programs before audiences in New York, Chicago, and
various cities in Florida. Performing the folk material provided Hurston
with the idea for her book *Mules and Men* (1935), the first volume of
black folklore by a black American. Hurston also contributed to the
theatre as a director and producer. In 1935 she was hired as a "drama
coach" for the New York Unit of the Federal Theatre Project and from
1939 to 1940 she was hired to organize a drama program for North
Carolina College for Negroes in Durham. Hurston collaborated with
Dorothy Waring, a white writer, on the musical comedy *Polk County* but
a scheduled 1944 Broadway production never materialized. According to
scholar Lynda Hill, Hurston became increasingly frustrated in her efforts
to pursue a theatre career and diverted her energy into her writing, where

the printed page became her primary stage for dramatizing the folkways and customs of black culture.

Zora Neale Hurston expressed herself as an artist by focusing on the rich cultural sources she found in the black community. Her strong commitment to self-help can be seen in the ways she wrote, produced, performed, flattered, and fought to sustain her life as an artist. Of all the playwrights, her energies stretch across the widest canvas, as if one form of artistic expression could not contain her creativity and talent. The life of Zora Neale Hurston continues to be an active force in the self-help/mutual support tradition. Many artists and writers draw on her life and work as a source of artistic inspiration and scholarly study. Laurence Holder drama-tized Hurston's life in *Zora Neale Hurston: A Theatrical Biography* (1978) and George C. Wolfe adapted and produced three of her short stories under the title, *Spunk* (1989). The recent discovery of ten typescripts of Hurston's plays at the Library of Congress has aroused great interest and excitement among scholars and artists (Triplett, "Hurston Plays," B2). Although Hurston was buried in an unmarked grave, novelist Alice Walker recently located the site and ensured the placement of a proper headstone that proclaims: Zora Neale Hurston: "A Genius of the South."

Sister playwrights

Other playwrights of the period were less prolific than Johnson, Miller, Spence, and Hurston but their contributions are of no less importance to the development of black drama and women's history in the American theatre. Space allows for only a few of these playwrights to be mentioned here but all of them participated in the self-help/mutual support tradition by focusing theatre's reflection of human life on the black community and creating self-defined images of black women.

Angelina Weld Grimké's *Rachel* (1916) is the earliest extant non-musical written, produced, and publicly performed by African Americans. Produced by the Drama Committee of the Washington DC branch of the NAACP, the play represents the first attempt to use the stage to enlighten the American public about the destructive effects of racism. *Rachel* focuses on the life of a young woman who learns that her father and brother were lynched in the South. Haunted by this past brutality, and witnessing how racism continues to destroy black lives, she vows never to become a mother. *Rachel* is the first full-length play representing the anti-lynching tradition in American drama. Grimké's play is a forerunner of later dramas, such as Georgia Douglas Johnson's one-acts, that speak out against the violence of lynching. *Mara* (1920), an unpublished play, also focuses on a young woman and her family who suffer the destructive effects of racism and the brutality of lynching.

Alice Dunbar-Nelson's *Mine Eyes Have Seen* (1918) captures the dilemma faced by many black men and their families during World War I. As black Americans the men were pulled between a call to serve their country in the American military while, at the same time, they knew African Americans were being subjected to Jim Crow laws, lynching, and denied the rights of full citizenship guaranteed by the Constitution. The one-act play was published in *The Crisis* and produced at Howard High School in Wilmington, Delaware where Dunbar-Nelson taught and served as head of the English department. *Gone White* (n.d.) treats the quagmire of self-denial and deceit light-skinned blacks faced when they chose to pass for white in order to achieve economic advantages. Dunbar-Nelson was an active participant in the crusade for women's rights and the anti-lynching movement. A writer of fiction, poetry, and newspaper columns, her recently published diary of 1921–31 reveals the ambitions and frustrations of a gifted black woman struggling to achieve her goals during the Harlem Renaissance era.

Mary Burrill's *Aftermath* (1919) portrays the anguish of a family whose father has been lynched and the spirit of revenge it inspires. It was published in the *Liberator* and produced by the Krigwa Players. *They That Sit in Darkness* (1919) deals with the struggles of a family living in poverty and denied access to knowledge of birth control. A very courageous play, and controversial in its time, it appeared in *The Birth Control Review*, a magazine advocating birth control rights for women.

Marita Bonner was one of the most innovative playwrights of the period. She did not write in the usual realistic style but created her own form of surrealistic or expressionistic drama. She specified that her first play, *The Pot Maker* (1927), was "A Play to be Read," not produced. The plot revolves around an unhappy marriage meeting a tragic end but the drama also functions as a morality play, commenting on human frailty and redemption. *The Purple Flower*, published in the 1928 issue of *The Crisis*, is the first drama to be written by a woman in the black revolutionary tradition. In this allegory of the black quest for freedom and happiness, Bonner sets her play in "The Middle of Things as They Are," divides the stage between the "Us's" and "the White Devils," and asks if black freedom is possible without violent revolution. Margaret Wilkerson has suggested that *The Purple Flower* is the "most provocative" play of the Harlem Renaissance era.[7] *Exit: An Illusion* (1929) deals with a jealous lover's revenge and the problem of acceptance of white ancestry in the black community.

Shirley Graham pursued a career in professional theatre as a playwright, composer, designer, and director. She studied music at Howard University and in Paris at the Sorbonne. Her three-act opera, *Tom Tom*, successfully produced in 1932 at the Cleveland Stadium, is the first black opera to be professionally produced. Reflecting Graham's knowledge of authentic African music, the opera examines how vestiges of African life and music have survived in the United States. *It's Morning* (1940) is a one-act tragedy based on the story of a slave mother who kills her daughter to prevent her being sold to a brutal slave master. *I Gotta Home* (1939) is a three-act comedy of family life set in a Negro church parsonage. The family's strong bonds and spiritual faith are reinforced by the visit of cousin Mattie Cobb, whose liveliness, flamboyance, and stroke of good luck help save the family from financial worries. *Track Thirteen* (1940) is a radio drama that takes a comic look at the ability of railroad porters to deal with their demanding passengers and catch an escaped thief while maintaining an attitude of "it's all in a day's work." When Graham married W. E. B. Du Bois in 1951 she gave up her aspirations in theatre and devoted her life to supporting his work for world peace and justice. She died in 1977 at the age of eighty in Peking, where she was working on a book about the women of China.

Other playwrights of the period who made important contributions were Ruth Gaines Shelton, Myrtle Smith Livingston, Helen Webb Harris, Maude Cuney Hare, Thelma Myrtle Duncan, Alvira Hazzard, and Mercedes Gilbert.

A focus on women and theatre in the Harlem Renaissance reveals how black women playwrights both relied upon and contributed to a tradition of self-help and mutual support. The self-defined images they created and their community involvement reflect a philosophy in which the concepts of self and community are unified. As they struggled to create the stories and images they wanted to see on the stage, they helped to shape a national black theatre movement and, by their significant numbers, recorded the collective entrance of African American women into the playwriting tradition.

NOTES

1 The name of the period and its dates are continuously under debate. See for example the introductions to Arthur P. Davis and Michael W. Peplow, *The New Negro Renaissance*; Victor Kramer, *The Harlem Renaissance Re-examined*; and Amritjit Singh, William Shiver, and Stanley Brodwin, *The Harlem Renaissance*.

2 A more recent anthology is Jennifer Burton, ed., *Zora Neale Hurston, Eulalie Spence, Marita Bonner, and Others: The Prize Plays and Other One-Acts Published in Periodicals*.

3 Audio-taped interview with May Miller, 1973. Hatch-Billops Collection, New York.
4 *Ibid.*
5 See Sandra L. Richards, "Writing the Absent Potential," for an analysis of the play as representative of a black folk aesthetic.
6 For a different interpretation of this play, see Addell P. Austin, "Pioneering Black Authored Dramas, 1924–1927."
7 Margaret B. Wilkerson, *9 Plays by Black Women*, xvii.

8

THOMAS P. ADLER

Lillian Hellman: feminism, formalism, and politics

Although a number of women who wrote for the American stage before Lillian Hellman, including Susan Glaspell, Rachel Crothers, and Sophie Treadwell, have recently been receiving serious attention from theatre scholars and historians, Hellman was the first woman playwright to be admitted to the previously all-male space of the canon of American dramatic literature – and that on the basis of two major successes from the 1930s which remain to this day the best known of her eight original plays: *The Children's Hour* (1934), which introduced Hellman to theatre audiences and provided the longest run (691 performances) of her thirty-year playwriting career; and *The Little Foxes* (1939), a perennial favorite with actresses that continues to be given star-studded Broadway revivals. While it may not seem particularly surprising that these same two works, sixty years or more after their New York premieres, continue to be the focus of critical commentary on Hellman, what is somewhat ironic, though perhaps not unexpected, is that they have become the center of contention among feminist scholars, for whom their canonized position is seen as deeply problematic.

The Children's Hour concerns accusations of lesbianism involving two teachers at a girls' boarding school; though the rumors are founded on the lies of a vicious child, without evidentiary proof, they fuel a campaign of vilification and hatred, leading ultimately to the broken engagement of one woman and the suicide of the other. Because the lesbian experience is described as socially disruptive, named by the community as "unnatural" – the designation most frequently appearing in the dialogue Hellman writes for her characters – and eventuates in the death of the abject sexual Other, recent criticism tends to regard the play as a "profoundly conservative text" whose adherence to realism's codes inscribes lesbianism as an "enigma" that must be "purged," and thus a play whose very canonization valorizes heterosexism and homophobia.[1] *The Little Foxes* tells of a conniving southern woman who gleefully rises to economic power and independence at the turn of the century over her two brothers and a husband whom she allows to die by withholding his medicine, but who as a result will suffer separation from her daughter and live emotionally destitute. The work has raised the larger issue of whether a feminist perspective that interrogates narrowly inscribed gender roles and seeks to subvert patriarchal hegemony can ever be compatible with traditional dramatic realism. Can a mimetic form that implies the existence of a stable, normative order; that has tended to erase the woman as subject and enshrine her as object; that even reflects male bodily experience in its structure of rising action and climax; and that has been subject to hierarchical production practices be instrumental for women in effecting social change?[2]

Though not lacking in sympathy for the feminist movement, Hellman saw the "woman question" in fairly narrow terms; as she writes in her first volume of memoirs, *An Unfinished Woman* (1969) – undoubtedly too sanguinely for some since she speaks from a position of money and success, even celebrity: "By the time I grew up the right for the emancipation of women, their rights under the law, in the office, in bed, was stale stuff" (36). What does interest her, however, is the power that comes with having enough money to control one's life: "I don't think it's of any great moment who carries out the garbage. I think it is important that people be economically equal. So that if somebody feels like walking out, there's a way for her to earn a living rather than suffering through a whole lifetime because she can't" (Bryer, *Conversations*, 205). (Not surprisingly, Hellman considered Brecht's *Mother Courage* the great play of her time.) And Hellman will, in several of her plays, dramatize the debilitating effects of economic dependency and the apparently empowering aspect of its opposite. In *The Little Foxes* and – though written later, the prequel to its action – *Another Part of the Forest* (1946), Hellman provides a Chekhovian snapshot of the agrarian South in 1880 and 1900 as it comes under the dominance of business and industry; if the cultured, genteel way of life now dying out was never as ideal as memory would have it (it was, after all, built upon the institution of slavery), neither does the more pragmatic and utilitarian society hold the promise that its adherents intimate, because it so easily falls into the carelessness of its individual members, whose prime value resides in their being negotiable commodities.

In *Forest*, the daughters of the two families – the Hubbards, who inhabit a southern Greek Revival mansion that fosters the deceptive appearance of a seat of learning and high principles, and the Bagtrys, whose plantation Lionnet has fallen into ruin under an antebellum economy – both suffer from their societally conditioned dependency on men. Birdie Bagtry, adrift in an impractical dream of somehow restoring the past, will instead end up marrying the dissolute Oscar Hubbard, who rides with the Klan; while Regina Hubbard will desert the father who has always adored her to side with her scheming brother Ben, who displaces the father through swindling and blackmail. Possessed, as Gayle Austin comments, of a "painful self-awareness ... of her subjugation" (*Feminist Theories*, 53), Regina capitulates to being traded in marriage to Horace Giddens in return for the financial holdings he will bring into the family; she must sacrifice love and erotic fulfillment in order to satisfy her ambition for power and influence.

The woman Hellman most valorizes in the heavily satiric *Forest* is the once-poor brutalized outsider, Lavinia Hubbard, who knows of her husband Marcus' illegal profiteering during the Civil War that inadvertently resulted in the slaughter of two dozen southern soldiers. That she appears almost blessed in her religious fanaticism and derangement indicates the depth of Hellman's condemnation of a society that delights in bartering human beings, whether they be daughters or black servants, for economic gain. By the time of *Foxes*, the physically abused, neurotic Birdie has retreated through alcoholism into a nostalgic remembrance of a past that never was; and Regina, for whom financial power has become a substitute for sex, has triumphed over her husband and brothers, in part as revenge for having been dispossessed by her father years before. The closing image in *Foxes* finds Regina's morally perceptive daughter Alexandra, newly emboldened by a social conscience not yet tested in the real world, predicting her mother's perpetual loneliness despite her financial triumph; it thus forms a diptych with the end of *Forest*, except that there Regina had been financially powerless as well as emotionally alienated.

A dependency that is essentially emotional, but one perpetuated through financial control, governs the lives of the two sisters in Hellman's last original work for the stage, *Toys in the Attic* (1960). The spinsters Anna and Carrie Berniers have literally lived and slaved for their brother Julian; their certainty of his need for them has been their entire purpose in life, extending, even after his marriage, to giving him financial support as a way of maintaining his dependency. When he comes back home flush from a lucrative business deal negotiated without their help, he turns the tables, bestowing upon them excessive presents. With their need to be needed now evaporated, their existence seems empty: sublimating their desire to be loved into an obsession to love, they had reduced themselves into objects who had importance only in the eyes of their brother, fooling themselves that Julian was dependent upon them, when really the opposite was true. So the relationship among the three siblings was in fact a psychologically infantile, tangled web of codependency, a destructive union in which controlling behavior masked a clinging insecurity, and power and powerlessness were confused. Even in the relationship between the two sisters, the lines of control had been blurred: although Anna appears to have been the dominant one, Carrie actually called the tunes for their life together. When Hellman remarks that "all women living together take on what we think of as male and female roles," but that these are sometimes "a rather puzzling mix-about" (*Pentimento*, 12), she would seem to be voicing the inevitability of the stronger/weaker, dominant/submissive bifurcation in all relationships, whether built on the power of love or the power of money. In the Berniers family, emotional feelings remained unspoken, even unadmitted, with human contact defined instead in the transaction of material goods, in a confusion of love with things.

In what has become a well-known "Introduction," originally written in 1942 for a volume containing her first four plays, Hellman enshrined the terminology that would generally govern discussions of her works for the next several decades, identifying herself as a moralist who employs the structural pattern of the realistic well-made social problem play within the generic mode of melodrama. All three of these tags – moralist, well-made, melodrama – carry with them associations that might appear seriously to box in Hellman's dramaturgical practices; furthermore, they impel audiences to expect an unambiguous closure with no strings left untied and just deserts meted out, while signaling for critics the appropriateness of readily applying a formalistic approach to the plays. As "a moral writer, often too moral a writer," Hellman confesses an inability to "avoid, it seems, that last summing up. I think that is only a mistake when it fails to achieve its purpose, and I would rather make the attempt, and fail, than fail to make the attempt" (*Six Plays*, viii–ix). Yet if for Hellman the dramatic form in no way hampers content ("what the author has to say"), it does, nevertheless, place certain restrictions on the "means of saying it," since "compared to the novel ... the theatre ... is a tight, unbending, unfluid, meager form in which to write" (x). Moreover, the realistic theatre that "has interested [Hellman] most" not only demands "tricks" – though these are "only bad" if they "stop you short" – but also is predicated upon the "vaguely awry ... pretense of representation ... the always rather comic notion that the audience is the fourth wall" (xi). And the well-made realistic play "whose effects are contrived, whose threads are knit tighter than the threads in life" for that very reason runs the risk of not, or of only partly, convincing the spectator (x). Having admitted these limitations to her chosen medium, Hellman at the same time rejects any too easy dismissal of the melodramatic mode and even attempts to rehabilitate it by emphasizing that, contrary to what some popularizers think, the "violence" employed to bring about the requisite happy ending may, in fact, be purposive: nothing inherent in the form requires that it "point no moral [or] say nothing, in say-nothing's worse sense" (xi).

More recently, Peter Brooks has outlined an expansive notion of the nature of melodrama in ways that might help elucidate Hellman's own understanding and practice. With no apologies for the overwrought tone of the melodramatic mode, with its "extravagant expression, moral polarization, emotional hyperbole, extreme states of being," Brooks proposes that this literary form may well be "heightened, hyperbolic [precisely] *because* the moral realm it wants to evoke is not immediately visible, and the writer is ever conscious of standing over a void, dealing in conflicts, qualities, and quantities whose very existence is uncertain" ("Melodramatic Imagination," 204–05). The melodramatic imagination becomes, then, a central means for realizing those "quests of the modern imagination ... to bring into the drama of man's quotidian existence the higher drama of moral forces" by "refus[ing] to allow that the world has been drained of transcendence ... [and by] locat[ing] that transcendence in the struggle of the children of light with the children of darkness, in the play of ethical mind" (211–12). When Brooks applies this method of "interrogat[ing] appearances" in order to delve beyond surface reality specifically to the novels of Henry James, he finds "that what is being played out within the realm of manners is charged with significance from the realm of the moral" (199). Mention of James in the same breath with Hellman may not be totally unwarranted or inappropriate, since oftentimes her drawing rooms – as sites where old-world values meet new, where naivete and innocence are challenged by experience and corruption, and where the goal of self-determination is pursued through moral (or immoral) choices – seem as much Jamesian as they do Ibsenian (in, for instance, *Watch on the Rhine* [1941]) or Chekhovian (in *The Autumn Garden* [1951]).[3] Furthermore, the nature of good and evil, of the light and dark, in Hellman's works allows for greater ethical subtleties than her totalizing comments (e.g., "The theme of *The Children's Hour* was good and evil") would at first imply.

The Children's Hour can serve as a case in point. Although critics have tended to focus on the fiendish Mary or the "abject" Martha in their discussions, Karen Wright might profitably be considered the focal character in the play; certainly she holds the audience's visual attention at play's end, and the complexities of her moral dilemma and development are more thoroughly – and ambiguously – charted. As Philip Armato has suggested, if one follows out as a central motif the play's opening presentation of the tension between mercy and justice in Portia's lines from Shakespeare's

7. Scene from *The Children's Hour* by Lillian Hellman

Merchant of Venice that the girls are reciting, then it is Karen, in her final confrontation with Mrs. Tilford, who becomes the chief exemplum for mercy in the play. As Armato claims, "Karen has destroyed the vicious cycle that has characterized human relations; her compassion is the ultimate good in the world of the play" ("Good and Evil," 447). Even Martha, when she admits her longstanding physical attraction to Karen, remains (as Armato also notices), harshly self-condemnatory, with Hellman's text having Martha confess to "feel[ing] dirty." Notions about gender roles and sexual orientation in the play are, however, socially constructed. Although Martha long guessed there was something "wrong" in her lack of physical desire for men, she had no clear conception of what it was, nor could she give a name to it until others did first. Yet once named, she feels guilty, accepting society's judgment that such feelings are abnormal and therefore evil.

If Martha's lesbian sexuality is socially constructed, Karen Wright's heterosexual identity in the play might be said to be deconstructed. Not only is she, in sequence, accused by the girls; (mis)named as deviant by Mrs. Tilford; and even doubted by her fiancé, Joe. But she is also leered at by the homophobic gaze of the delivery boy, before, finally, Martha confesses to her homosexual feelings for her. Once aware that she is the focus of the gaze, the object of lesbian desire, what must the effect be on Karen's subject position, on her sense of her own identity in a society where gender and sexuality are not constituted but must be negotiated, and where one is constructed by how others, rightly or wrongly, perceive and name them? Any stable identity is brought into question and indeterminacy results. Just before Joe haltingly asks – he never can utter the words, though Karen understands his meaning – whether the two women had ever "touched each other," Karen remarks that as a consequence of the paranoia now unleashed, "every word will have a new meaning … Woman, child, love, lawyer – [there are] no words that we can use in safety anymore" (*Collected Plays*, 61). All stable referents have broken down; all received notions are now called into question. As Anne Fleche comments, the old language is "no longer understood as referential but as constitutive, performative, constraining" ("The Lesbian Rule,"23), so what remains is a crisis of meaning.

A number of critics, including Fleche, have remarked on the way in which Karen's surname "Wright" (like the second half of the word "play-wright") is a homonym for both "right" and "write." Yet they have not explicated how Hellman consciously calls attention to this in the exchange between Mrs. Tilford and Karen that brings *Children's Hour* to its close. The older woman asks the younger if she will "be all right," to which Karen replies uncertainly, "I'll be all right, I suppose" (*Collected Plays*, 71). If "right" is not only an emotional state and a moral condition, but the possessing of a sexuality that is sanctioned by narrow societal mores, that is, not "unnatural," then can Karen ever again be totally sure of being straight, not gay – either from her self-knowledge or the perception of others? Mrs. Tilford goes on to ask Karen if "You'll write me sometime?" to which Karen rather mysteriously responds, "If I ever have anything to say" (71). The enlightened moral code that the writer (Karen? Hellman herself?) needs to signify – the understanding that transgressive sexuality may be just as "natural" and loving as heterosexuality rather than always to be denigrated as a flaw needing to be expunged – has as yet no acceptable signifier. When Karen, her back turned, "*raises her hand*" and, in the curtain line, utters a belated "Good-bye" to the woman who is no longer on stage (Mrs. Tilford? Martha?), she seems totally turned in upon herself, certain about nothing but uncertainty – all the once carefully boundaried values sanctioned by society now undermined. Karen remains in a state of tortured confusion about herself, reflecting the larger confusion of a society that must now at least admit the existence of, if not sanction, the previously inadmissible and transgressive.

When *The Children's Hour* was revived on Broadway late in 1952 under Hellman's own direction, it assumed a political meaning and resonance it did not originally have, since audiences and reviewers were quick to draw an analogy between the aftermath of events in the girls' boarding school and the widespread paranoia spawned by the anticommunist witch hunt undertaken by the House Committee on Un-American Activities – which itself found homosexuality almost as great a threat to the nation's security as the "Red Menace." And *Children's Hour* was not the only play on the New York stage in the early 1950s to be seen as speaking, however covertly, to the issue of character assassination through suspicion and innuendo, of impugning the reputation and ostracizing the Other for being somehow different: while Arthur Miller's dramatization of the Salem witch trials in *The Crucible* (1953) has long been considered the most obvious example, Robert Anderson's *Tea and Sympathy* (also 1953) and Tennessee Williams' *Cat on a Hot Tin Roof* (1955) – both initially more popular than Miller's play and both involving accusations of homosexuality – serve as examples as well. Earlier in the same year that she directed *Children's Hour*, Hellman herself had been called to testify before the Congressional body. Finding repellent what she would be asked to do, that is, name names of supposed fellow travelers, she declared she would waive the constitutional privilege afforded by the Fifth Amendment against self-incrimination on the condition that the Committee refrain from asking her anything about people other than herself. She expressed her position in a letter (circulated among the press during the hearing) that contained the now-legendary passage: "I cannot and will not cut my conscience to fit this year's fashions, even though I long ago came to the conclusion that I was not a political person and could have no comfortable place in any political group" (*Scoundrel Time*, 93).

As a writer employing dramaturgical constructs ("well-made play"; "melodrama") that foreground issues of narratology, of how she tells her stories, Hellman espouses and practices a formalistic poetics that would seem to invite as most immediately congenial a similar approach on the part of critics. Such an approach, one focusing on technique and structural design at the expense of content, one conceiving of literature as an autonomous aesthetic order transcending ideology, would appear, however, to be inimical to political engagement and the expression of a political position. And yet the two – formalistic poetics/political ideas – need not be mutually exclusive. As Frederic Jameson suggests in *The Prison-House of Language*, the disjunction between leftist politics and aesthetics was not characteristic of the Russian practitioners of Formalism in the way that it was of their modernist American and British counterparts; furthermore, if "one abandons the idea of technique and purpose, and speaks simply of dominant and secondary elements, or of a dominant constructional principle," then in any literary work there exists a rich dialectical tension – of foregrounding/backgrounding – not only between the narrative mode as it was practiced by and embodied in earlier influential writers and the current uses to which it is put, but more importantly between elements of other non-literary "systems" (e.g., socioeconomic, historiopolitical) that are absorbed by and/or used within "the purely literary system" and the literary artifact itself (45, 92–93). Applied to Hellman, this would suggest an adaptation of formalist principles that allows for the incorporation of overtly political elements, which at times may rise to ascendancy, while at other moments they may recede from focus and be submerged.

Of Hellman's five overtly political plays (three original works and two adaptations), *Watch on the Rhine*, which opened nine months before Pearl Harbor and went on to win the New York Drama Critics Circle Award, was the most successful with reviewers and audiences alike. A trumpet call to throw off isolationism and actively respond to the threat of fascism, it literally brings the European conflict into the upper-class American living room, this one in a suburb of Washington DC. After years of living abroad, Sara arrives with her husband, Kurt Muller, and their three children at the home of her mother, Fanny Farrelly, who is also entertaining Count Teck de Brancovis and his American-born wife, Marthe. Kurt, a hero who had fought in Spain and become an activist in Germany when he witnessed soldiers massacring people in the streets, is a member of the anti-Nazi underground movement, carrying with him a large sum of money to help others escape political captivity. When Teck, a sleazy and self-serving sympathizer with National Socialism, demands blackmail in return for not revealing his identity, Kurt finds it necessary to kill him. Fanny, who shares with Kurt a love of music and the piano, not only contributes money to her son-in-law's cause, but also, "shaken out of the magnolias" and happily "not put together with flower paste" – along with her son David – agrees to cover up for Kurt as he returns to Germany, fully aware of the "trouble [they are] in for" (*Collected Plays*, 276).

Kurt, talking with the children he will leave behind, refuses to excuse the killing as anything but "bad ... for whatever reason it is done, and whoever does it" in a "world [that] is out of shape" (275). His insistence that "all over the world there are men who are fighting ... In every town and every village and every mud hut in the world, there is a man who might fight to make a good world" in which the need to kill would no longer prevail, recalls the belief of Fanny's late husband and Sara's father, Joshua (whose portrait dominates the room) that for anyone, anywhere, to experience political or economic injustice or racial or ethnic intolerance diminishes everyone else and is everyone's fault: "'For every man who lives without freedom, the rest of us must face the guilt' ... We are liable in the conscience-balance for the tailor in Lodz, the black man in our South, the peasant in –" (249). This notion of a world community, and of the overarching responsibility of all those who survive without suffering, is one that Hellman shares with her slightly younger contemporary Miller, in plays as various as *All My Sons, Incident at Vichy*, and *After the Fall*.

For Vivian Patraka, the incursion of the deceased Joshua's traditional liberalism onto the stage evidences "the ideology of heroism and war conducted by men" that is part and parcel of "the text's reinscribing of the patriarchal narrative of the nuclear family," which in turn not only undermines "gender equality" and leaves "no space ... for female resistance" of a political nature, but may even, albeit inadvertently, "perhaps ... recuperate [fascism] into dominant ideology via the domestic scene" ("Lillian," 136–42). Yet once Kurt goes back to Europe and an uncertain future, perhaps never to return from his dangerous mission, the Farrelly drawing room becomes more a matriarchy than a patriarchy. Sara, moreover, assumes a larger, proactive role in pinpointing the educative nature of the events that are unfolding and of the way in which this might necessitate a changed understanding – not only by those in the drawing room on stage but by the spectators in the theatre as well – when she expresses the moral imperative to adopt "a few new [convictions], now and then" (*Collected Plays*, 240). A crisis in language (similar to the one Karen faced in *Children's Hour*) makes this, however, a considerable challenge, because world events are outstripping the stable referents that once underpinned the absolutes authorizing and setting boundaries upon socially and politically acceptable behaviour. As Sarah asserts, "I don't know the language of rooms like this anymore. And I don't want to learn it again" (232). To reject isolationism and kill in order to protect the free world against the Nazis and the fascists (as American soldier/sons will soon do) may in fact be, despite what Kurt told his children, a morally good and defensible, and not simply a necessary, action.

In her English versions of plays written by others, Hellman adds two more "political" heroes to her own Kurt Muller from *Watch on the Rhine*. Her adaptation of Emmanuel Robles' *Montserrat*, which opened under Hellman's direction in 1949 for a disappointing run of sixty-five performances, bears an uncanny resemblance in content and tone to Harold Pinter's overtly political plays of the 1980s, such as *One for the Road* and *Mountain Language*, that dissect the capriciousness of totalitarian regimes in which power, brutally exercised, is elevated as the only right. Centering on events during Simon Bolivar's 1812 insurrection against the Spanish army of occupation in Venezuela, *Montserrat* depicts the revolutionaries as pitting themselves against the unholy trinity of God, King, and Fatherland that has turned their colonized nation into a slaughterhouse. Instead of subjecting Montserrat himself to torture in order to discover Bolivar's whereabouts, the henchman of the unseen Excellency (whose beautiful piano music sounds while murders are committed in his name, demonstrating the ironic coexistence of culture with evil) indiscriminately pulls six people, a microcosm of the society, off the streets to be summarily executed if Montserrat does not talk. Since they are "guilty of nothing but innocence" (*Collected Plays*, 443–44), their fate might be linked to the rounding-up of victims during the Holocaust. Montserrat, despite refusing to waver until Bolivar has time to regroup the radicals for his next advance, nevertheless recognizes his responsibility to these people who will be executed because of his intransigence in the name of right. Furthermore, one of the play's minor characters embodies a position that, with Hellman's blacklisting from Hollywood screenwriting in the late 40s and early 50s and her interrogation by the House Un-American Activities Committee, seems applicable to the dramatist herself, by drawing a line of conscience that he will not violate, "reserv[ing] a space for what we will not do" (472) under pressure from any government, even one to which he otherwise remains loyal.

The "political" surfaces again in Hellman's second and better received adaptation, that of Jean Anouilh's treatment of St. Joan in *The Lark* (1955), which with its fluid handling of time, its mix of narrative and dramatic segments, and its gestures toward metatheatricalism is the least realistic in setting and most complex in structure of all her plays. Joan embodies the power of the individual to energize the social organism, as well as the absolute duty to follow one's conscience and disobey an established order that seeks to thwart the minority in its midst. If Hellman could not "cut [her] conscience," Joan cannot "when something is black ... say it is white" (*Collected Plays*, 610). When she temporarily recants the truth under pressure from the inquisitors, Joan understands that all she has done is "[eat] the dirt of lies" in order to gain "a few more years of unworthy life" (627). Hellman helped underscore the analogy between Joan and her inquisitors on the one hand, and the suspected communists and the House investigating committee on the other, by "scal[ing] down [Anouilh's] play [and] cut[ting] the comparisons to the World War II German invasion of France and the tributes to the French spirit"; furthermore, she allowed her own protofeminism to come through in the appeal of "Joan [who] was history's first modern career girl, wise, [and] unattractive in what she knew about the handling of men" (*Pentimento*, 202). Joan's response to authoritarian suppression reflects Hellman's own condemnation of the paranoid McCarthy era as a "shameless period" in American history.

The responsibility for the moral lassitude of that time lay, however, not solely at the feet of the witch hunters and Red baiters who actively hounded and persecuted others, but could also be attributed to the failure of the silent liberals, including Leftists, who found it easier to stand passively by. In the pages of *Scoundrel Time* – which Hellman's severest critics condemn as a self-serving revisionist reading of the period, fraught with half-truths or untruths – Hellman refuses to exonerate herself wholly from blame, at least for having been blind to "the sins of Stalin Communism – and there were plenty of sins and plenty that for a long time [she] mistakenly denied"; but, at the same time, she asserts that she "had, up to the late 1940s, believed that the educated, the intellectual, lived by what they claimed to believe; freedom of thought and speech, the right of each man to his own convictions, a more than implied promise, therefore, of aid to those who might be persecuted. But only a very few raised a finger when McCarthy and the boys appeared" (*Scoundrel Time*, 40). As Doris Falk emphasizes, such a failure to respond actively, "the inaction of bystanders [is] a cardinal sin in Hellman's morality" (*Lillian Hellman*, 70). Addie's stern observation in *Little Foxes* – "There are people who eat the earth ... I think it ain't right to stand and watch them do it" (*Collected Plays*, 188) – provides the most explicit gloss in all of Hellman's writings on this moral failure, which can be detected in the plays as early as Mrs. Mortar's complicity in *Children's Hour* with those who persecute others on the basis of insinuation and innuendo; out of spite and to avoid "unpleasant notoriety" she did not return to deny in court damaging remarks she had made about her niece, Martha.

An opposite moral choice, a refusal to remain passive, is taken by the servantwoman Hannah, in Hellman's second play, *Days to Come* (1936). Although Carl Rollyson comments that in *Days* "it is a moral argument, not a political one, that Hellman makes" (*Lillian Hellman*, 94) – as if the two were capable of separation for her – another of her biographers, William Wright, terms it her "most political" play, "written at a time when she herself was becoming staunchly political" because of a confluence of "ideological forces" and a series of events decisive for the liberal cause: the Depression; the Spanish Civil War; Hitler's anti-Semitism; and the lure of socialism and communism as responses to the apparent failure of capitalism (*Lillian Hellman*, 127–28). Not only does Hannah collect money from the other servants and take food from her employer's pantry for distribution to the workingmen on strike in his factory, but she also refuses his command to open the door to admit the strikebreakers and scabs, saying: "That's one bell I ain't going to answer. I can't help what other people do, but I don't have to help 'em out" (*Collected Plays*, 90). The company owner, Andrew Rodman, naively believing that the outmoded paternalism that had always before won respect within the community will continue to do so, expects his workers to acquiesce to lower wages that would ensure continued quality in the face of increasing competition. When the union leader, Whalen, arrives to organize the laborers, Andrew lets in the corrupt agitators, not understanding the likelihood of their stirring up violence that will result in bloodshed and death. Andrew is equally muddled about the failure of his marriage to Julie, who is desperate to discover a subject position for herself, a space where she will not simply be expected to "listen" but can "talk myself," where she can "do ... be ... want ... think ... believe," where she could "make something for [her]self, something that would be right for [her]" (103, 111, 130). Conscience-stricken over the murder he has unwittingly caused and aware of having permanently lost his standing in the community, Rodman eventually realizes that "Polite and blind, we lived" (132), and that his punishment "for all the days to come" will be the knowledge of his failure to see and respond positively in areas of personal and social responsibility.

The last of Hellman's three original political dramas, *The Searching Wind* (1944), is structurally the most complex of these works. The scenes occurring in the present are set in another Washington drawing room, this one home to former Ambassador Alex Hazen and his wife Emily, the daughter of a prominent, now-retired newspaper owner, Moses Taney. Three of the play's six scenes, however, flash back to decisive historical moments (involving the same central characters) leading up to World War II; these sequences dramatizing the past form meditations upon the failure of democratic societies and left-leaning intellectuals who fooled themselves about events that it was easier to countenance and condone than to openly challenge. The first of these takes place in the Italy of 1922, when King Victor Emmanuel and his government welcomed Mussolini and his troops into Rome; the second in the Berlin of 1923, when Jews were rounded up in an early pogrom; and the third in the Paris of 1938, when England and France gave the Sudetenland to Hitler through the Munich Pact. Throughout all of this time, Hazen, on the rise in US diplomatic circles, fails to see the situation as clearly as he should, and so falls prey to tolerating and temporizing about actions he should be condemning. In 1922, fascism seemed somehow preferable to a communist-inspired people's revolution over widespread misery and starvation. In 1923, he naively refused to believe that anyone was "bad enough to put up the money" for a vicious assault on the Jewish people; the coming Shoah is so cataclysmic as to have overpowered the ability of language to contain and express the "horror and disgrace," and therefore it seems beyond conception" (*Collected Plays*, 314–15). And in 1938, Alex is again unable to fathom that other democracies would be villainous enough to cut a deal with the Nazi leader – though preventing war at any and all costs, so that his son and those of others will not have to fight, helps make appeasement attractive.

Hazen's greatest failure and that of those like him is, in short, to feel impotent in the face of history, to "just sit back and watch" because he doubted that anything he might say or do "makes any difference" (330, 335). Paradoxically, his shortsightedness almost guarantees that he help write a history he did not realize he was writing – and one that almost certainly he never intended to write. Hellman's portrayal of Alex Hazen serves as an early reflection of the existentialist point of view she will voice in a central passage in *Autumn Garden* several years later. Expressing how the succession of choices one continually must make, or that one fails to make, finally creates, and thus determines, what one becomes, the content of one's character, she has General Griggs remark: "So at any given moment you're only the sum of your life up to then ... the turning point in your life, the someday you've counted on when you'd suddenly wipe out your past mistakes, do the work you'd never done, think the way you never thought, have what you'd never had – it just doesn't come suddenly. You've trained yourself for it while you waited – or you've let it all run past you" (*Collected Plays*, 568–69).

Alex's irresponsible personal life, including a dalliance over the past twenty years with his wife's best friend, Cassie, reflects the same myopia and self-absorption apparent in his politics. She (like the Cassandra of classical times) is the most clear-sighted of the three, understanding that they are "an ignorant generation. We see so much and know so little. Maybe because we think about ourselves so much ... Things mean so little to us"; this made them just "frivolous people" who "did things for a bad reason" (300, 333). In other Hellman plays, art, most often in the form of music, can sometimes bond people together (as it does Birdie and Alexandra in *Little Foxes*, Fanny and Kurt in *Watch on the Rhine*, or Carrie and Julian in *Toys in the Attic*); appreciation of art, however, is no guarantee of human decency (as in *Another Part of the Forest*, where it covers over venality, or *Montserrat*, where it provides a counterpoint with political executions). Here, in *Searching Wind*, Cassie realizes that Emily's piano playing is not only a helpless palliative, but indeed a blinding distraction or flight from the reality of the guns of war. It falls to representatives of the older and younger generations to put into sharpest perspective precisely what the major characters' inactivity and unresponsiveness in the face of evil has occasioned: Taney tauntingly reminds them that "There's nothing like a good compromise to cost a few million men their lives" (331–32), while Alex and Emily's soldier/son, Sam, home from the Front and ashamed of his father's mistakes and his mother's casual consorting with uncommitted European émigrées in the salons of the rich, faces the amputaton of his wounded leg. His body inscribed by war becomes one of the most potent of Hellman's stage symbols. Sam himself looks upon his shattered limb as a text that potentially will teach them all: "I don't like losing [a leg] at all. I'm scared – but everybody's welcome to it as long as it means a little something and helps to bring us out someplace" (337). This is Sam's way of not sitting around and watching, one which is more traumatic, though at the same time more effective, than Alexandra's youthful romantic flight at the end of *Foxes*.

The other innocent, stigmatized bodies in *Searching Wind* are those of the unseen Jews, terrorized on the streets of Berlin. Although Hellman herself acknowledged "the gift of being born a Jew" (Bryer, *Conversations*, 291), Kenneth Holditch calls her "one of the least Jewish of all Jewish authors" ("Another Part of the Country," 17), while Joan Mellen judges her "ambivalen[t] about her Jewish identity" partly because by making her Other it "robbed her of the acceptability she craved" (*Hellman*, 167). Yet Mellen goes on to quote from Hellman's speech in 1940 before an audience of two thousand at a meeting of the American Booksellers Association, when she declared: "I am a writer and also a Jew. I also want to be able to go on saying that I am a Jew without being afraid of being called names or end in a prison camp or be forbidden to walk down the street at night." Increasingly, as is true also of such plays as *All My Sons* and *The Crucible* by her fellow public intellectual, Arthur Miller, it seems that the Holocaust – and the universal responsibility everyone shares for that ultimate severing of the bonds of common humanity – is perhaps the most powerful subtext in Lillian Hellman's works for the stage from *Children's Hour* through *Watch on the Rhine* and *Searching Wind* to *Montserrat*. To name the Other as guilty, for whatever difference, be it ethnic or religious or racial, to round up the innocent as sacrificial scapegoats to a society's own fears and inadequacies is, in Hellman's moral encomium, the great evil. And for an individual or society to be complicitous by "stand[ing] and watch[ing]" is not only politically irresponsible but morally reprehensible. As Hellman wrote, looking backward from the perspective of the 1960s, "the McCarthys came, will come again, and will be forgotten ... It is eccentric, I suppose, not to care much about the persecutors and to care so much about those who allowed the persecution, but it was as if I had been deprived of a child's belief in tribal safety. I was never again to believe in it and resent to this day that it has been taken from me" (*Pentimento*, 225).

NOTES

1 Jill Dolan, "'Lesbian' Subjectivity in Realism: Dragging at the Margins of Structure and Ideology," 46–47. See also Anne Fleche, "The Lesbian Rule: Lillian Hellman and the Measures of Realism"; Lynda Hart, "Canonizing Lesbians?"; and Mary Titus, "Murdering the Lesbian: Lillian Hellman's *The Children's Hour.*"

2 For a thorough discussion of the relevant theoretical issues, see chapter 1 of Patricia R. Schroeder's *The Feminist Possibilities of Dramatic Realism*, 15–43.

3 Katherine Lederer mentions Hellman's novelistic imagination and the Jamesian connection in *Lillian Hellman*, 35, 57. For a standard treatment of Hellman as a disciple of Ibsen, see Jacob H. Adler, *Lillian Hellman.*

9

MARGARET B. WILKERSON

From Harlem to Broadway: African American women playwrights at mid-century

World War II ended in 1945, ushering in a mid-century decade of major change in the world and especially in the United States. The flowering of African American literature, known as the Harlem Renaissance, had seemed to fade as writers tried to cope with the Great Depression and a World War forcing them to a new understanding of their place in the world. While the US labor force adjusted itself in order to accommodate returning soldiers, African American soldiers returned to ambivalence at home. Women were displaced from the wartime jobs that they had taken on the domestic front, but white, not black, veterans replaced them. Segregation and discrimination still prevailed in jobs, housing, and schools.

But the 1950s would herald a measure of "progress," however conflicted. In 1954, the Supreme Court declared separate schools inherently unequal, and the Interstate Commerce Commission banned segregation in interstate travel. Later, in 1957, Congress passed the first Civil Rights Act since 1875. The world and the country settled uneasily into the new phenomenon of a Cold War in an atomic age, while Senator Joe McCarthy continued his hunt for communists and homosexuals at home. The lifestyle of American families was changing rapidly as whites fled the cities and settled into new suburban housing developments, made affordable by the GI Bill and the adaptation of the assembly line to housing construction, while blacks were kept out to a large degree. As women returned to their kitchens, the pressure increased for them to conform to traditional family expectations – those of wife and mother.

Harlem was the center of black political and cultural life in the country, but unemployment was high as in all of black America, twice the rate of that among white Americans, a phenomenon that would continue throughout the rest of the century. In a world where the United States had assumed global leadership and was locked in an ideological struggle with the Soviet Union and its satellites in "undeclared wars," African American women playwrights found a great deal to write about, much like their forebears in the Harlem Renaissance. But the "Red Scare," the hunt for subversives at home led by Senator McCarthy, had a chilling effect as the House Un-American Activities Committee held hearings and provoked testimony, however specious, that ruined the careers of many artists. Nevertheless, the Left organizations provided the only forum where issues regarding equality of African Americans were discussed among "progressives," a loose coalition of Left to radical people and groups often labeled as "communist" or "communist-front" organizations. Despite the danger, prominent African Americans such as Paul Robeson (whose passport was revoked for his so-called "pro-communist" statements and activities), and W. E. B. Du Bois, continued to speak out and attracted to the Progressive Movement young African Americans of like mind. Two of the most important African American women playwrights of the 1950s and 1960s, Alice Childress and Lorraine Hansberry, were nurtured in this movement and mentored by Robeson and Du Bois.

Both Childress and Hansberry emigrated to New York from other parts of the country. Alice Childress was born in Charleston, South Carolina, in 1920, but moved to Harlem five years later, where she grew up and graduated from high school. Hansberry, born in 1930, came to Harlem from Chicago in 1949 after two abortive years at the University of Wisconsin at Madison, the first of her family to attend a predominantly white university. Both were largely self-educated in the intellectually challenging circles of the Progressive Movement. Both were hired in 1950 to write for Paul Robeson's newspaper, *Freedom*, a monthly publication that covered domestic and international news of interest to African American communities across the country. Childress wrote a column on Mildred, a no-nonsense domestic with the feistiness of Childress herself, and Hansberry worked as associate editor, helping to shape the content of the paper and editing many of the articles. Hansberry and Childress, Hansberry's elder by ten years, became good friends and fellow artists.

By the time that Hansberry arrived in New York, Childress was already an established actor with the original American Negro Theatre (ANT) in Harlem. She appeared in *On Strivers Row* in 1940 and *Natural Man* in 1941, and performed in the original cast of the American version of *Anna Lucasta* in 1944. During the life of this show, a number of black actors would appear at one time or another: Hilda Simms, Earle Hyman, Frederick O'Neal, Canada Lee, Ossie Davis, Ruby Dee, and Sidney Poitier. Childress wrote her first produced plays for the American Negro Theatre. She was a very active member of ANT, at various times serving as drama coach, director, personnel director, and member of the board of directors. A year later, she adapted *Just a Little Simple* from Langston Hughes' collection *Simple Speaks His Mind*, which was produced at the Club Baron Theatre in New York. In 1952, with the Committee on Negro Arts' production of *Gold Through the Trees*, Childress became the first African American woman to have an original play produced Off-Broadway.

The play was performed in celebration of the 200-year-old struggle for freedom by South African blacks (Hatch and Abudullah, *Black Playwrights*, 46). Through a series of dramatic sketches, this musical revue tells of slavery and resistance throughout the African diaspora, from Africa to the Haitian Revolution, the British West Indies, and the United States. Hansberry reviewed the show in *Freedom*: "Alice Childress seems to know more about language and drama than most people who write for the theatre today, and the result is that . . . 'Gold Through the Trees' is probably the most worthwhile and entertaining show currently running in New York" (Hansberry, "CNA," 7).

Like African American women playwrights who preceded her, Childress was devoted to the authentic portrayal of black life, but as a Harlem resident of the 1950s, her stories carried an urban edge sharpened by the disappointments of blacks in postwar America. Her leftist politics were tempered by the humanity of her characters and their insistence on being treated with dignity. Because Childress was a single parent and had to work to support herself and her young daughter, Jean, she knew the difficulties faced by a working woman of color. Her many and varied jobs – salesperson, assistant machinist, insurance agent, and domestic worker – brought her a range of experience and contact with a variety of working-class people, some of whom found their way into her drama and fiction. Childress' primary focus was writing, particularly plays in the early years of her career, although she took a variety of jobs to support herself and her daughter. She learned and practiced her playwriting skills with the American Negro Theatre, studying for eight years with ANT teachers, performing in and observing the plays that the group produced. Her plays gave voice to black working-class women of the times. Florence, in Childress' play of the same name, eloquently defends her daughter's choice to pursue a career in acting, against the doubts and ridicule of a white, privileged woman whom she meets in a train station. Despite the economic pitfalls and the low status of her mother, who works as a domestic, Florence claims for her daughter the right and the talent to pursue her dream. This assertion in the midst of visible discrimination, a Jim Crow waiting room, and a social context of presumed inferiority, is typical of Childress' female characters and preceded others who were as independent and self-assured.

Angry at the arbitrary limitations placed on black actors, Childress extended the theme initiated with *Florence* to an insightful, provocative play on the problems of being a black actor in the theatre of white America. *Trouble in Mind* opened at the Greenwich Mews Theatre in New York on November 4, 1955 (Hatch and Abudullah, *Black Playwrights*, 47). A cast of black actors working with a white director experience all of the indignities, subtle and otherwise, known to people in the business. Wiletta Mayer, the aging actor and main character in the play, questions the subservience of her character to white supremacy implicit in the script. This and other disagreements with the director build to a climax as Wiletta tries to rally the cast to insist on changes that affirm the dignity of the race. But she loses her fight as the actors choose bread over principle. The play was a hit in Off-Broadway circles, and the rights to produce the play were sold to a Broadway producer, but it was abandoned after two years as too risky for commercial theatre. The play has been published with two different endings, one more palatable for white audiences, but Childress eventually withdrew this version, refusing to capitulate to Broadway's monied interests. This play would not be the last of her works to just miss Broadway production; however, it won an Obie award for best original Off-Broadway play of the year, making Childress the first black woman to be so honored (Brown-Guillory, *Wines in the Wilderness*, 99).

Childress was successful in having her book, *Like One of the Family: Conversations from a Domestic's Life*, published in 1956. The conversations were taken from the sketches which had appeared in *Freedom* and which continued in the *Baltimore Afro-American* in the column "Here's Mildred." Childress' Mildred is often compared to Jesse B. Simple, a character created by Langston Hughes, whose humorous commentary on black life was very popular in the *Chicago Defender* and was subsequently published in a series of books on Simple. Simple's sometimes biting humor/satire is often tempered by a straight man, Boyd, while Childress' Mildred, both in form and statement, takes a more confrontational stance. When her column on Mildred ended in 1958, Childress began to focus primarily on writing plays during the next decade.

Meanwhile, Lorraine Hansberry had settled into her new life in New York City, seeking "an education of a different kind," one that was filled with intellectual challenge in a context of political activism (Hansberry, *Young, Gifted*, 93). During her earlier years in Chicago, she had benefited from her family's middle-class status and a social life that brought major cultural and political figures to her family's dinner table. Her uncle, William Leo Hansberry, who was professor of African history at Howard University and contact person for exchange students from Africa, introduced her to young people from the African continent. Despite these opportunities, Hansberry knew the sting and danger of racism. A brick thrown by an angry mob protesting her family's move into an all-white neighborhood narrowly missed the eight-year-old Lorraine. Chicago was one of the nation's most segregated northern cities, the races kept apart by restrictive covenants that prevented blacks from buying homes in white neighborhoods. Carl Hansberry, Lorraine's father, used his knowledge and status as a real estate broker to open up marginal neighborhoods for the growing black population in Chicago, and fought a case challenging restrictive covenants all the way to the Supreme Court, where he won a limited ruling. He earned the name of "kitchenette king" for converting these large houses into apartments for multiple families. Hansberry would later use this setting in her first major play.

Hansberry came to know and admire working-class blacks through her father's tenants and her peers in public school. She was drawn to their independence and assertiveness, especially in the face of white arrogance. Breaking with her family's tradition of attending southern black colleges, she chose the University of Wisconsin at Madison, a predominantly white institution, where she integrated her dormitory, becoming the first black student to live there, and became politically active. She worked in the Henry Wallace presidential campaign and in the activities of the Young Progressive League, becoming president of the organization in 1949 during her last semester there. Perhaps the most important influence of the university was its effect on her artistic sensibilities. There she was deeply moved by a production of Sean O'Casey's *Juno and the Paycock*, a work that universalized human suffering. Later she wrote of the play: "The melody was one that I had known for a very long while. I was seventeen and I did not think then of writing the melody as I knew it – in a different key; but I believe it entered my consciousness and stayed there" (Hansberry, *Young, Gifted*, 87).

She moved to New York, where she would be surrounded with the rich and progressive social, political, and cultural life of Harlem and where she would be stimulated to begin writing short stories, poetry, and plays. Hansberry honed her writing skills as a journalist and essayist, working on *Freedom*, Robeson's newspaper, *New Challenge*, and other Left publications. Her experience with *Freedom* would have a lifelong effect on her thinking and writing. In addition to her avid reading of a variety of books and articles, the newspaper's focus on international as well as domestic affairs further educated Hansberry on the complex matters of the world that impacted on African Americans. Robeson and Du Bois (from whom she took a seminar on Africa and who frequently contributed to *Freedom*) understood that connection and involved Hansberry in reporting on developments in Africa, the Caribbean, and the United States. But Hansberry quickly discovered that the journalist's strict adherence to the facts was too limiting because it did not allow her to get at larger truths revealed through the imagination. So she began writing plays, as well as pageants and short sketches, for various demonstrations and to celebrate one of *Freedom*'s anniversaries. Most of these works focused on racial oppression, but on occasion, a strong female character would break through.

In 1953, Hansberry's ideas about women would be strongly influenced by a book from France, Simone de Beauvoir's *The Second Sex*. This work by the French existentialist partner of Jean-Paul Sartre would become Hansberry's reference book on the oppression of women throughout the world's cultures. She would later write in a commentary on *The Second Sex* that it was probably the most important book of the twentieth century (Hansberry, "Simone de Beauvoir," 129). In the same year, she married Robert Nemiroff, a young man of Jewish heritage who was in graduate studies at New York University, and who was also deeply involved in progressive demonstrations and other activities. Although they separated after a few years and divorced in 1964, they maintained a friendship and artistic relationship throughout the years. Stimulated by de Beauvoir's powerful work and her own experience, Hansberry wrote letters to lesbian and gay publications condemning homophobia, even as she attacked the oppression of blacks and the dangers of a nuclear age, and emphasized the need for activist intellectuals.

After her marriage, Hansberry moved to Greenwich Village, a haven for New York artists and intellectuals, and began working on several plays while taking a series of jobs including typist, tagger in the garment industry, program director at Camp Unity (a progressive, interracial summer program), teacher at the Marxist-oriented Jefferson School for Social Science, and recreation leader for the handicapped. But a sudden change in fortune made it possible for her to devote herself full time to her writing. Nemiroff and his friend Burt d'Lugoff wrote a folk ballad, "Cindy Oh Cindy," which became a hit and brought in enough money for Hansberry to quit part-time work (Carter, "Lorraine Hansberry," 123). She had found little support for her writing projects on women's oppression from her husband and friends, and, her concerns for the oppression of blacks fueled by the 1955 lynching of Emmett Till in the face of the 1954 Supreme Court decision against segregated schools, Hansberry began a project initially entitled *The Crystal Stair*. It was named for Langston Hughes' poem about the sacrifices of black mothers in order to advance the opportunities for their children. With the Civil Rights Movement heating up and non-violent demonstrations in the South over segregated lunch counters and schools, the nation's appetite was whetted for this play, which would eventually become *A Raisin in the Sun*.

Drawing from her knowledge of working-class black families who rented her father's apartments and with whose children she attended school, Hansberry crafted a realistic play that eloquently explored a theme from another Langston Hughes poem, "Harlem" (from *Montage of a Dream Deferred*), which asks: "What happens to a dream deferred? Does it dry up like a raisin in the sun? ... Or does it explode?" After hearing the play read, Phil Rose, a friend who had employed Nemiroff in his music publishing firm, decided to option the play for Broadway production. Although he had never produced a Broadway play before, Rose and co-producer David S. Cogan set forth enthusiastically with their fellow novices on this new venture. However, they found that the "smart money" considered a play about black life too risky a commercial venture. The only producer expressing interest required cast and directorial choices unacceptable to Hansberry, so the group raised cash through other means and took the show on tour without the guarantee of a Broadway house. Its success with audiences in New Haven, Connecticut, and Chicago, along with a last-minute rush for tickets in Philadelphia, finally made the case for acquiring a Broadway theatre.

A Raisin in the Sun opened at the Ethel Barrymore Theatre on March 11, 1959, and was an instant success with both critics and audiences. Set on Chicago's South Side in the 1950s, *A Raisin in the Sun* reveals the private life of a working-class black family in all its frustrations, humor, and pathos. Three generations of the Younger family live in a crowded kitchen-ette apartment: Lena Younger, who receives a $10,000 death benefit due to the recent death of her husband; Walter Lee, her son, who is frustrated with his chauffeur job and wants to advance his own and his family's economic fortunes by using the money to invest in a liquor store; Ruth, his faithful wife, who receives the brunt of Walter's anger and who faces the dilemma of pregnancy and a husband who is ambivalent about her condition; Beneatha, Lena's daughter and Walter's sister, who aspires to be a doctor; and Travis, Walter's son, whose future is the concern of everyone in the family. When Lena decides to place a down payment on a house in the belief that the family's struggles will be somewhat alleviated by living in a house that they own, the conflicting values of Walter and his mother come to a head. However, when Lena realizes how her decision has devastated her son's dreams, she gives him the balance of the money – a portion to be set aside for Beneatha's college education and the rest to be used by Walter as he wishes. Walter "invests" the money with a supposed "business partner" who steals it, leaving Walter to face his incredulous, devastated

8. Scene from *A Raisin in the Sun* by Lorraine Hansberry

family. Proving herself a master of American realism, Hansberry deftly uses this narrative to contrast the materialism of the American dream with its humanistic alternative. Lena speaks of her generation's victories over segregation, while Walter argues that the power of money is more important. How the family overcomes this tragedy through its own resilience and determination in the face of seeming defeat makes *A Raisin in the Sun* a remarkable expression of the human will to survive.

Walter Kerr, premier Broadway critic, wrote that Hansberry read "the precise temperature of a race at that time in its history when it cannot retreat and cannot quite find the way to move forward. The mood is forty-nine parts anger and forty-nine parts control, with a very narrow escape hatch for the steam these abrasive contraries build up. Three generations stand poised, and crowded, on a detonating-cap" (Kerr, "No Clear Path,"

1–2). Through the character of Beneatha, Hansberry introduces several firsts to the Broadway stage. Beneatha, attempting to identify with an African homeland and smitten with a young African intellectual, Asagai, dons native garb and wears her hair natural or unpressed. The Broadway production, however, wrapped her head in cloth because her haircut "was not properly contoured to suit" her features (Nemiroff, "Notes," xvi). Asagai became the first literate and un-stereotyped African character on the Broadway stage, and connected the struggle of African Americans and Lena's revolutionary ideals to that of their cohorts in emerging African nations. Hansberry also introduces class conflict into the play through another of Beneatha's suitors, George Murchison, who comes from a wealthy family and whose bourgeois values Beneatha cannot tolerate. The critics, however, did not comment on these nuances.

Overnight, Hansberry acquired the celebrity status that had eluded other African American women before her, but which at the same time was built on their courage and insights as well as her own talent. The play won the New York Drama Critics Circle Award in 1959, against such established playwrights as Eugene O'Neill and Tennessee Williams. Hansberry became the first black playwright, the youngest person, and the fifth woman to win that award. The original production boasted an outstanding cast composed of names now well known in American theatre and television: Sidney Poitier, already a film star at the time of the Broadway production, Ruby Dee, Claudia McNeil, Diana Sands, Lou Gossett, Jr., Glynn Turman, Ivan Dixon, and Ossie Davis, who later replaced Poitier.

During the next year, Hansberry would spend much of her time enjoying her new-found fame, using it to speak out for black civil rights. Then, in 1960, she was commissioned to write a television play on slavery as the opening segment for a television series commemorating the Civil War. After thorough research, Hansberry wrote *The Drinking Gourd*, a provocative television play that focused on slavery's effects on three classes of people – white master, black slave, and overseer recruited from among poor whites. This class analysis, which showed slavery as less a peculiar institution than an economic system out of control that brutalized all whom it touched, proved too controversial for NBC television executives. The play was shelved along with the entire project.

A Raisin in the Sun, however, was brought to mass audiences in 1961 by Columbia Pictures, which produced it as a film based on the screenplay written by Hansberry. Although Hansberry sharpened the play's attack on the effects of segregation and revealed with a surer hand the growing militant mood of black America, these additional scenes were edited out of the film and have yet to be produced. The original cast, with the exception of one, was used in the film.

James Baldwin wrote of Hansberry's play that the truths of black life had never been portrayed so authentically on the American stage. His sentiment was reflected in the generations of black artists who were inspired by her accomplishment and who would pursue a life in the theatre or in film because of her work. The play's extended success made Hansberry a much sought after public figure and popular speaker at a variety of conferences and meetings. One of her most notable speeches was delivered to a black writers' conference sponsored by the American Society of African Culture in New York. Written two weeks before the Broadway opening, "The Negro Writer and His Roots" is Hansberry's credo. "All art is ultimately social" (5), she declared, and challenged black writers throughout the world to be involved in "the intellectual affairs of all men, everywhere" (3). As the civil rights movement intensified during the early years of the 1960s, Hansberry made significant monetary contributions to the Student Non-violent Coordinating Committee (SNCC), a group of young people risking their lives on the front lines in southern states, and helped to plan fundraising events to support such organizations. Angry with the Red-baiting tactics of the House Un-American Activities Committee, she called for its abolition, and criticized President John F. Kennedy for bringing the world to the brink of nuclear war by his handling of the Cuban Missile Crisis.

As welcome as these opportunities for advocacy were for Hansberry, she longed for the time to continue other important writing projects. So she moved to Croton in upstate New York in 1962 in order to recapture her privacy. The previous year she had begun working on several plays, including a favorite project, an adaptation of *Masters of the Dew*, based on the novel by Haitian Jacques Romain. She had been asked to write the screenplay by a film company, but contractual disputes shelved the project after she had completed the screenplay. She also began working on a play that reflected her experiences living in Greenwich Village. *The Sign in Sidney Brustein's Window* would be her next and last play to be seen on Broadway during her lifetime.

In April 1963, Hansberry began to experience health problems. She was diagnosed with cancer of the pancreas and faced progressive decline in her condition. Nevertheless, she continued to work on *Sign* and to engage in political activities. Her writing schedule during the last years of her life included *Les Blancs*, a play warning that time for the liberation of black people in Africa was running out; *Laughing Boy*, a musical adaptation of the novel of the same title; *The Marrow of Tradition*, based on the novel,

Mary Wollstonecraft, on an early fighter for women's rights; and *Achnaton*, a play about the Egyptian pharaoh. Frequently hospitalized during this period, she nevertheless completed an essay for *The Movement: Documentary of a Struggle for Equality*, a photographic book on the civil rights struggle.

October 15, 1964, saw the opening of *The Sign in Sidney Brustein's Window*, a play that was based on the eviction of a young woman photographer in Greenwich Village for placing in her apartment window a sign that supported a political candidate challenging the *status quo*. In the play, the protagonist became a Jewish male, who almost capitulates to an ineffectual intellectualism unwilling to fight against graft, corruption, and other social wrongs. The play opened to mixed reviews (Nemiroff, "101," 148–53). Critics were surprised that this young spokesperson for the civil rights movement would write a play that did not place black concerns at its center and that contained only one black character – in a supporting role, no less. Some blacks felt betrayal that she had not written another play that portrayed black life and that offered employment in a racist theatre system where opportunities were few. But Hansberry, pursuing an artistic activism not limited by color, called intellectuals to get involved in social problems and world issues. A group of theatre artists, including Viveca Lindfors, Paddy Chayefsky, Sammy Davis, Jr., Anne Bancroft, and Mel Brooks, raised money to keep the show open, but it closed after 101 performances.

On January 12, 1965, the night that the play closed, Hansberry died at the age of thirty-four, cutting short a promising career in American theatre. However, her legacy would continue to build as her former husband and literary executor, Robert Nemiroff, whom she divorced a year before she died, devoted the rest of his life to promoting her name and her work. Despite the brevity of her life, Hansberry made a significant contribution to American theatre. *A Raisin in the Sun*, more than simply a "first," was the turning point for many black artists in the professional theatre. The continued timeliness and craft of the play have made it one of the most popular plays in America and one of the most frequently produced. In this and all of her plays, Hansberry consciously counters the drama of despair, affirming humanity's potential to transcend its brutality, and advocating its will to overcome.

Hansberry's influence would continue for many years in various forms. Her award-winning play would be produced on virtually every continent on the globe. Her creation, Walter Lee Younger, would affect subsequent portrayals of black males on the American stage. Audiences had not seen the restlessness and frustration of a black male such as Walter. Usually, such characters crossed the line into criminal behavior and could be dismissed as victims of their own or society's problems. But Walter is different. He makes a stupid error, but lives through it, reclaiming his dignity and his status in the family. Walter becomes the theatrical father of a number of black male characters who stride the boards in the 1960s, products of the militant Black Arts Movement, which carved out a more visibly activist role for theatre. Viewed as the cultural arm of the Black Nationalist Movement and the child, sometimes considered a wayward child, of the civil rights movement, the Black Arts Movement sought to define a black aesthetic which promoted the beauty of all things black. A heavily male-dominated movement, it offered limited roles for women in organizing as well as cultural portrayals. Alice Childress and Adrienne Kennedy would be strong voices in this changed context as would some of Hansberry's plays that were produced posthumously.

Alice Childress outlived her friend, Lorraine Hansberry, by many years and gave the 1960s theatre two important works that broke new ground in the discourse on racial matters. True to her determination to speak her mind regardless of the consequences, Childress wrote a play on interracial love between a black woman and a white man entitled *Wedding Band*, first produced in December 1966, at the University of Michigan in Ann Arbor. Subtitled *A Love/Hate Story in Black and White*, this play goes against the tradition in American theatre and literature of portraying such relationships as exotic, in sentimental, romantic stories in which at least one partner has considerable wealth. Set against the backdrop of South Carolina in 1918 just after World War I, the play begins at the ten-year anniversary of Julia's and Herman's love affair. Julia is a seamstress who has moved frequently from one depressed black area to another because of her relationship with Herman. Herman, a baker, is a man of very modest means. He brings Julia a wedding band (ring) to celebrate their years together and a cake, a gesture that emphasizes the clandestine nature of this relationship that is endorsed by none of their friends, family, or neighbors. And their love cannot be legally sanctioned because of South Carolina's prohibition against marriage between black and white.

The couple fantasize about running away to New York, but Herman's meager income and his declining health make it an impossible dream. Childress shapes these ordinary characters whose only distinction is their love across color lines and thereby emphasizes the ludicrousness of the racial baggage that we carry. In one of the play's dramatic moments, Herman and Julia berate each other, speaking simultaneously, and re-counting the pain of their racial experience. Neither actually listens to the other in this moment of utter frustration. The attitudes of many in the audience were reflected in the ambivalent impotence of Herman's sister and the dogmatic racism of Herman's mother, who comes to Julia's humble quarters in a black neighborhood to reclaim her son. Julia's black neighbors, while less caustic in their statements, still register their displeasure that she is involved with a white man, a figure whom experience has taught them to view only as exploiter. Again as with *Trouble in Mind*, this play by Childress was optioned for Broadway and held for a three-year period before being dropped from consideration. It was not until 1972 that the play was given a major production by Joseph Papp at the New York Shakespeare Festival. Lacking the sensationalism of most plays and films that address this subject, *Wedding Band* would wait until 1973 for a television production.

Several years after critiquing black and white attitudes toward interracial relationships, Childress would close out the 1960s by writing *Wine in the Wilderness*, a play that was commissioned by public television station WGBH in Boston, Massachusetts, for its series "On Being Black," and aired in 1969. A very popular play in schools and community theatres, *Wine in the Wilderness* critiques narrow definitions of the 1960s slogan, "black is beautiful." The play is set in the midst of a riot in the studio apartment of Bill, a painter, who is creating a triptych, a three-paneled picture entitled "Wine in the Wilderness." Each panel portrays an aspect of black womanhood: the first painting is of a "charming little girl in Sunday dress and hair ribbons"; the second is of a beautiful, idealized woman draped in African garb. The final panel remains empty because Bill is searching for the woman who is "unattractive" enough to symbolize "the lost woman ... what the society has made out of our women. She's as far from my African queen as a woman can get and still be female ... She's ignorant, unfeminine, coarse, rude ... vulgar ... a poor, dumb chick that's had her behind kicked until it's numb" (*Wine*, 126). Bill's middle-class friends bring him Tommy, a woman victimized by the riot outside, to be the model for the last panel, but during the course of the play, Tommy's ugliness and seeming ignorance turn into beauty and intelligence, as her true nature is revealed. Childress vests in Tommy knowledge about black history and culture that Bill and his friends, with all of their education (mostly an education of self-hatred, the play reveals) cannot match. In many ways, this play questions the preeminence of male attitudes. Although several women were prominent in the Black Arts Movement, their plays fit more comfortably within the prevailing ideology. Nevertheless, plays by Sonia Sanchez, Mari Evans, and Val Ferdinand captured the activism of black women as poets and artists in the effort to end second-class citizenship for black people. Childress' powerful and effective play, however, reminds the audience of the pervasiveness of white male attitudes in the formation of black ideologies.

During the 1960s, Childress also participated in a number of public forums, including a BBC panel discussion on "The Negro in the American Theatre," which included LeRoi Jones, Langston Hughes, and James Baldwin, all prominent writers of the time. In these presentations and discussions, she continued to speak candidly about poor and working-class people with a special focus on black life. Other black women such as Hazel Bryant of the Richard Allen Center, Vinette Carroll of the Urban Arts Corps, Rosetta Lenoire of Amas Repertory Theatre, Vivian Robinson of the Audience Development Committee (AUDELCO), Barbara Ann Teer of the National Black Theatre, Joan Sandler of the Black Theatre Alliance, and Val Gray Ward of Kuumba Theatre in Chicago, contributed to the development of black women playwrights by establishing and directing artistic organizations that supported and produced new work.

In this decade, Adrienne Kennedy, another African American woman playwright, came into prominence, reaching a somewhat different audience and approaching the development of plays from a more personal perspective. Although Adrienne Kennedy was only one year younger than Lorraine Hansberry, the first major production of one of her plays took place three years after *A Raisin in the Sun*. Born in 1931 in a comfortable, middle-class community in Cleveland, Ohio, Kennedy gave little indication of the intense, violent images that would become common to her plays. She grew up in an integrated neighborhood enjoying the rich cultural activities of Italians, blacks, Jews, Poles, and others. This supportive environment gave her confidence in the potential of racial harmony, despite important cultural differences. However, when she attended Ohio State University, a predominantly white institution, she was ill prepared for the racial hostility that she found there. White students kept themselves separate from other cultural groups, and most of the restaurants in Columbus, Ohio, where the university was located, were segregated. Like Hansberry, Kennedy chose a different educational path from her parents, who had attended historically black colleges.

Upon graduation, Kennedy married Joseph C. Kennedy, who was drafted and sent to Korea within a few months. Pregnant, she returned home to live with her parents until her husband's return. The loneliness of being a bride with a husband fighting in a dangerous war drove Kennedy to creative pursuits; she wrote her first plays, one based on a play by Elmer Rice, and another inspired by Tennessee Williams' *Glass Menagerie*. When her husband returned, he decided to pursue graduate studies at Columbia Teachers College and moved with his wife and their son to New York City.

Adrienne Kennedy used this opportunity to study creative writing and to develop her writing skills at Columbia University, the American Theatre Wing, and Circle-in-the-Square School with Edward Albee, one of American theatre's most prominent playwrights, during 1954 to 1962.

Funnyhouse of a Negro is Kennedy's best-known and among her longest plays (forty-five minutes playing time). Produced in 1962 by Circle-in-the-Square Theatre, this play established Kennedy as a poet of the theatre who uses surrealistic fantasy and sharply dense language to express the impact of the black and American experience on individual sensibilities. The self is the primary subject for Kennedy. Viewing writing as "an outlet for inner, psychological confusion and questions stemming from childhood," she uses this medium of expression as a way to figure out "the 'why' of things" (Wilkerson, "Adrienne Kennedy," 164). Kennedy writes from the inside out, basing her plays in personal autobiography. Like both Hansberry and Childress, she insists on candid, honest portrayal of her material, much of which comes from the subconscious. Arguing that the intellect is an imitation of oneself, she fights what she believes to be its censoring effect. The world of the subconscious that she reveals is terrifying, violent, and controversial as her characters live in multiple levels of consciousness and in political contexts that challenge our sense of our own conscious existence. Kennedy's language is rhythmic, intentionally repetitious, and filled with metaphors, images, and symbols. The theatre produced by her plays is intense and unique.

The inspiration for *Funnyhouse of a Negro* came during an extended trip that Kennedy took with her husband through Europe and Africa. A turning point in her life, this trip exposed her to the colonialist power of Europe epitomized by the mammoth statue of Queen Victoria that she saw in front of Buckingham Palace in London, and the effects of colonialism in Ghana, which she remembered as a place of immense beauty and ambiguity, through images of horses running on the beach and cloth imported from Holland bearing the face of Kwame Nkrumah, Ghana's premier. During her visit abroad, Patrice Lumumba, the first premier of the Republic of the Congo, was murdered. She began writing the play in West Africa, completing it in Rome while carrying her second son. The strong images from Africa and Europe gave her a new and powerful voice that had not been elicited by the works of Rice and Williams (Wilkerson, "Adrienne Kennedy," 165).

Funnyhouse of a Negro focuses on the identity crisis and confusion of Sarah, a sensitive young Negro woman, whose internal conflict is personified by various selves: a balding Queen Victoria and the Duchess of Hapsburg, who symbolize the colonial power of Europe and fear the return of the black father/husband; Patrice Lumumba/father/husband who resists the call to save his race; and an impotent Jesus Christ haunted by his inability to escape his blackness. The ambiguities and burdens of being black build in Sarah's subconscious until she commits suicide – or appears to; the act reported by her Jewish boyfriend Raymond may be yet another illusion of the mind. The play takes its title from the funnyhouse of an amusement park in Cleveland featuring two huge white figures perched on either side of a maze of mirrors, laughing hysterically at the confused patrons within.

The play is replete with oppositional symbols, such as black ravens and white doves, which reinforce Sarah's dilemma. Kennedy uses a character near the beginning of the play to confess that there is no plot:

> There is no theme. No statements. I might borrow a statement, struggle to fabricate a theme, borrow one from my contemporaries, renew one from the master, hawkishly scan other stories searching for statements, consider the theme then deceive myself that I held such a statement within me, refusing to accept the fact that a statement has to come from an ordered force. I might try to join horizontal elements such as dots on a horizontal line, or create a centrifugal force, or create causes and effects so that they would equal a quantity but it would be a lie. For the statement is the characters and the characters are myself. (*Funnyhouse of a Negro*, 195)

Ironically, this irrational premise produces a very coherent work of art. Kennedy's characters in this play have a double edge. Their stories are drawn from close family and friends, but they are transformed into metaphors for the ambiguous state of a people created out of the clash between African and European cultures.

Edward Albee, the prominent playwright to whom Kennedy submitted the play, believed in Kennedy's approach and work, even though the first production in the workshop at Circle-in-the-Square was received with mixed reactions. He optioned the play and two years later in 1964 opened the show at the East End Theatre in New York's Off-Broadway season. The play quickly became the cult play for theatrical circles, enjoying great success, until LeRoi Jones' *Dutchman* opened that same year. *Funnyhouse of a Negro* ran for forty-six performances, and won a 1964 Obie for distinguished plays along with works by Samuel Beckett, Edward Albee, and other better known playwrights. Like *A Raisin in the Sun*, this play had cross-over appeal for white audiences while attracting some black audiences, but was clearly not for those who were wedded to realistic portrayals on the stage. Howard Taubman of the *New York Times* along with other critics praised the new and unusual work. He wrote that Kennedy explored "relatively unknown territory" and dug "unsparingly into Sarah's aching psyche – and by extension into the tortured mind of a Negro who cannot bear the burden of being a Negro and who is too proud to accept the patronage of the white world." She reflects, he added, "what it is to be a sensitive Negro" (Wilkerson, "Adrienne Kennedy," 166). Like Childress' *Wine in the Wilderness*, this play exposed negative aspects of being black and critiqued the idea of the resilience of black individuals to overcome all odds.

In *Funnyhouse of a Negro*, Adrienne Kennedy found her theatrical voice. Six additional plays were completed in less than one year from the production of this first work. Hailed by critics as a fresh, unique voice, seven of her plays were professionally produced between 1963 and 1969. In writing these plays, she would continue to employ the technique she had mastered in this play. In *The Owl Answers* (1963), a long-time favorite of hers, she created composite characters who change slowly back and forth into and out of themselves in place of the multiple selves of *Funnyhouse of a Negro*. This play explores the desperate attempts of Clara, the major figure, to resolve her ambivalent emotions about black and white, and to cope with the oppositional power of purity and carnality. Clara is a composite character drawn from Adrienne herself, her mother, and her aunt, whom she described as a beautiful and brilliant woman who felt that she did not belong anywhere. Again, historical characters appear as powerful figures of influence as Clara encounters her mythical forebears: William Shakespeare, William the Conqueror, Geoffrey Chaucer, and Anne Boleyn. Powerful animal symbols such as the owl reflect mythological forces.

The Owl Answers, produced with *The Beast* by Joseph Papp under the title *Cities in Bezique*, ran for sixty-seven performances at the New York Shakespeare Festival. Papp considered it to be the best-written play he had produced to date. Critical reception was somewhat mixed, although Kennedy's talent remained undisputed. Critics Clive Barnes and Walter Kerr, both of the *New York Times*, differed over the coherence of the two plays, Barnes finding the design more successful than Kerr. Riding the wave of success from *Funnyhouse of a Negro*, Kennedy adapted a short play, *The Lennon Play: In His Own Write*, from John Lennon's books of poems and nonsense stories. It was fully produced in 1968 in London at Sir Laurence Olivier's National Theatre on a triple bill with works by John Arden, Margaretta d'Arcy, and Tom Stoppard.

A Rat's Mass, her last major play to be produced during this period, was rooted in her brother's injuries in an automobile accident and subsequent death. It was produced Off-Broadway in 1969 at the La Mama Experimental Theatre, and Kennedy based the play on a dream that she had while on a train from Paris to Rome. In the dream she was pursued by red, bloodied rats. Haunted by that image for many years, she finally captured it in *A Rat's Mass*. Kennedy explained in a 1977 interview that she is not in much control of the images and their sources. In this case, her brother's death evoked a memory of their childhood days, when they played in the attic, and her fears of what might lie behind the closet door in that attic. In the play, the love that Brother and Sister Rat have for each other is juxtaposed to their previous adoration for Rosemary – the white and beautiful "descendant of the Pope and Julius Caesar and the Virgin Mary" (Wilkerson, "Adrienne Kennedy," 168). Catholic symbols clash with blood as an ambiguous representation of religious sacrament and guilt. Again, the New York reviewers did not fully understand the play. Clive Barnes wrote that "it has a heart where its mind ought to be – and that heart, while pumping, is too dim with blood to be articulate" (Wilkerson, "Adrienne Kennedy," 168). Nevertheless, Kennedy's works were produced frequently during this period even though the audience that appreciated her plays was limited.

Childress, Hansberry, and Kennedy created multiple and multilayered voices for black women in American theatre. All of them built on the traditions inherited from earlier years of the twentieth century of speaking the concerns of African American communities from the perspective of women. Both Childress and Hansberry were nurtured intellectually and artistically in Harlem's cultural organizations, and Kennedy came to New York to study the craft of playwriting. However, unlike their predecessors, they became the trail-blazers for black women's entry into the Off-Broadway and Broadway stage. Where several of Childress' works just missed Broadway productions, largely because of the conservative values of producers, Hansberry was fortunate enough to have new and independent producers who promoted her work. Even so, *A Raisin in the Sun* took an unusual route to Broadway, facing early on producers' reticence to back a play about black life. The success of her work not only inspired a generation of young writers of many colors, but opened the door for more candid and authentic portrayals of black experience in the public arena of the theatre. Adrienne Kennedy's work represents the most experimental of the many works produced by these writers. Her exploration of the interior reality of her own self and that of others that she knew required a non-realistic style that confused and alienated some audiences. Yet many found hers to be a refreshing and expressive style that was able to comprehend the irrationality and ambiguities that inform racial matters.

The works of these three outstanding playwrights continued into the next decades of the century. After Hansberry's death in 1965, her literary executor and former husband, Robert Nemiroff, produced *Les Blancs* on Broadway, and *A Raisin in the Sun* on television with restored scenes cut from the Broadway production, and toured nationally *To Be Young, Gifted and Black*, based on Hansberry's life and writings, later produced for television. He also released for publication a number of her essays. Other plays and writings in Hansberry's archives await release to the public and publication. Childress continued as a prolific writer, but began to concentrate on novels because the economic risks of theatre became intolerable and impossible to negotiate. A film, "A Hero Ain't Nothin' But A Sandwich" based on her novel of the same title, was released in 1974 and won the Jane Addams Honor Award for a novel for young adults, among many other awards. However, up to her death in 1994, she regarded herself primarily as a playwright who wrote about poor, but resilient heroines. Adrienne Kennedy has continued to write plays and in the 1990s enjoyed the production of several new works at the New York Shakespeare Theatre, under the direction of George C. Wolfe, an African American playwright and director. During these years, she also published a book, *People Who Led to My Plays*, which reveals more secrets of her complex works. These women moved, though not without difficulty, from the "Harlem" of their predecessors to Broadway, opening the way for numerous African American women to enrich the American theatre with their talent, skill, and wisdom.

3
NEW FEMINISTS

10

JANET BROWN

Feminist theory and contemporary drama

What is a feminist drama? At first glance, this question suggests a binary split: a play is or is not feminist, depending on its rhetorical or didactic intention or, in other words, on its politics. But just as the feminist movement itself has, in this century, repeatedly emerged as a political movement and then seemingly disappeared, diffusing into the mainstream of American thought, so has feminism in American drama. Playwriting, performance, and dramatic theory today offer a feminist political critique through the act of dramatic speech, of costume and visual image, of performance itself. Just as feminists of the sixties and seventies discovered that "the personal is political," so in the nineties, the political nature of all performance has emerged as a major theme.

In the twentieth century, drama that is feminist in intention has exhibited a commitment to telling the stories of silenced and marginalized women, celebrating women's community and sense of connection through group protagonists, and expressing the moral concerns and societal criticisms that arise from women's experience.[1] The eighties and nineties have built on this tradition and added a broadened spectrum of political concerns, a questioning of language and of visual images and icons, and a specific concern with performance itself as an expression of gender and racial identity.

Giving voice to silenced women

A primary goal of twentieth-century feminist thought has been to give voice to women, especially to those at the margins of society, both past and present. Carol Christ, in *Diving Deep and Surfacing: Women Writers on Spiritual Quest*, begins with the words: "Women's stories have not been told ... The expression of women's spiritual quest is integrally related to the telling of women's stories" (1). Historian Gerda Lerner, in *The Creation of Patriarchy*, traces women's absence from written history back to the emergence of written history itself, in ancient Mesopotamia. In a resonant analogy, she compares recorded history to a drama in which both men and women

> act out their assigned roles ... Neither of them "contributes" more or less to the whole; neither is marginal or dispensable. But ... Men have written the play, have directed the show, interpreted the meaning of the action ... Men punish, by ridicule, exclusion, or ostracism, any woman who assumes the right to interpret her own role or – worst of all sins – the right to rewrite the script. (12–13)

Advocating specifically for African American women, Bell Hooks writes, "To understand that finding a voice is an essential part of liberation struggle – for the oppressed, the exploited, a necessary starting place – a move in the direction of freedom, is important for those who stand in solidarity with us" (*Talking Back*, 18).

In response to this exclusion, feminist scholars have taken up what Annette Kolodny, in her now classic essay, "Dancing Through the Mine-field," defines as the feminist literary critic's first task: the return to circulation of lost works by women (144–67). The nineties have brought a sharpened sense of the centrality of this mission to the goals of feminism. A new perception of Virginia Woolf as a feminist, perhaps as the primordial feminist critic of modern times, has brought with it a reminder of her emphasis on what has *not* been written by women as well as what has. Ellen Bayuk Rosenman cites Woolf's description of the empty book shelves where women's books should be: "Although there is nothing here, that 'nothing' still has meaning, just as rests have meaning in a system of musical notation. This is another version of re-vision: to see blank space as its own kind of historical record, just as she sees potential artists in madwomen and witches" (*A Room of One's Own*, 40).

Today, scholars continue to uncover women's creations where past historians saw only blank space. In drama, this has meant a broader definition of the body of women's work, one that encompasses the closet drama and the community theatre. Margaret Ezell, for instance, directly contradicts Woolf's assumption that the history of women writing in English began in the eighteenth century with Aphra Behn, simply because Behn was a professional playwright whose work was paid. She observes that even the male canon of Behn's era includes aristocrats who would have scorned to write "professionally." Feminist literary scholarship, she argues, should include manuscripts circulated informally, religious works, and works written collaboratively by women: "If in our anthologies we no longer impose modern literary hierarchies on women authors in the past, we open up the possibility of a new concept of women's literature ... [then]

the canon of [sixteenth and seventeenth century] women's literature ... will no longer be silenced, but will speak with many voices" ("Myth," 591).

Alice Walker, in "In Search of Our Mothers' Gardens," builds her essay specifically on Woolf's advocacy of "writing back through our mothers," and of reading even their silences. As she evokes and mourns these silenced African American women, she also celebrates their creations: "Yet so many of the stories that I write, that we all write, are my mother's stories ... through years of listening to my mother's stories of her life, I have absorbed not only the stories themselves, but something of ... the urgency that involves the knowledge that her stories – like her life – must be recorded" (240). Clearly, her essay has offered a sense of legitimacy and entitlement to the present generation of African American playwrights such as Dr. Endesha Ida Mae Holland, who bases the second act of her largely autobiographical play, *From the Mississippi Delta*, on Walker's image of "our mothers' gardens."

Selwyn R. Cudjoe observes that the African Americans' rich tradition of autobiography, dating back to slave narratives, is rooted in their historic powerlessness to control their external circumstances ("Maya Angelou," 8). "The speech of the Afro-American, then, is accorded an unusually high degree of importance and acts as an arena where a sense of one's personal and social liberation can be realized" (9). Furthermore, these autobiographies are often intended as public gestures, performances expressing violation and denigration as an impersonal condition, with each individual's tale told and heard as representative of the group.

A new perception of the act of speech itself has emerged in the nineties: performance is perceived as a political gesture, not merely a psychological or spiritual one. All performance arises from and expresses the community; it is public and therefore political in nature, impacting the larger society, and it operates in circular fashion, reaching backward in time to give speech to silenced forebears, and extending into the future, nurturing the next generation. Rosenman notes that the last of these elements was specific to Woolf's initial notion: "The process is not one of linear influence but of circularity and mutuality. The modern writer is legitimized and affirmed by her foremother, and the foremother is resurrected by the modern writer, who confirms her potential and perhaps rediscovers her" (*A Room of One's Own*, 86).

The expressly public nature of theatre, Lynda Hart notes, makes it both the riskiest and most effective of literary genres for bringing the silenced to speech: "As a form, the drama is more public and social than the other literary arts. The theatre is the sphere most removed from the confines of domesticity, thus the woman who ventures to be heard in this space takes a greater risk than the woman poet or novelist, but it may also offer her greater potential for effecting social change" (*Making a Spectacle*, 2).

In the nineties, then, the bringing to speech of the silenced and oppressed continues to be a major theme of feminist drama. Indeed, the political nature of this act is reinforced now, while the definition of the silenced and oppressed community has broadened and grown.

Merged egos and group protagonists

The presentation of the group protagonist in feminist drama dates back at least to Susan Glaspell's *Trifles* in 1916 and extends through Lorraine Hansberry's 1959 *A Raisin in the Sun*, presenting itself in troubling fashion in the split and suffering egos of Adrienne Kennedy's works of the 1960s. With the emergence of the second wave of feminism in the sixties, the consciousness-raising group, loosely based on Marxist theory, emerged as a central political practice. As Nancy Hartsock wrote, "the PRACTICE of small-group consciousness raising, with its stress on examining and understanding experience and on connecting personal experience to the structures that define our lives, is the clearest example of the method basic to feminism" (Donovan, *Feminist Theory*, 85).

Radical feminist theatre groups of the sixties and seventies often emerged from a consciousness-raising process, turning to theatre as praxis, or modeling their companies after the egalitarian consciousness-raising group process. Undoubtedly, these feminists were influenced by other British and American radical theatre groups of the sixties and seventies who attempted in Brechtian style to break down the barrier between audience and performers, sometimes by ensemble performances in which the same actor played several roles.

The typical feminist theatre group in the US in the seventies was a non-professional operation presenting highly didactic performances, often comprising a series of sketches or monologues. Some groups performed only for women, while others sought to raise the consciousness of the larger community. Individual playwrights, sometimes working with a performing ensemble, began in the seventies and eighties consciously to create plays with a group protagonist. Playwright Honor Moore dubbed these "choral plays," and contributed to the genre herself,[2] as did Susan Griffin with her radio play, *Voices*, and Ntozake Shange in *For Colored Girls Who Have Considered Suicide/When the Rainbow is Enuf*, as well as in much of her later work.

While some of the earliest writing by feminist theatre groups would seem impossibly naive today, the group protagonist has gained impetus in the eighties and nineties, not only in drama by women, but in many forms of fiction written by both women and men. Toni Morrison's divided protagonists come immediately to mind, and feminist theorist Hélène Cixous has observed that "split egos" are common in characters in contemporary fiction by both male and female authors.[3]

Certainly, the continuing strength of this notion owes as much to the voicing of previously silenced and oppressed groups as it does to the political practices of the sixties. Writing in 1985, Anthony Barthelemy placed Hansberry's modern classic, *A Raisin in the Sun*, into a historical and political context to identify the play's feminist intention. When Walter Younger fails his family, his female relatives remain loyal both to him and to their dreams of betterment. When Walter adopts a role of pride and responsibility, they are happy to defer to him. "It may seem strange to say Hansberry's intentions were feminist ... But the play endorses patriarchy not at the expense of female strength or female governance. Manhood in *A Raisin in the Sun* is wholly compatible with feminism. Lena [his mother] does not surrender judgment to Walter simply because he is a man; she acquiesces because Walter is right" ("Mother," 779). The entire Younger family forms a collective protagonist, in other words, expressive of each member and supportive of all.

Bell Hooks calls for "[d]iscarding the notion that the self exists in opposition to an other" and maintains that she learned the power of the merged ego "from unschooled southern black folks. We learned that the self existed in relation, was dependent for its very being on the lives and experiences of everyone, the self not as signifier of one 'I' but the coming together of many 'I's, the self as embodying collective reality past and present, family and community" (*Talking Back*, 31).

Notice that Hooks does not limit this discovery to the dependence of African American *women* on one another. She does speak eloquently of the dialogue between unempowered black women as the root, authentic talk of her early life:

> Unlike the black male preacher whose speech was to be heard, who was to be listened to, whose words were to be remembered, the voices of black women – giving orders, making threats, fussing – could be tuned out ... [But] [d]ialogue – the sharing of speech and recognition – took place not between mother and child or mother and male authority figure but among black women.
> (*Talking Back*, 6)

Yet the whole community – including the black male preacher, excluding no one – consists of individuals relying on one another for psychic as well as physical survival.

One logical extension of this notion of the merged ego can be found in the one-woman performances of contemporary theatre. In very different ways, both Lily Tomlin and Anna Deavere Smith have successfully entered the mainstream with *tour-de-force* solo performances of a wide variety of characters. In *The Search for Signs of Intelligent Life in the Universe*, written by Tomlin's partner, Jane Wagner, Trudi, a bag lady, explains that "I ... got a hookup with humanity as a whole. Animals and plants too ... It's like somebody's using my brain to dial-switch through humanity" (21–23). This "dial-switching" forms the framework of the play, which alternates between scenes from the lives of all the people who flash through Trudi's brain, and Trudi herself, making humorous, philosophical observations. Anna Deavere Smith bases her performances on interviews she has conducted, usually around some crisis such as the riots that followed Rodney King's beating in LA. Her technique is based on a theory of acting she developed, which counters the standard acting technique of finding the character within the self of the actor: "I wanted to develop an alternative to the self-based technique, a technique that would begin with the other and come to the self" (*Fires*, xxvii).

This recognition of interdependence by feminists of the eighties and nineties does not reflect a mere historic swing of the pendulum between women's solidarity and inclusiveness across genders. Advances in the fields of biology, psychology and ethical development have led feminists toward an encompassing recognition both of women's distinct experience and of our essential, shared humanity.

In *Myths of Gender*, Anne Fausto-Sterling examines biological theories about the differences between men and women. Fausto-Sterling notes that the controversies she discusses have arisen because scientists are themselves cultural products, "their activities structured, often unconsciously, by the great social issues of the day." After discussion of supposed gender-based brain differences, research on testosterone's relationship to aggression, and the effects of PMS and menopause on women's emotional stability, among other subjects, she concludes, "Bodies, minds, and cultures interact in such complex and profound ways that we cannot strip them down and compare them separately ... Male and female babies may be born. But those complex, gender-loaded individuals we call men and women are produced" (270). Thus, she, with other feminist scholars, denies the argument that accepted scientific knowledge supports a biologically determined patriarchy.

Also among those scholars must be counted Nancy Chodorow and Carol Gilligan. Chodorow's observation in 1978 that "The basic feminine sense of self is connected to the world, the basic masculine sense of self is separate," forced a rethinking of received notions of the universality of children's psychological development (*Reproduction*, 169). Chodorow speculated that, because women are almost universally the primary parents in our society, "Mothers tend to experience their daughters as more like, and continuous with, themselves. Correspondingly, girls tend to remain part of the dyadic primary mother–child relationship itself ... From very early, then ... girls come to experience themselves as less differentiated than boys, as more continuous with and related to the external object-world" (166–67).

In 1982, building in part on Chodorow's work, Carol Gilligan challenged the notion of a homogeneous moral development in male and female children. Instead, she derived from interviews with boys and girls discussing the same moral dilemmas, two separate moral stances. Possibly because, as Chodorow described, girls feel a greater sense of connection with others, they tend initially to "judge themselves in terms of their ability to care," rather than in terms of obeying rules and respecting rights, as boys do (Gilligan, *Different Voice*, 17). While the moral development of men involves a progression from a narrow "rules" orientation to a more mature sense of responsibility and concern for others, women come to maturity by "questioning the stoicism of self-denial and replacing the illusion of innocence with an awareness of choice ... Then the notion of care expands from the paralyzing injunction not to hurt others to an injunction to act responsively toward self and others and thus to sustain connection" (149).

Gilligan's ideas were immediately challenged, not only by the academic old guard, but also by feminists disturbed at her apparent reinforcement of old stereotypes. Linda Kerber commented that Gilligan's focus on the "care voice" in women recalls the "romantic sentimentalism of old voices in the women's movement, with their notions of women as more peaceable than men" (Prose, "Confident at 11," 38).

Josephine Donovan, for instance, outlining American feminist theory, traces what she calls "cultural feminism" back to nineteenth-century writers like Charlotte Perkins Gilman, who envisioned a culture with a "matriarchal value system." Cultural feminists of that time argued that women's suffrage was needed to clean up the corrupt world of masculine politics. Writing in 1985, Donovan described a new cultural feminism, born of women's unique biological and historical experience, which is "based on a fundamental respect for the contingent order, for the environmental context, for the concrete, everyday world ... Such an epistemology provides the basis for an ethic that is non-imperialistic, that is life-affirming, and that reverences the concrete details of life" (*Feminist Theory*, 173). But is this morally superior stance innate to women, regardless of their life experiences? Kerber, noting that Gilligan's initial studies were done with a group of girls and women from a fairly narrow racial and economic stratum, raises the possibility that social and moral attitudes might have less to do with gender than with power. "Marginality is the real issue," Kerber commented. "Women become critics of society because they're on the fringes of society" (Prose, "Confident at 11," 38).

In this light, women, like men, are seen as morally responsible individuals who are influenced by their experience, but are not merely its passive victims. Playwrights like Caryl Churchill in *Top Girls* and Theresa Rebeck in *The Family of Mann* have begun to examine the choices and moral dilemmas presented to women who, as successful competitors in the business world, are at least partially in the subject position in their lives.

As women's thinking emerges into the public sphere, in theatre as in other arenas, it impacts on the thinking of men as well. Jean Bethke Elshtain observed in 1981, "If it is the case that women have a distinct moral language, as Carol Gilligan has argued, one which emphasizes concern for others, responsibility, care and obligation . . . then we must take care to preserve the sphere that makes such a morality of responsibility possible and extend its imperatives to men as well" (*Public Man*, 335).

Interestingly, there is some evidence that such an extension of feminist ethics into the mainstream is already in progress in the US today. Paul H. Ray, reporting on eight years of social research surveys, describes a shift toward what he calls an emerging "Integral Culture." This culture will synthesize the ideas of the two predominant US subcultures, traditionalism and modernism. While the standard bearers of the new culture are a minority, they number 24 percent of American adults, or about 44 million people. Found in all regions of the country, "Cultural Creatives," as he terms these standard bearers, have a male–female ratio of 40:60. Among their key values is feminism. "Much of the focus on women's issues in politics comes from them – including concerns about violence and abuse of women and children, desire to rebuild neighborhoods and community, desire to improve caring relationships and concern about family" (Ray, "Rise of Integral Culture," 18). Ray adds, "Compared to the rest of society, the bearers of Integral Culture have values that are more idealistic and spiritual, have more concern for relationships and psychological development, are more environmentally concerned, and are more open to creating a positive future" (13). Furthermore, "this new subculture is busily constructing a new approach to the world. It is synthesizing a new set of concepts for viewing the world: an ecological and spiritual worldview; a whole new literature of social concerns . . . and an elevation of the feminine to a new place in recent human history" (14). In other words, Ray's research suggests that what Donovan described in 1985 as the new cultural feminism is, indeed, entering the mainstream of American politics and culture.

While Gilligan's more recent work has expanded its racial and economic bounds, it has also tended to focus more descriptively on the moral development of girls alone. Meanwhile, Mary Pipher has popularized Chodorow's and Gilligan's theories in *Reviving Ophelia*, a best-selling application of feminist ideas to the practical problem of raising daughters in contemporary society. Presumably read by thousands of "Cultural Creative" parents in the mainstream of American society, Pipher's book concludes by confidently invoking the foremost names in feminism in urging the subject position for girls:

> Simone de Beauvoir would say that strength implies remaining the subject of one's life and resisting the cultural pressure to become the object of male experience ... Gloria Steinem calls it "healthy rebellion." Carol Gilligan refers to it as "speaking in one's own voice," and Bell Hooks calls it "talking back." Resistance means vigilance in protecting one's own spirit from the forces that would break it. (*Reviving Ophelia*, 264)

Pipher would certainly recognize and agree with the societal critique of the Cultural Creatives, who bemoan the failures of modernism and seek instead to use old ideas and technologies in new ways, to find new stories that adequately explain our world and how we fit into it. In feminist drama, this struggle to find new stories and new forms in which to tell these stories must necessarily be central.

Finding a feminist form

Since at least Virginia Woolf, who imagined a "female sentence," women writers have searched for authentic feminist forms, for a way of reclaiming the English language from patriarchal paradigms. In the eighties, feminist critics identified particular plot patterns and genres as recurrent in women's literature. Carol Christ described a pattern of social and spiritual quest in which a woman moves from an experience of self-hatred and victimization to an awakening to a mystical identification with nature or with a community of women, followed by a new naming of self and reality reflecting a spiritual wholeness. This pattern, Christ observes, is not often linear, but recurs in a spiral pattern instead. Elizabeth Abel also describes a spiraling plot pattern, as well as a preference for a group protagonist, in what she calls "fictions of female development" (Abel, Hirsch, and Lang-land, *Voyage*). And Rachel Blau DuPlessis notes that twentieth-century women's fiction often presents a female hero representing a community that resists "the ending in death and ... the ending in marriage [as] obligatory goals for the female protagonist" (*Writing*, 142). Regina Barreca maintains that "For women writers, recognition replaces resolution. Resolution of tensions, like unity or integration, should not be considered viable definitions ... for women writers because they are too reductive to deal with the non-closed nature of women's writings" (*Last Laughs*, 142).

But is this "non-closed," spiraling quality feminist or merely modernist? Haven't modern male authors at least as far back as Arthur Miller's *Death of A Salesman* also turned away from traditionally noble tragic heroes engaged in linear plots? It is true that both modernists and feminists have called for new stories, new paradigms that more adequately represent lived experience.

Cognitive researchers describe the process by which human beings interpret their experience as one of fitting this information into the available paradigms or interpretive stories. But as Joanne S. Frye points out, this process is interactional. In other words, human beings "are also able to modify the initial paradigm in response to discrepant information. In this way, the conventions of literary narrative *can* act as an enclosing grid, a set of constraining interpretive paradigms that foreclose women writers' access to new interpretations of experience; but through the subversive voices of those same women, new conventions can also develop in response to the presence of discordant information in the lives of women" (Frye, *Living Stories*, 32). In other words, by subverting the forms and language of the patriarchy, feminist authors can begin to alter the interpretive paradigms themselves.

In contemporary drama, Suzan-Lori Parks offers one of the most striking examples of such subversion with her creation of an original dramaturgical technique that she calls "repetition and revision" or "rep and rev." Parks describes this technique as based on the principles of jazz:

> "In such pieces we are not moving from A–B but rather, for example, from A–A–A–B–A. Through such movement, we refigure A. And if we wish to call the movement FORWARD PROGRESSION, which I think it is, then we refigure the concept of forward progression." Parks says elsewhere that this is "what jazz musicians have been doing ... for years. They call it repetition and revision."
>
> (Rayner and Elam, "Unfinished Business," 44)

Critics Alice Rayner and Harry Elam observe that repetition and revision are critical to works such as *The Death of the Last Black Man in the Whole Entire World* (1990), a ritualistic funeral for the title character, who cannot rest in peace, struggling instead to reconcile the history of African American experience. "Parks refigures narrative history in a vertical spiral rather than a horizontal line. She demonstrates the ways in which the personal and political intersect such that so-called past events inhabit and haunt the present" (450). While Parks abandons traditional linearity, she plays constantly and savagely upon clichés and stereotypes, naming her central characters Black Man with Watermelon and Black Woman With Fried Drumstick, for instance. In so doing, she engages with and ultimately subverts traditional theatrical representations of African American women and men.

Such parodic subversion of dramatic conventions has become a predominant feminist technique of the nineties. Lynda Hart introduces a collection of essays on contemporary women's theatre with the words:

> By appropriating certain dramatic conventions and methods, subverting their customary usage and turning the lens of "objectivity" to re-present women through their own looking glasses, the women playwrights discussed in this book and the authors who call attention to their disruptions are canceling and deforming the structures that have held women framed, stilled, embedded, revoking the forms that have misrepresented women and killed them into art.
>
> (*Making a Spectacle*, 3)

Anita Plath Helle observes that this subversive power is especially striking in theatre, where live human behavior is the very medium of communication. Considering plays that present women authors, such as Susan Glaspell's *Alison's House* (on Emily Dickinson) and Edna O'Brien's *Virginia, A Play* (on Virginia Woolf), she states:

> The materiality of the stage offers unique opportunities for breaking out of the textual construct and context of masculine authority in two ways ... [First,] what women say and do onstage may ... contradict, exceed, or otherwise mark off a space of difference between the static symbolic construct, "women," and "women" as historical subjects. Second, theater sets up conditions for identification between actor and spectator that are different from those that obtain in the relation of texts to other texts that confer authority and meaning on them.   ("Re-Presenting Women Writers," 197)

The directness and physicality of theatre offer unique opportunities to break through symbolic constructs and into material reality. At the same time, theatre's materiality presents special dangers. Work that merely celebrates the traditionally feminine may be, in traditional fashion, diminished, while the presentation of women's bodies onstage is fraught with the potential of sexual objectification. Thus, Janet Wolff maintains, in considering feminist visual and performance art:

> The celebratory work, which often revives traditional female crafts ... or uses the female body itself as vehicle and subject-matter, is too often naively

essentialist. Moreover, it misses the point that in a patriarchal culture it is not possible simply to declare a kind of unilateral independence ... The guerilla tactics of engaging with that regime and undermining it with "destabilizing" strategies (collage, juxtaposition, re-appropriation of the image, and so on) provide the most effective possibility for feminist art practice today.

(*Feminine Sentences*, 82)

Language and the body

Language and the physical representation of the body, theatre's two means of communication, each present special problems to the feminist creator. The human body, unmediated by language, might seem to offer the best hope of a pure expression prior to socialization by the patriarchy. Feminist theorists from Virginia Woolf to Hélène Cixous have held out this hope, that "the body might provide the basis for a nonhierarchical difference, that it might serve as the origin of a distinctively female writing." Rosenman translates Cixous, "'Her flesh speaks true. She lays herself bare. In fact, she physically materializes what she's thinking; she signifies it with her body ... She draws her story into history' ... At these moments the body does seem to offer some hope of authenticity: it undoes the suppression of the narrator's feelings by presenting her with somatic symptoms, forcing her to read herself differently – indeed, to take herself, and not the books of experts, as her text" (*A Room of One's Own*, 86).

Yet from the first consciously feminist theatre of the sixties and seventies, a fear of "mis-reading" the female body has persisted, particularly in performances before a mixed-gender audience. In reprinting Charlotte Rea's 1979 article, "Women for Women," the editor, Carol Martin, dismisses such fears as of a particular "historical moment," which has now passed: Rea, she says, "spends a great deal of time worrying about men in the audience for feminist work, and assumes, along with her contemporaries, that *all* men would use the work in a prurient way" (*Sourcebook*, 7). Yet in the same anthology, a 1989 interview with Holly Hughes raises the question of whether Hughes' play, *Dress Suits to Hire* (1987), portraying the fantasies and role plays of a lesbian couple, "would be better served performed exclusively for women." The interviewer describes the discussion that followed its performance for a mixed audience, and the fear that, "for straight audiences it became ... entertainment; that straight audiences and specifically males in that context couldn't somehow 'read' the piece correctly" (Martin, *Sourcebook*, 245). Clearly, the question of authentic representation of the female body before the desiring male gaze is not yet settled.

Yet Hughes defends the value of performing before a mixed audience, arguing that because women's sexuality is terrifying to both men and women, it must be reclaimed in the interest of women's empowerment. "I am interested in talking about sexuality as a return, and a way of re-creating your life as a powerful thing, as a positive force. I'm interested in trying to invent new images for women sexually" (Schneider, "Holly Hughes," 245). Lynda Hart makes the same point, observing that "if the female body is at the root of male fear, the blank space that he must master, then it also has great power for the woman playwright as a medium for articulation" (*Making a Spectacle*, 6).

But how is the paradox to be resolved? Helen Michie maintains that while the problem is insoluble, the situation is not hopeless. All knowledge, even of our own bodies, comes to us filtered through language, a language based on a patriarchal culture:

> Full representation of the body is necessarily impossible in a language that depends for meaning on absence and difference, and literal representation impossible in a language that is itself a metaphor for thought. The work of Jacques Lacan tells us, furthermore, that a totalized body is not only rhetorically but psychically inaccessible; since our knowledge of the self is constituted in and by discourse, we can only construct for ourselves a body in pieces, a *corps morcelé*. Literary representation, then, is not the process through which the body is fragmented; the fragmentation has already occurred and is always already reoccurring in the necessary and constitutive encounter with the mirror. (*Flesh*, 149)

In other words, there is no pure representation, even of the voiceless body. Nevertheless, she maintains, "anything that foregrounds the inequities of representation, even if this is an admission of the impossibility of moving into a safe space beyond it, is feminist; anything that struggles against these inequities is essential" (150).

If even the physical body is mediated by language and culture, then how can language itself be used to struggle against the culture? Only by what Wolff terms "guerilla tactics," by putting the language of the dominant culture to subversive use. Returning to the example of Suzan-Lori Parks, here is a playwright who, in the tradition of Gertrude Stein and Adrienne Kennedy, uses the language and imagery of the dominant culture as a critique against itself. Parks describes her own use of language as further complicated by her African American culture:

> At one time in this country, the teaching of reading and writing to African Americans was a criminal offense. So how do I adequately represent not merely the speech patterns of a people oppressed by language (which is the simple question) but the patterns of a people whose language use is so complex and varied and ephemeral that its daily use not only Signifies on the

non-vernacular language forms, but on the construct of writing as well? If language is a construct and writing is a construct and Signifyin(g) on the double construct is the daily use, then I have chosen to Signify on the Signifyin(g).   (Solomon, "Signifying," 75–76)

Thus, though there is no discourse outside the culture, feminists find ways to enter and critique the discourse from within.

Realism vs. materialism

Since the 1960s, feminists have drawn on Marxist ideas and practices in developing their societal critique. The consciousness-raising group and the notion of a class critique of society, in which women form an oppressed class, were both central to the development of feminist theory at that time. Perhaps the greatest contribution of Marxist theory to feminism has been to "de-naturalize" the relations and roles of men and women, thus offering the possibility of social change in a way that cultural feminism at its simplest cannot. If women are placed in an "object" position by their gender, and if their identity and experience in this gender separate them from men at some essential level, then, as Elshtain pointed out, there can be no hope of societal transformation.

In the Marxist or materialist view, on the other hand, classes and hierarchies develop from economic and political pressures. As Monique Wittig points out, the existence of "a lesbian society pragmatically reveals that the division from men of which women have been the object is a political one and shows how we have been ideologically rebuilt in a 'natural group'" ("Point of View," 47). Otherwise, "Not only do we naturalize history, but also consequently we naturalize the social phenomena which express our oppression, making change impossible" (48).

It is the reinforcement of "naturalization" that has caused some feminist critics to reject the conventions of realism. Sue-Ellen Case, among others, criticizes realism for its insistence that the viewpoint of the playwright is the only "reality." "Realism makes the spectator see things its way," she argues ("Butch-Femme," 297). Similarly, Hart says that, "as the subject/ author records nature, eschewing selectively structured representations that are shaped by the personal experience and historical specificity of the perceiver, there is the persistent denial that 'objectivity' is simply one lens among many . . . this is the master's way of seeing" (*Making a Spectacle*, 4).

Instead, some critics have looked to Bertholt Brecht for a theatrical application of class theory. Elin Diamond defines Brechtian theory as "attention to the dialectical and contradictory forces within social relations, principally the agon of class conflict in its changing historical forms;

commitment to alienation techniques and nonmimetic disunity in theatrical signification; 'literalization' of the theater space to produce a spectator/ reader who is not interpellated into ideology but is pleasurably engaged in observation and analysis" ("Brechtian Theory," 121).

Brecht's "alienation effect" can be applied to gender through cross-dressing, as in Hughes' *Dress Suits to Hire*, when two lesbians try on the clothing of both genders for each other, "denaturalizing" them in the process. As a further consequence of this spectacle, the audience is allowed "to imagine the deconstruction of gender – and all other – representations," inviting "the participatory play of the spectator, and the possibility for which Brecht most devoutly wished, that signification (the production of meaning) continue beyond play's end, congealing into choice and action after the spectator leaves the theater" (Diamond, "Brechtian Theory," 125–26). The actors are detached from their characters in this style of theatre; they demonstrate but do not "become" their roles. Therefore,

> If feminist theory sees the body as culturally mapped and gendered, Brechtian historicization insists that this body is not a fixed essence but a site of struggle and change. If feminist theory is concerned with the multiple and complex signs of a woman's life: her color, her age, her desires, her politics – what I want to call her historicity – Brechtian theory gives us a way to put that historicity on view – in the theater.   (Diamond, "Brechtian Theory," 129)

Writing in 1988, Diamond presents this style of theatre, which she calls "gestic," as superior to realism because it "challenges the presumed ideological neutrality of any historical reflection."[4] By 1992, however, Diamond is writing in praise of Caryl Churchill, who has managed, in plays like *Top Girls*, to make a Brechtian comment while maintaining the traditional presentation of characters in "recognizable human fiction" ("(In)visible Bodies," 260).

In 1993, director Anne Bogart staged Clare Boothe Luce's *The Women* in San Diego.[5] Luce's realistic satire of thirties society women was treated to a highly Brechtian production, incorporating alienation techniques such as a narrator who comments on the action, and music designed to interrupt the characters and mood rather than reinforce them. While critics of the 1930s considered *The Women* anti-feminist, even misogynistic, Bogart's production highlighted the class differences that divide the female characters and the societal constraints that smother them, resulting in a clearly feminist performance. A realistic script presented in Brechtian style, like *Top Girls*, it incorporated both, pointing up the essentially performative nature of even realistic theatre, and the essentially political nature of all performance.

The performative is political

The political and performative nature of all identity has emerged in the nineties as a predominant theme, not only in feminist theatre criticism but in literary criticism and social theory as well. Bell Hooks' recent work has turned to the impact on identity of images and stereotypes in drama and film. In *Black Looks: Race and Representation*, she hails black female filmmakers who "employ a deconstructive filmic practice to undermine existing cinematic narratives even as they retheorize subjectivity in the realm of the visual … Opening up a space for the assertion of a critical black female spectatorship, they do not simply offer diverse representations, they imagine new transgressive possibilities for the formulation of identity" (131).

Sandra Gilbert and Susan Gubar, best known for their studies of nineteenth-century British women's novels, have focused their most recent work on the significance of cross-dressing among the modernists. While male modernists used cross-dressing as a negative symbol of the disintegration of civilization, "female modernists frequently dramatized themselves through idiosyncratic costumes, as if to imply that, for women, there ought to be a whole wardrobe of selves … as Woolf said, we are what we wear, and therefore, since we can wear anything, we can be anyone" (*No Man's Land*, 327).

Marjorie Garber has turned her attention from Shakespeare's women to "Cross-dressing and Cultural Anxiety," the subtitle of her encyclopedic study of transvestism in society and popular culture as well as in drama and other literature. Garber argues convincingly that the transvestite appears where "cultural category crises" occur in society, explaining, for instance, the popularity of early twentieth-century minstrel shows, in which whites did not only dress as blacks, but white men dressed as black women to play "wench" roles.[6]

In contemporary drama, cross-dressed characters have become commonplace, led, of course, by plays like Harvey Fierstein's *Torch Song Trilogy* (1982) and Tony Kushner's *Angels in America* (1992), which focused on open exploration of gay male characters and themes, bringing these into the mainstream for the first time. Plays like *Cloud Nine* (1979) by Caryl Churchill and *M. Butterfly* (1986) by David Henry Hwang employ cross-dressing as a central image for an examination of race, class, and culture as well as gender issues.

While Gilbert and Gubar translate cross-dressing as a sign of liberation, Garber argues for a more complex interpretation: "Transvestism can be a trickster strategy for outsmarting white oppression, a declaration of difference, a gay affirmative or a homophobic representation" (Garber,

Vested Interests, 303). Jill Dolan warns that cross-dressing by men can also be a way of co-opting female power into androgynous unity – while rejecting actual women.[7]

The essential insight of cross-dressing, as Anna Deavere Smith observes, is an insight into individualism. Smith, whose series of one-woman shows grapple with racial and cultural crisis points in contemporary American society, is specific in her intention not to take a stand, but instead to attempt to empathize with all parties. "If only a man can speak for a man, a woman for a woman, a Black person for all Black people, then we, once again, inhibit the *spirit* of theatre, which lives in the *bridge* that makes unlikely aspects *seem* connected. The bridge doesn't make them the same, it merely *displays* how two unlikely *aspects* are *related*" (*Fires*, xxix).

Twenty years ago, it seemed possible and important to divide feminists into clear-cut categories: the liberal individualists, the Marxist materialists, the new cultural feminists. Today, these divisions seem less clear. In a lively, continuing conversation, each party cautions the others, constantly building to a new synthesis. Elizabeth Fox-Genovese warns that the individualism on which the US was founded, available only to a few white, propertied males, is won with much greater difficulty for a much broader constituency. Yet to dismiss the differences between men and women as "an artifact of language and an abuse of power" is to insist that inequality is inescapable. Instead, she urges feminists to "reclaim man for historical understanding," recognizing that "the consequences of difference attributed by societies and polities are subject to constant reinterpretation" (*Feminism Without Illusions*, 238). While Wittig, the materialist, insists that women must develop class consciousness, she cautions that, "to become a class we do not have to suppress our individual selves, and since no individual can be reduced to her/his oppression we are also confronted with the historical necessity of constituting ourselves as the individual subjects of our history as well" ("Point of View," 51).

While Nina Rapi hopes to identify a "lesbian theater aesthetic," she eventually evolves a definition so broad that it nearly defines contemporary theatre itself. Indeed, as she herself observes, "how do lesbians, as hetero-geneous as we are, act? Like someone who is constantly making herself up" ("Hide and Seek," 148).

Thus every playwright and each performer invents her own form, expressive of the individual story she relates. While appreciating and maintaining our connections to the community of women, of feminists, of families, while struggling as a class for a more just and inclusive society, we nevertheless work as individual artists as well, constantly engaged in "making ourselves up," in the creation of something new.

NOTES

1 See Janet Brown, *Taking Center Stage*, 1–26.
2 See Honor Moore, "Woman Alone, Women Together," 186–91.
3 Hélène Cixous, "The Character of Character," 383–402.
4 Elin Diamond's article in Carol Martin, *A Sourcebook*, is reprinted from *TDR* (1988).
5 Bogart restaged *The Women* at the Hartford Stage Company in 1994, a production that I attended.
6 Marjorie Garber, *Vested Interests*.
7 Jill Dolan, "Gender Impersonation Onstage."

11

HELENE KEYSSAR

Feminist theatre of the seventies in the United States

American women have been writing plays for at least 150 years, and, if we are willing to look innocently (because he is not a woman) at early American drama, an argument could be made that Royall Tyler's *The Contrast* (1787) is the first feminist American play. More commonly, it is Anna Cora Mowatt's *Fashion*, written and performed in 1845, that has been considered to be the first popular play written by an American woman (but *Fashion* is not a *feminist* play). At least three other scripts compete for the position as "first feminist play": Lillian Hellman's *The Children's Hour* (1934), Lorraine Hansberry's *A Raisin in the Sun* (1959), and Megan Terry's *Calm Down Mother* (1965). There are various angles from which one can contest these selections. Plays written by American women were performed in the nineteenth century; some remain available in collections and paperback printings.[1] They occasioned much delight among their audiences, according to letters and news reports of their time, but hardly lasted beyond the moment or beyond a single tour of American cities. That, of course, is typical of Western drama (indeed, of most drama – not just American drama – or drama written by women). Leading the early one-act plays in the United States were the plays written by women: they authored "little" plays (usually one-acts) performed in towns, villages, and cities in the United States during the late nineteenth and early twentieth centuries.

I want to leap in this chapter from an acknowledgment of the hundreds of dramas written by American women (and often directed and produced, but rarely printed) to the more recent history of American drama by women, particularly the drama that is called "feminist drama." Over the last thirty years, since my early (1960s) involvement as teacher, critic, and director, with the women's movement and with the civil rights movement, a genre of work has appeared, especially in the United States and in Britain,[2] that is not only written by women, but calls itself "feminist theatre." In this new genre, writers struggle for appropriate forms and distinctive aesthetics to present issues of gender, race, and power, issues simultaneously raised

9. Scene from *Viet Rock* by Megan Terry

outside of the theatre in new and powerful ways. Definitions of "feminist theatre" tend to be vague and multiple. I abide with Honor Moore, an early participant in feminist theatre, whom I cited in *Feminist Theatre* as saying "there are now playwrights whose art is related to their condition as women."[3]

In the late sixties and the seventies, marches, "street theatre," and, in particular, ensemble theatres, were concerned with issues that were also being confronted in other contexts: race, poverty, sexism. As was true in the non-theatrical protest movements of the sixties, young people, especially, acted out of their concerns for racial and economic equality for all; many were vehemently opposed to the United States' leading role in the Vietnamese War. From the mid-sixties on, gender was named (mostly by women) as an issue equal to these others, but was at first less successful in provoking change than were non-gendered issues. The resistance often came from inside families: my parents called my college degree my "insurance policy" in case my "potential" husband became ill or other bad things happened that would require me to go into the working world. Generously, my father took on a second job and supported me at Pembroke for the full four years. At Brown, in the sixties, kernels of activity in support of civil rights eventually grew to include protests of gender inequalities and theatrical presentations such as skits.

Women from universities, and from activist work outside educational institutions, joined in the civil rights movement. Slowly, however, several of the activist feminists became frustrated by the writing of speeches and political position papers that were then presented in public by men in the movement, often without mention of the women authors. Many movement women were relegated to the kitchen. They became tired and distressed at being always the unseen researchers, the backstage crew, the seamstresses, the unnamed playwrights and actors and producer's crew, rarely, if ever, the voice heard and the persona presented. Several women who had been working hard within the sixties theatre groups withdrew from the better-known mixed-gender groups and founded alternative groups to create their own theatre without men or at least without the all-too-familiar productions in which, in the production process if not the script, women's roles were not given fair credit.[4]

Among these women there are three whose dramas I want to address in this chapter. Two of the three playwrights to whose work I turn were importantly involved in the politics and "new theatre "of the 1960s and seventies (when I refer to "the seventies," I am not talking precisely of the period 1970–79; rather, I urge that the idea of a decade in critical terms is not absolutely historical; I use the term to signify a period of challenge to the claims that American women's drama either was most successful as it mirrored realistic male drama and/or that it did not really change drama from the protest plays of the twenties and thirties until the 1980s). More generally, I want to call well-merited attention to the aesthetic and political distinctions and social contributions of plays by women that first broke the realistic, often melodramatic[5] traditions of modern American drama. Contrary to most American theatrical entertainments, then and now, several of the plays written by American women from the nineteenth and twentieth centuries called for changes in the ways women and men can see and hear as we move toward the twenty-first century.

The three women to whose plays I want to draw attention here are Megan Terry (1932–), Maria Irene Fornes (1930–), and Ntozake Shange (1948–). All three are women playwrights associated with "the seventies" (although Terry and Fornes both were active in theatre from the mid-fifties on); all three are still writing plays. All three have won major awards. Fornes and Terry were key members of the theatre groups they helped to create.[6] In 1972, Terry and Fornes joined with Rosalyn Drexler, Julie Bovasso, Adrienne Kennedy, and Rochelle Owens to form the Women's Theatre Council. Their initial goal was to produce in repertory one play by each of the founding members. They hoped not just to bring more attention than had been the previous case to their own work, but to encourage the production and publication of other plays by women. As a separate group of women playwrights, they existed only a year; by 1973, they had joined with seventeen other playwrights, including male American playwrights Ed Bullins, Sam Shepard, and John Ford Noonan to found the company Theatre Strategy. Several of the writings by men, like those of their women associates, resisted "straight" realism in the form and content of their works.

Terry, Fornes, and, within a few years, Shange, as well as several other American playwrights, were making theatre in non-conventional ways and spaces.[7] In most cases, efforts were made to spotlight the company, not a single star, male or female. Several of the women playwrights sought alternatives to the conventional realistic forms of modern playwrights. My choices are examples of the themes and shapes we find of concern to many theatre artists of the sixties and seventies, and to their audiences. But not everyone in the new theatre groups agreed on the need for new theatrical forms to present these political concerns; and what "new forms" meant was somewhat of a mystery or reduced to any mode that was not the now commonplace realism of theatre, and also of film and television. Several playwrights, men as well as women, started writing in the fifties and went on in the sixties, the seventies, and through the present to demonstrate that new times, new politics, and new economics required new forms. Megan Terry's theatre of transformation, in which characters, place, time, and action change rapidly, and actors switch roles, often regardless of gender, was particularly influential. It was not clear to everyone, however, that the transformations of the actors, physically and sometimes verbally, was a good – or sufficient – strategy for any drama, even when these plays were well thought-out and had carefully selected goals and strategies for actors and audiences.

The significance of unveiling on the stage volatile and politically pressing issues – the Vietnam war,[8] the power of language as well as the big political themes of power, injustice, ignorance, could rarely overcome the problem for the players and playwrights of insufficient funds. In part, this was a matter of a commitment to a larger and "poorer" audience (financially, educationally, stylistically) than that which attended Broadway and similarly costly urban commercial theatres. Despite the heralded hegemony of most of the new American theatre groups, there also emerged in the late sixties and seventies tensions among members themselves about race, poverty, gender, and target audiences. Few Americans actually saw, heard, or read the work of the "new" companies. Even the most loyal and financially supportive audiences gradually witnessed the demise of Theatre Strategy and similar companies as ongoing groups. Ironically, several of the male members went on alone to be leading American playwrights of the twentieth century. I think here of Imamu Amiri Baraka, Ed Bullins, and Sam Shepard. Two women, Megan Terry and Maria Irene Fornes, were members and mourners of Women's Theatre Council and Theatre Strategy. Following the brief lives of each of these companies, Terry and Fornes continued on, working individually at times or in connection with other theatre groups in and out of New York. Shange's playwriting did not come to production until 1974, and then it was on the West Coast initially. Biographically, the three women were each of different social worlds, yet they had many common goals: a new theatre that was political and feminist in its concerns, expressed in experimental forms and commitments to learn from each other.

Megan Terry was born in Seattle, Washington in 1932 and received a BA from the University of Washington in 1952; the summer of the same year, she was awarded Certificates in Acting, Directing, and Design. Her teaching experience, for which her education had supposedly prepared her, had an effect opposite to what she had imagined. She was appointed to a position, but was sufficiently distressed at the mechanical way in which she was expected to teach and at the condemnations by parents and administrators of what many saw as the "unorthodox" plays she was producing and writing for children. Terry quit her teaching position in 1956 and moved to New York City. There, for the next decade and a half, she found comrades in the emergent politically oriented theatre groups and began to write plays,[9] some of which remained conventional in structure but allowed her to address straightforwardly the topics that engaged her and brought her into the world of the new, experimental New York playwrights.[10]

Among these colleagues was Maria Irene Fornes. Born in 1930 in Havana, Cuba, Fornes emigrated with her sister and widowed mother to New York City. In 1951, she became a nationalized US citizen. Like Terry, and Shange, Fornes' origins were out-stream of commercial American theatre. Their family roots show in the plays they write: Terry's origins as a white female in Seattle; Fornes' first fifteen years as a Cuban living in Cuba; and Shange's urban San Francisco African American background led to different paths into theatre. Nonetheless, there is a common core among them: they each see themselves as poet-playwrights; they have been heralded around the world; each of these women has had significant success with her work outside the United States. In turn, these three playwrights have brought non-mainstream American conventions and views of society in the second half of the twentieth century to the American stage; their plays suggest the multiplicity and courage of Americans, especially American women. Each was also smart enough to know that there were precedents for what they were attempting: in Lorraine Hansberry's *A Raisin in the Sun* (1959), for example, the putative world of the stage demanded not just to be colored, male and female, but to alter its relationship with its actors and audiences.

Megan Terry's move in 1956 from her birthplace, Seattle, to New York City was a conscious attempt to unstick herself from conventional American drama in both form and content. In New York, she met and worked with other theatre people who were searching for significant changes in the forms of theatre, partially so that topics such as race, gender, and class could be approached dramatically by other means than realism. Maria Irene Fornes, Joseph Chaikin, Peter Feldman, and Barbara Vann were among those whose rejections of conventional theatre were taking positive, innovative forms in the workshops of the Open Theatre.[11] The group tried to work collectively and to explore old and new dangers in their performances. It was in and from this group context that Terry began to experiment with playwriting and new demands on performers: meanwhile, an African male character in *A Raisin in the Sun* was saying "the world's most liberated women are not liberated at all."[12]

Between 1956 and 1970, Terry wrote at least twenty-two plays, thus gaining her the title "Mother of American Theatre"; many of these were produced for the first time in the sixties. Her first play of the 1970s, *Approaching Simone*, brought to Terry a new kind of attention: almost all reviews of her play were positive; *Approaching Simone* won an Obie award for best play of the 1969–70 season. Terry had been fascinated since the fifties with the historical figure, Simone Weil, but it was more than a decade until she felt she could write the play she wanted about her heroine.

Approaching Simone is that play. It has fifteen named characters and the ensemble; as a director, I would have all of the spectacle and bit parts played by members of the ensemble. Much as in early Greek drama, Simone, the character, is drawn from a historically and mythically remembered woman whose brief life began in Paris in 1909 and ended in England in 1943. The *Encyclopedia Britannica* describes Weil as "a mystic, a social philosopher and activist in the French Resistance during World War II, whose posthumously published works had particular influence on French and English thought" (online, 1997).

Of the fifteen characters in *Approaching Simone*, all except Simone are played by a limited number of actors who repeatedly transform throughout the play. These actors perform like a chorus in a Greek tragedy, taking on not only several of the play's characters, but different elements of mood or environment and different elements of Simone herself.[13] The playscript intends that one actor play Simone, although this character lives through various transformations. The concept of one character's evolution as played by one actor is key.

The joining of the political and the spiritual in *Approaching Simone* is announced by the set: the flags of France, Nazi Germany, Russia, and the United States are draped at the top of the proscenium; in the center at the top of the proscenium arch and the flags is a "giant icon painted in muted, glowing colors and gold leaf" (Terry, *Approaching Simone*, 40). They reveal "God," as a flowing white beard at the top, with Jesus below Him. Downstage left and right are enormous papier-mâché cherubs, painted in gold; each cherub has golden rings on its umbilicus, and, from the rings flow golden cords. On the ceiling is a beautiful head with an open mouth. The spectacle includes actors whose appearance suggests great age: the men are in costumes that designate royalty and power; the women, in *haute couture* costumes of the 1930s, suggest identities as cultural and social leaders. As in many of the films of the thirties, this tableau of grandeur and wealth is in sharp contrast to the poverty experienced by many Americans during the Depression. From my perspective as a director, these figures could be constructed cutouts or actors who join the rest of the ensemble as it moves onstage.

Most of the acting company enters from the back of the theatre and proceeds to the stage. Each member of the company, except the actor playing Simone, takes one end of a golden chord and, once on stage, turns to the audience. The actor who plays Simone takes a position extreme stage left and stares out at the audience, while the chorus sings fragments of Simone Weil's biography – of darkness and light, horrendous migraine headaches, sugar she sent to French soldiers, the sensation that her mind was bleeding. A baritone from the chorus urges the audience and Simone to "reach out through the mind . . . [to find] 'mind ecstasy.'" The chorus sings or yells "Attention! Attention" while one female voice urges, twice, "Anyone can become" (41), and a male member of the chorus sings out (twice) "Anyone can know truth" (42). Each chorus member then sings alone until they all sing together: "ATTENTION, PULL WITH YOUR WILL/GENIUS IS INVISIBLE." First alone, then five times together, each actor sings the name "Simone." One member of the ensemble intones from an onstage platform: "Simone taught herself the art of perpetual attention" (42). After this enunciation (or denunciation), the entire cast, including Simone, exits.

The play begins as it will end – in ritual – or what Terry and others called "magic realism."[14] Moments of choral chanting and dancing are interrupted by short scenes from Simone Weil's life; many of these are internally realistic snapshots, but all scenes are nuanced by multiple role-playing;

onstage and offstage transformations move the scenes and characters from one time or place in Simone's life to another, beginning with her childhood exodus with her Jewish family to "the lodge," someplace in France, where they hope to be safe from a Nazi invasion. Here, and later in the play, these and comparable brief scenes cover much of Simone's life from age five to her death at thirty-four in 1943, but Terry requires that the actor playing Simone always look about thirty. This accentuates the non-realistic quality of the play for much of its duration.

The dialogue in the short scenes is realistic, transparent; the anecdotes that highlight Simone's life in this play reveal her political awareness and her charity. As political acts, she refuses to eat and insists on carrying her suitcase. In a notable scene she insists first on giving away her stockings and then on giving an envelope of scarce sugar to the soldiers at the Front. Simone's early life ends with an image of her suffering as she greets a painful migraine headache on the occasion of her first menstrual period. Her pain, reflected by the body positions and movements of the ensemble, introduces the mental and spiritual aspects of the scholar-philosopher-politician that Simone will become throughout her brief life.

In an often cited dramatic segment, "Simone at Fourteen – When and Why She Wants to Kill Herself," Simone interprets her migraines as aspects of self-hatred and loathing and as punishment for her particular life struggles. We are now, Terry's stage directions tell us, inside Simone's head. Ensemble members, identified in Terry's script only by numbers, close this section by wrapping Simone in increasingly large pieces of white cloth while shouting epigrammatic taunts that emphasize Simone's gender and demean her intellect and actions in the world: "You are unfit for this world" (as she is being mummified), "you're nothing but a girl, Simone," "You'll never amount to anything, Simone" (50). The verbal charge is juxtaposed to the visual act: "Number Thirty" of the ensemble ends the verbal laceration of Simone with the instruction, "Kill yourself, Simone" (52), as other ensemble members unwrap Simone from her bandages. The verbal charge to Simone – to kill herself – is contradicted by the visual image of her rebirth. A brief song, sung by The Singer, serves as a transition in an abrupt switch of context and style to a nightclub, where a more adult Simone rolls cigarettes for her companions (among them Jean-Paul and Albert and "Simone Two"). While the political conversation continues, Simone is chastised for insisting on heavy topics.

This and subsequent scenes revealing Simone's continuing "otherness," apparent both socially and in her sharply aware political sensibility, are played quickly. The section following "Simone at Fourteen" begins with a somewhat older Simone who wants to discuss sophisticated scholarship in physics, politics, philosophy, and economics. Her friends, all male here, do not wish to be serious at this point; Simone can be nothing but engaged in ideas and political actions. The tension between Simone and her friends is cut by the performance of a singer, Carolina, who leads the crowd in a long blues song that recalls images from other, mostly black, American music. Carolina attempts to teach Simone to dance, and, unsuccessful, exits the stage with the entire ensemble. As in a litany, Simone recites, "What I am, I endure ... I suffer" (62).

The play cuts to Simone and her mother in a truck comprised of the bodies of the ensemble. The following brief scenes show the departure of Simone's mother and present Simone's experiences as a teacher. She shows herself to be an excellent and provocative teacher, too much so for the private school. She is fired, and we see her at her next teaching job, where there are no desks, but there are the inquiring minds of students.

Simone declares her desire to teach her pupils to think. As part of this pedagogical challenge, she arranges a two-day camping trip with her students. Repeatedly, Simone takes risks that she assumes others will admire. In part because one female student almost dies on the camping trip crossing an icy river (the student cannot swim), this school's board fires her, too. Nonplussed, Simone announces that she is happily moving on to study the workers in fields and factories. She embraces the imagination as the key to learning in all disciplines; in a different but not contrary voice, Simone asserts that "property consists in reality of the power to dispose of goods." The act ends in a return to spectacle, recalling the ritual quality of the beginning of the play: a group from the ensemble, now appearing as old ladies, pull the gold chord on one of the huge, fabricated cherubs. The belly of the cherub opens, spilling jewels and candies on the audience. This absurd and ironically festive gesture concludes Act I.

Act II follows Simone, who continues as a teacher and field worker. She further demonstrates her intellectual acuity as she criticizes the war in Spain, World War II, and all wars. After Simone burns herself while cooking for the Anarchist troops, her parents appear and bring her home from the hospital, to a renewed contact with her family and a revelation of the spiritual work she has been doing, while her body heals. Simone speaks of a person as a body and a soul and reveals to her father (and the audience) her possession by Christ.

Act II is more overtly philosophical and intellectually polemical than Act I. At the same time, it is impressively, unusually dramatic: the ensemble forms and re-forms from the beginning of Act II; the actors first present themselves as human animations of mathematical ideas, formulae, and theories. These actor-created objects are not new to Terry's work. She has also used "soft sets," created mainly from quilted materials such as those made for *Approaching Simone*, in earlier plays, and she continues to work with soft sets when the script and context seem appropriate. This places an emphasis on women's work and art; sensitivity to the development of a distinct feminist form in all aspects of stage language is integral to most of Terry's plays.

As Simone continues to ask unanswerable or enigmatic mathematical questions, and to lecture as if in a trance, the ensemble moves toward the audience to lecture them. Echoing Simone, the ensemble move into the audience, reciting outrageous theories. Two of the ensemble, the "Soprano" and the "Baritone," respond to Simone with the affront, "You don't interest me" (85).

The Dionysian terror of that assertion is suggested to the audience by the ensemble chanting the word "Ecstasy." The ensemble sings, initially in conventional terms, but quickly in obscenities that are meant to be unsettling for the audience. Simone challenges her onstage audience, telling each member that "there is something sacred in every person" (86). Simone goes on to assert to that audience that "good and evil will be done to you" (90) (notably not *by* you). As the ensemble experiences "ecstasy," the actors chant and dance as in a thirties musical (Terry's directions). The ensemble members assert their power and urge others to "LEARN TO WALK LIKE YOU OWN THE WORLD" (91).

The next rapidly played set of scenes demonstrate what this last instruction means. Simone travels endlessly, from field to factories, to churches, helping people with their work and teaching them about the Russian Revolution. She urges her "brothers" to resist Joseph Stalin's dictatorship and to return to the vision of "Lenin's ideals" and a people's democracy. She is taunted by some, who call her a Trotskyite, by others because she seems always engaged in political actions. Simone now moves relentlessly to Spain and joins the Anarchist forces. (A bare stage refers the audience back to the flags hung above the proscenium.) Simone is finally stopped by her own physical pain and anger: while shouting and encouraging political work, she inadvertently spills hot oil on her leg.

Simone is rescued after the oil accident by her parents. While recuperating, she learns from her own burnt skin and from reading, how to "get outside her pain." A dialogue with a priest, initiated by Simone, again reveals her turn to mysticism and her constant urge to learn and teach, not didactically but through conversation and her own daring. Simone's ever transforming personhood provides her energy as she travels from factory to church to army camp. She dies refusing to eat; as long as others starve she feels immoral eating. Men and women remark her "strange" behavior; one woman comments that Simone's coffin must be awfully small. Words cease, and stage lights slowly dim to a pin spot on Simone, followed by a very slow fade to black. This suggests the work that the actor must do in playing the part of Simone: she must present a small body that gradually vanishes physically while evolving into a great spirit.

Audience members and professional critics responded strongly and positively to the power of that final moment of the play. I want to elaborate on this response. What does it mean to "approach Simone"? Jack Kroll, consistently a tough and apt theatre and film critic, called the shape of the play "a chronicle, grave, didactic, warm, filled with an incandescent interest in its subject."[15] Like Simone's soul, the vanishing point of light is at once enigmatic and seductive. Simone has died, but her writings, which had not yet been printed, would be published and read and translated into numerous languages.

Depending, of course, on different players, Simone can be a political embarrassment, a self-theatricalizing "typical woman," or a strong, tiny light beckoning others, especially women, to take on her struggle for freedom, action, and universal respect, man for woman, man for man, woman for woman, woman for man – none of these fully encompass Simone's vision. In her last speech, as she lies dying, Simone has a very clear sense of the world and of herself: "War is affliction," she declares. "It isn't easy to direct one's thoughts towards affliction, voluntarily" (*Approaching Simone*, 130). Thus alerted, the actor who plays Simone must seduce the audience without behaving seductively, must listen to her own political and spiritual convictions, must be neither bombastic nor weak.

Suicide is almost always a weak gesture.[16] In Terry's drama, Simone's suicide at the age of thirty-four appears as both weakness and strength. Simone is a martyr. Her own final words of instruction and her refusal to eat are Simone's "last words." Any suicide, and Simone's, particularly, is an act of vengeance against those still living, against a complacent society. In Simone's case, she leaves her audiences and readers outside the theatre to respond.

To think affliction, it is necessary to bear it in one's own flesh. Terry helps us understand this by bringing Simone in frequent contact with a variety of "Others." This play is an instance of the way in which the ensemble technique Terry learned in the sixties, the use of bodies to create place, time, and a multitude of characters, and the power of theatrical transformations (sometimes a meaningless device used to make a simple statement of the social as better than the individual, but aptly used here) make theatre a strange and important place to be. The title and the play, *Approaching Simone*, is perhaps determinedly ambiguous, a pointer for the audience to several urgings and what they mean: to try to be like Simone in her courage, her spirituality, and her radical politics; to come near Simone when she does not like to be touched; to be a martyr; to be a self-consuming fool; and to be a writer who Megan Terry believes can transport you "to the tree of life." (I think here of Samuel Beckett).

It may not seem so at a glance, but Maria Irene Fornes' *Fefu and Her Friends*, her best-known, prize-winning play, is in several ways – in structure and in political and aesthetic concerns – sister to Terry's *Approaching Simone*. Fornes' *Fefu*, first performed in May 1976 by the New York Theatre Strategy, has been and continues to be performed, mostly at colleges, universities, and community theatres, often outside the United States. Fornes has won eight Obie awards. If there were prizes for generating most discussion after a theatre performance, Fornes might win, but then, she would have to compete with Terry and Shange, an act, even a notion, that I believe none of these playwrights would accept.

Born in Cuba in 1930, Fornes moved to New York City in 1945 with her mother and sister. Her father had died of a heart-attack at the age of fifty-three, after cautioning his wife and two daughters about the dangers of New York. The women, nonetheless, moved to New York, a city crowded with Cuban emigrants in 1945. Little of Fornes' political activities or her spiritual beliefs were explicit until the mid-sixties, when she began writing plays which were often deliberately unfinished and sometimes only partially cast when rehearsals began. She served as director and writer, making changes as the cast developed and contributed. Fornes' plays increasingly were constructed in two phases: the first stage is "additive"; watching and playing with the cast, she "invites creativity and admits irrational ideas and images" to her scripts. Her second stage is "subtractive." As the term suggests, Fornes' second stage focuses on the elimination of the obvious from the script and on an emphasis on words and actions as they suggest the uncertainties, ambiguities, and ironies of characters on/in sets.[17]

Fefu and Her Friends metaphorically inhabits, and shares, the peak of a mountain which Fornes has climbed since the mid-sixties. *Fefu* is remarkably like Terry's *Approaching Simone*, and Shange's *For Colored Girls Who Have Considered Suicide/When the Rainbow is Enuf*. Written in the seventies, the three plays are alike in haunting ways: in each there are one or two characters who have notably more or less power than the others; in each there is an ensemble of women (and occasionally men), many of whom play several parts. There are strong urges in at least one of the characters to be both autonomous and together. All of the plays are written (at least for a moment) with some music and passages in verse; yet the feel is not of a poem. Each play occurs in the theatrical and historical past and present. Numerous changes of space and/or time dislocate the players and audience (even in the case of Simone, who lives doubly in pieces of her entire life and as Simone at thirty).

The key differences among these plays are in their aesthetic domains. In Terry's work, Simone and her thoughts (intended to be played by an ensemble) are historically and dramaturgically structured around a particular woman, Simone, and an ensemble of women and men (who play both specific minor characters – i.e. Simone's mother and father – and could, at times, participate in the ensemble) who create the outer and inner textures of Simone's worlds. Fornes' *Fefu and Her Friends* calls for a cast of eight women, another chorus of sorts, although all here have character names, and two, Fefu herself and Julia, set themselves apart from the others. Shange's *For Colored Girls* is performed by a female chorus of equals, although the story related by one of the seven, the lady in red, is more compelling than any other colored girl's tale in this play and marks the final similarities rather than differences among the three works.

If I appear here to be avoiding summaries of the plot lines, settings, and characters in *Fefu*, it is not my avoidance of a familiar mode of drama criticism, but my fear of reducing any of these plays to types and narratives. It is not the case, however, that the characters are indistinguishable each from another, within one work or among all three. The space both around and "inside" Simone is distinctive, historically and symbolically informed; it could not appear in the plays and spaces of Fornes or Shange. The characters of *For Colored Girls* live in various and vague places, mostly on the street and in tenements in Harlem. The house that Fornes and her friends built should be readily recognized as a house, somewhere ... The latter also requires at least four distinct playing areas within the onstage house.

The women who arrive at different times at Fefu's house (including Fefu herself, and Julia) convey to the audience only the vaguest sense of a reason why each is there; we and they know generally that they have come together to plan a charity event, but anyone offstage is meant to be increasingly uncertain about every dimension of the characters and the situation. In Act II, in which we, the audience, are led from room to room of the playing space, "Fefu's house," we might wonder if we are in *The X Files*, the television series where time and place slip sufficiently that they can easily and deliberately disorient the audience. There is a limited world in *Fefu and Her Friends* that functions in continuity with the material world as we have known it. It is worth making a full list of what we know about this time, this place, and these characters but only to be sure of the failure of certainty by the end of the play. Nothing, including my own sense of stability as a spectator, remains constant or steady in this play. Julia, the friend who punishes Fefu by accusing her of responsibility for the accident that put Julia in a wheelchair, may or may not be crazy as others on stage and off conclude, but all of us have to encounter Julia's departure from her wheelchair and her ability to walk at the end of the play.

Beyond this, in *Fefu and Her Friends*, is an experience of increasingly troubled ambiguity for the audience. Or is there? My answer has been and remains, I hope so. In earlier writings about *Fefu*, I have urged that initially *Fefu and Her Friends* conforms to the conventions of traditional theatre.[18] A small group of women come together for a reunion meeting to rehearse a series of presentations for a public event. Fornes' play preserves the unities of time, place, and action: all events occur during one day, in one house, among a group of people who form a temporary community. From the start, however, the differences among the women's voices are striking, as are their abilities to reaccentuate each other's lives and the meanings of each other's utterances. Fefu opens the play, declaring to no one in particular: "My husband married me to have a constant reminder of how loathsome women are." "What?" Cindy (one of the visitors) asks. "Yup," Fefu responds. Often, one or another of the women do not understand each other, but what one says to another changes the other before our eyes.

Central among these women are Fefu, the hostess in whose house the gathering occurs, and Julia, a friend of several of the women, including Fefu. Julia's confinement to a wheelchair is the result of a bizarre accident in which a hunter shot a deer; after falling as if shot herself, Julia found herself to be paralyzed. Julia and Fefu are the most complex and perplexing of the characters, but each of the other women assembled has her own specific voice, her own desires, and differences. In a 1985 interview with Scott Cummings, Fornes described her relationship to these characters in the context of a change in style in her work: "The style of *Fefu* dealt more with characters as real persons rather than voices that are the expression of the mind of the play" (Cummings, "Seeing with Clarity," 53). Fornes goes on to say that instead of writing in a "linear manner" she "would write a scene and see what came out" and then "I would write another as if I were practicing calligraphy" (53).

It is not just, however, in the autonomy and multiple fields of vision of the characters that I find Mikhail Bakhtin's notion of the dialogic imagination at work in Fornes' drama. The second part of *Fefu and Her Friends* elaborates the differences among the voices of the women but also removes them and us to separate spaces. During Part 2, four different scenes occur simultaneously in four different spaces: the lawn, the study, the bedroom, and the kitchen. The audience is divided into four groups, each of which is guided to a different space where one or more of the women is speaking. After a scene is completed, the audience moves to the next space, and the scene that has just occurred in that space is repeated until all members of the audience have viewed all four scenes. The remarkable achievement of this device is to move the spectator from his or her single, unified perspective without destroying theatre itself by removing the footlights. Fornes has created a dramatic correlative for the multiple points-of-view narrations of the modern novel or the parallel montages of film.

My experience as an audience member for several different productions of *Fefu and Her Friends* is that the audience is disconcerted, not only by being moved from our stable and familiar positions, but by our proximity to each other and to the characters; we are *in* their spaces but not of them. Their world remains separate from ours, and there is nothing we can do to make a difference in their world. We are thus not in the distracting position of the kind of interactive theatre that emerged in the sixties, where the divisions between the world of the stage and the world of the theatre were wholly destroyed and where I did not know to whom I was talking – an actor or a character. Instead, in each viewing of each scene of *Fefu* our position as audience members is reaccentuated and our relationship to the characters is remediated. My experience is similar to that of my reading William Faulkner's *The Sound and the Fury*; each character's telling of the tale remediates my relationship to all of the characters and their various meanings.

The most difficult and disturbing scene in Part 2 of *Fefu and Her Friends* is that in which we witness Julia lying on a mattress on the floor so that we must look down upon her. Julia speaks what the other characters refer to as her "hallucinations." The setting itself is a hybrid place, a mixture of cultural artifacts that do not normally belong together: "There are dry leaves on the floor although the time is not fall" (*Fefu and Her Friends*, 33), the stage directions indicate. Julia speaks of "they" – they who clubbed her, tore out her eyes, took away her voice. Then her pronoun changes to "he." "He said that women's entrails are heavier than anything on earth and to see a woman running creates a disparate and incongruous image in the mind. It's anti-aesthetic" (33–34).

Julia' s hallucination is the discourse of an other, a male other, ventrilo-quated by Julia.[19] That this is a specifically and ominously gendered discourse we hear in an utterance from Julia's lips that she calls a prayer:

> The human being is of the masculine gender. The human being is a boy as a child and grown up he is a man. Everything on earth is for the human being. Woman is not a human being. She is 1. A mystery. 2. Another species. 3. As

yet undefined. 4. Unpredictable; therefore wicked and gentle and evil and good which is evil. (35)

In the midst of these hallucinations, Julia has cried out of concern for Fefu. The "voices" appear to be telling her they will have to kill Fefu. What "they" want from Fefu is her light. Julia has become aware of herself as one person in an alien culture, but she also fears that that "other" culture has good reason to dominate, control, and destroy her own different voice. It is not anything that Julia has done or had done to her that makes her speak so strangely or that causes her paralysis. She is no more or less mad, no more or less paralyzed than Hamlet. She is like the figure whom Nietzsche presents in *The Birth of Tragedy*, the figure for whom Shakespeare's Hamlet stands as the paradigm, the one who experiences nausea in his own knowledge and in that knowledge cannot move. Like Hamlet, Julia is paralyzed from too much knowledge, and she fears that Fefu is approaching the same state. Julia is always conscious of death; death is constantly present, and it is only because "something rescues us from death at every moment of our lives" (*Fefu and Her Friends*, 52) that she remains alive. But Julia is also threatened by the knowledge that "they" who control insist that "the human being is of the masculine gender" (35), and she suffers because she can neither believe nor resist that dictum. Those whom she calls the "judges" have told her that once she believes the prayer that denigrates women, she will be well. They tell her that all women have come to believe the prayer.

Fefu and Her Friends is a dialogic drama, and is, more precisely in Mikhail Bakhtin's terms, "an intentional novelistic hybrid" (Bakhtin, *Dialogic Imagination*, 360). In an intentional novelistic hybrid differing points of view on the world collide within one cultural form: "the novelistic hybrid is an artistically organized system for bringing different languages in contact with one another" (Bakhtin, *Dialogic Imagination*, 361). The world that Fornes has created in *Fefu* is one in which not only Julia and Fefu herself but each of the women struggles with her own voice and brings into the conversation the diverse historical elements of her own linguistic consciousness. Emma, the incomparable performer, pontificates in the inflated rhetoric of a long passage from "The Science of Educational Dramatics" by Emma Sheridan Fry; Paula weeps her contempt for "those who having had everything a person can ask for, make such a mess of it" (*Fefu and Her Friends*, 57). Her American plain style tale of her own early envy of the rich might be heard as sentimental in another context, but, here, as one utterance in an authentic conversation, it interanimates the whole of the drama.

To sustain this distorted heteroglossia is dangerous; it is dangerous to the living of daily life and to drama itself. In the end, Fefu can no longer bear the multiple voices in her head. She goes outdoors and shoots a rabbit; indoors, blood appears on Julia's forehead, and Julia dies. The women surround Julia in a protective circle and the lights fade. Few in the audience (including critics who have written about this play over two decades) agree on what this ending "means." Somewhat earlier in the play, yet another of the women, Christina, asked if she liked Fefu, responded that she did but that Fefu confused her. "Her mind," Christina says, "is adventurous. I don't know if there is dishonesty in that. But in adventure there is taking chances and risks, and then one has to, somehow, have less regard or respect for things as they are. That is, regard for a kind of convention, I suppose" (31).

In this play, Fefu kills Julia and reconstructs the primacy of monologue only in the end and only as a last, desperate effort to ward off the threat to her own stability of consciousness. Other modern plays have ended similarly. Lula kills Clay at the end of Baraka's *Dutchman* because he has broken the conventions of his servile pseudo-discourse, the white middle-class discourse of the New York subway that still demands (even if it is now losing) its dominance. At the end of Beckett's *Krapp's Last Tape*, Krapp's lips move, but there is no sound: "Past midnight. Never knew such silence. The earth might be uninhabited" (28). Only the tape runs on in silence.

Beckett, perhaps not unlike Bakhtin, foresees, proclaims, the end of drama. Why? Because there are not two words, two different utterances to speak? Because if you kill the conventions you kill the form? Bakhtin proclaims the dialogic novel to be different, to transcend other forms because, for him, as rearticulated by Michael Holquist, "Other genres are constituted by a set of formal features for fixing language that pre-exist any specific utterance within the genre" (Bakhtin, *Dialogic Imagination*, xxix). In contrast, Holquist argues, "the 'novel' is the name Bakhtin gives to whatever force is at work within a given literary system to reveal the limits, the artificial constraints of that system" (Bakhtin, *Dialogic Imagination*, xxi). Should we, then, give the name "novel" to *Fefu and Her Friends* or *Approaching Simone* or *Krapp's Last Tape* because they reveal the "artificial constraints" of the system we call drama, reveal and disrupt those constraints? The obvious answer is yes and no. While there remain artificial constraints in all three of the plays I discuss here, our attention is called to the authorial emplacement of restraints, not the naturalness of constraints. This holds, even, with death, as the "death" of Julia suggests in *Fefu and Her Friends*.

"What are the salient features of this novelization of other genres suggested by us above?" Bakhtin asks. "They become more free and flexible, their language renews itself by incorporating extraliterary hetero-glossia and the 'novelistic' layers of literary language, they become dialo-gized, permeated with laughter, irony, humor, elements of self-paradox and finally – this is the most important thing – the novel inserts into these other genres an indeterminacy, a certain semantic openendedness, a living contact with unfinished, still-evolving contemporary reality (the open-ended present)" (Bakhtin, *Dialogic Imagination*, 6–7).

I read my own words and those of Fornes' and find that, counter to my claims, printed previously, non-traditional polyphony remains at the end of *Fefu and Her Friends* and powerfully so.

Power, and its current place in the drama, are related to the subject as well as the effect of the third play I want to address, Ntozake Shange's *For Colored Girls*. Here, performance power is divided among seven women, articulated by colors, as in "lady in red," "lady in blue," "lady in yellow" until the rainbow is complete. Shange calls the piece a "choreopoem." It was performed first in San Francisco and Berkeley by Shange and four other black women, on a very lean budget. While making changes in script and cast, the ensemble moved the show to New York City, where, after further changes, including an increase in the number of actors to seven, the show played short stints at the Henry Street Theatre and the Public Theatre. The production then moved to the Booth Theatre on Broadway and has continued playing at theatres across the country, with no foresee-able end to performances.

For Colored Girls is in structure and values close to Terry's *Approaching Simone*, and, more elusively, recalls Fornes' *Fefu and Her Friends*. *For Colored Girls* calls forth historical figures not as characters, but as references. There is no Simone or Fefu, only seven women each identified by a different color of the rainbow. Just as in nature's rainbow there is no white, there is no "lady in white" in *For Colored Girls*. All women – perhaps, all people – face some of the issues confronted by the colored girls in this play. No group of people, no matter what their skin color, is any more "colored" than another group.

Despite Shange's own naming of the play as a "choreopoem," none of its special features is unusual to drama, especially feminist drama: there are women in all three plays I have been discussing who sing, dance, and speak. Each has at least one particular story to tell; together they bring us a performance that is at once narrative and ritualistic. Shange and designer Ming Cho Lee have emptied the stage for *For Colored Girls* with the exception of a large bright red fabricated rose, hung upstage left. The "colors" of the women are displayed in simple, dance-like costumes: leotards and skirts in each one's designated hue. The set is painted black.

Dancing, posing, moving her body in consonance with her voice, each character of *For Colored Girls* introduces her place and "sings her sighs." The women announce to the audience where each is from. (African American males, especially, call people from their home towns, no matter how far away, "home boy.") Each woman speaks of her origins and her youth, mostly talking about growing up, and about the importance of love and sex. The first introductory sequence ends with all of the characters dancing and referring to sexual experiences. The dialogue moves rapidly until two sudden light changes cue rapidly paced dialogue from the ladies in red, blue, and purple. A change in music signals the end of this section of the play.

For Colored Girls is intended to move on to the next stage of these women's lives without interruption. Each woman-girl now speaks and dances a story of some "colored girl." Her colleagues on stage are quiet; they become her first audience, and we the audience for the whole cast. The lady in brown tells of Toussaint L'Ouverture, the Haitian hero with whom she fell in love, secretly, reading books under the covers at night. The lady in red, speaking as if she is narrating another woman's story, describes the complexity of "her" days and nights, creating a vivid, double-voiced speaker who smiles and sings her history as transformation from a sensuous young girl-whore to a sophisticated, powerful woman-whore. The lady in red goes on at some length, narrating the story of a woman who seems in control of her life. She concludes her story and this first sequence of the play by telling how "she" sent away the man who had been in her bed, wrote in her diary of her "exploit," placed a silk rose behind her ear, and cried herself to sleep.

The world these women are creating is sometimes solitary, sometimes augmented by other members of the cast. Each woman takes her turn talking, reciting, and, with time, each one's words become connected stories, stories that build a world that is first confessed by one actor, then integrated with the others when they hear each other out. The women of this rainbow sing and dance together of their own beauty, of their magic, of their Saturday nights. They, too, like the choruses of *Fefu* and *Approaching Simone*, close the first dramatic section singing together of the qualities of their lives, which concludes with all (but with the lady in red speaking first) chanting together the words, "and complicated."

These "colored girls" go on telling their stories of growing up, of moments of pleasure and moments of pain. They elaborate the "complications" they have named, and begin to find themselves. The lady in green tells a tale at once funny and gripping: "somebody almost walked off wid alla my stuff" (Shange, *For Colored Girls*, 49), she declares, and continues a monologue that is second by second funnier while simultaneously more frightening than entertaining. All of her stuff includes her whimsy and her independence as well as material objects. Near the end of her monologue, the lady in green confesses that until this incident she did not know how easily she gave herself way.

The stage becomes increasingly quiet, the players intense and aware as they listen to each other in a way they have taught each other to listen. In drama, as in music, silence can be palpable, can be at once joy and pain. As characters the actors teach us to listen, bringing quiet to the audience. The women dance and come together, draw each other into communal anger and strength and tenderness. Then the play nears its end, with the lady in red's story of "crystal," and her children and the children's father, "beau willie," who has just finished serving in the Vietnam war. "Beau willie" declares that he wants crystal and her children back; crystal resists, having given in to this man too many times before.

In nervous rushes and bursts of recollected terror, the lady in red concludes her story of crystal and her children (crystal tells the other women and us that beau has picked up their children and is standing near a window): "i stood by beau in the window / with naomi reachin for me / and kwame screamin mommy, mommy from the fifth story / but i cd only whisper / & he dropped em" (60). For the other women on stage and for the audience, something has happened. They can no longer stand alone or be without feeling. Isolation and fear bring the women together: they approach each other, touch each other, lay their hands on each other, form a circle and become silent.

For a moment there is only silence. The women come together at the close of the play provoked by the lady in red's underplayed revelation that crystal's story was her story, not a fiction, not a history of someone else: without any unique gesture or emphasis, the woman in red just switches from talking about crystal as another to "i stood by beau in the window."

This change of voice to the first person by the lady in red allows the other women on stage, and perhaps later the women and men in the audience, to speak. The words that follow the story of crystal allow the other women onstage to speak their final words of the play: singly and together the women urge other women to be strong, to find good in themselves, to love fiercely and to go on, softly, repeating the words of the lady in red: "i found god in myself & i loved her / i loved her fiercely" (63).

For Colored Girls ends with the ladies singing first to each other, then to the audience and "After the song peaks the ladies enter into a closed tight circle" (Shange's directions, 64). There remains a final coda, spoken by the lady in brown: "& this is for colored girls who have considered suicide / but are movin to the ends of their own rainbows" (64).

It is a lot to ask. Despite the women's movement, and the civil rights movement, many women remain or have become unsure of how to be in the world. Yet perhaps, as the lady in brown says at the end of *For Colored Girls*, women (and not only "colored girls," it is important to acknowledge,) are in the process of moving to the end of their own rainbows.

NOTES

1 See Helen Krich Chinoy and Linda Walsh Jenkins, *Women in American Theatre*, for the best list of plays of American women up to 1980. For playwrights and plays written before and after 1980, see also Rachel France, *A Century of Plays by American Women* and Emilie Kilgore, *Contemporary Plays by Women*, 590–93.

2 It is important to note here, as several other writers have done, that neither "the sixties" nor "the seventies" were congruous with a conventional calendar of feminist theatre events. The attempt to bring theatre into alternative venues and forms, the conception of the theatre company as author, performers, etc. arose as in conjunction with sixties politics, but reached well into the seventies. One critic (Sara Evans, *Personal Politics*) suggests that this occurred because the women of the American theatre, as was the case of many theatres and times, did not organize their efforts by calendar decades; thus it is not inappropriate to include women like Terry and Fornes. The latter both began working in oppositional American theatre in the early sixties, and withdrew from theatre companies in which women found themselves demeaned because they were women. For example, Tom Hayden delivered the speeches that Casey Hayden wrote, without reference to the "source." This may have seemed to be appropriate to some of the seventies theatre groups, in which "credit" was not to be important. But for the women, it was not just their absence on the playbill, but their absence publicly from the various public stages that made a significant negative difference.

3 See Helene Keyssar, *Feminist Theatre*, and Honor Moore, *The New Women's Theatre*.

4 See Evans, *Personal Politics*.

5 I urge readers to look at the bibliographies in France, *A Century of Plays*, Enoch Brater, ed., *Feminine Focus*, and Chinoy and Jenkins, *Women in American Theatre*.

6 These included Women's Theatre Council and New York Theatre Strategy.

7 See note 2 above. Women had difficulties establishing their own companies. Among reasons given were inexperience and the difficulty of the long work hours.

8 In the late sixties, Megan Terry was the first playwright to write and have produced a play that challenged the values and questioned the merits of the Vietnam war.

9 Terry's plays written during this period include: *Calm Down Mother, Comings*

and Goings, American Kings' English for Queens, Babes in the Bighouse, Ex-Miss Copper Queen on a Set of Pills, Home, Hothouse, Keep Tightly Closed in a Cool Place, Kegger.

10 Obviously, not all New York theatre in the sixties and seventies was experimental or unconventional in its themes, characters, or relation to audience.

11 By innovative, I refer to the language games, soft props, provocative approaches of actors to audience, and transformations that became key to experimental theatre in workshops and performances in the sixties and seventies. For more on this topic see my book, *Feminist Theatre*, 64–66.

12 See *ibid.*, 35ff., for more detail on sexism and racism as critiqued in Hansberry's plays.

13 See the introduction by Phyllis Jane Wagner to *Approaching Simone* for further detail on the historical figure, Simone Weil.

14 Terry refers to "magic realism" in the sense that it is used in reference to visual arts, especially painting, rather than to fiction such as that by Garcia Marquez and Borges. It appears to be first used in Germany in the 1920s, when a realistic yet socially critical style, "the veristic," emerged as a tool of social criticism in contrast to the then-prevalent styles of expressionism and abstractionism (see *Encyclopedia Britannica* online, 1997).

15 Jack Kroll, "Waiting for God," *Newsweek* 75 (March 16, 1970), 64. Finally, I have a chance to express my respect and gratitude to Jack Kroll. His reviews of film and theatre almost always provoke and please me; his obituary to Alan Schneider, my friend and colleague who taught me much about theatre, made me able to weep at Alan's death.

16 This is a controversial assertion to make. I know that my grandfather committed suicide in France in 1933, when Hitler came to power in Germany. My grandfather had been active in socialist movements for many years and had endured Siberian prisons for his efforts. When my friend, John William Ward, President of Amherst College while I was teaching there and subsequently head of the ACLS, committed suicide in the 1980s, another friend, angry at Ward, taught me why anger was an appropriate response on the friend's part. In every play I address in this chapter there is a suicide (or its equivalent in *For Colored Girls*). Perhaps Simone, in *Approaching Simone*, Julia in *Fefu*, and all of the women in *For Colored Girls* should encounter each other, their acts, and the meanings of suicide – on a stage.

17 Assunta Kent, *Maria Irene Fornes and Her Critics*, 115–17. Several areas of my interest and concern in Fornes' work are also discussed by Kent.

18 See my *Feminist Theatre*, 123–25.

19 See Michael Holquist, "The Politics of Representation," 162–83 for this specialized use of "ventriloquation," a term I and others have come to use frequently as if it were one of Bakhtin's own terms.

12

LAURIN PORTER

Contemporary playwrights/traditional forms

A story is always a question of desire. But whose desire is it that speaks, and whom does that desire address?

Teresa de Lauretis, *Alice Doesn't*, 112.

The appearance of significant women dramatists ... is a real reflection of a change in women's attitudes towards themselves. It is a sudden understanding that they can be, and indeed are, the central characters in their own lives.

Marsha Norman, in Betsko and Koenig, *Interviews*, 338.

In the 1980s, a striking phenomenon occurred on the American stage. In an eight-year span, three women dramatists, Beth Henley, Marsha Norman, and Wendy Wasserstein, were awarded the Pulitzer Prize, approaching the total of five Pulitzers awarded to women for the previous sixty years.[1] This same period saw the production of new plays by Tina Howe, Maria Irene Fornes, Emily Mann, Ntozake Shange, and Wendy Kesselman, among others, as well as the establishment of avant-garde, alternative women's theatre companies, both in New York and around the country.[2] In a 1992 *New Republic* article entitled "What Do Women Playwrights Want?" Robert Brustein refers to the "spate of plays by, for, and about women that have multiplied in the last decade," saying that "in terms of numbers, if not in broadness of theme, American women playwrights now represent a significant movement that is surely unprecedented in history" (28). I would like to examine how three women playwrights, Henley, Norman, and Howe, drawing on realistic modes, use these traditional forms to dramatize feminist perspectives.

It is necessary first, however, to define what it is that makes a play "feminist," a topic which has received considerable attention in the literature. Jill Dolan begins her important study, *The Feminist Spectator as Critic*, with a statement that parallels Laura Mulvey's point about film, namely that the theatre spectator has traditionally been assumed to be white, middle class, heterosexual, and male. While the male spectator is perceived as an active subject and encouraged to identify with the male hero in the narrative, women spectators and actors are relegated to marginal status; they are regarded as "passive, invisible, and unspoken subjects" (2). From this perspective, any play which moves women to the center of the narrative, foregrounding women's experience and concerns, can be considered feminist.

This focus on the content of the play as definitive is the key factor for many critics. Others, such as Helene Keyssar, for instance, emphasize the mode of presentation, stressing structure and performance as the crucial elements. These theorists tend to privilege non-realistic modes of representation, focusing on the work of avant-garde feminist theatres and experimental plays (Schroeder, "Locked," 104). Still others focus on different schools of feminist thought and the agenda each proposes. Both Dolan and Sue-Ellen Case, for instance, themselves writing from a materialist feminist position, make careful distinctions between liberal, radical, and materialist feminism and the political position each brings to the theatre, as does Patricia R. Schroeder in *The Feminist Possibilities of Dramatic Realism*.[3]

I find it helpful to conceive of plays as situated on a continuum from the least to the most feminist. A play that foregrounds women's experience, granting women subject status and moving their narratives to center stage, emerges from a feminist perspective. One that also exposes the patriarchy as a controlling force and the culture as defined, determined, and shaped by men, thus limiting women's development and range of life choices, makes the case more forcefully and moves toward more radical conclusions. To quote Janelle Reinelt, such works "underscore the social construction of gender, the male-gendered subject position and the corresponding space of the Other left for women in dominant bourgeois discourse," revealing and arguing against the historical nature of gender oppression ("Feminist Reconsideration," 49). A play which takes the argument to its limit insists, either implicitly or explicitly, on a restructuring of society and thus enters the arena of the political.

Of these three playwrights, Beth Henley by any measure is the least feminist in her content and intent as well as the most traditional in her use of dramatic structures. If her plays privilege women's narratives and occasionally reveal the destructive nature of patriarchal institutions and attitudes, in the last analysis Henley's female characters survive by adapting to the patriarchy and only dimly understand, if *at all*, the extent to which their lives have been shaped by a male-determined world. Henley's plays never seriously challenge the oppressive cultural structures themselves that have "cabin'd, cribb'd [and] confin'd" (*Macbeth* III.4.23–24) her female characters.

Crimes of the Heart, Henley's first play and smash hit, is a case in point. The 1981 Pulitzer Prize and Drama Critics Circle Award winner, it took the stage by storm, with critics lauding the "new voice" on Broadway. Set in Hazelhurst, Mississippi, it tells the story of the three Magrath sisters: the eldest, thirty-year-old Lenny, who looks after Old Granddaddy in the family homestead; Meg, a singer with beautiful eyes and a sad voice who went to LA to seek her fortune and ended up working for a dog food company; and Babe, the youngest, who just shot her rich and powerful husband Zachary Botrelle because she "didn't like his looks" (17). In the course of the reunion precipitated by Babe's dilemma, all three confront demons from the past. The operative archetype is that of the quest: each searches for a revelation that will explain her unhappiness and allow her to move forward. What is noteworthy here is that (1) although the play appropriates the typically male quest formula, the focus is on female experience and (2) the transformations of the sisters are grounded in an all-female community.

Further, their problems derive from patriarchal assumptions. Lenny sees herself as rapidly approaching spinsterhood. Her chief defect, in her mind, is the fact that she has a "shrunken ovary" and cannot bear children, which prompted her to end a relationship with Charlie Hill, whom she met through an ad in a dating service. At a critical moment in the play, she shouts at Meg, "It's so easy for you – you always have men falling in love with you! But I have this underdeveloped ovary and I can't have children ... so what man can love me?" (80). Her self-worth is determined by her value to men, which in turn is measured by her fertility.

The beautiful Meg simply represents the other half of the coin. One of Henley's promiscuous women (a common stereotype in her plays), Meg is described by Cousin Chick as "known all over Copiah County as cheap Christmas trash" (6). A more fundamental problem is the fact that she has lived her life trying to please Old Granddaddy, striving to fulfill his ambitions for her and telling him elaborate lies when she fails. Meg, too, has to rid herself of a male-defined identity. Babe, finally, has also been shaped by the dictates of a patriarchal society. Although according to Old Granddaddy Zachary was "the right man for her whether she knew it now or not" (22), he has emotionally and physically abused Babe for years.

In focusing upon women's narratives and revealing their problems to be the result of patriarchal values, *Crimes* is informed by a feminist perspective. One further manifestation of feminism is Henley's adaptation of the traditional romantic comic structure. Typically this pattern follows the familiar "boy meets girl, boy loses girl, boy gets girl" paradigm. In *Crimes of the Heart* this familiar formula is worked out in the context of an all-female world. The play begins with Lenny alone, celebrating her birthday in isolation from any community. Soon her sisters come home, however, and the action focuses on their relationships and separations, both minor (Meg's spending the night with her former boyfriend Doc Porter) and potentially catastrophic (Babe's attempted suicide). But they are reunited in the end, as Meg and Babe give Lenny a birthday cake that says, "Happy birthday, Lenny – A Day Late," enacting through this gesture comedy's traditional celebration of union and fertility. That this formula is played out in terms of women's relationships instead of the usual heterosexual ones reinforces the point made earlier, that the problems of the Magraths are resolved, at least superficially, within the bonds of sisterhood.[4]

Ultimately, however, the play fails to challenge patriarchal structures or even acknowledge that they have been the root of the problem. Lenny returns to Charlie, who she discovers doesn't want children. The fact that Lenny's value has been defined by her reproductive status never comes into focus; she is "redeemed" from infertility because Charlie, a prospective mate, doesn't care. Meg's breakthrough comes after she begins to sing again following her night with Doc, which has shown her that she can love and still endure, even if she loses the love-object. Two things here: Meg's problem, it is inferred, stems from her fear of loving, implying that for a woman, love relationships are determinative. Further, it is this experience with Doc rather than the support and solidarity she experiences with her sisters that enables her to finally stop lying to Old Granddaddy.

Babe's situation, particularly the immediate prospect of a jail sentence, is also resolved within the context of a heterosexual relationship, as she pairs off with Barnette Lloyd, her young lawyer. Although Henley provides a conveniently masculine symbol in the saxophone Babe is learning to play, the fact is that Babe has not appropriated any phallic power. It is Barnette who saves her from a life in prison, sacrificing his own vendetta against Zachary when he falls in love with Babe. And he alone calls her by her given name, "Becky," symbolically conferring a new identity upon her – hardly a feminist perspective.

Thus while Henley may replace male narratives and characters with female ones, she still writes for the male gaze, not challenging the bipolar definition of gender or essentialist definitions of womanhood. Couples pair off in heterosexual fashion; women undergo transformations only within the context of love relationships; and a male ultimately rescues the maiden in distress. To make matters worse, mothers, by and large, are villainized in this play. Their mother's suicide has obviously been psychologically devastating to all three Magrath sisters, who are abandoned at a tender age and left to Old Granddaddy, and Chick, portrayed as the villain of the melodrama whom Lenny literally runs off with a broom, is a "bad mother" who cannot control her children. But it is perhaps Henley's use of comic structure that most limits whatever feminism this play aspires to. By its very nature, comedy is conservative, upholding the *status quo*. There are no societal reconfigurations in the comic scheme of things, just resolutions that set everything to rights once again. Although she does assign all-female roles within a typically heterosexual narrative structure, in the end this is nullified by the play's male–female pairings and relationship-determined transformations.

The Wake of Jamey Foster (1982), Henley's next play, follows a similar pattern. The action takes place in the home of Marshael Foster, a young mother of three who is burying her husband, Jamey, who had left her for another woman. Marshael has been supporting her family by sewing drill team uniforms and selling "household improvement ornaments" since Jamey, threatened by her strength, left her. The night of the wake finds Marshael with her wayward sister Collard (another Meg), her brother's girlfriend Pixrose, and her prim and proper sister-in-law Katty, who has locked herself in the bathroom in despair over her empty marriage. To entice her to come out, the women take turns telling stories about their most humiliating experience. It is Marshael's that finally does the trick. She describes a time when she went to visit Jamey in the hospital and he insulted her in his new lover's presence, which, she says, "fiercely hurt me and my pride, like I wasn't even a woman." At that, Katty emerges from the bathroom, saying, "Oh, Marshael, honey, you are a woman. A beautiful woman. Don't let anyone tell you different from that" (*Four Plays*, 51).

As in *Crimes of the Heart*, this experience of female solidarity is presumably the impetus for transformation. Although Katty ultimately returns to her subservient relationship with her husband, both Marshael and Collard undergo significant reversals. Shortly after the scene described above, Marshael finally enters the parlor and confronts her dead husband: "You're gonna face me!" she shouts. "You cheat! I've got t'have something … redemption … something" (59). And the next day at the funeral, Collard, bolstered by her sister's faith in her, assumes the responsibility of taking Marshael's children to the funeral when Marshael refuses to go, speaking, the stage directions tell us, "with a new sense of command and warmth" (65).

It seems that at least two of these women have been empowered by female solidarity. A closer look, however, reveals that patriarchal structures remain solidly in place. Immediately after Marshael insists to the dead

Jamey that she must have "redemption," she says, "I'm so scared. I'm scared not to be loved" (59). That need is fulfilled by the minor character Brocker Slade, a bumbling but likeable man twenty years her senior. The play ends with his singing Marshael a lullaby as she drifts off to sleep, thus positioning her in the role of child. This relationship, ostensibly, will be the source of her "redemption." The play is further compromised by its treatment of motherhood, never seriously questioning the value society confers on motherhood as women's *raison d'être* nor challenging Katty and Marshael's need to be "fulfilled" by having babies. Gender roles remain unchallenged in this play, with a romantic comic structure, again heterosexual, pairing Brocker and Marshael and reestablishing the *status quo*.

The Miss Firecracker Contest (1984), Henley's next play, holds forth the promise of a feminist critique of society. Its protagonist, Carnelle, is competing in the "Miss Firecracker" beauty contest of Brookhaven, Mississippi – a contest her beautiful cousin Elaine won years before – thereby hoping to transcend her reputation for promiscuity and establish her true worth. This offers Henley the opportunity to critique beauty pageants and other institutionalized rituals which offer women up as commodities for consumption. Unfortunately, Carnelle loses the pageant when her rowdy former lovers call out her nickname, "Miss Hot Tamale," and pelt the stage with peanuts. When Elaine argues that the contest is meaningless, Carnelle shouts, "I wanted to win that contest ... It was important to me" (*Four Plays*, 128). Any possibility of exposing the pageant's inherent sexism is lost at this point. Carnelle never understands how being labeled "Miss Hot Tamale" by the very men she gave her body to validates a system which insists that women are to be used and then discarded. There is no insight or transformation, just Carnelle's decision to carry on. Henley's subsequent plays, *The Lucky Spot* (1987) and *Abundance* (1989), are if anything less successful dramatically and certainly no more feminist in content than *Miss Firecracker* or *Jamey Foster*.[5]

Of the playwrights discussed here Marsha Norman comes closest to being awarded canonical status. Indeed, much of the criticism revolves around whether this canonization, itself debated, represents an assault on the male-only bastion of American drama or a capitulation to white, heterosexual, male standards. Although not all of Norman's plays foreground women's narratives (*The Holdup* and *Traveler in the Dark*, for instance), the two for which she is best known, *Getting Out* and *'night, Mother*, plus a minor work, *Third and Oak* (two one-acts, *The Laundromat* and *The Pool Hall*), present a strong feminist vision, exploring what happens when women are allowed to author their own stories.

These plays, though quite different in setting, plot, and outcome, are alike in significant ways. All three revolve around the relationships of two women: Jessie Cates and her mother Thelma in *'night, Mother*; Deedee Johnson and the older, unrelated Alberta Johnson in *The Laundromat*; and Arlene and Arlie Holsclaw in *Getting Out*. The nature of the relationship, in each case, is that of mother–daughter, either literally or figuratively.[6] Finally, these plays pursue identical themes: taking control, choosing an identity rather than accepting one ready-made. As such, they challenge patriarchal values and reveal the social construction of gender.

Getting Out, Norman's first play, was originally produced at the Actors Theatre of Louisville in 1977 and moved to New York the following year.[7] It portrays the struggles of Arlene, newly released from an eight-year prison term, as she begins her life on the "outside," an ordeal made more difficult by relationships and incidents from her past. This relationship of past to present is suggested by the play's symbolic staging. Arlene's dingy one-room apartment in Louisville, Kentucky is framed by an elevated catwalk with a prison cell on stage right, to which it is connected by stairs. The actor playing Arlie variously occupies the cell, an area downstage, and another stage left, boxing in the apartment and suggesting that the present is limited by the past. To further reinforce this suggestion of imprisonment, a guard is stationed on the catwalk, so that the play literally takes place under a male gaze.

The action begins with two voices heard in sequence over the loud-speaker. The first, a woman's, reads various directives meant for the prisoners regarding kitchen workers, the exercise teacher's new baby, and the beauty school picnic lunch, which, as Jenny Spencer points out, "characterize the limited sphere of approved female activity both inside the prison and out" ("Marsha Norman," 154). The second voice, representing male authority, is that of the warden announcing Arlene's parole. It names her as subject, describes her life-narrative in terms it sees as definitive, and pronounces her "completely rehabilitated": "The Alabama State Parole Board hereby grants parole to Holsclaw, Arlene, subject having served eight years at Pine Ridge Correctional Institute for the second-degree murder of a cab driver ... Crime occurred during escape from Lakewood State Prison where subject Holsclaw was serving three years for forgery and prostitution ... Subject now considered completely rehabilitated" (Norman, *Four Plays*, 6).

This sets the stage for the action of the play, Arlene's determination to achieve subject status in the face of a patriarchal society which reserves that right for itself. This agon is dramatized by her encounters with Bennie and Carl. Bennie is a "benevolent" guard who has resigned from his job to drive Arlene to her new apartment, and Carl is her former pimp; both want to appropriate her body for their own ends. Bennie wants to assume the role of caretaker. He offers to get take-out chicken while she gets "fixed up." When Arlene insists that she "ain't gonna do no fixin'," he replies, with a knowing smile, "I know how you gals are when you get in the tub" (13). He legislates her desire as he sets the scene for seduction.

This scene is juxtaposed with one in the prison cell where Caldwell, another guard, brings Arlene her food, insisting that she has to eat. When she asks why he cares whether she eats or not, he tells her that they have a two-way mirror in the shower room and adds, "We sure do care if you go gittin' too skinny ... Yes ma'am. We care a ... hog-lickin' lot" (14). The whole patriarchal system, up to and including the Department of Corrections (the name is telling), subject her to male desire.

Arlene's former pimp Carl, though more odious than Bennie, operates from the same assumption: Arlene is his to use as he pleases. He's escaped from jail and come to take Arlene to New York with him, assuming she'll acquiesce: "We're goin' to the big city, baby. Get you some red shades and some red shorts an' the johns be linin' up fore we hit town. Four tricks a night. How's that sound? No use wearin' out that cute ass you got" (26). When she insists that she wants to go straight and get a job, his response puts Arlene's finances in perspective: as a prostitute she can make in one night what it would take her six eight-hour days to make washing dishes. Arlene's body is a valuable commodity in this culture; it's all she has worth selling.

The appropriation of Arlene's body began, we learn, when the child Arlie was raped by her father. Even the chaplain who first called her "Arlene" and gave her hope can be seen as manipulative in telling her that she had to kill Arlie, her "hateful self." This advice has enabled her to get out of prison, but something is lost in the bargain. Though anti-social at best and vicious at worst, Arlie at least fought to maintain her sense of self, whatever the cost. Arlene has learned that "the meek, them that's quiet and good" (52), are the ones that survive.

The only hope in this otherwise grim play comes from Arlene's association with Ruby, the ex-con who lives upstairs. Of all the characters in the play, only Ruby listens to Arlene, respects her pain, and tells her the truth. When Arlene, close to despair, says she thought life on the outside was going to be different, Ruby replies, "Well, it ain't. And the sooner you believe it, the better off you'll be" (52). Ruby's presence when Carl returns gives Arlene the courage to refuse him, and she is also there when Bennie drops by with some flowers. After he leaves, Arlene quietly tears up his phone number and accepts Ruby's offer to come upstairs, appropriately suggesting a game of Old Maids. Spencer feels that for Arlene, "getting out involves a giving up of the very strength she would seem to need outside" ("Marsha Norman," 154), but that combativeness is replaced at least in part by her budding friendship with Ruby. That, along with her courage in rejecting both Bennie and Carl, makes possible the final scene in which Arlie addresses Arlene directly for the first time. Arlie tells a story about her childhood in which she was locked in the closet and in rebellion "peed in all Mama's shoes." Arlene smiles as she listens, and they both say in unison, recalling their mother's reaction, "Arlie, what you doin' in there?" (Norman, *Four Plays*, 56). The lights dim on Arlene's "fond smile" as Arlie laughs once more. It is a fragile reconciliation, but it's a start. By integrating Arlie into her present life, Arlene will learn to mother herself.

Getting Out, in my opinion, is the most feminist of Norman's plays. Not only does it focus on a woman's struggle for self-determination in the face of powerful patriarchal forces; it documents the social construction of gender. Arlie's identity is shaped by a father who rapes her and a mother, herself abused, who fails to protect her; a pimp who uses her body for profit and prison guards who use it for pleasure. Her identity, then, is directly linked to her sexual identity. As Spencer notes, "no separation is made (or possible) between self and sexual identity. Arlie's sex determines the particular forms of abuse she suffers, just as Arlene's rehabilitation depends on the management of her sexual behavior and the appearance of a presentably feminine demeanor" ("Marsha Norman," 154). The role of "good" woman in this culture is associated with domesticity (kitchens and quilts) and making oneself attractive (exercise classes and beauty school). Her ability to invent herself, to discover who she is and who she wants to become, depends on her own inner resources, her integration of Arlie's energy and strength, and her newly forged bond with Ruby.

Norman's one-act play *The Laundromat* was written in 1980 as a companion piece to *The Pool Hall*, written two years earlier (the two were published together under the title *Third and Oak* in 1985). The plays are mirror images of one another. *The Laundromat* is about a brief encounter between two strangers, Deedee and Alberta, both doing their laundry at 3 a.m. in a dreary laundromat. No one else appears on stage except for a brief intrusion by a disc jockey named Shooter, who stops to do his laundry after his late night shift, then goes to the pool hall next door. *The Pool Hall* focuses on Shooter's relationship to Willie, the owner and a father-figure; the only other character who appears is Deedee, who serves as intruder in *this* plot. The spaces are obviously gendered: laundromats for women, pool halls for men – one, an extension of the private sphere and identified with domesticity and service; the other, a public and primarily social sphere identified with pleasure. Although they are more character studies than fully developed plays, both reveal Norman's understanding of the ways in which gender shapes identity.

Deedee and Alberta are another of Norman's mother–daughter pairs, figuratively if not literally. Though they are presented as complete opposites – Alberta, a retired schoolteacher, tidy, private, and reserved, and Deedee, sloppy, uneducated, and talkative – they are united by their loneliness and the fact that they are women. It may not seem like much of a basis for a relationship, but it proves to be enough.

Deedee's husband Joe, we learn, has been cheating on her. She is washing his shirts at 3 a.m. to escape their small apartment since he still isn't home from "working overtime" at the Ford plant. On Sundays they go to the garage and Deedee watches him work on his car, which he dreams of drag racing. She addresses envelopes for a company in New Jersey, but she can't spend her money or Joe would know she had a job, which he won't tolerate. Perhaps the most pathetic revelation is her story about a two-foot tall doll she had made by a company that imprinted a picture of her face on it. When she gave it to Joe for their anniversary, he "laughed so hard he fell over backward out of the chair and cracked his head open on the radiator" (*Four Plays*, 69). He later gave the doll away.

It is evident from these examples that Deedee's world is patriarchally determined. Joe's dreams are the definitive ones, not hers; her job is to watch and wait. Like Ibsen's Nora, she is financially dependent, not free to make or control her own money. The doll (also recalling Ibsen's play) is an icon of what the culture teaches women to be: pretty playthings.[8] Although Alberta has more resources to draw upon, her husband's recent death has left her alone, also. Having come to the laundromat in the middle of the night to wash his clothes, she tells Deedee she hasn't cried in forty years, and we believe her.

In the course of this evening, Deedee's chatter draws Alberta out, and Alberta, in turn, listens to Deedee with compassion. Their tentative relationship is disrupted, however, at the entrance of Shooter, the disc jockey whose seductive voice is heard over the radio at the play's beginning.[9] Deedee's attention immediately shifts to him, as they engage in flirtatious discussions, and Alberta withdraws coldly. Shooter becomes a magnet for the attention of Deedee, who intuits that this is where the power resides. Significantly, after Shooter leaves and Alberta and Deedee "make up," Alberta finally tells Deedee about her husband's death. She, in turn, listens to Deedee with compassion and concern. Before she leaves, she tells Deedee, "You don't have to put up with what he's [Joe] doing. You can if you want to, if you think you can't make it without him, but you don't have to" (80). Alberta has been able to provide the acceptance and encouragement that Deedee's own mother withheld. In using a romantic comedy pattern to structure the action, with Shooter the intruder who temporarily comes between Alberta and Deedee, Norman underlines the importance of women's solidarity and the extent to which their common experiences allow them to understand one another. Like Arlene in *Getting Out*, Deedee must believe in her ability to make her own life choices.

'night, Mother, a powerful drama about a woman's decision to commit suicide, is undoubtedly the play for which Norman is best known. Of all her dramas, it enjoyed the longest continuous run and generated a great deal of critical response, much of which polarized around gender differences, as Jill Dolan points out.[10] Some feminist critics who see *'night, Mother* as a play about defeat try to find an explanation for Jessie's decision: her lifetime struggle with epilepsy, her failed marriage, her delinquent son. Others debate Jessie's motive in telling her mother Thelma that she is going to kill herself – is it loving or hostile? – while still others focus on Thelma herself as a survivor.[11]

I would argue that Jessie has resolved the central issue of the play before the curtain rises. She's "through talking," as she tells her mother. Death is "exactly what I want" (18). When Thelma asks why, she says, "I'm just not having a very good time and I don't have any reason to think it'll get anything but worse" (28). In a much-quoted passage, she compares life to a bumpy ride on a crowded bus with fifty blocks still to go: "I can get off right now if I want to, because even if I ride fifty more years and get off then, it's the same place when I step down to it" (33). Later she compares her life to a radio with nothing on she wants to listen to. "It's all I really have that belongs to me and I'm going to say what happens to it," she says (36). This is her decision, and she regards it as an affirmation. When Mama pleads with her not to give up, to try something else, Jessie responds, "I'm not giving up! This *is* the other thing I'm trying ... *This* will work. That's why I picked it" (75).

Upsetting though the outcome may be, Jessie's narrative is about taking control. One can analyze the emptiness of her life from a feminist perspective, and certainly she has few options; one can argue, as Spencer does, that Jessie's suicide "is defined primarily in terms of the absent men to which most of the dialogue refers," men like her brother Dawson, her father, her husband, and son, though I find this position over-stated ("Marsha Norman," p. 156). But in the end, this is a play about female empowerment. Norman herself takes this position when pressed on the issue of Jessie's suicide as defeat: "Jessie has taken an action on her own behalf that for her is the final test of all that she has been. That's how I see it" (Betsko and Koenig, *Interviews*, 339). This is the crux of *'night,*

Mother's feminism. It is not a critique of the social conditions that led to Jessie's decision; indeed, for the most part, Norman strips such cultural markers from the text. It does not, like *Getting Out* and, to a lesser extent, *The Laundromat*, expose the cultural construction of gender so much as it tells the story of a single woman who finds the courage to write the last chapter of her life story in her own way.

This in no way diminishes the extent of Norman's achievement. Simply dramatizing Jessie's tragedy in a culture accustomed to valorizing male action is a bold move. We take Willy Loman's plight seriously and regard Oedipus' self-blinding as cosmic in its implications, but as Norman points out, our culture does not accord this stature to women's crises: "The things that we as women know best have not been perceived to be of critical value to society" (Betsko and Koenig, *Interviews*, 338).

For some critics, Norman's use of realistic modes and structures excludes her from the feminist canon.[12] Materialist feminists like Dolan and Jeanie Forte, for instance, take this stance. Forte's position is typical. "Classic realism," she writes, "always a reinscription of the dominant order, could not be useful for feminists interested in the subversion of a patriarchal social structure" ("Realism," 116). She argues for the connection between realist narratives and the oppression of women by identifying the Oedipal plot as traditional narrative's motivating force. Applying this definition to *'night, Mother*, Forte argues that "the play ultimately reinscribes the dominant ideology" (117). In "Mimesis, Mimicry, and the 'True-Real,'" Elin Diamond makes a similar point. Defining mimesis as a style which "posits a truthful relation between world and word, model and copy, nature and image, or, in semiotic terms, referent and sign, in which potential difference is subsumed by sameness" (58), she argues that realism, the "modern theater's response to mimesis," remains problematic for feminists because it "insists on a stability of reference, an objective world that is the source and guarantor of knowledge" and thus "surreptitiously reinforces (even if it argues with) the arrangements of that world" (60–61). This position is most succinctly summed up by the title of Audre Lorde's article in *This Bridge Called My Back*: "The Master's Tools Will Never Dismantle the Master's House" (Moraga and Anzaldua, *This Bridge Called My Back*).

While I understand the dangers implicit in appropriating a form which has been used to reinforce the patriarchy, I agree with Patricia Schroeder, Janet Haedicke, and others who argue that realism is a tool, not an ideology, and as such can serve a useful purpose.[13] Schroeder insists, for instance, "Feminists are in no position to discard the equipment at their disposal, to overlook any tool of resistance, even one – like realism –

inherited from the fathers who may have used it against us" (*Feminist Possibilities*, 43). A flexible and multi-faceted form, realism can be adapted to a wide range of purposes.

Consider Henley's use of realistic style and comic plots. Although laced with fairly strange characters and bizarre circumstances, her worlds are ones we recognize as "real," by and large, and her plots follow the traditional realist praxis of presenting problems to be resolved. Norman's plays, which presume a tragic sensibility, bend realism to quite different ends. *Getting Out*, while it follows a conventional narrative line in telling Arlene's story, intercuts with segments of "Arlie's" past. Juxtaposing these episodes with present action represents the relationship between past and present, as does the expressionistic set design. Further, the fact that Arlie enters Arlene's area unseen by the other characters, intruding upon her space–time continuum, requires that the audience adjust to a non-realistic convention, underscored by the fact that Arlene and Arlie are played by two different actors.

The Laundromat, as noted above, is more a one-act than a fully developed play. *'night, Mother*, though considerably longer, is also structured as a one-act, not just because it is played without an intermission, but in its handling of the narrative. In this play, Norman departs from traditional narrative strategies in announcing the outcome of the play within the first five minutes when Jessie tells Thelma of her decision to kill herself. Although the audience may cling to the hope that Jessie will change her mind, there is never any real doubt about her suicide. In giving up suspense, one of traditional realism's chief tools, Norman invites us to focus on other elements – character, motive, and theme. Thus though the play's technique is admittedly realistic, its structure breaks with a principal realistic convention.

Playwright Tina Howe pushes the limits of dramatic realism even further. Her plays, by and large, are not structured as problems to be resolved or events building to a climax, nor do they typically revolve around a central protagonist. *Birth and After Birth* (1973), for instance, which deals with the interaction of two couples, the one childless and the other with a four-year-old son, has no single protagonist.[14] *Museum* (1976) takes place in an art museum, with various groupings of visitors who simply comment on the art and pass through. *The Art of Dining* (1979) employs a similarly unconventional structure. Ellen and Cal, a married couple, have just opened an exclusive new restaurant with Ellen serving as chef, and Cal, the *maître d'*. As Ellen cooks real food before our eyes, tantalizing the audience with the smells of savory meats and rich sauces, various pairs and trios on the restaurant half of the stage eat their dinners and conduct conversations.

No narrative thread links these disparate groups of people; their only connection is the fact that they're dining in the same restaurant.

Neither of the latter two plays was kindly received by the critics, and Howe could not even find a producer for *Birth*. With *Painting Churches* (1983), her best-known work to date, Howe quite deliberately chose a more traditional plot. "I knew that *Painting Churches* was my last chance after the review of *The Art of Dining*," she said, admonishing herself: "'You better put a play in a conventional setting. You've got to stop all this fancy horsing around and settle down'" (Betsko and Koenig, *Interviews*, 323). Yet even this play, a three-character study of an artist who helps her aging parents move from the family home on Beacon Hill to a Cape Cod cottage, is as much about art as it is about the parent–child relationship. Mags, a talented portrait artist, agrees to help with the move if her parents, the famous poet Gardner Church and his eccentric wife Fanny, consent to sit for a portrait. As the play proceeds, the house is progressively dismantled as the portrait takes shape. The transformations of the personae, meanwhile, are even more profound. Mags comes to terms with the steady dissolution of her father's once formidable intellect and her mother's growing desperation while they, in turn, finally recognize her considerable talent.[15]

In his review in *The New York Times*, Frank Rich calls the play "a theatrical family portrait that has the shimmer and depth of the Renoir portraits the Churches so much admire" ("Painting Churches," 13). It is an apt metaphor. The entire play resembles an impressionist painting, or better, a series like Monet's haystacks or the Rouen cathedral, with each scene revealing the relationships and nuances of feeling in a slightly different light. Though there is admittedly a moment of resolution at the play's end, when Fanny and Gardner, enchanted by Mags' portrait of them, dance around the empty living room in an imitation of a Renoir café scene and Mags watches them, "moved to tears" (83), it is simply that – a moment, precious precisely because it is transitory.

On one level all of Howe's plays are about art and creativity. It is worth noting, in this regard, that most (though not all) of the artists in her plays are women: Ellen, the master chef of *Dining*; Mags in *Painting Churches*; Holly Dancer, the photographer in *Coastal Disturbances* (1987); Charlotte Blossom's dying aunt Olivia, a famous postmodern artist in *Approaching Zanzibar* (1988); and Dinah, a costume designer in Howe's latest play, *One Shoe Off* (1992).[16] Although the issues which the plays foreground are not, by and large, overtly feminist in nature and Howe doesn't self-identify as a feminist, the stories that she tells do revolve around women and women's lives. *Birth and After Birth*, for instance, focuses on both the problems that come with having a child and those that come with being childless, pitting parents Sandy and Bill Apple against their childless friends Mia and Jeffrey Freed, anthropologists who study children in exotic cultures. This play comes the closest of any in her canon to examining what might be construed as feminist issues: the difficulties of being left at home with a small child, the pressures on women to produce children as a badge of worth. But its intent is not so much to reveal oppressive patriarchal structures as it is to expose the limitations of both professional motherhood and careerism.

While her subsequent plays, like *Birth*, do focus more on women than men, the emphasis is primarily on issues of creativity rather than specific details of these women's lives. We don't know (or care) about Ellen as an individual or even about her relationship with her husband in *The Art of Dining*; what upsets us is the fact that he devours the hollandaise sauce and eats the grapes that were to garnish the duck. The play becomes a metaphor for the ways in which critics (Cal) sabotage the artist's creative efforts. Similarly, *Museum* is a fascinating exploration of consumerism in art, with viewers altering its shape and meaning as they respond to it – in the final scene, literally so, as museum visitors voraciously dismember an artist's soft sculpture for souvenirs. The list could continue. My point is that unlike Norman in *Getting Out* or *The Laundromat* or even, to a lesser extent, Henley in *Crimes of the Heart*, Howe's dramas are only tangentially informed by a feminist agenda.[17]

They are, however, unique in their departure from traditional "masculine" narrative structures dependent upon logic and linearity. In dealing with this aspect of Howe's dramas, Kenneth E. Johnson elaborates on the realist tradition referred to above. He notes that nineteenth-century realism is "dominated by a logic that imposes a particular subordination of one set of ideas, values, or beliefs on another set. In traditional dramaturgy this logic manifests itself in plot linearity to which events are related by cause and effect, constituting a trajectory that leads from 'development' to 'climax' to 'denouement'" ("Tina Howe," 15–16). Howe's plays subvert that tradition by refusing to privilege one position over another; indeed, they eschew the notion of conflict altogether. The result is a celebration of individual differences and their interplay rather than a search for conflict resolution.

Thus devices usually employed in structuring dramas are noticeably absent in Howe: for example, an agon or series of trials a protagonist must undergo, obstacles which must be overcome, demons from the past which must be confronted. The oppositional logic which informs the many variations on traditional patterns – either *A* will win, or *B*; the protagonist will either triumph or go down in defeat – does not inform Howe's plays. *Churches*, for instance, presents memories from the past, most notably Mags' story about the fiasco Fanny caused by her flamboyant behavior at her first group exhibition in Soho and the poignant tale about the gigantic wax sculpture she created out of melted crayons when for months as a child she was banished from the dinner table. While these are moving moments and help fill in some details about Mags' conflicted relationship with her parents, they are not essential to the action *per se*, nor do they ever come up again. They are simply presented as part of the portrait. Moreover, the relationship between Mags and her parents is not framed as a conflict where one or the other will prevail; rather, all three of them come to regard one another with greater tolerance and appreciation.

Howe's treatment of time also breaks with conventions of realism. Linear structures assume that the order in which events take place is key – a *sine qua non* of causality. In Howe, the opposite is true. Although her plays end with scenes that provide a sense of closure, one could rearrange the order of events – the dinner table conversations in *Dining* or the museum-goers' visits in *Museum*, for example – with no effect upon the outcome. The same can be said for the various visitors to the beach in *Coastal Disturbances*. These plays are more like a series of snapshots, taken in random order – or simultaneously, for that matter – than a narrative.[18]

In considering the critical and commercial response to these three play-wrights, the evidence supports the position of critics like Schroeder, Haedicke, and Judith Barlow, who argue that those who dismiss realism as ideologically incompatible with feminist objectives may be throwing out the baby with the bathwater.[19] To reject realism out of hand denies access to a wide spectrum of the theatregoing public. When one compares the reception of plays by Henley, Norman, and Howe, placed on a continuum of the most to the least realistic in structure and style, it is no accident, I think, that Henley's plays had the longest Broadway runs, followed by Norman and Howe, in that order. After its original run of two weeks, *Crimes of the Heart* reopened for a continuous run of fifteen months; *Miss Firecracker*, Henley's second most commercially successful play, ran for six (non-continuous) months. *Getting Out* ran for a combined Broadway and Off-Broadway total of six months, while *'night, Mother*, in different productions, enjoyed a total of thirteen. Howe's plays have been the least popular with audiences, though *Painting Churches* ran for six months at Lamb's Theatre after its initial brief production at The Second Stage, and *Coastal Disturbances* ran for eleven months.[20] Howe is, interestingly, the only one of the three not to receive a Pulitzer Prize. While popular success is obviously not a reliable index of artistic merit or a worthy objective in and of itself, it is one measure of a work's potential for making an impact. At the very least, it speaks to the possibility of reaching an audience.

The plays of Henley, Norman, and Howe, while all classified as dramatic realism, encompass a diversity of modes and moods, from the southern gothic comedies of Henley to the somber *'night, Mother*; from traditional comic structures to one-acts to Howe's non-linear forms; from a strictly mimetic style to the expressionism of *Getting Out* or the absurdism of *Birth and After Birth*. It is perhaps the very plasticity of dramatic realism that makes it such a powerful tool, one which serves these playwrights well. In the last analysis, I would argue, it is a combination of the conceptual content of the plays, i.e., their depiction of the culture, and the way in which the individual playwright manipulates dramatic form, that leads to either a reinforcement of the *status quo* or an exposure of patriarchal oppression. The answer to Brustein's question, "What do women playwrights want?" is simply that they want to be able to tell their own stories in whatever way they choose.

NOTES

1 The following women playwrights received the Pulitzer Prize for Drama between 1921 and 1958: Zona Gale for *Miss Lulu Bett* (1921), Susan Glaspell for *Alison's House* (1931), Zoë Akins for *The Old Maid* (1935), Mary Chase for *Harvey* (1945), and Ketti Frings for *Look Homeward, Angel* (1958). See Kathleen Betsko and Rachel Koenig, *Interviews with Contemporary Women Playwrights*, 456.

2 Patricia R. Schroeder writes about the emergence of feminist drama in the 1970s, "In 1978, Pattie Gillespie counted some forty feminist theatres in the United States alone ... Just three years later, in 1981, Helen Krich Chinoy and Linda Walsh Jenkins listed 112 American feminist theatres." See "Locked Behind the Proscenium: Feminist Strategies in *Getting Out* and *My Sister in This House*," 104.

3 Schroeder, The *Feminist Possibilities of Dramatic Realism*, chapter 1, and Sue-Ellen Case, *Feminism and Theatre*, chapters 4 and 5. See also Janelle Reinelt, "Feminist Theory and the Problem of Performance," 48–57, and Janet Brown, *Taking Center Stage: Feminism in Contemporary US Drama*, 5–11.

4 For a fuller treatment, see my "Women Re-Conceived: Changing Perceptions of Women in Contemporary Drama," 55.

5 Jonnie Guerra takes a similar position. See Guerra, "Beth Henley: Female Quest and the Family-Play Tradition," 118–30.

6 *Getting Out* presents two mother–daughter relationships, the dysfunctional relationship which Arlene has with her real mother and the more nurturing and significant one which she tentatively moves toward with Arlie. Norman's novel, *The Fortune Teller* (1987), also revolves around a mother–daughter relationship.

7 *Getting Out* won the John Gassner Playwriting Medallion, the *Newsday* Oppenheim Award, and a special citation from the New York Drama Critics Circle.

8 Spencer also makes this connection with *A Doll's House* ("Marsha Norman," 161). Interestingly, Thomas P. Adler invokes this play in reference to Jessie's final slamming of the door in *'night, Mother*. See *Mirror on the Stage: The Pulitzer Plays as an Approach to American Drama*, 8.

9 It is no accident that the last song Shooter plays, the strains of which we hear just before his sign-off, is "Stand by Your Man," a succinct statement of women's assigned role in this culture.

10 See Dolan's tracking of gender bias in reviews of *'night, Mother* in "Bending Gender to the Canon," in Hart, ed., *Making a Spectacle*, 326–34. For a breakdown of feminist responses to the play as liberal, cultural, or materialist, see Dolan, "Bending Gender," 336–37, and Janet V. Haedicke, "Margins in the Mainstream: Contemporary Women Playwrights," 213.

11 See, for example, Katherine H. Burkman, "The Demeter Myth and Doubling in Marsha Norman's *'night, Mother*," 254–63.

12 For a helpful discussion of realism as a dramatic mode, see Schroeder, *The Feminist Possibilities of Dramatic Realism*, chapter 1.

13 *Ibid.*, and Haedicke, "Margins in the Mainstream," 204–05.

14 Howe acknowledges her absurdist tendencies. In *Birth*, for instance, the role of four-year-old Nicky Apple is played by an adult actor. For a discussion of the absurdist influence in Howe's canon, consult Rosette C. Lamont, "Tina Howe's Secret Surrealism: Walking a Tightrope," 27–37. See also the interview with Howe in John L. DiGaetani, *A Search for a Postmodern Theatre: Interviews with Contemporary Playwrights*, 151.

15 *Painting Churches* won an Obie Award for Distinguished Playwriting, the Outer Critics Circle Award, and a Rosamond Gilder Award and was televised on American Playhouse in 1986.

16 Male artists include Gardner Church, a poet; Wally Blossom, a composer; and the sculptor in *Museum*.

17 Along with *Birth and After Birth*, Howe herself identifies *Approaching Zanzibar* as "a very female play," a "descent into that strange, haunted female landscape" (DiGaetani, *Interviews*, 153). While this is true, the focus of this play, it seems to me, remains primarily on the creative process.

18 Kenneth E. Johnson makes the interesting point, in this regard, that though all of Howe's central characters are artists in some way, "they are artists of non-narrative genres, genres that do not depend on the linearity of language and the logic that language can achieve" ("Tina Howe," 18).

19 See Schroeder, *Feminist Possibilities*; Haedicke, "Margins in the Mainstream"; and Judith Barlow, "Into the Foxhole: Feminism, Realism, and Lillian Hellman," 157.

20 Thanks to Jeffrey D. McMurtry for this information and other invaluable assistance.

13

JAN BALAKIAN

Wendy Wasserstein: a feminist voice from the seventies to the present

As a young girl growing up in Brooklyn, and later in New York, Wendy Wasserstein experienced the conspicuous double standards between boys and girls that ignited her feminist instincts. While her brother received Richard Halliburton's *Complete Book of Marvels* – a travel guide to spectacular places around the world – for his Bar Mitzvah, she was reading *Eloise* and *Madeline*. And, to instill a sense of feminine etiquette in her daughter, her mother sent her to the Helena Rubinstein Charm School. Moreover, to make her well rounded, she enrolled her in the June Taylor School of Dance. If that were not bad enough, when Wendy showed up everyday in the same work shirt at the Calhoun School on the Upper West Side of Manhattan, the headmistress would call her mother to tell her that she should get dressed up and wear pink (Bennetts, "An Uncommon Dramatist," 5). Indeed, she has always felt angry about the importance placed on women's appearance.

The marginalization of women also became apparent to her in the television shows she was watching as a girl in the fifties. Her favorite television show, *Bachelor Father*, depicting a debonair, suave small screen "Cary Grant," convinced her that she would "rather wear a dinner jacket than perform the routine housewife duties of Mrs. Danny Thomas, Mrs. Father Know Best, or especially June Cleaver." She felt compelled to find a female counterpart for the bachelor father, "a woman who possessed all the vitality of a Broadway musical, whose charms would beguile even Helena Rubinstein, and who never closed herself off from the possibility of adventure" (Wasserstein, *Bachelor Girls*, 6). Consequently, she became fascinated by Doris Day films, films about bright, self-motivated, charming, willful women, who approached life with guts and gusto.

The role of women became even more problematic for her at Mount Holyoke in the seventies. First they told young women to graduate and marry lawyers, then to become lawyers, but then women turned around and started having families. "They changed the rules in the middle of the game, and what you get is both confusion and liberation. You realize that you're free to make your own choice of whatever works for you" (Bennetts, "An Uncommon Dramatist," 5). While Betty Friedan's *Feminine Mystique*, the writings of Kate Millet, and Germaine Greer revolutionized the sensibilities of the class of '69 by shattering the conventional notions of being a mother and wife, Mount Holyoke forced these same women to wear hostess gowns and engage in the ritual of tea hour and milk and crackers in the evening while other college campuses were the sites of virulent anti-war protests. When she entered college, women were being "pinned," a ritual whereby men would give their dates a pin to wear as an emblem of their commitment, suggesting a possible engagement, but by the time she graduated, no one would be caught dead with a pin. Yet, they were afraid to say that they would become professional women (Rothstein, "After the Revolution," 28). On the one hand, the class of '69 was shouting "Suburbia Screw," but on the other, they later bore secret pain and loss about not having a family (Wasserstein, *Bachelor Girls*, 145). Wasserstein has astutely observed a self-recrimination that women feel for not having become a certain kind of woman because they pursued independent lives (*Bachelor Girls*, 148). Coming of age in the sixties, she recollects a feeling of solidarity, "a sense of we were going to change things. The whole sense of the women's movement was that it [would] change women's expectations of themselves, both externally and internally. Eventually that 'have-it-all' optimism imploded"; women began judging themselves harshly if they did not have a family and a wonderful job by the time they were forty (O'Connor, "Wendy Chronicles," 2).

Consequently, Wasserstein's plays dramatize women caught between these two conflicting sets of values and struggling to define themselves in a "post-feminist" America that still suffers from the backlash of sexism, of homophobia, and of traditional values. *Isn't it Romantic* and *The Heidi Chronicles* both reflect the problem of being told how to live one's life in the face of constantly changing values. Indeed, all of her plays reflect the fact that she came of age in the midst of the women's liberation movement, during which she attended feminist consciousness-raising meetings, where feminists asserted that "you either shave your legs or you don't" (*Bachelor Girls*, 17). These feminist meetings shaped the way she saw the world, assuring her that she did not have to marry a doctor and live in suburbia. It gave her the courage to become a playwright despite her perception that "there were no women playwrights when I was a girl" (Ouderkirk, "Human Connections," 10). "I never knew that you could legitimately go into the theater" (Clippings, Kaufman, *Wall Street Journal*, A12). The fifties in which Wasserstein grew up was a world of *How to Marry a*

Millionaire, in which Betty Grable brings home to Lauren Bacall and Marilyn Monroe an oil man she met in the fur department of Bergdorf's (*Bachelor Girls*, 165). Paradoxically, she longs for the fifties when things were simpler for women. Still, she turned her back on the fifties woman, but not without some sacrifice in her personal life. Indeed, Geoffrey in *The Sisters Rosensweig* addresses this dilemma, which is at once feminist and comes with the territory of being an artist: "We must work even harder to create the best art, the best theater, the best bloody book we can ... and the rest, the children, the country kitchen, the domestic bliss, we leave to others who will have different regrets" (*The Sisters Rosensweig*, 84).

Wasserstein's talent as a playwright resides in her ability to make personal conflict political and comedic as she chronicles baby-boomer history. A social historian, she tracks social change in a generation both cynical and hopeful, self-aware and confused. Her women characters have a metaphysical angst as they try to figure out how to live their lives in the face of so many options. Emotionally insecure, they are torn between conventional romantic expectations and career goals (Rosen, *Theatre Week*, 17). Helen Gurley Brown, Jacqueline Kennedy Onassis, Nora Ephron, Gloria Steinem, Judy Blume, Susan Isaacs, and Marlo Thomas flocked to the early run of *The Heidi Chronicles* because it crystallized their experiences as women (Maychick, "Heidi," 51). And it is no accident that Wendy Wasserstein is Hillary Clinton's favorite playwright (Clippings, London *Observer*, 5). Both she and Hillary come from a transitional time in America, when women were just beginning to gain their liberation. Wasserstein remarks, "if Hillary had graduated a few years later, she might not have thought she had to marry the guy who was going to become the president. She could have said, 'I want to be a senator'" (Balakian, "Interviews," 67). She grapples with the post-women's movement question, "where do we go from here" (Garfield, "Wendy Chronicles," 52). Although she is a social chronicler, who is consistently interested in the traps of being a well-educated woman, her worldview is also profoundly existential: "Most of the things my friends want in their lives will eventually come to pass through hard work, perseverance, privilege. Our lives are not totally random. We make commitments; we cause things to happen" (*Bachelor Girls*, 145).

If there was confusion about women's roles at Mount Holyoke, there was also a conspicuous voicelessness of women at the Yale School of Drama in 1973. As a student of playwriting, Wasserstein studied no plays by women, nor did she meet one woman director. In fact, at the first reading of *Uncommon Women* at Yale, a male student remarked to Wasserstein that he did not know if he could "get into" her play because "it was about women." Wasserstein thought, "well I had gotten into Hamlet and Lawrence of Arabia, so why don't you try this on for size" (Sweet, "Making It Specific," n.p.). Reading a lot of Jacobean dramas where men would kiss the lips of women, and then drop dead because of the poison, she thought, "this doesn't represent anyone I possibly know. I felt left out" (Isenberg, "Writing," 90). She also recalled that the plays that her parents took her to see either had few girls in them, or they depicted "dumb girls in slips." "There was nobody I could grow up to be" (Isenberg, "Writing," 90). Equally disturbed by Hollywood's negative and stereotypical representation of women, Wasserstein was determined to prove that a woman need not be insane, desperate, or crazy in order to be stageworthy. "Three middle-aged women on a stage who are accomplished and successful and not caricatures in our culture is still a surprise. And that's why I wanted to write this play" (Balakian, "Conversation," 382).

Although the women's movement helped to liberate women, Wasserstein continues to see the problems of sexism in contemporary America, where she says "the pressure is still on the woman to somehow make it all work" (Balakian, "Conversation," 384). She observes that to be a woman in the nineties demands "enormous resilience, energy, strength, and self-reliance" (Papazian, "Everywoman," 23). Moreover, she cannot understand why successful men in their forties are considered desirable, while successful women in their forties are deemed threatening. "Who made that up?" she asks. "Why are women's problems considered secondary to men's?" (Balakian, "Conversation," 384). Indeed, the crisis of The Heidi Chronicles is a uniquely female crisis. She remarks sardonically, "Baby boomer women are now content buying condos alone at the beach, having artificial insemination, going to Tom Cruise movies on Friday nights with women friends. Bachelor Girls under thirty enjoy temporary happiness with older, wiser, wealthier men, or with much younger tennis stars" (Bachelor Girls, 55). Furthermore, she is concerned that Elizabeth Dole, Tipper Gore, and other "new" political wives, who have acquiesced to taking a back seat to their husbands' careers, in contrast to Geraldine Ferraro, are setting a bad example to the new generation of women. "Women haven't come a long way if the ultimate privilege is being a first-class support system" (Bachelor Girls, 13). She recalls that her former boyfriend left her because she was spending more time with the production of Isn't it Romantic at Playwrights Horizons than with him (O'Connor, "Wendy Chronicles," 2). And she resents the fact that corporate America "depends on forty well-groomed women who maintain twenty-three inch waist lines and up to the minute invitation lists" (Bachelor Girls, 128). Finally, she is convinced that the "mommy track" is not equal to men's career tracks (Ouderkirk, "Human

Connections," 10). Wasserstein, however, resists being labeled a feminist playwright because she insists that good playwriting is about character, rather than about a political philosophy, that feminism is really humanism. In fact, her plays are all character-driven, rather than driven by plot.

Uncommon Women and Others (1977) explores the lives of five twenty-seven-year-old women who meet in 1978 at a New York restaurant and then travel back six years to their senior year at Mount Holyoke, where they perform the ritual of "gracious living" – a formal tea hour – discuss their future careers, men, sex, marriage, and the fact that society is patriarchal. Privileged, well-educated women struggle to make decisions that will enable them to be fulfilled socially and professionally in a patriarchal world. Having failed to reach such contentment in the present, in a Chekhovian refrain they look forward to a time when they will be "pretty amazing," though the age when they will attain their success moves farther and farther into the future. Serving as a segue to these flashbacks, the college president, represented by a man's voice, which, in the last scene, fades into a woman's, proclaims the ideals of the college: producing women with personal dignity, intelligence, competence, flexibility, maturity, responsibility, gaiety, femininity, a capacity for giving, stimulated by demands, intellectual curiosity, diligence, adventure, a conception of the good life, and the spirit of systematic disinterested inquiry. The woman's voice, however, recognizes the overwhelming obstacles to achievement and the limited set of options that women still encounter, despite progress in women's rights. Indeed, their elite education at Mount Holyoke has not prepared them for the complexities of the world outside their college dorms. As in all of Wasserstein's work, her female characters preoccupy themselves with "having it all." In effect, the play grapples with defining feminism. The action and conflict of the play consist of young women expressing their confusion about their lives. And for this reason alone, *Uncommon Women* was a landmark; it was the first time that contemporary women's issues were staged with seriousness Off-Broadway and then on public television. Wasserstein moved us from a literary tradition of men's locker rooms to the inside of a woman's dormitory. When asked whether she thinks *Uncommon Women* is a feminist play, Wasserstein responds, "the point of my play is that there is no 'wrong choice.' All you have to do is find what works for you" (Sturgeon, "Phoenix," n.p.).

Uncommon Women establishes the feminist concerns that Wasserstein continues to probe in each of her later plays. In addition, the strength of her writing derives from her characters' humorous discussions of sex, sexism, relationships, and careers. The play cleverly satirizes the dated traditions of all women's colleges, a world of "gracious living," peanut-butter-and-marshmallow-fluff study breaks, and elves. With references to lesbian rock bands, birth-control pills, the Cambodia strike, Judy Collins, James Taylor, the Beatles, EST, Bette Davis movies, the Dave Clark Five, and *Ms.* magazine, *Uncommon Women and Others* is a wistful social documentary about the confusion and aspirations of well-educated women in the late sixties and seventies.

Like *Uncommon Women and Others*, *Isn't it Romantic* (1983) explores upper-middle class, expensively educated, single women, but Janie and Harriet are six years older than their counterparts in *Uncommon Women*, and they are not simply sitting around a dorm room, talking about the future. They are out in the world, searching for love and professional fulfillment in Manhattan. According to Wasserstein, the play grapples with women being told how to live their lives, with the rules changing every six months (Gold, "Wendy," 30). The answering machine becomes a theatrical device, the icon of the eighties by which characters communicate their most intimate concerns. While Janie is the daughter of neurotic, overprotective Jewish parents, who desperately want her to get married, Harriet is the daughter of a professional, WASP mother, Lillian, who encourages her to pursue her career more than a marriage. Janie meets Marty Sterling, a Jewish doctor with a specialization in kidneys, doing his residency at Mount Sinai, who wants to marry Janie and move to Brooklyn. She feels suffocated by him, however, because he never consults her about moving, and views her as his future wife, rather than as an individual with her own aspirations. Janie takes a part-time job at *Sesame Street*, while Harriet, a Harvard MBA, gets promoted at the Colgate-Palmolive Company. Harriet first has an affair with her boss's boss, and then dumps him for her head-hunter, Joe Stine, whom she marries. Janie feels abandoned and betrayed by her best friend, who always vowed the importance of independence and considered herself Janie's "family." While Janie and Harriet are negotiating their relationships with men and with each other, we hear the recorded phone messages of Meryl Streep's desperate voice as Cynthia, Janie's old friend, blurting into the phone her rejection by the Upper West Side male population. With wit Wasserstein again probes serious issues: the complexity of relationships and marriage, the price of independence, the turbulence of growing up and finding one's identity, the question of whether women can have it all, the dynamics between mothers and daughters, the Jewish sensibility, and the problem of sexism in the early eighties.

The strength of *Isn't it Romantic* derives from its humorous and astute dramatization of feminist growing pains. Wasserstein has cleverly decided to have Harriet and Marty first meet in a class at Harvard called

"Twentieth-Century Problems," because these characters' lives are frustrated, not romantic. Contrary to Erica Munk's criticism that the play fails as a social play (Munk, *Village Voice*, 109), in fact it gives us more than a glimmer of the world outside by looking so astutely at the world inside – at the complex conflicts between mothers and daughters, between men and women, between women and within women, between what America tells women they should want, and what they need in order to feel fulfilled, between being American and being Jewish. As we watch Wasserstein's women make and break relationships, we are looking at America in transition, from a time when women lived vicariously through their husbands, to a time when they began asserting their own identities and negotiating the demands of their professions and their families. For Wasserstein's characters, growing up is painful and turbulent, and when Janie and Harriet confront each other in their climactic scenes, their anguish surfaces. Her writing is strongest when she pits two strong women against each other, who debate the pros and cons of marriage and independence. These are not the cartoon characters that critics often accuse her of writing. Instead, they are full of paradox, and when they finally disclose their values, they find out that best friends are not exactly the people they thought they were. Furthermore, she creates poignant moments, such as the ones toward the end when Janie refuses the mink coat her parents bring her because it is not true to her identity, when she tells them that she cannot compromise and marry someone she does not love, when her parents tell her they wish she wanted to see them, and she responds, "all you have to do is trust me a little bit" (150). For all of its light-hearted humor, *Isn't it Romantic* is a serious play about a young woman who learns to trust herself and to live alone rather than please others.

More political than *Isn't it Romantic, The Heidi Chronicles* (1988) explores the wistful character of Heidi Holland, a witty, unmarried art history professor at Columbia University, approaching middle age and becoming disillusioned with the collapse of the idealism that shaped the sixties. Spanning twenty-three years, the play begins with Heidi's slide lecture in which she affirms the neglect of women artists, and then it skates back to a 1965 Chicago high school dance where she meets several lifelong friends who inspired her interest in the women's movement. At college, Heidi and her friends become ardent feminists and radicals, and we see them at a 1968 Eugene McCarthy rally in New Hampshire, a 1970 Ann Arbor consciousness-raising session when Heidi is a Yale graduate student, and a 1974 protest for women artists at the Chicago Art Museum.

Heidi's friends become swept away by the materialism and narcissism of the Reagan eighties, leading the vacuous lives they once denounced. Heidi, however, remains adamantly committed to the ideals of feminism and feels stranded. At her high school alumni luncheon, the climax of the play, she delivers a long, impromptu confession concerning her feelings of abandonment and her disappointment with her peers. "I thought the point was we were all in this together" (232), she exclaims. By the end of the play in 1988, however, Heidi feels a little less alone and depressed in her New York apartment, having adopted a daughter as a single parent. She hopes that her daughter will feel the confidence and dignity that were the aims of the women's movement. In effect, the play subtly parallels aspects of the original Heidi novel by Joanna Spyri, in which Heidi learns while traveling and then "uses what she knows" (236).

Many feminist critics assaulted the play by insisting that it is not really a feminist play because Heidi "sells out" in the end by adopting a baby. They argued that "this unmotivated conclusion compromised Heidi's antecedent values," and that the true cause of her depression was her manlessness. In fact, when the play was being considered for film production in Hollywood, LA producers said, "we just have trouble with the main character, the second act and the ending" (Berson, "Women," 14). Wasserstein, however, retorts that Heidi adopts a baby because that choice is consistent with her character: "How can they say, 'we find the choice in your life politically incorrect. Give your baby back.' I thought feminism was turning against itself. She is a woman who wants a baby. It takes enormous courage to do what she does" (Balakian, "Conversation," 389). But beyond this particular complaint, critics argued that in general *The Heidi Chronicles* was perfect for a middle-class Broadway audience because it was not really subversive (Hodgson, "Heidi," 605–06). It evades serious feminist issues because it never raises the question of abortion or of women's rights in a real context (Robins, "Betrayals," 10), and that Wasserstein's choice to depict her protagonist as an art historian undermines Heidi's validity because her profession has little effect on anyone's life (Robins, "Betrayals," 10). The *Village Voice* critic similarly charged that Heidi assures us that intelligent, educated women are funny for the same traditional reasons women have always been funny: they hate their bodies, cannot find a man, and do not believe in themselves. Moreover, National Public Radio's Laurie Stone objected that Heidi rejects the word "feminist" in favor of "humanist," as if fighting for women's rights were diminishing (Rosen, *Theatre Week*, 17). Furthermore, Iska Alter argues that at the end, when mother and child are photographed in a slide, Heidi holding daughter Judy in front of a museum banner for a Georgia O'Keefe retrospective, we are left with an image of triumph, not necessarily its reality or realization, because Georgia O'Keefe consistently acted against the feminine grain and the feminist expectation

(Alter, "Wendy," 7). While it is clear that the play is not radically feminist (even Heidi regrets that she never torched lingerie), it is a mistake to read the ending so literally. Heidi and her daughter become icons for a future generation of women who will have a stronger sense of self in a more equal society. Carol Rosen assesses the play more accurately when she says that *The Heidi Chronicles* catapulted Wasserstein into another league; she could no longer be dismissed as early Neil Simon in drag because beneath her clever banter she confronts the anguish of women caught in the dilemma between love and work (Rosen, *Theare Week*, 17).

These negative critics overlook the bold and epic project that Wasserstein undertakes in *The Heidi Chronicles*. This was the first Broadway play to grapple with the collapse of the feminist movement during two decades of change. The play grew out of Wasserstein's strong feminist sentiments: "I wrote this play because I had this image of a woman standing up at a women's meeting saying, 'I've never been so unhappy in my life ...' The more angry it made me that these feelings weren't being expressed, the more anger I put into that play" (Shapiro, "Chronicler," 90). A "mordant comedy of manners" (Gold, "Wendy," 30), the play exposes the marginalization of women artists, egregious sexism, women's loss of identity, the collapse of marriage as a sacred contract, the difficulty that women face in negotiating between fulfilling professional and personal lives, and the lost idealism of early feminism.

The play may also be considered feminist in a structural and aesthetic sense. Feminist critics like Rachel DuPlessis, who argue that the female, literary aesthetic, written from a position of marginality, attempts to overturn dominant forms of knowing, and is therefore non-hierarchic, non-linear, and multiclimactic, could claim that the flashbacks that rocket us back and forth from the sixties to the eighties in *The Heidi Chronicles* are part of a feminine aesthetic. And, as Iska Alter notes, these devices continually pull the action back into the past, producing the ironic gaps between promise and realization, hope and disillusion that the events of the play announce (Alter, "Wendy," 7). Mimi Kramer has pointed out that the "moving-snapshot style of theatre is most often used to chronicle disillusionments and disappointments" (Kramer, "Portrait," 19).

When asked to define feminism, Wasserstein says that she cannot understand why gender imposes limitations on people's lives. "Who said that men who are forty-eight and successful are extremely desirable, and women who are forty-eight and successful are scary, threatening, and sad? ... WHY? Who made that up?" (Balakian, "Conversation," 391). If what the larger women's movement seeks is a transformation of the structures of a primarily male power which now order our society,[1] then *The Heidi*

Chronicles is in some ways a feminist play. Heidi's adoption of a baby certainly subverts the traditional family structure because she remains a single woman supporting herself as a professional. Perhaps Wasserstein's comedy is an intrinsic part of her female aesthetic. As she has said, "for me humor has always been a way to be likable but removed" (Shapiro, "Chronicler," 90). This is the same kind of distance that she associates with the female sensibility. Her humor "eases the way" for us to take a hard look at the problems of a sexist society and to recognize the fact that women's liberation still has a long way to go. By dramatizing the dissolution of the feminist movement, *The Heidi Chronicles* moved Wasserstein to the ranks of the serious social critics.

In her next play, Wasserstein moves from post-feminist America to 1989 London at the moment of the Soviet coup. *The Sisters Rosensweig* (1992) dramatizes the disparate lives of three sisters, Sara, Pfeni, and Gorgeous, as they congregate to celebrate Sara's fifty-fourth birthday. The oldest sister, Sara Goode, divorced three times, recovering from a hysterectomy, is a successful banker in a Hong Kong bank. She has moved to London to efface her Jewish identity by acquiring a phony British accent and a protective English last name from her second ex-husband, and naming her daughter Tess, after Thomas Hardy's novel, *Tess of the D'Urbervilles*. WASPier than a WASP, Sara relishes the openly repressed nature of English society. At first she is a cold woman, who resists falling in love again, until she meets Merv Kant, a Jew from Brooklyn and a world leader in synthetic animal protective covering. After a night with the furrier, Sara reembraces the Jewish identity that she had sublimated. Wasserstein wanted to write a play about two people who actually get together in the end, in contrast to her earlier plays in which her female protagonists remain alone. In short, the play affirms the possibility of love for middle-aged women. And, unlike the men in *Uncommon Women and Others*, and *Isn't it Romantic*, the men in this play are positive forces, with the exception of Nick Pym, Sara's English male friend, whom everyone accuses of being a Nazi. Sara leaves him for Merv.

Sara's daughter, Tess, is doing a biography of her mother's early years for her school summer project. Her exploration of her family history provides a context for each character's quest for their identity. While Tess longs to return to her Connecticut home, she plans to go to Lithuania to support the Lithuanian independence movement with her working-class boyfriend, Tom Valiunus. Sara adamantly opposes Tess' relationship and her journey. In the end, Tess decides not to go to Lithuania, not because of her mother, but because she ultimately does not feel sincerely connected to the Lithuanian movement.

While Sara is a self-loathing Jew, her youngest sister, Gorgeous, is an unabashedly practicing Jew, a yenta, who encourages Sara to fall in love again. She is in London not just for her sister's birthday, but because she is leading the Temple Beth El sisterhood on a trip to see the Crown Jewels. Married to an attorney, who, she later reveals, has lost his job and is writing mystery novels in the basement, she seems to have the most conventional life of the sisters, a mother of four, who lives in Newton, Massachusetts. But Gorgeous has an unusual career. A kind of Dr. Ruth Westheimer, she has a call-in radio show where people discuss their love lives. Her humor dominates the play.

Pfeni, the middle sister, is a forty-year-old journalist, dating a bisexual theatre director, Geoffrey, who leaves her because he misses men. The wandering Jew, Pfeni has renounced her political writing for travel writing because she feels that she is exploiting the people whose problems she records, and because her career does not meet her deceased mother's expectations. As Howard Kissel puts it, she has "secularized her Jewish idealism in radical journalism" ("Family Circus"). Sara helps her understand that she has turned her back on her true calling.

Although the three sisters are from the same place, they lead vastly different lives. In effect, the play is about the journey that each woman takes to discover herself: at the end, Sara discovers love again and acknowledges her Jewish roots, proclaiming, "My name is Sara Rosensweig." Gorgeous takes responsibility for her life and cashes in her Chanel suit in order to send her son to college. Pfeni returns to political journalism. Tess discovers that she does not have to go to Lithuania to find out who she is. Thus, the larger political backdrop of Eastern Europe's democratization parallels the evolving autonomy and liberation of each woman.

Wasserstein's sisters, who yearn to find their "Moscow," their place in the world, overtly echo Chekhov's *Three Sisters*. Wasserstein acknowledges her debt to Chekhov:

> Like Chekhov, I wanted to write a play dealing in time, obsessing about time. I wanted to write something about the end of the century when everything was breaking up. Setting it at the time of the Russian coup was important because there was great hopefulness then, before things fell apart. I also wanted to write about [the fact that] time has passed and you're not going to be all those persons you might have been; you have a history, you've chosen a road, and yes, you did know what you were doing.
>
> (Darling, "Wendy Generation," 12)

The play is also Chekhovian in the way it balances comedy and melancholy. While examining serious questions about identity, family, relationships, the democratization of Eastern Europe, the American recession, the plight of homelessness in London, bisexuality, and the predicament of women in mid-life, the play still manages to sustain a comic tone.

Wasserstein set out to write a play in which, for once, her female protagonist would not remain alone, but would connect with a man, "especially in a culture that tries to deny the possibility of love to women over thirty-five" (Darling, "Wendy Generation," 12). She also wanted to place women of dignity on stage. In an interview Wasserstein has said, "the fact is, three middle-aged women on a stage who are accomplished and successful and not caricatures in our culture is still a surprise. And that's why I wanted to write this play" (Balakian, "Conversation," 382). The play questions whether all women should want to marry. It also asks whether women's issues should be ghettoized.

The Sisters Rosensweig is Wasserstein's most skillfully written play to date. Even though it is a quintessentially New York play, full of New York and Jewish references, it grabbed audiences outside New York because it tells a well-structured story about three sisters who revel in telling stories. Unlike her previous plays, this one is a one-set, non-episodic play, complete with the unities of time, place, action, and with two stock characters who represent the polarities of English society: an upper-class snob, Nick Pym, and a young, working-class radical, Tom Valiunus. Its brilliance lies in its balance of humor and the serious issues of identity, self-hatred, and the possibility of romance and love when it seems no longer possible, or, sadder yet, no longer necessary. Wasserstein felt strongly about creating a role for a woman over forty who falls in love with a nice man at first sight. This is a play of possibilities, not just in terms of a middle-aged love, but in its exploration of characters who discover who they are. *The Sisters Rosensweig* is a Broadway play of the sort Wasserstein saw as a girl in New York, one that makes us laugh a little, sigh a little, and go home feeling that despite life's confusion and pain, things will somehow work out.

Nevertheless, Wasserstein is fully aware that life does not work out for all women. In 1994, riveted by the harassment experienced by Zoe Baird, Lani Guinier, Kimba Wood, Hillary Clinton, and later by the media hype surrounding Secretary of State Madeleine Albright (Franklin, "Time," 64), Wasserstein headed to Washington DC to do research for the most overtly political work of her career, a play about a woman in politics, *An American Daughter*. The Zoe Baird debacle was foremost in her mind. Baird, a corporate lawyer, nominated to be Attorney General, was forced to withdraw after it was learned that she and her husband had hired illegal aliens as domestic help. To Wasserstein, this excuse for denial of high office insulted all women of ambition and reminded her that "ingrained prejudices about women's roles die hard" (Marks, "Outsider," 5). Moreover, the play also reflects her troubled awareness that women still hold only about 10 percent of the seats in Congress, and that politicians and journalists view issues like child care and sexual harassment as being "women's issues" rather than everyone's concern. "There's a danger in that kind of thinking," says Wasserstein (Marks, "Outsider," 5). Part political satire, part morality tale, *An American Daughter* (1996) not only takes a hard look at the media's destruction of the woman nominee for Surgeon General, but it also dramatizes the predicament of two different kinds of women coming to mid-life and having regrets, as well as the new generation of feminists.

In addition to examining Wasserstein's concern about sexism, in this play she scrutinizes the problems with liberalism for the first time. In fact, she had long wanted to compose a play about the liberal establishment (Marks, "Outsider," 10), and, with President Clinton in office, the moment seemed right. She turned to her friend and former editor of *The New Republic*, Michael Kinsley, to check the play for accuracy. *An American Daughter* was also a first in another sense; this was the first of Wasserstein's plays to go directly to Broadway without an initial Off-Broadway run.

The play takes place in 1994 at the Georgetown home of Lyssa Dent Hughes (Kate Nelligan), the great-granddaughter of Ulysses S. Grant. Lyssa Hughes is an idealistic, liberal doctor in her early forties who has just been nominated as Surgeon General by a Democratic president. She seems to have it all – a prominent sociologist for a husband, a comfortable George-town home with two children, and a medical career. On the other hand, her best friend, Dr. Judith Kaufman (Tony award-winning Lynne Thigpen), a black, Jewish oncologist, is desperately trying to conceive a child. Divorced from a gay, Jewish psychiatrist whose new partner is a florist-opera singer-doctor, and profoundly depressed about not having children, she tries to drown herself in the Potomac. But Lyssa's life does not turn out much more auspiciously. Her gay, politically conservative friend, Morrow, reveals to the media that she failed to respond to a jury notice, and thereby destroys her prospect for becoming Surgeon General. Moreover, her husband, Walter Abrahmson (Peter Riegert), a professor of sociology and author of an influential book on liberalism called *Towards a Lesser Elite*, cheats on her with his former student, the flashy, superficial feminist, Quincy Quince (Elizabeth Marvel). A Naomi Woolf-second-generation feminist, she has written a best-seller, *The Prisoner of Gender*. Timber Tucker (Cotter Smith), the journalist reminiscent of Forrest Sawyer, interviews Lyssa so ruthlessly that he forces her to withdraw her nomination for Surgeon General. Not even the spin doctor, Senator Hughes' assistant, who is called in to coach Lyssa about how to present herself before the media, Billy

Robbins (Peter Benson), can salvage her career. Lyssa's father, the famous Republican senator from Indiana, Alan Hughes, based on the former Wyoming senator, Alan Simpson (Hal Holbrook), wishes that he could have prevented his daughter from withdrawing her nomination, but she tells him about her decision only after she has decided to withdraw. The senator's socialite fourth wife, Charlotte "Chubby" Hughes (Penny Fuller), represents the generation of women before the feminist movement. In the end, both Lyssa Dent Hughes and Judith Kaufman have failed to achieve their aspirations. Nevertheless, Lyssa refuses to accept defeat and pronounces the words of her great-grandfather, Ulysses S. Grant, to his daughter, as she walks up the stairs to see her children, "our task is to rise and continue" (*An American Daughter*, 105).

The play concerns itself most centrally with the problems that accompany being a successful, intelligent, powerful woman in the public arena. Dr. Judith Kaufman is convinced that "a woman's life is all about boundaries," that "women don't have heads, necks, or throats" (6), and she affirms that if Lyssa were a man, her failure to do jury duty would be a non-issue, an oversight. Quincy Quince, who believes that "sweet women are trapped by their own hostility" (5), has written *The Prisoner of Gender*, referring to it as "sexism made simple" (5). Quincy is convinced that Dr. Hughes is a prisoner of her gender. Because she assumed so many obligations, she overlooked her public obligation of responding to her jury notice. "The best intentions in females often become the seeds of their own destruction," she explains. Still, she acknowledges that women have come a long way: "women in the twenties and thirties were [only] able to excel in show business, cosmetology, and aviation" (4). Believing that women have transcended the need for women mentors in the nineties, she has no problem with the fact that her academic mentor is a male professor, Walter. Without realizing it, however, she, too, is a prisoner of gender in her drive to "have it all." Having two books to write, wanting to start her family before she focuses on her public life, concerned about restoring women's sexual identity, she plans to write another book called *Venus Raging*. "Sex for Lyssa's generation became just something else to be good at ... We, on the other hand, want to come home to a warm penis" (35). Quincy, however, does not represent a hopeful future for the new generation of feminists. Only concerned with her fame, and lacking ethics, she has an affair with Lyssa's husband, her former professor. When Lyssa withdraws her nomination, she glibly remarks, "she's still gotten a lot of heat out of it" (81). Further, this nineties "feminist" is hardly articulate, using "like" before nearly every phrase she speaks.

Once again, then, Wasserstein explores the price that women pay when they try to "have it all." Dr. Judith Kaufman prefers "the reliable variables of science" to the precariousness of public life, and Lyssa's experience with a muck-raking media drives her to conclude that she "does not know what really smart means anymore" and that "the Lyssa Dent Hughes generation is still twisting in the wind" (96).

Consequently, the play asks where a woman should go to find a role model. Lyssa has no such model in her family because she lost her mother at an early age. Her father asserts that Amy Fisher should have been her role model, instead of Eleanor Roosevelt and Florence Nightingale.[2] Lyssa wishes her father could console her the way he did when she was a little girl: "I'd give anything for you to show up and say, 'everything's going to be fine. Here's an awful red coat'" (102). Her father is powerless to help her in the face of social forces that destroy her. Dr. Kaufman also wants contemporary women role models on whom she can rely. The only noteworthies, however, were Mamie Eisenhower, Dorothy Kilgallen, and Lena Horne.[3] But since she knew she wanted to be a scientist, only Marie Curie came close to her aspirations. Therefore, she had to invent herself.

While Lyssa is trying to bring feminism into the twenty-first century, Walter suggests that maybe feminism "should cease and desist in the twentieth century, like Soviet communism or the rotary dial" (41). Indeed, the spin doctor seems to verify this idea when he coaches Lyssa to emphasize her family values and her midwestern humility as opposed to her liberal, eastern, elitist political views. Lyssa is keenly aware that she has to play the role that the public demands, but she also insists on being true to herself: "I'm a senator's daughter, so I can put [the headband] on and I can take it off ... I won't be hung out to dry ... even if I have to wear a headband, bake cookies, or sing lullabies to do it" (83). When Lyssa takes off her headband, she takes off the pretense of being someone other than who she is.

Yet, her inability to be someone other than herself ultimately prevents her from assuming the position of Surgeon General. As director Dan Sullivan says, "the question that Lyssa confronts turns 1960s idealism on its head: can an ethical, progressive person enter public life without having to betray her values? ... to be a politician, everyone has to turn into someone else." From a feminist point of view, however, the play is about women as outsiders (Marks, "Outsider," 5).

Charlotte, Lyssa's stepmother, represents the sensibility of women before the women's movement. For her, being a feminist means managing the Southampton Golf Club and being the first to host the Dinah Shore Classic. Similarly, Lyssa describes her mother as an ordinary Indiana housewife, who "took pride in her icebox cakes and cheese pimento canapes" (45).

And when American women hear her describe her mother in this fashion, they feel assaulted and diminished. Lyssa represents the generation between her mother and Quincy, whom, Walter says, that Quincy must think of as "one of those seventies good girls who came to prominence in the nineties and schedules half an hour a day for spontaneity" (41).

Dr. Judith Kaufman represents the other polarity of the nineties woman, the one that gravitates to the conventional role of women, despite her accomplishment as a physician. She regrets the fact that she can neither "make life or stop death" (99), that she has let her life pass without having children. Her failed quest for fertility coincides with Lyssa's withdrawal from her nomination. Accordingly, the play is set during the festival of regrets. Their only consolation, then, is their friendship and moving on "with the second part of [their] lives."

The play *An American Daughter* makes clear that women's liberation has a long way to go. Not only does Lyssa know that classic rock is "very paternal," and represents the female body in misogynistic ways, but she is on a crusade to educate the public about women's health care and advocates reproductive rights. Indeed, a woman's vulnerability is most clearly evident in the health problems that are unique to women. Dr. Judith Kaufman is an oncologist, specializing in women's breast cancer. Rather than working together, however, women compete against each other, obstructing larger, political progress for women. For instance, the female public opinion is running against Lyssa Dent Hughes four to one, in part because she is successful, attractive, and has two great kids. Further, American women find her condescending and elitist. After watching her on television, her children tell her that the public thinks that their mother is "what's wrong with America" (71). As Walter says, "in the heartland that means you're one prissy privileged, ungrateful to her mother, conniving bitch" (64). For this reason, Lyssa's stepmother cautions her to protect her family and marriage because jealous or disappointed people will destroy her. She knows that trying to impress the public will ruin Lyssa's life, so she advises her to find a way "to move forward gracefully" (68).

America betrays both women. Not only can women not count on other women to support them, but they also cannot rely on their close friends. Morrow, the conservative gay man, who is supposed to be a close family friend, reveals the fact that Lyssa failed to do jury duty, claiming "I forgot they were people I know and like" (78). The journalist is equally pernicious. His interview with Lyssa consists of brutal questions about whether she resented her mother, whether she is too perfect for the American public, whether she likes her father's fourth wife. Further, he pits Lyssa against her father. The talk show becomes the nineties vehicle for betrayal. Lyssa retorts that her answers to these questions have nothing to do with her potential competence as Surgeon General. American women, she boldly asserts, should instead concern themselves with retaining their reproductive rights, with the fact that breast cancer, ovarian cancer, and uterine cancer research are grossly underfunded compared to prostate cancer, and with teenage drug addiction and pregnancy. After the televised interview, Timber tells Lyssa, "I tried to warn you" (94), but his remark merely reinforces his unethical behavior. Thus, the play dramatizes the power of the media to ruin lives, and the voices of the media at the doorway infiltrate the living room each time the senator enters.

As much as the play attacks sexism, it assaults liberalism. Judith points out that Morrow and the brightest minds misguidedly believe that "sexual preference is the reason for all personal and societal happiness" (26). Gay awareness, however, will not solve all social problems. "There won't be a national health insurance or decent schools because of where you choose to place your penis" (26). Moreover, she complains that AIDS receives more attention than women's cancer. Wasserstein makes a bold dramatic decision in having her gay character destroy her protagonist's career. Morrow has converted to the far right "because of the inconsistency of the left." He is convinced that "left-wing rage for selective privilege or self-righteous entitlement" (27) is far more insidious than his conversion to the right. Indeed, he attributes Lyssa's oversight of her jury notice to her liberal sense of entitlement; she was too busy with her professional and political duties to fulfill her civic ones. Morrow, however, is more concerned about his immediate well-being than with the larger social direction of America, just as the media is.

If social forces betray Lyssa Dent Hughes, feminists might also argue that the play betrays radical feminist values by espousing rather traditional values for women. After all, Lyssa's father tells her that she read too many books about Eleanor Roosevelt and Florence Nightingale when she should have found more sensible heroines like Arianna Huffington[4] and Amy Fisher. While Lyssa tells Dr. Kaufman that "all lives don't have to be about children" (11), she nevertheless confesses that her "greatest privilege is my family" (90). Her stepmother also advises her to protect her family and marriage before her career, and she confides to her husband, "I never intended for our lives to become about me" (71). It is also curious that Lyssa's two children are boys rather than girls. At the end we hear them yelling for Mom, as if to say, "Mom, where are you??!" as if suggesting that Lyssa's ultimate responsibility, like the fate of many professional mothers, lies with her children.

Critics accurately point out that, in *An American Daughter*, Wasserstein is "one of the few American playwrights since S. N. Behrman to create a commercial comedy of manners with moral and social heft" (Brantley, "Hostile Glare," C14–16). A *New York Magazine* critic wrote that "Wasserstein valiantly juggles several genres: drawing-room comedy, comedy of manners, political satire, a social problem play, and a domestic infidelity drama" (April 28, 1997, 102–03). Some critics, however, claimed that the play does not know where it is going, despite Wasserstein's ear for dialogue and sense of craft. On the contrary, the play's direction is quite clear: the media destroy the career of a dedicated public servant, not because of her qualifications, but because of a minor oversight. As Wasserstein says, "what happens to women, sometimes, is blatantly unfair" (Balakian, "Interviews," 70). The play is about the sadness of a generation in a personal and a political sense. It probes questions about women's identity and self-determination. Well into their forties, the characters in *An American Daughter* have found that being amazing has its own disappointments. Whereas her earlier plays had to do with women in the process of making choices, now her characters find themselves in predicaments as a result of the choices they have made. But whatever their obstacles and disappointments, they persevere. Finally, Wasserstein insists on the American quality of the Lyssa Dent Hughes predicament. A descendant of Ulysses S. Grant, whose family is "American and has been for generations" (103), Lyssa should have inherited the right to life, liberty, and the pursuit of happiness. Instead, she is a prisoner of her gender. In a choral moment, her father the senator says, "there's one idea of America out there right now I just can't grab onto … It's certainly not our most illuminating or honest hour" (101).

Each of Wasserstein's plays, then, wistfully explores the predicament of well-educated women trying to have it all – fulfilled personal and professional lives – within a sexist society. She is convinced that "the issues of women would not be taken care of unless women take care of them" (Balakian, "Interviews," 66). The plays reflect her stinging awareness that girls are taught to be nice, to make things work for people, at the expense of themselves. And they all have a distinctly New York, Jewish flavor. Moreover, with the exception of Lyssa Dent Hughes in *An American Daughter*, her characters never experience cataclysmic tragedies, but rather a Chekhovian, middle-class combination of melancholic sadness, moments of regrets, and moments of comedy. They affirm that there are possibilities in life, along with great sadnesses. *Uncommon Women and Others* attempts to define feminism as it dramatizes the confusion and aspirations of women graduating from college. In effect, it conveys that the women's movement has really not been successful. *Isn't it Romantic* explores the complexity of relationships, the price of independence, the difficulty of finding one's identity, and being Jewish in New York. *The Heidi Chronicles* grapples with the collapse of the feminist movement during two decades of change, while *The Sisters Rosensweig* comes to terms with being Jewish and with the possibility of love for a middle-aged woman in the context of the Russian coup. Her darkest and most searing play to date, *An American Daughter*, reveals the harassment experienced by women in politics, while also attacking liberalism. Thus, in each play, Wasserstein is a kind of sociologist, probing the psyche of "serious, good" American women (Balakian, "Interviews," 70), who have questions about their identity and self-determination, in a society that continues to impose double standards on them. However tortured her characters are, their humor sustains them.

NOTES

1 See Annette Kolodny, "A Map for Reading: Gender and the Interpretation of Literary Texts."

2 Amy Fisher (1974–) was sentenced to prison for first degree assault against Mary-Jo Buttafuoco. She allegedly had an affair with Buttafuoco's husband. Eleanor Roosevelt (1884–1962) began her own political work in support of her husband, the future president Franklin Delano Roosevelt, in 1921, the year he was stricken with polio. A humanitarian and social worker, she served as one of the first delegates to the United Nations, and was one of the most influential and beloved first ladies in American history. Florence Nightingale (1820–1910) was an English nurse, the founder of modern nursing.

3 Mamie Eisenhower (1896–1979) was the wife of President Dwight D. Eisenhower. White gloves were so integral to her public image as first lady that they became emblematic of a lady-like female middle-class ideal in the 1950s. Dorothy Kilgallen (1913–65) was a journalist and television personality in the fifties. In 1936 she had challenged and beaten Nellie Bly's biggest stunt, breaking the record of Jules Verne's hero in *Around the World in Eighty Days*. Lena Horne (1917–) is a singer and actress. In 1943, she became the first black performer to have a long-term contract with a major movie studio.

4 Arianna Huffington is a well-known author, lecturer, and broadcaster. Her books include *The Female Woman*, on the feminist movement, biographies of Maria Callas and Pablo Picasso, works on Greek mythology, and on the intersection of politics and culture. She also wrote *The Fourth Instinct*, on the longing for meaning in a secular world. She is a frequent guest on national television and speaks often on culture and politics. A Senior Fellow at the Progress and Freedom Foundation, she chairs its Center for Effective Compassion.

4

FURTHER READING

14

CHRISTY GAVIN

Contemporary American women playwrights: a brief survey of selected scholarship

During the 1960s and 1970s, the women's movement and experimental theatre were vital forces in providing women a public space to challenge patriarchal values and to dramatize the rare, unseen inner life of woman. Beginning in the late 1970s, as the two major bibliographical works on women dramatists and theatre, Steadman's *Dramatic Re-Visions: An Annotated Bibliography of Feminism and Theatre 1972–1988*, and my own *American Women Playwrights, 1964–1989* will attest, scholars began responding to women's plays – uncovering neglected writers, discovering new ones, and developing theories to evaluate playwrights and performance.

Reclaiming the presence of women playwrights

Four notable volumes document the formation of the canon of women playwrights and feminist theatre: Chinoy and Jenkins' sourcebook, *Women in American Theatre*; *Notable Women in the American Theatre: A Biographical Dictionary*; Betsko and Koenig's landmark *Interviews with Contemporary Women Playwrights*; and, especially welcome, Burke's *American Feminist Playwrights: A Critical History*, which places women playwrights within a critical and historical context.

Feminist critiques of drama, theatre, and performance

The earliest critical methodologies were based on rhetorical analyses reflected in the work of Gillespie ("Feminist Theatre"), Brown (*Feminist Drama*), and Natalle (*Feminist Theatre*). But such rhetorical methods failed to inspire feminist theories; rhetorical analyses are "man-made" constructs that fail to take into account the interests peculiar to feminism. A shift to a more theatrical approach occurred with Keyssar's *Feminist Theatre*, in which she examined transformational drama, a dramatic strategy used to resist realist drama's tendency to subvert possibilities for a true metamorphosis of self and society.

A breakthrough in the development of critical methodology came in the late 1980s with two groundbreaking monographs: Case's *Feminism and Theatre* and Dolan's *The Feminist Spectator as Critic*. Unlike the earlier theoretical discussions of Keyssar and Natalle, Case's and Dolan's works reflect the increasing influence of film and literature theory as well as international feminist theorists. Both monographs signal a shift from a focus on the dramatic text as a work of art to the material and ideological conditions that determine representation on stage. Case's articulations of the major feminisms (liberal, radical, and material) and their application to gender-constructed representation, are excellent. Aston draws from Case's work in *An Introduction to Feminism and Theatre*, in which she explains the highly theorized area of feminism and theatre.

Like Case's study, Dolan's study reflects her pioneer work in feminist performance theory and lesbian representation. Although Dolan's ideological sympathies clearly lie with the materialist feminists, she does not slight the others in her discussions. Stimulating the most attention is her representation of lesbian desire. While some considered Dolan's thesis on lesbian desire compelling, others criticized her for focusing too much on lesbian theatre. Dolan's subsequent monograph, *Presence and Desire*, reflects her development as a critic, as she revisits and revises some of her previous positions.

In "American Drama, Feminist Discourse, and Dramatic Form: In Defense of Critical Pluralism," Schroeder's survey of trends and their controversies in feminist dramatic theory, she warns that, while advocating a particular theory is appropriate, feminists should not become so prescriptive as to exclude other perspectives.

Recently, a spate of collected essays reflect current issues in feminist drama and theatre: further exploration of the European theorists, Brechtian theory, mimesis, and lesbian representation. These include Case's *Performing Feminisms*, and *The Performance of Power: Theatrical Discourse and Politics*, co-edited with Reinelt; *Sourcebook for Feminist Theatre and Performance*, edited by Martin; *Critical Theory and Performance*, edited by Reinelt and Roach; *Performativity and Performance*, edited by Parker and Sedgwick; *Gender in Performance: The Presentation of Difference in the Performing Arts*, edited by Senelick; and *Acting Out: Feminist Performances*, edited by Hart and Phelan. As in most collections, the quality of research, thinking, and writing is uneven, ranging from excellent to mediocre.

Despite the proliferation of critical texts on performance theory, several recent volumes indicate a continued interest in close readings of texts, such as Austin's well-organized *Feminist Theories for Dramatic Criticism*, which provides succinct explanations of a variety of feminist theories, from literary to anthropological, and applies them to selected plays. While she provides a good deal of insight in applying theory to text, her suggestions (gender reversal and masks) of feminist interventions of productions of male-authored texts tend to be superficial. Schroeder's *The Feminist Possibilities of Dramatic Realism* responds convincingly to those feminists who argue that realism has no place in conveying feminist values. Additional volumes that offer close readings of plays are Hart's *Making a Spectacle: Feminist Essays on Contemporary Women's Theatre*; Brater's *Feminine Focus: The New Women Playwrights*; Schlueter's *Modern American Drama: The Female Canon*; and *Theatre and Feminist Aesthetics*, edited by Laughlin and Schuler. Although each has a different focus, they all offer essays providing historical and critical perspectives on women playwrights.

Critical reception of major women playwrights

From the early 1960s female avant-garde dramatists were largely dismissed by some white male critics as angry, bra-burning feminists while other critics touted plays that moved beyond "women's subjects" and feminist polemics to topics acceptable to the male canon such as psycho-social problems and such "unlikely areas as polar expeditions, the prison systems and men in battle" (Gussow, "Women," C3). Experimentalists such as Alice Childress, Megan Terry, Maria Irene Fornes, Rosalyn Drexler, Rochelle Owens, Myrna Lamb, Adrienne Kennedy, and Ntozake Shange recognized that conventional forms of realism were ill suited for conveying women's experiences because realism is filtered by the "male gaze." To shift the "gaze" to women in the subject position, these playwrights had to develop new theatrical language, gestures, forms. Yet others, including Pulitzer Prize-winners Marsha Norman, Beth Henley, and Wendy Wasserstein, felt more comfortable foregrounding their women within traditional realism.

The following highlights the scholarly activity related to major playwrights who have sustained a long record of scholarship that coincides with the continued interest in the staging of their plays.

Alice Childress

Known for her uncompromising approach to race and feminism, Alice Childress introduced themes such as miscegenation to the stage. In *Alice*

Childress, the first full-length examination of Childress, Jennings describes Childress as a transitional writer whose female-centered plays anticipated the work of Ntozake Shange and Sonia Sanchez. And, in the first major study of black women playwrights (*Their Place on the Stage: Black Women Playwrights in America*), Brown-Guillory points out that Childress was instrumental in bringing new images for females to the stage, avoiding the typecast roles of the black woman as fallen woman, frigid, domineering, or helpless. In her *Southern Quarterly* article, Austin emphasizes that Childress' plays are important in the study of feminist critical theory because of her refusal to express relationships (black/white, male/female, north/south) in binary oppositions "with their implications that one is superior to the other" ("Alice Childress," 53). Curb ("An Unfashionable Tragedy") argues that the greatness of Childress' play about miscegenation, *Wedding Band*, is that she does not portray the protagonists entirely as innocent victims – they too have their defects. Wiley's intriguing reading of *Wedding Band* ("Whose Name") emphasizes a feminist approach rather than one that focuses on interracial heterosexual politics. She argues that the play is more concerned with the relations among black women and those between black and white women than with miscegenation. And Hay contends that, unlike Tennessee Williams and Arthur Miller, Childress "does not reveal the theme through characterization but through argumentation" ("Alice Childress's Dramatic Structure," 119).

Megan Terry

A writer as well as a director, Megan Terry is known for her early use of transformation, an experimental strategy that demystifies attitudes toward gender, sexism, and patriarchy. Critics Schlueter ("Keep Tightly Closed"), Breslauer and Keyssar ("Making Magic Public") show how Terry uses transformation to redefine "self" on the stage; transformational shifts in character and situation challenge actors and spectators to rethink stereotypes that exist within patriarchal institutions. Diamond ("[Theoretically] Approaching Megan Terry") examines Terry's plays within the context of the problem of whether a woman can maintain her femaleness without retaining the "significations" associated with gender. Klein ("Language and Meaning") observes that Terry's approach to language in her musicals differs from that of the absurdists who devalued or abandoned language. Terry refuses to allow the idea of "meaninglessness to mask the uses made of language, action, and meaning" (574). In "Historical Re-Vision: Women Heroes on the American Stage," Laughlin shows that Terry's hero in *Approaching Simone* is a traditional masculine hero disguised as female, a representation criticized by many feminists for its reinforcing conventional notions of the hero. Terry's hero takes center stage but with an awareness of her marginality and subsequent constraints put upon her.

Maria Irene Fornes[1]

Despite being a multi-Obie award winner, Fornes remains on the fringes of American theatre. Fornes attributes her invisibility to mainstream audiences to her penchant for experimenting with dramatic styles. Schuler ("Gender Perspective") disagrees with Fornes' reasoning, maintaining that Fornes remains on the fringe because her female characters challenge the popular and romantic notions of what it is to be a real man. And Robinson (*The Other American Drama*) asserts that Fornes' and Kennedy's rejection of linear plot allows them a keen sensitivity to language, subjectivity, and emotion.

Several scholars have addressed Fornes' unique treatment of character. Gruber's two works ("Individuality and Communality" and *Missing Persons*) explore Fornes' development of a new type of character, one that employs an ego that is more mythic, communal, and public, than a private, isolated self. And in *Missing Persons* Gruber asserts that while Brecht is interested in political ideology, Fornes' ideological concerns "are subsumed [by] enactments of self" (159). Austin ("The Madwoman in the Spotlight") points out that Fornes is that rare dramatist who foregrounds the character of the madwoman so that she can represent herself. Cohn ("Reading and Teaching") offers unique insights on how Fornes and Churchill stage language: Fornes reveals the inner life of her characters by presenting on stage images of the written word. Geis ("Wordscapes of the Body" and "'Takin' a Solo'") explores how Fornes and Shange use the gestic monologue to define and embody their characters and to position their subjectivity. And in "Fornes's Odd Couple: *Oscar And Bertha* at the Magic Theatre," Cummings contends that Fornes' interest in characters is less psychological than ontological.

Adrienne Kennedy

Bryant-Jackson and Overbeck's *Intersecting Boundaries: The Theatre of Adrienne Kennedy* represents the growing scholarly recognition of Kennedy's *oeuvre*. This first full-length volume of essays on Kennedy includes personal interviews and critical interpretations of her plays.

Kennedy's major plays are unpredictable, highly personal, and surreal. Within the context of Kennedy's memoir, *People Who Led to My Plays*, Sollors, in a pair of essays ("People Who Led" and "Owls and Rats"), shows how Kennedy weaves autobiographical elements of family history, racial ambivalence, and cultural icons to shape her aesthetic vision.

Early on, scholars focused on Kennedy's tormented psychic characters.

Curb ("'Lesson I Bleed'") explores Kennedy's metaphorical use of blood and its relationship to the trauma of a girl's transition to womanhood. Tener ("Theatre of Identity") asserts that the owl in *The Owl Answers* is the controlling metaphor that secures the protagonist's "problem of identity." And Diamond ("Mimesis in Syncopated Time") provocatively uses mimesis to examine Kennedy's imbricated treatment of identity and identification. Mimesis is also central to Barnett's essay ("This Fundamental Challenge"), in which she discusses its implications and Julia Kristeva's notion of women's time for pregnancy and birth in Kennedy's work. Kintz's study, also based on Kristeva's cultural theories, argues that the insistence on "subjectivity . . . proves to be abnormal, rather than the resistance to an artificial unity" (*The Subject's Tragedy*, 7) of character.

Several critics have focused on Kennedy's unique brand of expressionism. Wilkerson ("Diverse Angles of Vision") compares Lorraine Hansberry's and Kennedy's use of realism and expressionism, respectively, to dramatize the sociopolitical forces imposed on individuals. In "'For the Characters of Myself,'" Brown examines Kennedy's use of expressionistic and surrealistic modes to dramatize the hostility of modern society toward a young woman's struggle for possession of her self. Elwood ("Adrienne Kennedy") contends that German expressionism informs Kennedy's early plays despite the fact that Kennedy's perception of reality differs from that of expressionists. Benston ("*Cities in Bezique*") asserts that Kennedy's expressionistic plays anticipated Amiri Baraka in breaking away from materialism.

Other scholars focus on the political rather than the personal in Kennedy's plays. Instead of examining the playwright's protagonists as tragic individuals, Forte explores, in "Kennedy's Body Politic," how they resist racist acculturation and deconstruct historical views on race. And Meigs ("No Place but the Funnyhouse") argues that Kennedy's fragmented protagonists represent the sociopolitical forces of white society that disrupt the construction of a viable black community.

Ntozake Shange

It took Ntozake Shange's smash hit *For Colored Girls Who Have Considered Suicide/When the Rainbow Is Enuf* to jolt mainstream theatre critics and academicians into an awareness of the work of black female dramatists. Major studies of Shange by Lester (*Ntozake Shange*) and Brown-Guillory reinforce the notion that *For Colored Girls* was a "breakthrough" play for black female theatre artists that established Shange, along with Childress and Hansberry, as "crucial links in the development of black playwriting" (Brown-Guillory, *Wines in the Wilderness*, 1). Shange's play inspired heated debate, especially in the black community, over its treatment of black men. Bond ("*For Colored Girls*"), Staples ("The Myth of Black Macho"), Peters ("Some Tragic Propensities"), and Rushing ("*For Colored Girls*") complain that Shange portrays black men as shallow, ominous beasts and accuse her of neglecting to dramatize the material reasons for oppression. However, several scholars defend Shange's portrayal. Olaniyan ("Ntozake Shange") examines Shange's work within the context of the anti-imperialist, masculinist plays of Amiri Baraka and others who assume that the same cultural identity speaks for both black men and black women. Murray ("Facing the Camera's Eye") examines Shange and Kennedy to show how male entrapment is as oppressive as is racism. For other spirited discussions, see Levin and Flowers ("Black Feminism") and 1979 issues of *The Black Scholar*.

Other scholars focus on material issues. DeShazer observes that Shange dramatizes the two sides of the "re-visioned" warrior – her characters' rage at their situation, as they struggle against racial, sexual, and economic oppression yet resist destruction by "nurtur[ing] ... strong selves and communities" ("Rejecting Necrophilia," 91). Mitchell ("'A Laying on of Hands'") argues that Shange's portrayal of community as "dog eat dog" repudiates Paul Tillich's vision of community. And Timpane ("The Poetry of a Moment") contends that although Shange's plays are anchored in a specific historical time targeted toward a specific audience, they are "open" texts accessible to diverse audiences.

Pinkney, Cronacher, and Thompson-Cage look at Shange's language and mythic forms. Pinkney ("Theatrical Expressionism") argues that Shange replaces dramatic conflict with a series of dramatic statements conveyed through poems, monologues, and vignettes. Shange replaces traditional text and dialogue with a "coded language" that best expresses the experiences of blacks and other Third World peoples. According to Thompson-Cage, Shange creates a set of mythic images, grounded in African American traditions, that challenges Western political and social structures; Shange's characters use magic "to formulate survival strategies that may or may not make sense to anyone else" (Thompson-Cage, "Superstition," 40). Cronacher examines Shange's feminist use of the minstrel show in *spell #7*. Minstrelsy reveals nothing of the reality of the African American experience, but tells plenty about "that dark continent of the white male phobias and desires, and the 'horror, the horror' of the white male's experience of gender and racial difference" (Cronacher, "Unmasking," 178).

Some scholars deal with Shange's approach to a woman's spirituality. Waxman examines Shange's use of dance to express spiritual healing, self-affirmation, and self-acceptance. Dance obfuscates traditional modes of dramatic expression. Shange has altered the course of dance and drama in

America in that she uses dance "exclusively for women's pleasure, control and solidarity" ("Dancing," 98). According to Richards, one of Shange's most effective dramatic strategies is the dialectic of "awareness of social oppression and commitment to struggle ... [and] a desire to transcend or bypass, through music and dance, the limitations of social and human existence" ("Conflicting Impulses," 73). Christ ("'i found god in myself'") observes that Shange, through a spiritual rite of passage, moves her women through pain and defeat to hope and rebirth.

Marsha Norman

Pulitzer Prize-winner Marsha Norman shapes her stories according to conventional rules, yet they are informed by her feminist values. Some critics, such as Dolan (*The Feminist Spectator*), charge that Norman's use of male-oriented realism compromises her feminism. Others disagree. Brown and Stevenson ("Fearlessly") argue that Norman's feminist aesthetic encompasses a variety of feminist views and that she creates works that are popular with mainstream audiences yet are socially effective. And Demastes (*Beyond Naturalism*) considers Henley and Norman as representing the second wave of "new realists," who challenge "classic realist" assumptions.

Several critics have focused on female subjectivity in Norman's dramas. Kintz (*The Subject's Tragedy*) addresses Norman's Oedipal protagonists, as does Spencer in "Norman's *'night, Mother*: Psycho-drama of Female Identity." Spencer uses psychoanalytic theory to explain gender differences in interpreting female identity issues on stage. And in a later article ("Marsha Norman's She-tragedies") Spencer examines Norman's plays within the context of the eighteenth-century *she-tragedies*. Norman's mother–daughter relationships are the focus of several studies. The symbiotic yet ambivalent relationship between mother and daughter in *'night, Mother* is pursued by Browder ("'I Thought You Were Mine'"). Hart ("Doing Time"), Burkman ("The Demeter Myth"), and Morrow ("Orality and Identity") address Norman's use of food, hunger, and appetite as controlling metaphors and its relationship to mother–daughter relationships. Miner, Scharine, and Murray address the political aspects of *Getting Out*. Miner ("'What's These Bars Doin' Here?'") sees the play as radical in its feminist critique of capitalism and patriarchal ideology. Scharine ("Caste Iron Bars") and Murray ("Patriarchal Panoticism") address key questions relating to the effect of institutional norms on the individual.

Beth Henley

The focus of many critiques is on Henley's themes of self and the bonds of family. Guerra ("Beth Henley") argues that Henley's theme of the female quest is undermined by her use of the male-oriented form of the family drama, which perpetuates expectations about women's representation on stage that are inherently restrictive. While Laughlin ("Criminality, Desire, and Community") agrees that *Crimes of the Heart*'s conventional form compromises Henley's theme, she suggests that the significance of the play lies in the subtext, its hidden layers of patriarchal oppression. Contrary to those who dismiss Henley's plays as light comedies, Hargrove ("Tragicomic Vision") asserts that through comedy, Henley conveys a tragicomic vision of the human condition. Harris ("Delving") and Harbin ("Familial Bonds") agree with Hargrove's conclusion that pain empowers Henley's protagonists in that it causes them to embark on a quest for meaning and self-fulfillment. Kullman ("Beth Henley's Marginalized Heroines") sees Henley's protagonists as existentialists seeking meaning in an absurd and dangerous world. And Haedicke ("Population") and Shepard both address the issue of violence in Henley's plays; Haedicke examines family violence in *Crimes* and Sam Shepard's *A Lie of the Mind*, and Shepard argues that while Henley's heroines "relish murderous ... fantasies, they repudiate them" ("Aborted Rage," 97).

Emerging playwrights

Although Wendy Wasserstein and Emily Mann have been producing for years, scholars have only recently begun critiquing their work. Emerging scholarship on Wasserstein has appeared in essays by Watermeier ("The Search for Self"), Balakian ("Conversation"; "*The Heidi Chronicles*"; "Interviews"), Mandl ("Feminism"), and Carlson ("Comic Textures"). Much of this work reflects scholars' ambivalence toward Wasserstein's feminism. Mann, also an accomplished director, has not received the critical attention she deserves. However, two recent essays by Kolin ("Public Facts") and Laughlin ("Historical Re-Vision") appear in *Public Issues, Private Tensions: Contemporary American Drama*, edited by Roudané.

To ensure the continuity and vitality of the critical canon of female playwrights, scholars need to explore the work of women whose plays are regularly produced and anthologized, such as Lynn Alvarez, Jane Chambers, Pearle Cleage, Velina Houston, Tina Howe, Wendy Kesselman, Karen Malpede, Cherrie Moraga, Suzan-Lori Parks, Sonia Sanchez, Milcha Sanchez-Scott, and Wakao Yamauchi.

NOTE

1   The first full-length volume on Fornes' work, Diane Lynn Moroff's very recent *Fornes: Theatre in the Present Tense*, was unavailable for review.

15

CHRISTINE R. GRAY

Discovering and recovering African American women playwrights writing before 1930

Thus when the white [person] says, "This is American reality," the Negro tends to answer... "Perhaps, but you've left this out, and this, and this."
(Ralph Ellison, "Twentieth-Century Fiction and the Black Mask of Humanity," 25)

Few scholars of American drama would deny the importance of Eugene O'Neill, Elmer Rice, or Susan Glaspell, playwrights active in the early decades of this century. Materials on these playwrights and their work for the stage are readily accessible through preserved notes, letters, reviews, photographs, and production records. Indeed, if one were to leaf through bibliographies of American plays and playwrights prior to 1930, it would seem that only white Americans were writing for the stage and thereby grinding the lens through which American life and culture could be viewed. By relying only on the reflection of American life and culture presented by white playwrights, however, one would have a warped picture, one that presented a monocular view of the United States and its drama of the early twentieth century. In 1987, Richard Bernstein, theatre columnist for the *New York Times*, wrote, "The tradition of a Black American Theatre is not a long one, going back only a generation or so to the work of such playwrights as Amiri Baraka [in 1970]" ("August Wilson's Voices," 34). Little realized by Bernstein, theatre students, and scholars of American drama is that 100 African American playwrights, thus far identified, wrote 350 plays before 1930. Of these playwrights 47 were women. Yet how many scholars of American drama can name more than a few, if any?

Although only a handful of plays by black American women in the nineteenth century have been uncovered, in 1916 black women became actively engaged in writing serious plays for the non-musical stage. Through these early plays, readers today gain a very different perspective on American life and culture in the early twentieth century, one not found in plays by the canonized American playwrights of that same period.

Written by Angelina Grimké (1880–1958), *Rachel* was the first significant play by an African American woman. It opened in March 1916 before an audience of blacks and whites at the Myrtill Minor School in Washington DC. Five acts long and highly melodramatic, *Rachel* focuses on an unmarried black woman, Rachel Loving, and her decision not to marry and bear children. Her father and brother, she learns, were lynched several years earlier. Rather than risk the same fate for her unborn children, her "brown babies," she breaks off her engagement and chooses to remain single.

Rachel is significant for several reasons. In addition to its condemnation of lynching, the play hoped to reach white mothers to show them the plight black women and mothers faced for their skin color. Moreover, *Rachel* revealed the gross prejudice that educated blacks faced in seeking meaningful employment, for even with a college degree Rachel's fiancé can find employment only as a waiter. In addition, Grimké's play sought to neutralize the corrosive depictions in minstrel shows of blacks as lazy, ignorant, and superstitious. The play countered these images with black characters who were middle class, educated, and soft-spoken. In this regard, *Rachel* also challenged the stereotypes of African Americans in the racist movie *Birth of a Nation*, which had, despite protests by the NAACP, played in Washington the previous fall. Perhaps most important, Grimké opened the door for African American women playwrights, who stepped over the threshold and began creating different images of African Americans for the American stage in the ensuing years. It is, therefore, with good reason that theatre historian James V. Hatch points to Grimké as the "Mother of African American Drama" (letter to the author, October 6, 1992).

By 1930, only fourteen years after Grimké's play, forty-six African American women had written plays, thereby adding another dimension to American drama. Although not all of the early plays have been located, scholars have identified Georgia Douglas Johnson, credited with twenty-two plays, as the most prolific. Other African American female playwrights active to a high degree include May Miller (fourteen plays), Zora Neale Hurston (thirteen plays), Eulalie Spence (thirteen plays), and Thelma Duncan (nine plays). These and other black women had purposes similar to Grimké's in that, for the most part, they used the stage to educate, rather than entertain, African Americans, to protest against the injustices pinned on the black race, and to uplift the race by showing its strength and will to endure against adversity. As theatre scholar Elizabeth Brown-Guillory notes, black women "were able to turn theatres into nurseries where the black race [was] given roots, nurtured, tested, healed, and provided with the spirit to survive" (*Their Place on the Stage*, 5).

Few subsequent plays written by black women before 1930 were in the genteel tradition of *Rachel*. That is, the characters, often speaking in dialect, were uneducated, and their homes, unlike the Lovings', do not have paintings and sewing machines. Usually one-act long, most of the plays written by African American women during that period drew instead on the folk tradition, which can be defined as the literature, customs, beliefs, and values held by members of a particular community, one which is usually isolated. The folk tradition traveled to northern cities with family bibles, pots, pans, and quilts in the move from Georgia and the Carolinas.

Often set in the rural South, folk drama reflects the lives of uneducated people dependent on the land and the cycle of the seasons. Through the plays of African American women, folk culture was given dignity and thereby validated through the heroism of the characters on stage, despite the submissive identity nurtured by whites outside the theatre doors. Further, reaped from the soil of slavery, the African American folk tradition distinguished African American plays from those derived from a European aesthetic and tradition, for slavery was not part of white culture. Nor had whites made the migration north, which began in the late nineteenth century, that American blacks had.

In addition to writing of experiences in America unlike those of whites, African American women had a different purpose in writing their plays: these dramatists sought to create a black voice. Abena Busia, an African American scholar, points out, "By giving [African Americans] a voice through our literature, we introduce into the masquerade of the traditional Western literary canon the dialogue we insist upon ... Our writers do not simply rewrite or recreate literature of the [white] ruling class in black face, but strive for something 'other'" ("Words Whispered," 15–16). African American women hoped to carry onto the African American stage the black voice – the "other" to which Busia refers – by telling their race's own unvarnished story. In their struggles to claim a voice, one without European echoes, African American women welded a theatre tradition out of materials with which they were familiar – the folk tradition and the black family. The folk tradition that black women drew from was the source and the location of the black voice for the early black stage.

African American writer Maya Angelou has noted that "all African Americans find their roots in the South" (*By River*). Whether in emigrating from it and leaving behind their kinfolk, in visiting relatives who still lived there, in attempting to return, or in longing for it, the South is knit into the fabric of nearly all of these early plays. In drawing from their folk heritage, black women playwrights acknowledged the links of African Americans everywhere – even the blacks who disavowed such humble roots – to the southern folk tradition culturally, spiritually, historically, emotionally, and socially. The migration north was not a distant memory for many of the African Americans who sat in school auditoriums or church basements watching Georgia Johnson's lynching play *A Sunday Morning in the South* (1925). Many audience members could understand the mixed feelings of a mother who allows her unborn child to die rather than face the possibility of lynching. With World War I being fought, many could relate to *Mine Eyes Have Seen* (1918) by Alice Dunbar-Nelson. The play focuses on whether a young black man has an obligation to serve his country in time of war, despite his father's lynching by a white mob in the South.

Discussions of African American literature from roughly 1920 to 1930 often rely on the term "Harlem Renaissance" to demarcate geographically the spirit and activity of the period. Although Harlem was seen as a Mecca for aspiring black writers and artists, it was not a hub for plays by African American women. Slices of black life and culture were reflected in works viewed in less public surroundings than Harlem. Many of the plays by black women were written by black literary groups in other locations and were produced in Philadelphia, Chicago, Baltimore, Cleveland, Boston, and Washington. Georgia Johnson's S Street Salon in Washington was one such group.

Indeed, a revolution was going on in the meeting rooms of black churches, in the basements of public libraries, and in the auditoriums of black colleges and schools throughout much of the United States. In a sense, the black women formed an underground movement in that their works, unlike those by writers associated with the Harlem Renaissance, were never part of the mainstream (read white) culture, nor were they intended to be. Instead, the plays produced by black American women were attempts both to preserve the African American folk tradition and, through it, to reenact via the stage the problems and situations blacks encountered. Through their plays, black women recorded and reenacted the story of Africans in America. It was in the plays produced in church basements that many African Americans learned black history, not in the flash and adventure of the Harlem writers.

Generally, the black women playwrights wrapped their plots around highly dramatic elements. Poverty, miscegenation, passing for white (with its inevitable tragedy), and lynching were common topics. These aspects of America's past, however, were, in a sense, embraced by the playwrights, for these struggles showed what African American families had survived and still battled against. A new estimation of the race by African Americans bloomed, to a great extent, through the plays written by African American women. The forbearance of the protagonist and her community distinguished the plays by African American women, as it revealed the strength of the black race in America.

Although the plays by black women reached out to their audiences through a variety of topics, the dramas were often linked by their concern for the family, for nearly every play is somehow involved with either a family's survival or its dissolution. In Mary Burrill's play *Aftermath* (1918), for example, a decorated black serviceman returns to his rural southern home from the war in Europe to find that his father has only recently been lynched by a white gang. In Johnson's play *A Sunday Morning in the South* (1925), an innocent young black man is taken from his family on a Sunday morning and hanged by a white mob that suspects him of flirting with a white woman. Myrtle Livingston Smith's *For Unborn Children* (1926) concerns the choice a young black man must make regarding his engagement to a white woman. Despite his love for her, he breaks off the engagement so that his unborn children will not have to contend with ostracism and the problems of mixed parentage. At the play's close, he exits his cabin, leaving behind his grandmother and sister, and offers himself to the waiting white lynch mob. Johnson's *Plumes* (1927) features a mother who must choose between giving her ill daughter the remote chance of a cure or putting that money into a grand funeral, complete with plumed horses, for her child. In Marita Bonner's *The Pot Maker* (1927) a black man is killed by his wife for his emotional battering of her. In Johnson's play *Safe* (1929), a black mother gives thanks for her infant's death, for it precludes the possibility of his ever being lynched by whites.

The color of one's complexion was an explicit topic of the plays by black women. Ottie Graham's *Holiday* (1923) features a woman who passes as white so she can further her stage career. On finding her actress-mother years later, her daughter, hurt by her mother's abandonment, commits suicide. Zora Neale Hurston's *Color-Struck* (1925) concerns a woman distraught with the darkness of her complexion and so jealous of light-skinned women that she drives away the one man who loves her. The complications of miscegenation are considered in Johnson's *Blue Blood* (1926). A marriage is prevented only hours before the ceremony when the young black couple learn about their parentage. The respective mothers, in boasting about the light complexions of their children, discover that their offspring have the same white father.

In addition to such themes, plays by African American women often rely on white characters as the force opposing or undermining the success, livelihood, and, frequently, the very lives of black characters. African Americans were prey to whites in any number of situations represented on stage: victimized or lynched by white gangs, ensnared by white landlords, or discriminated against after moving to "the Promised Land" of the industrial North. Most explicit in criticizing discrimination and in portraying anti-white sentiments is *The Purple Flower* (1929) by Marita Bonner. An expressionistic play, it virulently condemns the "white devils" and their intrusion on a black community and its beliefs. In these respects, such plays are obvious precursors to Lorraine Hansberry's *A Raisin in the Sun* (1959) whose Younger family is pressured by the white community's representative not to move into the white neighborhood in which they have recently purchased a house.

Whether drawn from Africa or its descendants living in the United States, black history provided another source of dramatic material for African American women. Denied and excluded from the privileges of white America, omitted from white textbooks and history books, freed barely fifty years earlier, African Americans, especially those emigrating from the South, were able to consider the ramifications of freedom and the nearly spiritual necessity of locating their own history. Primed by W. E. B. Du Bois's pan-African movement and Marcus Garvey's call for blacks to return to Africa, African Americans more than ever became curious about their past: what was black history? Was there even a black history, one worth recovering, before the Middle Passage? And where would this be found? How would one learn about black heroes? For African American writers, however, these queries could be subsumed under one overarching question: as African Americans, who are we?

Many African American women responded to these questions through pageants and plays. Through stage presentations, black female dramatists sought to uplift blacks by reminding the audience, or perhaps informing some members for the first time, of the culture's heritage. A theatre form rarely seen today, African American pageants centered on characters and incidents important in black history. Dorothy C. Guinn's pageant *Out of the Dark* (1924) presents tableaux of blacks in Africa, as slaves, and as a freed people. In Frances Gunner's *Light of the Women* (1925), actors portraying notable women in African American history, Frances E. W. Harper, Phillis Wheatley, Sojourner Truth, and Harriet Tubman, appear on stage to address the audience. In Maud Cuney Hare's play *Antar of Araby* (192?), audiences learned of a black warrior and hero. May Miller co-edited the collection *Negro History in Thirteen Plays* (1935); her history plays include *Sojourner Truth* and *Harriet Tubman*.

Only within the past fifteen or so years have plays by African Americans received the critical attention accorded to African American poetry and prose fiction. Before the plays can be discussed critically, however, they must first be made available. To this end, several anthologies of the plays have been published, a list of which is located at the end of this chapter. Scholars working with the early plays note, however, the many hurdles that lie in the way of compilation and publication. Freda Scott Giles, a theatre professor at the University of Georgia, points to the lack of coverage by the press during the 1920s outside of New York City as posing research problems. Without reviews and commentary from the period, Giles notes, it is difficult to piece together production histories. She raises several questions concerning research in African American drama: where were the plays performed? What did productions look like? How were they received by the audience? Who was the audience? (email to author, April 14, 1997). James V. Hatch, one of the first and most authoritative scholars of African American drama, in noting a lack of documentation on plays by black women, remarks that in order to locate reviews, commentaries, and production notes, one would "have to go through piles of microfilm of black newspapers of the twenties, but the women are in there" (email to author, April 14, 1997). Scholar of African American theatre Judith Stephens remarks that "many times African American female playwrights are still ignored even after their importance to theatre in this country has been documented" (email to author, May 14, 1997).

Recovery work, which precedes publication, is the term used to describe the process of locating and editing materials that have been lost, neglected, or forgotten. Recovery requires sifting through archival materials, contacting families, leafing through newspapers for theatre reviews, going through African American journals prior to 1930, poring over biographies and autobiographies, and reading early dissertations and theses. All of this detail work is done in the hope of locating a clue, no matter how slender, that will lead to a reference to a play or playwright. Recovery work is often difficult and frustrating, for many primary materials have been lost, inadvertently discarded, or misfiled; some have simply crumbled with age. For example, notes from one drama group in Washington during the 1920s were thrown out when, in 1970, the owner's family moved him to a home for the elderly. Library archives often hold valuable materials, unknown at times to librarians, who may not realize the importance of papers by little-known writers in their holdings. Although 350 African American plays written before 1930 have been identified, their locations or whether they have even been preserved is not always known. Once a play is recovered, obtaining permission to publish it can be problematic as families are often reluctant to part with or make public unpublished materials, especially if they are in holograph, or handwritten, form.

Zora Neale Hurston's plays provide examples of recovery work. In spring 1997, ten play scripts by Hurston were discovered by chance at the

Library of Congress. Although it had been known that Hurston had written the newly discovered plays, their whereabouts unknown, they were presumed lost. These plays will, no doubt, be republished and the canon of Hurston's work in general will be enhanced through an enriched perspective on the writer. In working with materials that did not initially relate to the research at hand, Harvard scholar Henry Louis Gates recovered the full manuscript of *Mule Bone*, a play Hurston co-wrote with Langston Hughes in 1931. Available only to scholars, the play had lain in manuscript form among the papers of Alain Locke, editor of *The New Negro* (1925), in the Moorland-Spingarn Research Center at Howard University in Washington. After reading about the play in Hughes' autobiography *The Big Sea* (1940), Gates had the play republished in 1991.

Locke's papers hold other leads in recovering plays by African American women. Among his unpublished papers are his comments on black women dramatists during the 1920s and his thoughts on *Rachel* as the prize-winning play in the NAACP drama contest in 1916. Indeed, in searching Locke's papers, one finds records of the drama group at the university, reads of squabbles among its members, and comes across several letters female drama students wrote to Locke.

Reliance on secondary sources, rather than primary, often creates further problems for scholars. Grimké's unpublished play, *Mara* (1916?) provides an excellent example. The Moorland-Spingarn Research Center, which holds Angelina Grimké's materials, has designated a draft of this play as "complete." Researchers on Grimké have, it seems, taken this to mean that the draft designated as complete is Grimké's final draft of the play. In doing so, they have written about *Mara* as a lynching play, which this one draft is. Subsequent scholars of Grimké's work have based their comments on *Mara* on work by earlier researchers and replicated the belief that *Mara* is a lynching play. The Moorland-Spingarn's designation of "complete" is, however, misleading. The *Mara* archive holds multiple drafts; it is not known which version Grimké considered final or complete. Indeed, in looking through the sizeable file of Grimké's holographic materials, one might conclude that Grimké was never satisfied with any of her drafts of this play, for she never, from what we know, sought publication for any version of it.

Although the draft designated as "complete" is that of a lynching play, the other draft gleaned from the file containing *Mara* is quite different. Its plot concerns a tragic affair between Mara, who is an African American, and a white man. The other draft relies heavily on the Arthurian tale of Elaine and Lancelot as drawn from Tennyson's *Idylls of the King*. In scanning the backs of the play's handwritten pages, one sees Grimké's references to her play

Rachel, which indicate that Grimké may have been working on *Mara* in 1915, as she wrote *Rachel*, not in 1926 as is generally believed.

Much work awaits scholars in the field of plays by African American women. For example, in 1935, playwrights May Miller and Willis Richardson edited the collection *Negro History in Thirteen Plays*; invaluable in the history of American drama, this volume has yet to be republished. Also, little attention has been paid to the audiences of the early plays. We know from the few available letters, production records, and interviews that the plays were usually produced by little theatre groups, but records are difficult to come by. Further, scant attention has been given to the pageants produced in the 1920s, yet several black magazines provide clues to their existence through a passing reference to or review of them. Photographs are of immeasurable value in discussions of the early audiences, yet very few photographs of the early productions by African American men or women have been found.

Plays by several other African American women have yet to be uncovered. Still to be reprinted is Mary Burrill's play *Unto the Third and Fourth Generation*. Active in Harlem during the 1920s, West Indian Eulalie Spence relied on urban settings for many of her plays, yet only a few of the thirteen plays she wrote have been located, and few have received critical attention or been published. The plays of African American women Ollie Burgoyne, Carrie Law Morgan Figgs, and Valai Snow may never be located.

As is evident, much has been omitted from the picture of America depicted on the stage in the early twentieth century. Our full and accurate understanding of American drama can come about only if the early plays by African Americans are included in the canon of American drama. Recovery of the contributions of the African American women playwrights makes apparent that black drama has a tradition, one that began many decades ago. Alice Childress, Lorraine Hansberry, Ntozake Shange, and others have built their plays on the foundations laid by pioneers Angelina Grimké, May Miller, Georgia Johnson, Eulalie Spence, Mary Burrill, and many others.

Keeping in mind Ralph Ellison's remark, which opened this chapter, one can see that the picture of American culture offered by white playwrights is inaccurate; it is only one tile of the cultural and historical mosaic that makes up the United States. By gathering what has been left out of the history of American drama – the plays by African American women – we see another picture of America in the early twentieth century emerge. By familiarizing ourselves with the works of the black women who put their work on the American stage, we enrich our understanding of this genre, of this country, and of its citizens.

ANTHOLOGIES OF PLAYS WRITTEN PRIOR TO 1930 BY AFRICAN AMERICAN WOMEN

Brown-Guillory, Elizabeth, ed. *Wines in the Wilderness: Plays by African American Women from the Harlem Renaissance to the Present.* New York: Praeger, 1990.

Burton, Jennifer, ed. *Zora Neale Hurston, Eulalie Spence, Marita Bonner, and Others: The Prize Plays and Other One-Acts Published in Periodicals.* New York: G. K. Hall. 1996.

Hamalian, Leo, and James V. Hatch, eds. *The Roots of African American Drama: An Anthology of Early Plays, 1858–1938.* Detroit: Wayne State University Press, 1991.

Hatch, James V. and Leo Hamalian, eds. *Lost Plays of the Harlem Renaissance: 1920–1940.* Detroit: Wayne State University Press, 1996.

Hatch, James V. and Ted Shine, eds. *Black Theatre, USA: Forty-Five Plays by Black Americans: 1847–1974.* 2 vols. New York: Free Press, 1974.

Locke, Alain and Montgomery Gregory, eds. *Plays of Negro Life: A Source-Book of Native American Drama* (1927). Westport, CT: Negro University Press, 1970.

Perkins, Kathy, ed. *Black Female Playwrights: An Anthology of Plays before 1950.* Bloomington: Indiana University Press, 1989.

Perkins, Kathy and Judith Stephens, eds. *Strange Fruit: Plays on Lynching by American Women.* Bloomington: Indiana University Press, 1997.

Richardson, Willis, ed. *Plays and Pageants from the Life of the Negro* (1930). Introduction by Christine R. Gray. Jackson: University Press of Mississippi, 1993.

Richardson, Willis and May Miller, eds. *Negro History in Thirteen Plays.* Washington DC: Associated Publishers, 1935.

SOME COLLECTIONS HOLDING EARLY PLAY SCRIPTS AND RELATED MATERIALS BY AFRICAN AMERICAN WOMEN

Hatch-Billops Collection, New York City.

Moorland-Spingarn Research Center, located at Howard University, Washington, DC.

Schomburg Center for Research in Black Culture, New York City.

WORKS CITED

Abel, Elizabeth, Marianne Hirsch, and Elizabeth Langland, eds. *The Voyage In.* Hanover, NH: University Press of New England, 1983.

Abramson, Doris. "Rachel Crothers: Broadway Feminist." In Schlueter, ed., *Modern American Drama*, 55–65.

Adler, Jacob H. *Lillian Hellman.* Austin, TX: Steck-Vaughn, 1969.

Adler, Thomas P. *Mirror on the Stage: The Pulitzer Prize Plays as an Approach to American Drama.*West Lafayette, IN: Purdue University Press, 1987.

Alter, Iska. "Wendy Wasserstein, *The Heidi Chronicles* and the Evasion of History." Paper presented at "Women In Theatre" Conference, Hofstra University, October 6, 1994.

Armato, Philip M. "Good and Evil in Lillian Hellman's *The Children's Hour.*" *Educational Theatre Journal* 25 (1973), 443–47.

Aston, Elaine. *An Introduction to Feminism and Theatre.* London: Routledge, 1995.

Austin, Addell P. "Pioneering Black Authored Dramas, 1924–1927." PhD dissertation, Michigan State University, 1986.

"The Opportunity and Crisis Literary Contests, 1924–27." *CLA Journal* 32 (1988), 235–346.

Austin, Gayle. "Alice Childress: Black Woman Playwright as Feminist Critic." *Southern Quarterly* 25 (1987), 53–62.

"*The Doll House Show*: A Feminist Theory Play." *Journal of Dramatic Theory and Criticism* 7 (1993), 203–07.

Feminist Theories for Dramatic Criticism. Ann Arbor: University of Michigan Press, 1990.

"The Madwoman in the Spotlight: Plays of Maria Irene Fornes." In Hart, ed., *Making a Spectacle*, 76–85.

Bakhtin, M. M. *The Dialogic Imagination.* Ed. Michael Holquist. Trans. Caryl Emerson and Michael Holquist. Austin: University of Texas Press, 1981.

Balakian, Jan. "A Conversation with Wendy Wasserstein." In *Speaking on Stage: Interviews with Contemporary American Playwrights.* Tuscaloosa: Alabama University Press, 1995, 378–91.

"*The Heidi Chronicles*: The Big Chill of Feminism." *South Atlantic Review* 60 (1995), 93–101.

"Interviews with Wendy Wasserstein." *The Journal of American Drama and Theatre* 9.2 (1997), 58–84.

Bank, Rosemarie K. "Theatre and Narrative Fiction in the Work of Nineteenth-Century American Playwright, Louisa Medina." *Theatre History Studies* 3 (1983), 55–67.

Barlow, Judith E. "Into the Foxhole: Feminism, Realism, and Lillian Hellman." In Demastes, ed., *Realism and the American Dramatic Tradition*, 156–72.

Barlow, Judith E., ed. *Plays by American Women: 1900–1930*. New York: Applause, 1985.

Barnett, Claudia. "Adrienne Kennedy and Shakespeare's Sister." *American Drama* 5 (1996), 44–56.

"'This Fundamental Challenge to Identity': Reproduction and Representation in the Drama of Adrienne Kennedy." *Theatre Journal* 48 (1996), 141–55.

Barreca, Regina, ed. *Last Laughs*. New York: Gordon and Breach, 1988.

Barthelemy, Anthony. "Mother, Sister, Wife: A Dramatic Perspective." *The Southern Review* 21.3 (1985), 770–89.

Beckett, Samuel. *Krapp's Last Tape and Other Dramatic Pieces*. New York: Grove, 1960.

Belsey, Catherine. "Constructing the Subject: Deconstructing the Text." In Newton and Rosenfelt, eds., *Feminist Criticism and Social Change*, 45–64.

Bennetts, Leslie. "An Uncommon Dramatist Prepares Her New Work." *New York Times* (May 24, 1981), sec. 2, 5.

Benston, Kimberly W. "*Cities in Bezique*: Adrienne Kennedy's Expressionistic Vision." *CLA Journal* 20 (1976), 235–44.

Ben-Zvi, Linda. "Susan Glaspell's Contributions to Contemporary Women Playwrights." In Brater, ed., *Feminine Focus*, 147–66.

Bernstein, Richard. "August Wilson's Voices from the Past." *New York Times* (March 27, 1988), H-34.

Berson, Misha. "Women at the Helm." *American Theatre* (July 1994), 14–21.

Betsko, Kathleen and Rachel Koenig, eds. *Interviews with Contemporary Women Playwrights*. New York: Beech Tree Books, 1987.

Bigsby, C. W. E., ed. *Plays by Susan Glaspell*. Cambridge and New York: Cambridge University Press, 1987.

Bond, Jean Carey. "*For Colored Girls Who Have Considered Suicide*." *Freedomways* 16 (1976), 187–91.

Booth, Michael R. *Theatre in the Victorian Age*. Cambridge: Cambridge University Press, 1991.

Brandt, Ellen B. *Susanna Haswell Rowson: America's First Best-Selling Novelist*. Chicago: Serbra Press, 1975.

Brantley, Ben. "In the Hostile Glare of Washington, the Media Define and Defy." *New York Times* (April 14, 1997), C11, 16.

Brater, Enoch, ed. *Feminine Focus: The New Women Playwrights*. New York: Oxford University Press, 1989.

Breslauer, Jan and Helene Keyssar. "Making Magic Public: Megan Terry's Traveling Family Circus." In Hart, *Making a Spectacle*, 169–80.

Bromley, Dorothy Dunbar. "Feminist–New Style." *Harper's Monthly* 155 (1927), 552–60.

Brooks, Peter. "The Melodramatic Imagination." *Partisan Review* 39 (1972), 195–212.

Browder, Sally. "'I Thought You Were Mine': Marsha Norman's '*night, Mother*." In

Mickey Pearlman, ed., *Mother Puzzles; Daughters and Mothers in Contemporary American Literature*. New York: Greenwood Press, 1989, 109–14.

Brown, Elsa Barkley. "Womanist Consciousness: Maggie Lena Walker and the Independent Order of Saint Luke." In Micheline Malson et al., *Black Women in America*. Chicago: University of Chicago Press, 1988, 173–96.

Brown, Janet. *Feminist Drama: Definition and Critical Analysis*. Metuchen, NJ: Scarecrow Press, 1979.

   Taking Center Stage: Feminism in Contemporary US Drama. Metuchen, NJ and London: Scarecrow Press, 1991.

Brown, Janet and Catherine Barnes Stevenson. "Fearlessly 'Looking Under the Bed': Marsha Norman's Feminist Aesthetic in *Getting Out* and *'night, Mother*." In Laughlin and Schuler, eds., *Theatre and Feminist Aesthetics*, 182–99.

Brown, Linda Ginter, ed. *Marsha Norman: A Casebook*. New York: Garland, 1996.

Brown, Lorraine A. "'For the Characters Are Myself': Adrienne Kennedy's *Funnyhouse of a Negro*." *Negro American Literature Forum* 9 (1975), 86–88.

Brown-Guillory, Elizabeth. *Their Place on the Stage: Black Women Playwrights in America*. New York: Greenwood Press, 1988.

Brown-Guillory, Elizabeth, ed. *Wines in the Wilderness: Plays by African American Women from the Harlem Renaissance to the Present*. New York: Praeger, 1990.

Brustein, Robert. "What Do Women Playwrights Want?" *The New Republic* 206 (April 13, 1992), 28–30.

   "Women in Extremis." *New Republic* 200 (April 17, 1989), 32–34.

Bryant-Jackson, Paul K. and Lois More Overbeck, eds. *Intersecting Boundaries: The Theatre of Adrienne Kennedy*. Minneapolis: University of Minnesota Press, 1992.

Bryer, Jackson R., ed. *Conversations with Lillian Hellman*. Jackson: University Press of Mississippi, 1986.

Burke, Sally. *American Feminist Playwrights: A Critical History*. New York: Twayne, 1996.

Burkman, Katherine H. "The Demeter Myth and Doubling in Marsha Norman's *'night, Mother*." In Schlueter, ed., *Modern American Drama*, 254–63.

Burton, Jennifer, ed. *Zora Neale Hurston, Eulalie Spence, Marita Bonner, and Others: The Prize Plays and Other One-Acts Published in Periodicals*. New York: G. K. Hall & Co., 1996.

Busia, Abena P. B. "Words Whispered over Voids: A Context for Black Women's Rebellious Voices in the Novel of the African Diaspora." *Studies in Black American Literature* 3 (1988), 1–41.

By River, by Rail: The Great Migration North. Narrated by Maya Angelou. CBS. WBAL, Baltimore. December 28, 1994.

Calinescu, Matei. *Five Faces of Modernity*. Durham, NC: Duke University Press, 1987.

Campbell, Jane. "Pauline Elizabeth Hopkins." In Trudier Harris and Thadious M. Davis, eds., *Afro-American Writers Before the Harlem Renaissance. Dictionary of Literary Biography*. Vol. L. Ed. Trudier Harris. Detroit: Gale, 1986, 182–89.

Carlson, Susan L. "Comic Textures and Female Communities 1937 and 1977: Clare Boothe and Wendy Wasserstein." *Modern Drama* 27 (1984), 564–73.

Carr, Mary. *The Fair Americans*. In Kritzer, ed., *Plays by Early American Women*, 183–215.

Carroll, Kathleen L. "Centering Women Onstage: Susan Glaspell's Dialogic Strategy of Resistance." PhD dissertation, University of Maryland, 1990.

Carter, Steven R. "Lorraine Hansberry." In Trudier Harris and Thadious M. Davis, eds., *Afro-American Writers after 1955: Dramatists and Prose Writers. Dictionary of Literary Biography.* Vol. XXXVIII. Detroit: Gale, 1985, 120–34.

Case, Sue-Ellen. *Feminism and Theatre.* New York: Methuen, 1988.

"Toward a Butch-Femme Aesthetic." In Hart, ed., *Making a Spectacle*, 282–300.

Case, Sue-Ellen, ed. *Performing Feminisms: Feminist Critical Theory and Theatre.* Baltimore, MD: Johns Hopkins University Press, 1990.

Case, Sue-Ellen and Janelle Reinelt, eds. *The Performance of Power: Theatrical Discourse and Politics.* Iowa City: University of Iowa Press, 1991.

Chafe, William H. *The Paradox of Change: American Women in the Twentieth Century.* New York: Oxford University Press, 1991.

Childress, Alice. "Wine in the Wilderness." In Brown-Guillory, ed., *Wines in the Wilderness.*

Chinoy, Helen Krich and Linda Walsh Jenkins. *Women in American Theatre.* Rev. edn. New York: Theatre Communications Group, 1987.

Chodorow, Nancy. *The Reproduction of Mothering.* Berkeley: University of California Press, 1978.

Christ, Carol P. "'i found god in myself . . . i loved her fiercely': Ntozake Shange." In *Diving Deep and Surfacing: Women Writers on Spiritual Quest.* Boston: Beacon Press, 1980, 97–117.

Cixous, Hélène. "The Character of Character." Trans. Keith Cohen. *New Literary History* 5: 2 (1974), 383–402.

Clark, Barrett H., ed. *America's Lost Plays.* 21 vols. Bloomington: University of Indiana Press, 1940.

Clark, Suzanne. *Sentimental Modernism: Women Writers and the Revolution of the Word.* Bloomington: Indiana University Press, 1991.

Cohn, Ruby. "Reading and Teaching Maria Irene Fornes and Caryl Churchill." In *Anglo-American Interplay in Recent Drama.* Cambridge: Cambridge University Press, 1995.

Cole, Carole L. "The Search for Power: Drama by American Women, 1909–1929." PhD dissertation, Purdue University, 1991.

Collins, Patricia Hill. *Black Feminist Thought: Knowledge, Consciousness, and the Politics of Empowerment.* New York: Routledge, 1990.

Cott, Nancy F. "Across the Great Divide: Women in Politics Before and After 1920." In Louise A. Tilley and Patricia Gurin, eds., *Women, Politics, and Change.* New York: Russell Sage, 1990, 153–76.

Cronacher, Karen. "Unmasking the Minstrel Mask's Black Magic in Ntozake Shange's *spell #7.*" *Theatre Journal* 44 (May 1992), 177–193. Rpt. in Keyssar, ed., *Feminist Theatre and Theory*, 189–212.

Crothers, Rachel. Clippings file. Billy Rose Theatre Collection, New York Public Library for the Performing Arts.

Expressing Willie and Other Plays. New York: Brentano's, 1924.

A Man's World. In Barlow, ed., *Plays by American Women*, 1–70.

Mary the Third, "Old Lady 31," A Little Journey. New York: Brentano's, 1923.

Nice People, Expressing Willie and Other Plays. New York: Brentano's, 1924.

"Ourselves." Ts. Special Collections, University of Pennsylvania Libraries.

"Young Wisdom." Unpublished script. Billy Rose Theatre Collection, New York Public Library for the Performing Arts.

Cudjoe, Selwyn R. "Maya Angelou and the Autobiographical Statement." In Mari Evans, ed., *Black Women Writers, 1950–1980: A Critical Evaluation.* Garden City, NY: Anchor Press/Doubleday, 1984, 6–24.

Cummings, Scott T. "Fornes's Odd Couple: *Oscar and Bertha* at the Magic Theatre." *Journal of Dramatic Theory and Criticism* 8 (1994): 147–56.

"Seeing with Clarity: The Visions of Maria Irene Fornes." *Theater* 17 (Winter 1985), 51–56.

Curb, Rosemary. "Fragmented Selves in Adrienne Kennedy's *Funnyhouse of a Negro* and *The Owl Answers.*" *Theatre Journal* 32 (1980), 180–95.

"'Lesson I Bleed': Adrienne Kennedy's Blood Rites." In Chinoy and Jenkins, eds., *Women in American Theatre,* 50–56.

"Re/cognition, Re/presentation, Re/creation in Woman-Conscious Drama: The Seer, the Seen, the Scene, the Obscene." *Theatre Journal* 37.3 (1985), 302–16.

"An Unfashionable Tragedy of American Racism: Alice Childress's *Wedding Band.*" *Melus* 7 (1980), 57–68.

Darling, Lynn. "The Wendy Generation." *Fanfare* (October 18, 1992), 12, 23.

Davis, Arthur P. and Michael W. Peplow, eds. *The New Negro Renaissance: An Anthology.* New York: Holt Rinehart and Winston, 1975.

De Koven, Marianne. *Rich and Strange: Gender, History, Modernism.* Princeton, NJ: Princeton University Press, 1991.

De Lauretis, Teresa. *Alice Doesn't: Feminism, Semiotics, Cinema.* Bloomington: Indiana University Press, 1984.

Demastes, William W. *Beyond Naturalism: A New Realism in American Theatre.* New York: Greenwood Press, 1988.

"Jessie and Thelma Revisited: Marsha Norman's Conceptual Challenge in *'night, Mother.*" *Modern Drama* 36 (1993), 109–19.

Demastes, William W., ed. *Realism and the American Dramatic Tradition.* Tuscaloosa: University of Alabama Press, 1996.

DeShazer, Mary K. "Rejecting Necrophilia: Ntozake Shange and the Warrior Re-Visioned." In Hart, ed., *Making a Spectacle,* 86–100.

Diamond, Elin. "Brechtian Theory/Feminist Theory: Toward a Gestic Feminist Criticism." In Martin, ed., *A Sourcebook of Feminist Theatre and Performance,* 120–30.

"(In)visible Bodies in Churchill's Theatre." In Hart, ed., *Making a Spectacle,* 259–81.

"Mimesis, Mimicry, and the 'True-Real.'" *Modern Drama* 32.1 (1989), 58–72.

"Mimesis in Syncopated Time: Reading Adrienne Kennedy." In Bryant-Jackson and Overbeck, eds., *Intersecting Boundaries,* 131–41.

"(Theoretically) Approaching Megan Terry: Issues of Gender and Identity." *Art and Cinema* 1 (1987), 5–7.

"Rethinking Identification: Kennedy, Freud, Brecht." *The Kenyon Review* 15 (1993), 86–99.

Dickinson, Thomas H. *Playwrights of the New American Theater.* New York: Macmillan, 1925.

DiGaetani, John L. *A Search for a Postmodern Theater: Interviews with Contemporary Playwrights.* New York, Westport, CT: Greenwood Press, 1991.

Dolan, Jill. *The Feminist Spectator as Critic*. Ann Arbor, MI: UMI Research Press, 1988.

"Gender Impersonation Onstage." In Senelick, ed., *Gender in Performance*, 4–13.

"'Lesbian' Subjectivity in Realism: Dragging at the Margins of Structure and Ideology." In Case, ed., *Performing Feminisms*, 40–53.

Presence and Desire: Essays on Gender, Sexuality, Performance: Critical Perspectives on Women and Gender. Ann Arbor: University of Michigan Press, 1993.

Donovan, Josephine. *Feminist Theory*. New York: Frederick Ungar, 1985.

"Drama." *Life* 63 (January 22, 1914), 150–51.

Du Bois, W. E. B. "Krigwa Players' Little Negro Theatre: The Story of A Little Theatre Movement." In Hatch and Hamalian, eds., *Lost Plays*, 446–52.

DuPlessis, Rachel Blau. *Writing Beyond the Ending*. Bloomington: Indiana University Press, 1985.

Ebert, Teresa L. "Gender and the Everyday: Toward a Postmodern Materialist Feminist Theory of Mimesis." In Glynnis Carr, ed., *"Turning the Century": Feminist Theory in the 1990s*. Bucknell Review. Lewisburg: Bucknell University Press, 1992, 90–122.

Ellison, Ralph. "Twentieth-Century Fiction and the Black Mask of Humanity." In *Shadow and Act*. New York: Quality Paperback, 1994, 24–44.

Elshtain, Jean Bethke. *Public Man, Private Women*. Princeton, NJ: Princeton University Press, 1981.

Elwood, William R. "Adrienne Kennedy Through the Lens of German Expressionism." In Bryant-Jackson and Overbeck, eds., *Intersecting Boundaries*, 85–92.

Emerson, Ralph Waldo. "The Poet." *Selections from Ralph Waldo Emerson*. Ed. Stephen E. Whicher. Boston: Houghton Mifflin, 1960, 222–41.

Encyclopedia Britannica online, 1997.

Engle, Sherry. "New Women Dramatists in America, 1890–1920: Martha Morton and Madeleine Lucette Ryley." Unpublished dissertation, Austin: University of Texas, 1996.

Evans, Sara. *Personal Politics: The Roots of Women's Liberation in the Civil Rights Movement and the New Left*. New York: Knopf, 1979.

Ezell, Margaret J. M. "The Myth of Judith Shakespeare: Creating the Canon of Women's Literature." *New Literary History* 21 (1990), 579–92.

Falk, Doris V. *Lillian Hellman*. New York: Ungar, 1978.

Fausto-Sterling, Anne. *Myths of Gender: Biological Theories About Women and Men*. New York: Basic Books, 1985.

Felski, Rita. *Beyond Feminist Aesthetics: Feminist Literature and Social Change*. Cambridge, MA: Harvard University Press, 1989.

The Gender of Modernity. Cambridge, MA: Harvard University Press, 1995.

Fleche, Anne. "The Lesbian Rule: Lillian Hellman and the Measures of Realism." *Modern Drama* 39.1 (1996), 16–30.

Fletcher, Winona. "Georgia Douglas Johnson." In Harris and Davis, eds., *Afro-American Writers*, 153–63.

Flynn, Joyce and Joyce Occomy Stricklin, eds. *Frye Street and Environs: The Collected Works of Marita Bonner*. Boston: Beacon Press, 1987.

Fornes, Maria Irene. *Fefu and Her Friends*. New York: Dramatists Play Service, 1980.

Forrey, Carolyn. "The New Woman Revisited." *Women's Studies* 2 (1974), 37–56.

Forte, Jeanie. "Kennedy's Body Politic: The Mulatta, Menses, and the Medusa." In Bryant-Jackson and Overbeck, eds., *Intersecting Boundaries*, 157–69.

"Realism, Narrative, and the Feminist Playwright – a Problem of Reception." *Modern Drama* 32.1 (1989), 115–27.

Fox-Genovese, Elizabeth. *Feminism Without Illusions*. Chapel Hill: University of North Carolina Press, 1991.

France, Rachel, ed. *A Century of Plays by American Women*. New York: Richards Rosen, 1979.

Frank, Glenda. "The Struggle to Affirm: The Image of Jewish Americans on Stage." In Marc Maufort, ed., *Staging Difference: Cultural Pluralism in American Theatre and Drama*. New York: Peter Lang, 1995, 245–57.

Franklin, Nancy. "The Time of Her Life." *The New Yorker* (April 14, 1997), 63–71.

Freedman, Estelle B. "The New Woman: Changing Views of Women in the 1920s." In Lois Scharf and M. Jensen, eds., *Decades of Discontent: The Women's Movement, 1920–1940*. Westport, CT: Greenwood Press, 1983, 21–44.

Friedman, Sharon. "Feminism as Theme in Twentieth-Century American Women's Drama." *American Studies* 25 (1984), 69–89.

Frye, Joanne S. *Living Stories, Telling Lives: Women and the Novel in Contemporary Experience*. Ann Arbor: University of Michigan Press, 1986.

Gale, Zona. *Miss Lulu Bett*. In Barlow, ed., *Plays by American Women*, 87–162.

Garber, Marjorie. *Vested Interests*. New York: Routledge, 1992.

Gardner, Vivien and Susan Rutherford, eds. *The New Woman and Her Sisters: Feminism and Theatre 1850–1914*. Ann Arbor: University of Michigan Press, 1992.

Garfield, Kim. "The Wendy Chronicles." *The Advocate* (July 18, 1989), 52–53.

Gavin, Christy. *American Women Playwrights, 1964–1989: A Research Guide and Annotated Bibliography*. New York: Garland, 1993.

Geis, Deborah R. "Wordscapes of the Body: Performative Language as *Gestus* in Maria Irene Fornes's Plays." *Theatre Journal* 42 (1990), 291–307. Rpt. in Deborah R. Geis. *Postmodern Theatric(k)s: Monologue in Contemporary American Drama*. Ann Arbor: University of Michigan Press, 1993.

"'Takin a Solo': Monologue in Ntozake Shange's Theater Pieces." In *Postmodern Theatric(k)s: Monologue in Contemporary American Drama*. Ann Arbor: University of Michigan Press, 1993.

Gilbert, Sandra and Susan Gubar. *No Man's Land*. Vol. 1. New Haven, CT: Yale University Press, 1988.

Gillespie, Patti. "Feminist Theatre: A Rhetorical Phenomenon." *Quarterly Journal of Speech* 64 (1978), 284–94.

Gilligan, Carol. *In a Different Voice*. Cambridge, MA: Harvard University Press, 1982.

Glaspell, Susan. *Alison's House*. New York: Samuel French: 1930.

Bernice. In *Plays*. Boston: Small, Maynard, 1920, 158–230.

Inheritors. In Bigsby, ed., *Plays by Susan Glaspell*, 103–57.

The Outside. In Bigsby, ed., *Plays by Susan Glaspell*, 47–55.

The People. In *Plays*. Boston: Small, Maynard, 1920, 32–59.

The Road to the Temple. New York: Frederick A. Stokes, 1927.

Trifles. In Bigsby, ed., *Plays by Susan Glaspell*, 35–45.

The Verge. In Bigsby, ed., *Plays by Susan Glaspell*, 57–101.

Woman's Honor. In *Plays*. Boston: Small, Maynard, 1920, 120–56.

Gold, Sylviane. "Wendy, the Wayward Wasserstein." *Wall Street Journal* (February 7, 1984), 30.

Gottlieb, Lois C. *Rachel Crothers*. Boston: Twayne, 1979.

Gruber, William E. "Individuality and Communality in Maria Irene Fornes's *The Danube*." In Roudané, ed., *Public Issues, Private Tensions*, 179–94.

Missing Persons: Character and Characterization in Modern Drama. Athens: University of Georgia Press, 1994.

Guerra, Jonnie. "Beth Henley: Female Quest and the Family-Play Tradition." In Hart, ed., *Making a Spectacle*, 118–30.

Hadden, Briton and Henry R. Luce, eds. *Time Capsule/1927*. New York: Time-Life Books, 1968.

Haedicke, Janet V. "Margins in the Mainstream: Contemporary Women Playwrights." In Demastes, ed., *Realism and the American Dramatic Tradition*, 203–17.

"'A Population [and Theater] at Risk': Battered Women in Henley's *Crimes of the Heart* and Shepard's *A Lie of the Mind*." *Modern Drama* 36 (1993), 83–95.

Halttunen, Karen. *Confidence Men and Painted Women: A Study of Middle-Class Culture in America, 1830–1870*. New Haven: Yale University Press, 1982.

Hamalian, Leo and James V. Hatch, eds. *The Roots of African American Drama: An Anthology of Early Plays, 1858–1938*. Detroit: Wayne State University Press, 1991.

Hammond, Percy. Review of *The Goat Song*, *Hedda Gabler*, and *The Great God Brown*. *New York Tribune* (January 31, 1926).

Hansberry, Lorraine. "CNA Presents Exciting New Dramatic Revue: *Gold Through the Trees*." *Freedom* (May 1952), 7.

To Be Young, Gifted and Black: An Informal Autobiography of Lorraine Hansberry. Adapted by Robert Nemiroff. New York: Signet, 1970.

"The Negro Writer and His Roots." *The Black Scholar* (March/April 1981), 2–12.

"Simone de Beauvoir and *The Second Sex*: An American Commentary (An Unfinished Essay-in-Progress)." In Beverly Guy-Sheftall, ed., *Words of Fire: An Anthology of African American Feminist Thought*. New York: The New Press, 1995, 125–42.

Harbin, Billy J. "Familial Bonds in the Plays of Beth Henley." *Southern Quarterly* 25. 3 (1987), 81–94.

Hargrove, Nancy D. "The Tragicomic Vision of Beth Henley's Drama." *Southern Quarterly* 22. 3 (1984), 54–70.

Harris, Laurilyn J. "Delving Beneath the Stereotypes: Beth Henley's *The Miss Firecracker Contest*." *Theatre Southwest* (May 1987), 4–7.

Harris, Trudier and Thadious M. Davis, eds. *Afro-American Writers from the Harlem Renaissance to 1940*. Dictionary of Literary Biography, vol. LI. Detroit: Gale, 1987.

Hart, Lynda. "Doing Time: Hunger for Power in Marsha Norman's Plays." *Southern Quarterly* 25. 3 (1987), 67–79.

"Canonizing Lesbians?" In Schlueter, ed., *Modern American Drama*, 275–92.

Hart, Lynda, ed. *Making a Spectacle: Feminist Essays on Contemporary Women's Theatre*. Ann Arbor: University of Michigan Press, 1989.

Hart, Lynda and Peggy Phelan, eds. *Acting Out: Feminist Performances*. Ann Arbor: University of Michigan Press, 1993.

Hatch, James V. and Omanii Abdullah. *Black Playwrights, 1823–1977: An Annotated Bibliography of Plays*. New York: R. R. Bowker, 1977.

Hatch, James V. and Leo Hamalian, eds. *Lost Plays of the Harlem Renaissance, 1920–1940*. Detroit: Wayne State University Press, 1996.

Hatch, James V. and Ted Shine, eds. *Black Theatre USA: Plays by African Americans, 1847–1938*. New York: Free Press, 1974.

Black Theatre, USA: Plays by African Americans. New York: Free Press, 1996.

Haun, Harry. "Is It Or… 'Isn't It Romantic.'" *Showbill* (March 1984), 5–6.

Havens, Daniel F. *The Columbian Muse of Comedy: The Development of a Native Tradition in Early American Social Comedy, 1787–1845*. Carbondale: Southern Illinois University Press, 1973.

Hay, Samuel. "Alice Childress's Dramatic Structure." In Mari Evans, ed., *Black Women Writers, 1950–1980: A Critical Evaluation*. Garden City, NY: Anchor Press/Doubleday, 1984, 117–28.

Hayes, Michael and Anastasia Nikolopoulou, eds. *Melodrama: The Cultural Emergence of a Genre*. New York: St. Martins Press, 1996.

Height, Dorothy. "Self-Help – A Black Tradition." *The Nation* 249 (July 24–31, 1989), 136–38.

Helle, Anita Plath. "Re-Presenting Women Writers Onstage: A Retrospective to the Present." In Hart, ed., *Making a Spectacle*, 195–208.

Hellman, Lillian. *The Collected Plays*. Boston: Little, Brown, 1972.

Pentimento: A Book of Portraits. Boston: Little, Brown, 1973.

Scoundrel Time. Boston: Little, Brown, 1976.

Six Plays by Lillian Hellman. New York: Modern Library, 1960.

An Unfinished Woman. Boston: Little, Brown, 1969.

Henderson, Jessie. "Interview with Viola Allen." *Boston Herald* (January 28, 1912).

Henley, Beth. *Beth Henley: Four Plays*. Portsmouth, NH: Heinemann, 1992.

Crimes of the Heart. New York: The Viking Press, 1982.

Hill, Lynda Marion. *Social Rituals and the Verbal Art of Zora Neale Hurston*. Washington DC: Howard University Press, 1996.

Hodgson, Moira. "The Heidi Chronicles." *The Nation* 248 (May 1, 1989), 605–06.

Holditch, Kenneth. "Another Part of the Country: Lillian Hellman as Southern Playwright." *Southern Quarterly* 25.3 (1987), 11–35.

Holquist, Michael. "The Politics of Representation." In Stephen J. Greenblatt, ed., *Allegory and Representation: Selected Papers from the English Institute*. Baltimore, MD: Johns Hopkins University Press, 1981, 162–83.

Hooks, Bell. *Black Looks: Race and Representation*. Boston: South End Press, 1992.

Talking Back. Boston: South End Press, 1989.

Hopkins, Arthur. *How's Your Second Act?* New York: Samuel French, 1931.

Howard, Lillie P. "Zora Neale Hurston." In Harris and Davis, eds., *Afro-American Writers*, 133–45.

Howe, Tina. *Coastal Disturbances: Four Plays*. New York: Theatre Communications Group, 1989.

Painting Churches. New York: Samuel French, 1982.

Hull, Gloria T. *Color, Sex, and Poetry: Three Women Writers of the Harlem Renaissance*. Bloomington: Indiana University Press, 1987.

Hull, Gloria T. ed., *Give Us Each Day: The Diary of Alice Dunbar-Nelson*. New York: W. W. Norton, 1984.

The Works of Alice Dunbar-Nelson. 3 vols. New York: Oxford University Press, 1988.

Huyssen, Andreas. *After the Great Divide: Modernism, Mass Culture, Postmodernism*. Bloomington: Indiana University Press, 1986.

Isenberg, Barbara. "Writing 'Bout Her Generation." *The Los Angeles Times* (October 7, 1990), Calendar, 48–55.

Jameson, Fredric. *The Prison-House of Language: A Critical Account of Structuralism and Russian Formalism*. Princeton, NJ: Princeton University Press, 1972.

Jennings, La Vinia Delois. *Alice Childress*. New York: Twayne, 1995.

Johnson, Charles S., ed. *Ebony and Topaz: A Collectanea*. New York: National Urban League, 1927.

Johnson, Georgia Douglas. *The Selected Works*. Ed. Claudia Tate. New York: G. K. Hall & Co., 1997.

Johnson, Kenneth E. "Tina Howe and Feminine Discourse." *American Drama* 1.2 (1992), 15–25.

Jones, Ann. *Women Who Kill* (1980). Boston: Beacon Press, 1996.

Jones, Jacqueline. *Labor of Love, Labor of Sorrow: Black Women, Work, and the Family from Slavery to the Present*. New York: Vintage, 1985.

Jones, Jennifer. "In Defense of the Woman: Sophie Treadwell's *Machinal*." *Modern Drama* 37 (1994), 485–96.

Kable, William S. "South Carolina District Copyrights: 1794–1820." *Proof: The Yearbook of American Bibliographical and Textual Studies* 1 (1971), 180–98.

Kaplan, Amy. *The Social Construction of American Realism*. Chicago: University of Chicago Press, 1988.

Keightley, Cyril. Scrapbook. Chamberlain and Brown Theatrical Agency. Billy Rose Theatre Collection, New York Public Library for the Performing Arts.

Kennedy, Adrienne. *Funnyhouse of a Negro*. In Clinton F. Oliver and Stephanie Sills, eds., *Contemporary Black Drama*. New York: Scribner, 1971.

Kent, Assunta Bartolomucci. *Maria Irene Fornes and Her Critics*. Westport, CT: Greenwood, 1996.

Kerber, Linda. "The Republican Mother: Women and the Enlightenment – An American Perspective." *American Quarterly* 28 (1976), 187–205.

Women of the Republic: Intellect and Ideology in Revolutionary America. New York: Norton, 1980.

Kerr, Walter. "No Clear Path and No Retreat." *New York Herald Tribune* (March 12, 1959), 1–2.

Keyssar, Helene, ed. *Feminist Theatre: An Introduction to the Plays of Contemporary British and American Women*. New York: Grove, 1985.

Feminist Theatre and Theory. New York: St. Martin's, 1996.

Kilgore, Emilie, ed. *Contemporary Plays by Women*. New York: Prentice Hall, 1991.

Kintz, Linda. *The Subject's Tragedy: Political Poetics, Feminist Theory, and Drama*. Ann Arbor: University of Michigan Press, 1992.

Kiper, Florence. "Some American Plays from the Feminist Viewpoint." *Forum* 51 (1914), 921–31.

Kissel, Howard. "Family Circus." *Daily News* (October 23, 1992), 73.

Klein, Kathleen Gregory. "Language and Meaning in Megan Terry's 1970s 'Musicals'." *Modern Drama* 27 (1984), 574–83.

Kobler, John. *The Trial of Ruth Snyder and Judd Gray*. Garden City, NY: Doubleday, Doran, 1938.

Kolb, Deborah S. "The Rise and Fall of the New Woman in American Drama." *Educational Theatre Journal* 27.2 (1975), 149–60.

Kolin, Philip C. "Public Facts/Private Fictions in Emily Mann's Plays." In Roudané, ed., *Public Issues, Private Tensions*, 231–48.

Kolodny, Annette. "Dancing Through The Minefield: Some Observations on the Theory, Practice, and Politics of a Feminist Literary Criticism." In Showalter, ed., *The New Feminist Criticism*, 144–67.

"A Map for Rereading: Gender and the Interpretation of Literary Texts." In Showalter, ed., *The New Feminist Criticism*, 46–62.

Kramer, Mimi. "Portrait of a Lady." *The New Yorker* 64 (December 26, 1988), 81–82.

Kramer, Victor, ed. *The Harlem Renaissance Re-examined*. New York: AMS Press, 1987.

Kritzer, Amelia Howe, ed. *Plays by Early American Women, 1775–1850*. Ann Arbor: University of Michigan Press, 1995.

Kullman, Colby H. "Beth Henley's Marginalized Heroines." *Studies in American Drama, 1945–Present* 8 (1993), 21–28.

Lamont, Rosette C. "Tina Howe's Secret Surrealism: Walking A Tightrope." *Modern Drama* 36.1 (1993), 27–37.

Laughlin, Karen L. "Criminality, Desire, and Community: A Feminist Approach to Beth Henley's *Crimes of the Heart*." *Women & Performance* 3 (1986), 35–51.

"Historical Re-Vision: Women Heroes on the American Stage." In Roudané, ed., *Public Issues, Private Tensions*, 143–60.

Laughlin, Karen L. and Catherine Schuler, eds. *Theatre and Feminist Aesthetics*. Madison: Fairleigh Dickinson University Press, 1995.

Lederer, Katherine. *Lillian Hellman*. Boston: Twayne, 1979.

Leeson, Richard M. *Lorraine Hansberry: A Research and Production Sourcebook*. Westport, CT: Greenwood, 1997.

Lerner, Gerda. *The Creation of Patriarchy*. New York: Oxford University Press, 1986.

Lester, Neal A. *Ntozake Shange: A Critical Study of the Plays*. New York: Garland, 1995.

Levin, Toby and Gwendolyn Flowers. "Black Feminism in *For Colored Girls*." In Günter H. Lenz, ed., *History and Tradition in Afro-American Culture*. Frankfurt: Campus Verlag, 1984, 181–93.

Littell, Robert. "Chiefly About *Machinal*." *Theatre Arts* 12 (1928), 774–80.

Locke, Alain, ed. *The New Negro* (1925). New York: Arno, 1968.

Locke, Alain and Montgomery Gregory, eds. *Plays of Negro Life: A Source-Book of Native American Drama*. Westport, CT: Negro University Press, 1970.

Lyons, Bonnie. "Lillian Hellman: 'The First Jewish Nun on Prytania Street.'" In Sarah Blacher Cohen, ed., *From Hester Street to Hollywood: The Jewish-American Stage and Screen*. Bloomington: Indiana University Press, 1983, 106–22.

MacGowan, Kenneth. "'He and She.'" New York *Globe and Commercial Advertiser* (February 13, 1920).

Makowsky, Veronica. *Susan Glaspell's Century of American Women*. New York: Oxford University Press, 1993.

Mandl, Bette. "Feminism, Post Feminism and *The Heidi Chronicles*." *Studies in the Humanities* 17.2 (1990), 120–28.

Mantle, Burns. "'He and She.'" *New York Evening Mail* (February 13, 1920).

Marks, Peter. "An Outsider Goes Inside the Beltway." *New York Times* (March 23, 1997). Late New York edn., 5+.

Martin, Carol, ed. *A Sourcebook of Feminist Theatre and Performance*. London: Routledge, 1996.

Maychick, Diana. "The 'Heidi Chronicles' Strikes a Familiar Chord with the Playwright's Diehard Fans." *New York Post* (March 5, 1989), 51.

McConachie, Bruce. *Melodramatic Formations: American Theatre and Society, 1820–1870*. Iowa City: University of Iowa Press, 1992.

McDonnell, Lisa J. "Diverse Similitude: Beth Henley and Marsha Norman." *Southern Quarterly* 25. 3 (1987), 95–104.

McKay, Nellie, "What Were They Saying?: Black Women Playwrights of the Harlem Renaissance." In Kramer, ed., *The Harlem Renaissance Re-examined*, 129–46.

Meigs, Susan E. "No Place but the Funnyhouse: The Struggle for Identity in Three Adrienne Kennedy Plays." In Schlueter, ed., *Modern American Drama*, 172–83.

Mellen, Joan. *Hellman and Hammett: The Legendary Passion of Lillian Hellman and Dashiell Hammett*. New York: HarperCollins, 1996.

Meserve, Walter J. *An Emerging Entertainment: The Drama of the American People to 1828*. Bloomington: Indiana University Press, 1977.

Michie, Helena. *The Flesh Made Word*. New York: Oxford University Press, 1989.

Miller, Jeanne-Marie A. "Georgia Douglas Johnson and May Miller: Forgotten Playwrights of the New Negro Renaissance." *CLA Journal* 33 (1990), 349–67.

Miller, Judith. "The Secret Wendy Wasserstein." *The New York Times* Sunday Section 2 (October 18, 1992), 1.

Miner, Madonne. "'What's These Bars Doin' Here?' – The Impossiblity of Getting Out." *Theatre Annual* 40 (1985), 115–37.

Mitchell, Carolyn. "'A Laying on of Hands': Transcending the City in Ntozake Shange's *For Colored Girls*." In Susan Merrill Squier, ed., *Women Writers and the City: Essays in Feminist Literary Criticism*. Knoxville: University of Tennessee Press, 1984, 230–48.

Moore, Honor. "Woman Alone, Women Together." In Chinoy and Jenkins, eds., *Women in American Theatre*, 184–90.

Moore, Honor, ed. *The New Women's Theatre: Ten Plays by Contemporary American Women*. New York: Vintage, 1977.

Moraga, Cherrie and Glorie Anzaldua, eds. *This Bridge Called My Back: Writings by Radical Women of Color*. Watertown, MA: Persephone Press, 1981.

Moroff, Diane Lynn. *Fornes: Theatre in the Present Tense*. Ann Arbor: University of Michigan Press, 1996.

Morrow, Laura. "Orality and Identity in *'night, Mother* and *Crimes of the Heart*." *Studies in American Drama, 1945–Present* 3 (1988), 23–39.

Mowatt, Anna Cora. *Fashion; or, Life in New York. A Comedy with Music in Five Acts* (1845). New York: French, 1964.

Munk, Erika. "Isn't It Romantic." *Village Voice* (December 27, 1983), 109.

Murphy, Brenda. *American Realism and American Drama, 1880–1940*. Cambridge and New York: Cambridge University Press, 1987.

Murray, Judith Sargent. *The Gleaner*, vols. I–III. Boston, 1798. Rpt. in Schenectady, *The Gleaner*. NY: Union College Press, 1992.

The Traveller Returned. In Kritzer, ed., *Plays by Early American Women*, 97–136.

Murray, Timothy. "Facing the Camera's Eye: Black and White Terrain in Women's Drama." *Modern Drama* 28 (1985), 110–24. Rpt. in Henry Louis Gates, ed., *Reading Black, Reading Feminist: A Critical Anthology*. New York: Meridian Books, 1990, 155–75.

"Patriarchal Panoticism, or The Seduction of a Bad Joke: *Getting Out* in Theory." *Theatre Journal* 35 (1983), 376–88.

Natalle, Elizabeth. *Feminist Theatre: A Study in Persuasion*. Metuchen, NJ: Scarecrow Press, 1985.

Nemiroff, Robert. "Notes on This New Edition." In Lorraine Hansberry, *A Raisin in the Sun/The Sign in Sidney Brustein's Window*. New York: Vintage Books, 1995.

"The 101 'Final Performances' of *Sidney Brustein*: Portrait of a Play and Its Author." In Lorraine Hansberry, *A Raisin in the Sun/The Sign in Sidney Brustein's Window*. New York: Vintage Books, 1995.

Newton, Judith Lowder, and Deborah Rosenfelt, eds. *Feminist Criticism and Social Change: Sex, Class and Race in Literature and Culture*. New York: Methuen, 1985.

New York Magazine (April 28, 1997), 102–03.

Nietzsche, Friedrich. *Beyond Good and Evil: Prelude to the Philosophy of a Future*. Trans. Walter Kaufmann. New York: Vintage, 1966.

Norman, Marsha. *Four Plays*. New York: Theatre Communications Group, 1988.

'night, Mother. New York: Hill and Wang, 1983.

O'Connor, Colleen. "The Wendy Chronicles." *The Dallas Morning News* (February 7, 1994), C2.

Odell, George C. D. *Annals of the New York Stage*. 15 vols. New York: Columbia University Press, 1927–49.

Olaniyan, Tejumola. "Ntozake Shange: The Vengeance of Difference, or the Gender of Black Cultural Identity." In *Scars of Conquest/Masks of Resistance: The Invention of Cultural Identities in African, African American, and Caribbean Drama*. New York: Oxford University Press, 1995, 116–38.

Olauson, Judith. *The American Woman Playwright: A View of Criticism and Characterization*. Troy, NY: Whitston, 1981.

Ouderkirk, Cathleen Stinson. "Human Connections – A Playwright's View." *The Christian Science Monitor* (October 10, 1989), 10.

Ozieblo, Barbara. "Rebellion and Rejection: The Plays of Susan Glaspell." In Schlueter, ed., *Modern American Drama*, 66–76.

"Susan Glaspell." In Clive Bloom, ed., *American Drama*. New York: St. Martin's, 1995, 6–20.

Papazian, Rita. "Everywoman Comes to Town and Takes it by Storm." *Westport News* (August 4, 1993), 23.

Parker, Andrew and Eve Kosofsky Sedgwick. *Performativity and Performance*. New York: Routledge, 1995.

Parker, Patricia L. *Susanna Rowson*. Boston: Twayne, 1986.

Patraka, Vivian M. "Lillian Hellman's *Watch on the Rhine*: Realism, Gender, and Historical Crisis." *Modern Drama* 32.1 (1989), 128–45.

Patterson, Ada. "A Chat with the Dean of America's Women Playwrights." *Theatre Magazine* 10 (1909), 126–30.

Perkins, Kathy A. ed. *Black Female Playwrights: An Anthology of Plays before 1950*. Bloomington: Indiana University Press, 1989.

Peters, Erskine. "Some Tragic Propensities of Ourselves: The Occasion of Ntozake Shange's *For Colored Girls*." *Journal of Ethnic Studies* 6 (1978), 79–85.

Pinkney, Mikell. "Theatrical Expressionism in the Structure and Language of Ntozake Shange's *spell #7*." *Theatre Studies* 37 (1992), 5–15.

Pipher, Mary. *Reviving Ophelia*. New York: Grosset/Putnam, 1994.

Pogson, Sarah. *Essays Religious, Moral, Dramatic, and Poetical*. Charleston: V. Hoff, 1818.

    The Female Enthusiast. In Kritzer, ed., *Plays by Early American Women*, 137–81.

Pollack, Arthur. "Plays and Things." *Brooklyn Daily Eagle* (September 30, 1928).

Porter, Laurin. "Women Re-Conceived: Changing Perceptions of Women in Contemporary American Drama." *CCTE Studies*, 54 (1989), 53–59.

Prose, Francine. "Confident at 11, Confused at 16." *New York Times Magazine* (January 7, 1990), 38.

Quinn, Arthur Hobson. *A History of the American Drama from the Civil War to the Present Day*. Rev. edn. 2 vols. New York: Appleton-Century-Crofts, 1936.

"Rachel Crothers's Play." *New York Times* (November 14, 1913), 11.

Rapi, Nina. "Hide and Seek: The Search for a Lesbian Theater Aesthetic." *New Theatre Quarterly* 9 (1993), 147–58.

Ray, Paul H. "The Rise of Integral Culture." *Noetic Sciences Review* 37 (1996). Rpt. in *Artsearch* (December 1996–January 1997).

Rayner, Alice and Harry J. Elam, Jr. "Unfinished Business: Reconfiguring History in Suzan-Lori Parks's *The Death of the Last Black Man in the Whole Entire World*." *Theatre Journal* 46: 1 (1994), 447–61.

Reinelt, Janelle. "Beyond Brecht: Britain's New Feminist Drama." *Theatre Journal* 38.2 (1986), 154–63.

    "A Feminist Reconsideration of the Brecht/Lukacs Debate." *Women and Performance Journal* 7.1 (1994), 123–39.

    "Feminist Theory and the Problem of Performance." *Modern Drama* 32.1 (1989), 48–57.

Reinhardt, Nancy. "New Directions for Feminist Criticism in Theatre and the Related Arts." In Elizabeth Langland and Walter Gove, eds., *A Feminist Perspective in the Academy: The Difference It Makes*. Chicago: University of Chicago Press, 1983, 25–51.

Rich, Frank. "Painting Churches." *New York Times* (November 23, 1983), III, 13.

Richards, Sandra L. "Conflicting Impulses in the Plays of Ntozake Shange." *Black American Literature Forum* 17 (1983), 73–78.

"Writing the Absent Potential: Drama, Performance, and the Canon of African American Literature," in Andrew Parker and Eve Kosofsky Sedgwick, eds., *Performativity and Performance*. New York: Routledge, 1995.

Richardson, Willis, ed. *Plays and Pageants From the Life of The Negro* (1930). Jackson: University Press of Mississippi, 1993.

Richardson, Willis and May Miller, eds. *Negro History in Thirteen Plays*. Washington DC: Associated Publishers, 1935.

Ritchie, Anna Cora Ogden Mowatt. *Autobiography of an Actress* (1854). New York: Arno Press, 1980.

Roberts, Vera Mowry. *The Nature of Theatre*. New York: Harper and Row, 1971.

Robins, Corrine. "Betrayals." *American Book Review* 11.5 (November/December 1989), 4.

Robinson, Alice M., Vera Mowry Roberts, and Milly S. Barranger. *Notable Women in the American Theatre: A Biographical Dictionary*. New York: Greenwood, 1989.

Robinson Locke Collection. Billy Rose Theatre Collection, New York Public Library for the Performing Arts.

Robinson, Marc. *The Other American Drama*. Cambridge: Cambridge University Press, 1994.

Rohan, Pierre de. "*Machinal* Ugly But Great Play." *New York American* (September 8, 1928).

Rollyson, Carl. *Lillian Hellman: Her Legend and Her Legacy*. New York: St. Martin's, 1988.

Rosen, Carol. *Theater Week* (November 2–8, 1992), 17.

Rosenman, Ellen Bayuk. *A Room of One's Own: Women Writers and the Politics of Creativity*. New York: Twayne, 1995.

Rothstein, Mervyn. "After the Revolution, What? The Daughters of Feminism." *New York Times* (December 11, 1988), 1, 28.

Roudané, Matthew C., ed. *Public Issues, Private Tensions: Contemporary American Drama*. New York: AMS Press, 1993.

Rowson, Susanna. *Slaves in Algiers; or, A Struggle for Freedom*. In Kritzer, ed., *Plays by Early American Women*, 55–95.

Ruhl, Arthur. "Off-Stage and On." *New York Herald Tribune* (September 20, 1928). "Second Nights." *New York Herald Tribune* (September, 16, 1928).

Rushing, Andrea Benton. "*For Colored Girls*: Suicide or Struggle." *Massachusetts Review* 22 (1981), 539–50.

Sayler, Oliver M. Review of *Machinal*. *Footlights and Lamplights* (September 17, 1928).

Scharine, Richard G. "Caste Iron Bars: Marsha Norman's *Getting Out* as Political Theatre." *Themes in Drama* 11 (1989), 185–97.

Schlueter, June. "Keep Tightly Closed in a Cool Dry Place: Megan Terry's Transformational Drama and the Possibilities of Self." *Studies in American Drama, 1945–Present* 2 (1987), 59–69. Rpt. in Schlueter, ed., *Modern American Drama*, 161–71.

Schlueter, June, ed. *Modern American Drama: The Female Canon*. Rutherford, NJ: Fairleigh Dickinson University Press, 1990.

Schneider, Rebecca. "Holly Hughes: Polymorphous Perversity and the Lesbian Scientist." In Martin, ed., *A Sourcebook of Feminist Theatre and Performance*, 239–53.

Schroeder, Patricia R. "American Drama, Feminist Discourse, and Dramatic Form: In Defense of Critical Pluralism." *Journal of Dramatic Theory and Criticism* 7 (1993), 103–18.

The Feminist Possibilities of Dramatic Realism. Madison, NJ: Associated University Presses: 1996.

"Hearing Many Voices at Once: The Theatre of Emily Mann." In Roudané, ed., *Public Issues, Private Tensions*, 249–65.

"Locked Behind the Proscenium: Feminist Strategies in *Getting Out* and *My Sister in This House*." *Modern Drama* 32.1 (1989), 104–14.

Schuler, Catherine. "Gender Perspective and Violence in the Plays of Maria Irene Fornes and Sam Shepard." In Schlueter, ed., *Modern American Drama*, 218–28.

Senelick, Laurence, ed. *Gender in Performance: The Presentation of Difference in the Performing Arts*. Hanover: University Press of New England, 1992.

Shafer, Yvonne B. "The Liberated Woman in American Plays of the Past." *Players Magazine* 49 (1974), 95–100.

Shange, Ntozake. *For Colored Girls Who Have Considered Suicide/When the Rainbow is Enuf: A Choreopoem*. New York, Macmillan, 1977.

Shapiro, Walter. "Chronicler of Frayed Feminism." *Time* 133 (March 27, 1989), 90–92.

Shepard, Alan Clarke. "Aborted Rage in Beth Henley's Women." *Modern Drama* 36 (1993), 96–108.

Showalter, Elaine, ed. *The New Feminist Criticism*. New York: Pantheon, 1985.

Singh, Amritjit, William Shiver, and Stanley Brodwin, eds. *The Harlem Renaissance: Revaluations*. New York: Garland, 1989.

Smith, Anna Deavere. *Fires in the Mirror*. New York: Doubleday, 1993.

Smith, Raynette Halvorsen. "*'night Mother* and *True West*: Mirror Images of Violence and Gender." In James Redmond, ed., *Violence in Drama*. Cambridge: Cambridge University Press, 1991.

Sollors, Werner. "People Who Led to My Plays: Adrienne Kennedy's Autobiography." In Bryant-Jackson and Overbeck, eds., *Intersecting Boundaries*, 13–20.

"Owls and Rats in the American Funnyhouse: Adrienne Kennedy's Drama." *American Literature* 63 (1991), 507–34.

Solomon, Alisa. "Signifying on the Signifyin': The Plays of Suzan-Lori Parks." *Theatre* 21 (1990), 73–80.

Spence, Eulalie. "A Criticism of the Negro Drama as it Relates to the Negro Dramatist and Artist." In Hatch and Hamalian, eds., *Lost Plays*, 465–67.

Spencer, Jenny S. "Marsha Norman's She-tragedies." In Hart, ed., *Making a Spectacle*, 147–65.

"Norman's *'night, Mother*: Psycho-drama of Female Identity." *Modern Drama* 30 (1987), 364–75.

Staples, Robert. "The Myth of Black Macho: A Response to Angry Black Feminists." *Black Scholar* 10 (March/April 1979), 24–32.

Steadman, Susan M. *Dramatic Re-Visions: An Annotated Bibliography of Feminism and Theatre 1972–1988*. Chicago: American Library Association, 1991.

Stephens, Judith L. "The Compatibility of Traditional Dramatic Form and Feminist Expression." *Theatre Annual* (1985), 7–23.

"From Positive Image to Disruptive Apparatus: Feminist Perspectives in American Plays and Dramatic Criticism." *Pennsylvania Speech Communications Annual* 44 (1988), 59–67.

"Gender Ideology and Dramatic Convention in Progressive Era Plays, 1890–1920." *Theatre Journal* 41.1 (1989), 45–55.

Stowe, Harriet Beecher. *Uncle Tom's Cabin.* 1852. New York: Penguin, 1987.

Stowell, Sheila. "Rehabilitating Realism." *Journal of Dramatic Theory and Criticism* 6.2 (1992), 81–88.

A Stage of Their Own: Feminist Playwrights of the Suffrage Era. Ann Arbor: University of Michigan Press, 1992.

Sturgeon, J. M. "The Phoenix Focus Talks to Wendy Wasserstein." The Phoenix Theatre Program 1977, n.p.

Sullivan, Victoria and James Hatch. *Plays By and About Women: An Anthology.* New York: Random House, 1973.

Sutherland, Cynthia. "American Women Playwrights as Mediators of the 'Woman Problem.'" *Modern Drama* 21 (1978), 319–36.

Sweet, Jeffery. "Making It Specific: Five Playwrights on their Craft." *Backstage* 29 (1994), n.p.

Tener, Robert L. "Theatre of Identity: Adrienne Kennedy's Portrait of the Black Woman." *Studies in Black Literature* 6 (1975), 1–5.

Terry, Megan. *Approaching Simone.* Old Westbury, NY: Feminist Press, 1973.

Thomas, Augustus. *As a Man Thinks.* In George Pierce Baker, ed., *Modern American Plays.* New York: Harcourt Brace, 1921.

Thompson-Cager, Chezia. "Superstition, Magic and the Occult in Two Versions of Ntozake Shange's Choreopoem *For Colored Girls* ... and Novel *Sassafrass, Cypress and Indigo.*" *MAWA Review: A Quarterly Publication of the Middle Atlantic Writers* 4 (1989), 37–41.

Timpane, John. "The Poetry of a Moment: Politics and the Open Form in the Drama of Ntozake Shange." *Studies in American Drama, 1945–Present* 4 (1989), 91–101. Rpt. in Schlueter, ed., *Modern American Drama,* 198–206.

Titus, Mary. "Murdering the Lesbian: Lillian Hellman's *The Children's Hour.*" *Tulsa Studies in Women's Literature* 10.2 (1991), 215–32.

Treadwell, Sophie. *For Saxophone.* Ts. n.d. University of Arizona Library Special Collections.

"Girl Slayer of Van Baalen Awaits Trial." 1914. Clipping, University of Arizona Library Special Collections.

Machinal. In Barlow, ed., *Plays by American Women,* 171–225.

Machinal. Ts. n.d. University of Arizona Library Special Collections.

"The Playwright as Actor." Ts. 1925. University of Arizona Library Special Collections.

"Producing a Play." Ts. 1925. University of Arizona Library Special Collections.

"Writing a Play." Ts. 1925. University of Arizona Library Special Collections.

Treduell, Sofi (Sophie Treadwell). "Avtor o postanovke <<Mashinal'>>." *Vecherniaia Moskva* (May 22, 1933). In Thomas Joseph Torda. "Alexander Tairov and the Scenic Artists of the Moscow Kamerny Theater 1914–1935." PhD dissertation, University of Denver, 1977.

Triplett, William. "Hurston Plays Discovered: Find at Library of Congress May Shed New Light on Black Writer." *Washington Post* (April 24, 1997), B2.

Valgamae, Mardi. *Accelerated Grimace: Expressionism in the American Drama of the 1920s.* Carbondale: Southern Illinois University Press, 1972.

Wagner, Jane. *The Search for Signs of Intelligent Life in the Universe.* New York: Harper and Row, 1986.

Wainscott, Ronald H. *The Emergence of the Modern American Theater, 1914–1929.* New Haven, CT: Yale University Press, 1997.

Walker, Alice, ed. *I Love Myself When I Am Laughing ... and Then Again When I Am Looking Mean and Impressive: A Zora Neale Hurston Reader.* New York: The Feminist Press, 1979.

In Search of Our Mothers' Gardens. San Diego, CA: Harcourt Brace Jovanovich, 1983.

Wall, Cheryl A. *Women of the Harlem Renaissance.* Bloomington: Indiana University Press, 1995.

Wandor, Michelene, ed. *Strike While the Iron Is Hot: Three Plays on Sexual Politics.* London: Journeyman Press, 1980.

Wasserstein, Wendy. *Bachelor Girls.* New York: Random House, 1990.

Clippings File. Billy Rose Theatre Collection, New York Public Library for the Performing Arts.

The Heidi Chronicles, Uncommon Women and Others & Isn't it Romantic. New York: Vintage, 1991.

The Sisters Rosensweig. New York: Harcourt Brace, 1993.

Interview with Charlie Rose. *The Charlie Rose Show.* WNET, New York (April 17, 1997).

An American Daughter. New York: Harcourt Brace, 1998.

Watermeier, Daniel J. "The Search for Self: Attachment, Loss, and Recovery in *The Heidi Chronicles.*" In Marc Maufort, ed., *Staging Difference: Cultural Pluralism in American Theatre and Drama.* New York: Peter Lang, 1995, 351–62.

Watts, Richard, Jr. "Applying the Pulmotor to Modernist Drama." *New York Herald Tribune* (September 23, 1928).

Waxman, Barbara Frey. "Dancing Out of Form, Dancing into Self: Genre and Metaphor in Marshall, Shange, and Walker." *Melus* 19 (1994), 91–106.

Weil, Dorothy. *In Defense of Women: Susanna Haswell Rowson (1762–1824).* University Park: Pennsylvania State University Press, 1976.

Wentworth, Marion Craig. *The Flower Shop.* Boston: Gorham Press, 1912.

Wiley, Catherine. "Whose Name, Whose Protection: Reading Alice Childress's *Wedding Band.*" In Schlueter, ed., *Modern American Drama,* 184–97.

Wilkerson, Margaret B., "Adrienne Kennedy." In Trudier Harris and Thadious M. Davis, eds., *Afro-American Writers after 1955: Dramatists and Prose Writers. Dictionary of Literary Biography.* Vol. XXXVIII. Detroit: Gale, 1985, 162–69.

"Diverse Angles of Vision: Two Black Women Playwrights." *Theatre Annual* 40 (1985), 91–114.

"Introduction." *9 Plays by Black Women.* New York: Mentor Books, 1986, xiii–xxv.

Wilson, Edmund. *The American Earthquake.* Garden City, NY: Doubleday, 1958.

Wittig, Monique. "The Point of View: Universal or Particular." *Feminist Issues* (1983), 63–69.

Wolff, Janet. *Feminine Sentences: Essays on Women and Culture.* Berkeley: University of California Press, 1990.

Woollcott, Alexander. "'He and She.'" *New York Times* (February 13, 1920), 16.

Worthen, W. B. "Still Playing Games: Ideology and Performance in the Theatre of Maria Irene Fornes." In Brater, ed., *Feminine Focus,* 167–81.

Wright, William. *Lillian Hellman: The Image, the Woman.* New York: Simon and Schuster, 1986.

Wynn, Nancy Edith. "Sophie Treadwell: The Career of a Twentieth-Century American Feminist Playwright." PhD dissertation, City University of New York, 1982.

INDEX